Women in Convent Spaces and the Music Networks of Early Modern Barcelona

This book presents the first study of music in convent life in a single Hispanic city, Barcelona, during the early modern era. Exploring how convents were involved in the musical networks operating in sixteenth-century Barcelona, it challenges the invisibility of women in music history and reveals the intrinsic role played by nuns and lay women in the city's urban musical culture.

Drawing on a wide range of archival sources, this innovative study offers a cross-disciplinary approach that not only reveals details of the rich musical life in Barcelona's nunneries, but shows how they took part in wider national and transnational networks of musical distribution, including religious, commercial, and social dimensions of music. The connections of Barcelona convents to networks for the dissemination of music in and outside the city provide a rich example of the close relationship between musical networks, urban society, and popular culture.

Addressing how music was understood as a marker of identity, prestige, and social status and, above all, as a conduit between earth and heaven, this book provides new insights into how women shaped musical traditions in the urban context. It is essential reading for scholars of early modern history, musicology, history of religion, and gender studies, as well as all those with an interest in urban history and the city of Barcelona.

The book is supported by additional digital appendices, which include:

- Records of inquiries into the lineage of Santa Maria de Jonqueres nuns
- Development of the collections of choir books belonging to the convents of Santa Maria de Jonqueres and Sant Antoni i Santa Clara.

Ascensión Mazuela-Anguita is Associate Professor of Music at the University of Granada, Spain.

Routledge Research in Music Series

Music by Subscription
Composers and their Networks in the British Music-Publishing Trade, 1676–1820
Edited by Simon D.I. Fleming and Martin Perkins

Early English Composers and the Credo
Emphasis as Interpretation in Sixteenth-Century Music
Wendy J. Porter

Music and Performance in the Book of Hours
Michael Alan Anderson

The Politicized Concert Mass (1967-2007)
From Secularism to Pluralism
Stephanie Rocke

Singers, Scores and Sounds
Making New Connections and Transforming Voices
Ellen Hooper

Schubert's Workshop: Volume 1
Towards an Early Maturity
Brian Newbould

Schubert's Workshop: Volume 2
Mastery and Beyond
Brian Newbould

Musical Topics and Musical Performance
Edited by Julian Hellaby

Women in Convent Spaces and the Music Networks of Early Modern Barcelona
Ascensión Mazuela-Anguita

For more information about this series, please visit: <https://www.routledge.com/Routledge-Research-in-Music/book-series/RRM>

Women in Convent Spaces and the Music Networks of Early Modern Barcelona

Ascensión Mazuela-Anguita

NEW YORK AND LONDON

First published 2023
by Routledge
605 Third Avenue, New York, NY 10158

and by Routledge
4 Park Square, Milton Park, Abingdon, Oxon, OX14 4RN

Routledge is an imprint of the Taylor & Francis Group, an informa business

© 2023 Ascensión Mazuela Anguita

The right of Ascensión Mazuela-Anguita to be identified as author of this work has been asserted in accordance with sections 77 and 78 of the Copyright, Designs and Patents Act 1988.

All rights reserved. No part of this book may be reprinted or reproduced or utilised in any form or by any electronic, mechanical, or other means, now known or hereafter invented, including photocopying and recording, or in any information storage or retrieval system, without permission in writing from the publishers.

Trademark notice: Product or corporate names may be trademarks or registered trademarks, and are used only for identification and explanation without intent to infringe.

Library of Congress Cataloging-in-Publication Data
Names: Mazuela-Anguita, Ascensión, author.
Title: Women in convent spaces and the music networks of early modern Barcelona / Ascensión Mazuela-Anguita.
Description: [1.] | New York, NY: Routledge, 2022. | Series: Routledge research in music series | Includes bibliographical references and index.
Identifiers: LCCN 2022038549 (print) | LCCN 2022038550 (ebook) | ISBN 9781032273617 (hardback) | ISBN 9781032273631 (paperback) | ISBN 9781003292371 (ebook)
Subjects: LCSH: Music in convents--Spain--Barcelona--History--16th century.
 | Music--Social aspects--Spain--Barcelona--History--16th century. | Nuns--Spain--Barcelona.
Classification: LCC ML3047.8.B37 M39 2022 (print) | LCC ML3047.8.B37
 (ebook) | DDC 780.9467/209031--dc23/eng/20220830
LC record available at <https://lccn.loc.gov/2022038549>
LC ebook record available at <https://lccn.loc.gov/2022038550>

ISBN: 9781032273617 (hbk)
ISBN: 9781032273631 (pbk)
ISBN: 9781003292371 (ebk)

DOI: 10.4324/9781003292371

Typeset in Times New Roman
by Deanta Global Publishing Services, Chennai, India

Access the Support Material: <www.routledge.com/9781032273617>

To my mother

Contents

List of Figures   viii
List of Tables   xv
Note for the reader: eResources   xvii
Acknowledgements   xviii
Abbreviations   xx

Introduction   1

1 Mapping convents' sound in the city   6

2 Music as a commodity: Music, convents, and the economy of the city   55

3 Music as a symbol of political power and social status   117

4 Music to reach heaven   154

5 Beyond the city: Religious orders as national and international music networks   203

Epilogue   239

Bibliography   241
Index   280

Figures

1.1. Location of the female convents active in sixteenth-century Barcelona. Map of sixteenth-century Barcelona (copy) [Markers are the author's]. AHCB, Fons Gràfics, Reg. 2980   9
1.2. Female religious institutions active in sixteenth-century Barcelona on the current map of Barcelona city centre   10
1.3. Drawing (watercolour and graphite pencil on paper) of the bastion of Jonqueres (close to the convent of Santa Maria de Jonqueres) at the city wall of Barcelona (1825), by Adolphe Hedwige Alphonse Delamare (Paris, 1793–1861), Barcelona, Museu Nacional d'Art de Catalunya, depósito de la Generalitat de Catalunya, Col·lecció Nacional d'Art, 2017. © Museu Nacional d'Art de Catalunya, Barcelona, 2022   11
1.4. The parish church of the convent of Sant Pere de les Puel·les as it survives today. Photograph by the author   13
1.5. Pieces from the low cloister of the convent of Sant Pere de les Puel·les (after 1187). Barcelona, Museu Nacional d'Art de Catalunya, depósito de la Generalitat de Catalunya, Col·lecció Nacional d'Art, 1879. © Museu Nacional d'Art de Catalunya, Barcelona, 2022   14
1.6. Location of the convent of Sant Antoni i Santa Clara adjacent to the gate of Sant Daniel (no. 9). Detail from: Johann Stridbeck (1666–1714), 'Barcelona, die Haupt Statt des Fürstenthums Catalonien' (1714), in *Curioses Staats und Kriegs Theatrum* (Augsburg: Johann Stridbeck, 1714). Barcelona, Institut Cartogràfic i Geològic de Catalunya. Creative Commons   15
1.7. Detail from: Jean Boisseau, *Nouvelle description de la fameuse ville de Barcelone cappitalle de la province de Catalogne* (Paris: chez Lou. Boissevin a la rue St Iaques a limage Ste Geneviesve, 164[5]). The location of the convent of Valldonzella is marked with 'V'. Barcelona, Institut Cartogràfic i Geològic de Catalunya. Creative Commons   15

1.8. Location of the convent of Santa Maria de Jonqueres. Detail from: Johann Stridbeck (1666–1714), 'Barcelona, die Haupt Statt des Fürstenthums Catalonien' (1714), in *Curioses Staats und Kriegs Theatrum* (Augsburg: Johann Stridbeck, 1714). Barcelona, Institut Cartogràfic i Geològic de Catalunya. Creative Commons   16

1.9. Location of the convent of Santa Maria de Jonqueres. Detail from: Georg Braun (1541–1622) and Joris Hoefnagel (1542–1601), *Barcino, quae vulgo Barcelona dicitur, urbis est apud Hispanos celeberrima* ([s.l.]: [s.n.], 1572). BNE, R/22249(1) PL. 6. Public Domain   17

1.10. The convent of Santa Maria de Jonqueres in its original situation, in a drawing by Francesc Soler Rovirosa (1864). AHCB, Fons Gràfics, Reg. 01047   17

1.11. Drawing (watercolour and graphite pencil on paper) of the convent of Santa Maria de Jonqueres on 2 September 1827, by Adolphe Hedwige Alphonse Delamare (Paris, 1793–1861), when the building turned into a military hospital (from 1810). Barcelona, Museu Nacional d'Art de Catalunya, depósito de la Generalitat de Catalunya, Col·lecció Nacional d'Art, 2017. © Museu Nacional d'Art de Catalunya, Barcelona, 2022   18

1.12. The convent of Santa Maria Magdalena in a drawing by Eduard Gràcia (1910–1915). AHCB, Fons Gràfics, Reg. 01667   20

1.13. Current church of the Carme in Barcelona, built in the space previously occupied by the Jeronymite nunnery. Photograph by the author   23

1.14. The convent of Santa Margarida la Reial in a 1906 drawing made by Eduard Gràcia. AHCB, Fons Gràfics, Reg. 01662   24

1.15. Book containing records of visitations (1536–1726), belonging to the convent of Santa Maria de Jonqueres. ACA,ORM, Monacales-Universidad,Volúmenes,169, fol. 2v (visitation of 1538)   27

1.16. 1572 file of the inquiry into the blood purity of Agraïda Grimau (d.1614), choir director of Santa Maria de Jonqueres convent. AHN, OM-RELIGIOSAS_SANTIAGO,Exp.291   30

2.1. Barcelona Jeronymite nunnery in an 1868 drawing by Francesc Soler Rovirosa. AHCB, Fons Gràfics, Reg. 01054   61

2.2. AMSP, Col·lecció de cantorals, no. 11, fol. 21r. Photograph by the author   67

x *Figures*

2.3. AMSP, Col·lecció de cantorals, no. 11, fol. 27v. Photograph by the author — 67
2.4. AMSP, Col·lecció de cantorals, no. 11, fol. 31v. Photograph by the author — 68
2.5. AMSP, Col·lecció de cantorals, no. 6, fol. XLIr. Photograph by the author — 68
2.6. Sixteenth-century antiphonary belonging to the convent of Sant Pere de les Puel·les. It shows interesting signs of use. On the left margin: 'lo segon es de la scolana que li toca la llamentacio' ('the second is for the choir girl in charge of performing the lamentation'). AMSP, Col·lecció de cantorals, no. 4, fol. 3v. Photograph by the author — 69
2.7. Detail from: Kyrie in plainchant book no. 2 (1600) from the convent of Sant Antoni i Santa Clara. AMSBM, Cantoral no. 2. This detail is on the last page and forms part of a fragment with no date. Photograph by the author — 72
2.8. Rubric and beginning of the hymn *Gloria, laus et honor* included in a processional which belonged to the nunnery of Sant Antoni i Santa Clara in Barcelona. BC, Ms. 1458, fol. 33r. Public Domain — 75
2.9. Rubric and beginning of the antiphon *Populum tuum obliviscere*, included in a processional copied for the use of an unidentified Poor Clare nunnery which might be that of Sant Antoni i Santa Clara in Barcelona. BC, Ms. 865, fol. 6v. Public Domain — 77
2.10. 'Nuns in Procession', in *Collection of moral tracts* (MS, c.1290), probably commissioned by the Cistercian nunnery of Notre-Dame-la-Royale at Maubuisson in France. London, British Library, Yates Thompson MS 11. Public Domain — 81
2.11. *Missa pro Mulieribus Pregnantibus* and annotation about the book owner in a plainchant notebook used by Sor Maria Dominga Pinós, a Capuchin nun in Barcelona. ADB, Jurisdicción Castrense 14, pp. 144–145, and blank sheet at the beginning. Photograph by the author — 82
2.12. [Breviary from the convent of Santa Maria de Jonqueres (Lyon: Bernard Lescuyer, 1521)], Common of the Saints, fol. 1r. Barcelona, Biblioteca Pública Episcopal, Res. 264-13 Bre. Image from: Altés 1990: 61 — 89
2.13. Francesc Valls (c.1671–1747), 'Deidades del abismo', *tono* for two tiples and accompaniment to be sung during a profession of vows. BC, M 1686/26. Public Domain — 96

Figures xi

2.14. First folio of the first alto part of the profession of vows villancico 'Angélicos giros' (1740) by Josep Pujol. BC, M 1470/19. Public Domain — 97

2.15. Title page of the printed lyrics of the villancicos sung at the convent of Sant Pere de les Puel·les for the profession of Maria Josefa de Vilallonga i Ialpi. BC, F.Bon. 9484. Public Domain — 98

2.16. Book of proceedings of the confraternity of booksellers in Barcelona (1579–1583). 'Llibre d'actes de la confraria de Sant Jeroni dels llibreters de Barcelona'. AHPB, 409/88. Photograph by the author — 103

2.17. Saint Maurice, patron saint of the cloth dyers guild in Barcelona. Copy of a sixteenth-century image preserved in Barcelona, Gremi de Tintoreres y Bugaders. enciclopedia.cat — 105

2.18. Agreement between the convent of Santa Maria de Montsió and the confraternity of *verguers* and *porters* in 1524. Barcelona, AHP, 278/43. Photograph by the author — 106

3.1. Josep Dalmau's *Relación de la solemnidad con que se han celebrado en la ciudad de Barcelona las fiestas a la beatificación de la madre S. Teresa de Jesús [...]* (Barcelona: Sebastià Matevad, 1615), title page. BC, 16-I-87. Public Domain — 130

3.2. Location of the three Carmelite convents in Barcelona — 131

3.3. Circle of Giovanni Balducci, 'il Cosci' (c.1560-1631), *Procession of Nuns and Novices Honoring a Male Saint*, 166 x 412 mm. Chicago, Art Institute, The Leonora Hall Gurley Memorial Collection, 1982.269. Public Domain — 136

3.4. First page of the 'Llibre de las Ceremonias del Cor fet per Dona Juana de Argensola Religiosa y Cabiscola de esta Casa de nostra señora de Junqueras; fet en lo Any 1640', in *Libro de la fundación, traslado y visitas*, ACA,ORM,Monacales-Universidad,Volúmenes,244, fols. 84r–95v — 138

3.5. Location of the convent of Santa Maria de Valldonzella (number 19 on the map). Detail from: Johann Stridbeck (1666–1714), 'Barcelona, die Haupt Statt des Fürstenthums Catalonien', in *Curioses Staats und Kriegs Theatrum* (Augsburg: Johann Stridbeck, 1711–1714). Barcelona, Institut Cartogràfic i Geològic de Catalunya. Creative Commons — 140

3.6. The gate of Sant Antoni. Detail from: Georg Braun (1541–1622) y Joris Hoefnagel (1542–1601), *Barcino, quae vulgo Barcelona dicitur, urbis est apud Hispanos celebérrima* ([s.l.]: [s.n.], 1572). BNE, R/22249(1) PL. 6 — 141

xii *Figures*

3.7. Baltasar del Hierro, *Los triumphos y grandes recebimientos dela insigne ciudad de Barcelona ala venida del famosissimo Phelipe rey delas Españas &c. Con la entrada de los serenissimos principes de Bohemia* (Barcelona: Iayme Cortey, 1564), title page. Barcelona, Universitat de Barcelona, Biblioteca de Reserva, B-44/3/13-2. Public Domain — 143

4.1. Diego Pérez de Valdivia, *Tratado de alabança de la castidad* (Barcelona: Iayme Cendrad, 1587). Rome, Biblioteca Universitaria Alessandrina, Q a 66. Public Domain — 160

4.2. Choir of the convent of the Mare de Déu dels Àngels in Barcelona (photographed in 1918). BC, Fons fotogràfic Salvany. Creative Commons — 161

4.3. Portrait of Saint Christina Mirabilis (c.1150–1224). Vienna, Österreichische Nationalbibliothek, PORT_00113353_01. Public Domain — 164

4.4. Dimas Serpi, *Tratado del purgatorio contra Luthero y otros herejes con singular y varia dotrina de mucho provecho y muy útil para predicadores, curas, religiosos y para todos los estados* (Barcelona: Iayme Cendrat, 1604 [Barcelona: Gabriel Graells y Giraldo Dótil, 1600]). Monistrol de Montserrat (Barcelona), Biblioteca de la Abadia. Public Domain — 166

4.5. Richard the Hermit (Richard Rolle), in 'The Desert of Religion', ink and pigments on vellum, 1425. London, British Library, Cotton MS Fastina B VI, vol. II, fol. 8v — 167

4.6. Account book containing records of anniversaries celebrated at the Barcelona convent of Sant Pere de les Puel·les between 1506 and 1540. 'Despensa feta per la anima de la señora Johana de Paguera y Aldonsa de Paguera'. AMSP, Llibres d'abadesses, no. 178, fols. 14v–15r. Photograph by the author — 172

4.7. 'Llibre en lo qual estan continuats los officis y Aniuersaris que per lo discurs del any celebran la Señora Abadessa y Señoras Monges del Monastir de Sant Pere'. AMSP, Llibres de fundacions, no. 1, fol. 69r. Photograph by the author — 173

4.8. Signs of use, calculating the total amount of Saint Gregory's Masses, in a copy of the 1604 edition of Dimas Serpi's *Tratado del purgatorio* (1600), p. 364. Madrid, Universidad Complutense de Madrid. Public Domain — 183

4.9. Fernando de Zárate, *Comedia famosa. De las Missas de San Vicente Ferrer* [no editorial details, written in 1661]. Madrid, Real Academia Española, 41-IV-59(7). Creative Commons — 186

4.10. Fra Angelico, *The Burial of the Virgin and the Reception of Her Soul in Heaven* (1434–1435), tempera and gold on panel, 26 x 53 cm. Philadelphia, Museum of Art, John G. Johnson Collection, 1917, Cat. 15 — 187

4.11. Illustration of the burial of Ignatius of Loyola, in Pedro de Ribadeneira (1527–1611), *Vita beati patris Ignatii Loyolae religionis societatis Iesv fvndatoris* (s.n., 1611). BNE, ER/6049 ILUSTRACIONES. Public Domain — 189

4.12. Engraving by Gustave Doré depicting a festive wake for a child. 'Une danse funébre (*jota*), à Jijona (province d'Alicante)', in Barón Davillier and Gustave Doré, *Le Tour du Monde, Voyage en Espagne 1862 a 1873* (Paris: Typographie Lahure, 1875), p. 317. Creative Commons — 190

4.13. Francisco Oller, *El velatorio* (The wake) (1893), oil on canvas, 269.5 x 412 cm. Río Piedras (Puerto Rico), Museo de Historia, Antropología y Arte. Creative Commons — 190

4.14. Family tree (and detail) included in Honorat Ciuró (1612–1674), *Camins traçats* (MS, 1642). Perpignan, Archives Communales de Perpignan, Fons Enric Pull, 17 S 1, fol. 26r ['Felix died at his parents' home when he was four or five days old; he was buried with polyphonic singing in the new tomb of the chapel of Our Lady of the Conception on 8 March 1650' (*mori felix en casa sus pares de edat de quatro o sinch dias enterrat a cant dorga y collocat dins la noua sepultura en la capella de n[ostr]a s[enyor]a de la concepcion als 8 de mars 1650*)] — 192

5.1. Plainchant treatise belonging to the Poor Clare convent in Valencia. *Ars cantus plani*, MS (fifteenth century). BC, M 1327 G. Fol, fols. 72v–89r, fol. 80r. Public Domain — 206

5.2. Guillem Caçador, *Ordinarium Barcinonense* (Barcelona: Claudium Bornat, 1569), title-page and fol. 246v. BC, 10-III-1. Public Domain — 207

5.3. Poem by Agraïda Grimau (d.1614), included among the preliminary material of: Vicente Miguel de Moradell, *Historia de S. Ramon de Peñafort frayle de Predicadores en coplas Castellanas* (Barcelona: Sebastián de Cormellas, 1603), s. fol. BC, 8-II-29. Public Domain — 214

xiv *Figures*

5.4a and 5.4b. Sonnet and gloss by Agraïda Grimau (d.1614), in Luis Díez de Aux, *Retrato de las fiestas que á la Beatificacion de la Bienaventurada Virgen y Madre Santa Teresa de Iesus, Renouadora de la Religion Primiua del Carmelo, hizo, assi Ecclesiasticas como Militares y Poeticas: la Imperial Ciudad de Zaragoça* (Saragossa: Iuan de la Naja y Quartanet, 1615), pp. 86, 98–99. BNE, R/457. Public Domain — 216

5.5. Alfonsa de Salazar (d.1639–1641) playing the harp and singing, in Miguel Toledano, *Minerva Sacra* (Madrid: Iuan de la Cuesta, 1616). Santiago de Compostela, Biblioteca de la Universid ade, Biblioteca Xeral 8756. Public Domain — 224

5.6. Title page of *Cancionero de Nuestra Señora: en el qual ay muy buenos romances, canciones y villancicos: aora nueuamente añadido* (Barcelona: en casa de la biuda de Hubert Gotart, 1591). BC, 6-VI-16. Public Domain — 225

5.7. Onofre Almudéver, *Coplas en alabança de la Virgen nuestra Señora al tono de ya tiene saya blanca, con otras dos canciones muy deuotas* (Barcelona: Sebastián de Cormellas, 1609). BC, 3-VI-8/12. Public Domain — 227

5.8. Beginning of the anonymous three-voice Catalan villancico 'Bella, de vos som amorós' at the *Cancionero de Uppsala* (RISM 1556/30), fols. 17v–19r, fols. 17v–18r. Uppsala, Uppsala Universitetbibliotek, Uka Utl.vok.mus .tr. 611. Public Domain — 228

5.9. Songbook belonging to the Barcelonan Carmelite nunnery (late sixteenth to nineteenth centuries). Barcelona, Arxiu de les Carmelites descalces, Ms. s.n. Photograph by Mercè Gras — 229

5.10. Diego de Mendoza, *Chronica de la provincia de San Antonio de los Charcas del orden de nuestro seraphico padre San Francisco en las Indias Occidentales Ryeno del Peru* (Madrid: s.n., 1665), title-page. New York, The New York Public Library, *KB+ 1665. <https://digitalcollections.nypl.org> — 232

5.11. Antonio de la Calancha, *Coronica [sic] moralizada del orden de San Augustin en el Peru, con sucesos egenplares en esta monarquia* (Barcelona: Pedro Lacavalleria, 1638), frontispiece. Madrid, Biblioteca AECID, 3GR-7118. Creative Commons — 233

Tables

1.1.	Urban nunneries active in sixteenth-century Barcelona	7
1.2.	Main male religious houses active in sixteenth-century Barcelona city	12
1.3.	Records of the visitations to the convent of Santa Maria de Jonqueres	28
1.4.	Contents of the report from the investigation into Angelina de Lupià's lineage in 1578	39
2.1.	Extraordinary payments to priests for the celebration of solemn Offices and Masses at the church of Sant Pere de les Puel·les convent	57
2.2.	Members of the community of priests at the convent of Sant Pere de les Puel·les in 1582. AMSP, Llibres de visites, no. 1, fol. 9r	58
2.3.	Organists hired by the convent of Sant Pere de les Puel·les in the sixteenth century according to the account books	62
2.4.	Organists hired at the convent of Santa Maria de Jonqueres between the fifteenth and the seventeenth centuries	63
2.5.	Earliest handwritten chant books preserved in the convent of Sant Pere de les Puel·les	66
2.6.	Excerpts bound together in chant book no. 3 of the convent of Sant Pere de les Puel·les	70
2.7.	Books included in a 1422 inventory of the convent of Sant Antoni i Santa Clara. 'Memorial de desapropis i càrrecs', AMSBM, box 15, no. 640/20 (1422), fol. 7v	74
2.8.	Handwritten plainchant books for processions belonging to individual nuns that are preserved in the archive of the convent of Sant Antoni i Santa Clara	78
2.9.	Legacies of procession plainchant notebooks recorded in wills of Santa Maria de Jonqueres convent. 'Libro de desapropio (testamento)' (1411–1741), ACA,ORM,Monacales-Universidad,Volúmenes,241	83

2.10.	Some of the plainchant books to be used in the choir belonging to the convent of Santa Maria de Jonqueres, according to inventories included in visitation books	86
2.11.	Participation of external chapel musicians (*capillas*) in the singing of villancicos on the occasion of nuns' professions at sixteenth-century Barcelona convents	90
2.12.	Female printers and booksellers in sixteenth-century Barcelona	100
2.13.	Examples of confraternities instituted in Barcelona nunneries	102
3.1.	Examples of royal visits to the convent of Santa Maria de Jonqueres in the sixteenth century	123
4.1.	Prayers *sine intermissione* to be said in Barcelona convents every day to ask God for a victory in Hungary, according to the resolution made by the city councillors on 13 August 1532 (*Manual de novells ardits...*, vol. 3, pp. 453–454)	156
4.2.	Examples from: 'Asientos de los aniversarios y misas cantadas de devoción en el año 1661 que se celebran en Santa Maria de Jonqueres, hechos por Sor Agraida Pons y Turell'. ACA,ORM,Monacales-Universidad,Legajos,8,3, fols. 1r–13v	178
4.3.	Ceremonies founded by Eugènia Grimau in her will (1636). 'Llibre de desapropis' (1411–1741), ACA,ORM,Monacales-Universidad,Volúmenes,241, fol. 270r–272r	181
4.4.	Post-mortem liturgical celebrations in honour of *albats* at the convent of Santa Maria de Jonqueres. 'Barcelona, convento de Santa Maria de Jonqueres. Libro de cuentas'. ACA, ORM, Monacales-Universidad,Volúmenes,381, fols. 1r–6v	191
4.5.	Some of the devotional Masses with music celebrated at Santa Maria de Jonqueres convent at Corpus Christi Octave for the nuns themselves. 'Memoria de totas las misses de deuocio que an de celebrar en la octaua de Corpus de las señoras religiosas de esta casa', in 'Asientos de los aniversarios y misas cantadas de devoción en el año 1661 que se celebran en Santa Maria de Jonqueres, hechos por Sor Agraïda Pons y Turell', ACA,ORM,Monacales-Universidad,Legajos,8,3, fol. 14r	194
5.1.	Visitors sent to the convent of Santa Maria de Jonqueres	209
5.2.	Lyrics to be sung *al tono de* at the *Cancionero de Nuestra Señora: en el qual ay muy buenos romances, canciones y villancicos: aora nueuamente añadido* (Barcelona: en casa de la biuda de Hubert Gotart, 1591)	226
5.3.	Lyrics devoted to the profession of particular Carmelite nuns in 1603–1608 and 1619 included in the songbook Barcelona, Arxiu de les Carmelites descalces, Ms. s.n.	230

Note for the reader: eResources

The appendices for this book are available through a digital eResource page. To access the appendices, visit <https://www.routledge.com/9781032273617>.

Digital appendices

Appendix 1. Records of inquiries into the linage of Santa Maria de Jonqueres nuns
Appendix 2. Development of the collections of choir books belonging to the convents of Santa Maria de Jonqueres and Sant Antoni i Santa Clara
    2.1. Santa Maria de Jonqueres nunnery
    2.2. Sant Antoni i Santa Clara nunnery
Appendix 3. Villancicos performed by external musicians on the occasion of nuns' profession of vows in Barcelonan convents (seventeenth and eighteenth centuries)
Appendix 4. Original language transcription of selected documents
    4.1. Books ownership and foundation of liturgical celebrations in Santa Maria de Jonqueres nuns' wills
    4.2. References to music and the convents under study in the *Dietaris de la Generalitat de Catalunya* (fifteenth to mid-seventeenth centuries)
    4.3. Musical references in Sebastià Roger's 1598 book on the different professions in Sant Antoni i Santa Clara nunnery and their obligations
Appendix 5. List of selected archival documents

Acknowledgements

This book presents some of the results of my work on the project 'Urban musics and musical practices in sixteenth-century Europe' (CIG-2012-URBANMUSICS no. 321876), funded by the Marie Curie Foundation and directed by Tess Knighton at the Spanish National Research Council in Barcelona. This four-year project finished in November 2016 and aimed to open up new perspectives on urban musical culture through the lens of the city of Barcelona, its external European music networks and internal musical dynamics, as well as the more general question of urban musical experience in the early modern period. As a postdoctoral research assistant for this project, I focused my research on the study of Inquisition records as evidence of the presence and moral status of music in urban daily life, the analysis of the integration of music at urban festivities such as beatifications and *autos de fe*, and an inquiry into the role of female convents in the soundscape of sixteenth-century Barcelona, which is the topic of this monograph. It was a great honour to participate in this project and to do research in such a stimulating and warm atmosphere. I cannot thank Tess Knighton enough for her generosity and for all that I have learnt.

I would like to express my appreciation to Núria Jornet, a professor at the department of library and documentation studies at the University of Barcelona, who provided me with helpful suggestions to undertake research at convent archives and put me in contact with Irene Brugués, the head archivist of the Service of Archives of the Catalan Federation of Benedictine Nuns (*Servei d'Arxius de la Federació Catalana de Monges Benedictines*), which includes the archives of the nunneries of Sant Pere de les Puel·les and Sant Antoni i Santa Clara in Barcelona, and that of Sant Daniel in Girona. I am very grateful to Irene for her orientation and service at the archive of Sant Pere convent, and also to Sor Coloma Boada, secretary of the Service of Archives, who welcomed me at the convent of Sant Benet de Montserrat, where the documental collection of the Barcelona convent of Sant Antoni i Santa Clara is preserved. I would like to thank the staff of the archives where I worked, including the Arxiu de la Corona d'Aragó, Arxiu Diocesà, and Arxiu Històric de Protocols in Barcelona, as well as the Arxiu Nacional de Catalunya (Sant Cugat del Vallès, Barcelona) and the Archivo Histórico Nacional (Madrid), for their kindness and support. I am also very grateful to Joan Roca, director of the Museu d'Història in Barcelona, for his interest in my research, and to Colleen Baade, Mercè Gras, Verònica Zaragoza, and Eduardo Carrero for their wonderful conversations. Sincere thanks to James Ritzema and Micah Neale for their diligent proofreading of my text, and to the Martin Picker Fund of the American Musicological Society, supported in part by the National Endowment for the Humanities and the Andrew W. Mellon Foundation, for awarding me with a subvention for the publication of this book.

Abbreviations

ACA	Barcelona, Arxiu de la Corona d'Aragó
ADB	Barcelona, Arxiu Diocesà
AHCB	Barcelona, Arxiu Històric de la Ciutat
AHN	Madrid, Archivo Histórico Nacional
AHPB	Barcelona, Arxiu Històric de Protocols
AMP	Barcelona, Arxiu del Monestir de Pedralbes
AMSBM	Barcelona, Arxiu del Monestir de Sant Benet de Montserrat
AMSP	Barcelona, Arxiu del Monestir de Sant Pere de les Puel·les
ANC	Sant Cugat del Vallès, Barcelona, Arxiu Nacional de Catalunya
BC	Barcelona, Biblioteca de Catalunya
BNE	Madrid, Biblioteca Nacional de España

Introduction

Our perception of musical life in sixteenth-century convents is largely shaped by the insightful scholarship on Italian nunneries carried out by Robert Kendrick (1996), Craig Monson (1995, 2010, 2012), Colleen Reardon (2001), and Laurie Stras (2017a, b, 2018), as well as Geoffrey Baker's work (2003) on Cuzco, Alejandro Vera (2020) on Santiago de Chile, Dianne Hall (2003) about Ireland, Barbara Eichner (2011) on Germany, Colleen Baade (1997, 2005, 2011) on Castile, or Antónia Fialho Conde (2013, 2016, 2019) on Portugal. These studies, among many others, demonstrate that nuns' music was not only a means of praising God but was also involved in the musical life of the city. It has often been claimed that the musical life of Italian nuns and women in general was much livelier than it was in Spain (Ramos 2005: 117). Nevertheless, this view might be distorted by the scarcity of Spanish sources preserved, and this study aims to nuance this assumption by presenting the first study of music in convent life in a single Hispanic city, namely Barcelona, following on from other works in the field of urban musicology focused on Iberian cities.[1] Seventeen female convents have been identified as being active in the city in the sixteenth century, a period often overlooked in the existing bibliography. Some of these convents were very centrally located, near the main centres of musical activity in Barcelona, and they were important settings for social networking and meetings between nuns and laywomen, who were able to display social status through devotional musical celebrations. This book analyses how nunneries were involved in the musical networks operating in the city and how both nuns and laywomen contributed to musical life by using these spaces in the broad sixteenth century.

In 1977 the French economist Jacques Attali argued that different musical networks represented distinctive types of social and economic relations. He proposed four successive types of distribution networks for music linked to four categories of social organisation (Attali 1977: 110; Fuhse 2009; Leyshon 2014). The first two types are relevant to sixteenth-century Barcelona: in the first, named sacrifice, music is considered as a part of oral tradition and intrinsic to religion, while the second type of musical network, called representation, operated after the invention of the printing press, when music became broadly commercialised and acquired a trade value. An exploration of how convents were involved in the musical networks operating in sixteenth-century Barcelona demonstrates an

DOI: 10.4324/9781003292371-1

overlapping of these two types of distribution for music which help to illuminate its role in this urban society. Music was a commercial product which involved patrons, audiences, musicians, instrument-makers, scribal activity, printers, and music books. Yet this book argues that the essential roles women played in musical networks—in Barcelona, but also nationally and transnationally—had motivations that stemmed from other values attributed to music: as a marker of identity, prestige, and social status, but above all, as a conduit between earth and heaven. This latter belief has deep philosophic roots, some of which predate Christianity, and was integral to popular religiosity. The connections of Barcelona convents to the networks which disseminated music in and outside the city serve as an example of the close relationship between musical networks, urban society, and popular culture.

In the early modern period, Barcelona was an important urban centre in both Iberian and European contexts. Studies of its musical activity have focused on important institutions such as the cathedral (Gregori 1987), the use of instrumental music in ceremony (Kreitner 1995), and sources of notated polyphony (Ros-Fábregas 1992, 2015; Puentes-Blanco 2018). Through the project 'Urban musics and musical practices in sixteenth-century Europe' (URBANMUSICS), Tess Knighton has developed in-depth studies of the soundscape of early modern Barcelona, from perspectives such as the citizens' sound experience, drawing on concepts borrowed from social anthropology or sound studies, such as 'acoustic community', defined by Barry Truax as 'any soundscape in which acoustic information plays a pervasive role in the lives of the inhabitants'.[2] Moreover, she is currently writing a 'history from below' of the musical life of the city, based on notarial documentation.

Barcelona's nunneries have received attention from several disciplines, with a focus on the periods before and after the sixteenth century.[3] For instance, the project CLAUSTRA (University of Barcelona) has catalogued and mapped the spaces of feminine spirituality in medieval Catalonia,[4] while several other studies have analysed the productions of nun writers.[5] However, the musical connections between female convents and the city remained generally unexplored for sixteenth-century Barcelona. Because of the disappearance of most of these convents, the geographic dispersion or destruction of their archives, and the lack of sixteenth-century musical sources beyond chant books, this study proves challenging and indirect approaches are required to study the imbrication of convents in the city's musical and cultural life. Methodologically, this destruction or dispersion of sources inevitably leads a researcher to explore 'convents without a memory of their own', by searching for scattered details in documentary records.[6]

This research is based on close reading of a variety of archival documents— mostly in archives located in Barcelona and Madrid—such as account books, wills, inventories, contracts, books of anniversaries and foundations, rules of religious orders, chant books, literary sources, books of pastoral visitations, reports on particular events, biographies of nuns and friars, letters, diaries, and books of ceremonies, among others. Musical sources have been examined for clues about processes of musical exchange—for instance, signs of use—and interpreted as artefacts derived from the material culture of the period. However, the inherent problems of these diverse source materials require a variety of methodologies from outside musicology to be used, including practices from book history, the history of popular culture, historical anthropology, cultural theory, gender studies, philosophy, religious history, and digital humanities. Traces of convent musical practices are often found in sources not usually considered by musicologists, detectable only via the 'oblique' methods employed by historians of popular culture (Burke 1978: 65).

While it has traditionally been claimed that the absence of women from historical records was caused by their confinement within a domestic or conventual milieu, the boundaries between 'private' and 'public' are far from being clear, and it is precisely when a blurring between private and public occurs—as in the case of nuns' musical performance in urban contexts—that traces of women's musical practices in private settings emerge. Invoking the concept of 'networks', and studying spaces where not only 'public' and 'private', but also written and oral overlap—such as the printing of lyrics intended to be sung to orally transmitted tunes—helps to make women's musical practices more visible, as well as offering a different window onto the musical culture of a city. One objective of this study is to challenge the invisibility of women in music history by studying, from a cross-disciplinary perspective, the participation of women in the configuration of music networks within and outside the city of Barcelona, drawing especially on convent spaces. Networks for the dissemination of musical artefacts, musicians, musical discourse, and oral traditions of music will be considered.

The role of convents in networks for distributing music has been studied by establishing parallels between the history of women's music and the history of religion, through the methodology of the history of popular culture. James Amelang has drawn attention to the relevance of studying the history of religion as an approach to the history of women, particularly in the Iberian world, since 'religion provided women with a rich and expressive vocabulary, and served as a system of social communication in which, for diverse reasons, women were distinguished as especially active participants'.[7] In recent decades, the Council of Trent has been reinterpreted 'within a continuity of Catholic reform and popular devotional movements spanning many generations'.[8] This book aims to show that the influence of the Tridentine prescriptions on the musical life of Barcelona nunneries was unequal and gradual and that the sixteenth century was a period of constant reform but also of resistance, both of which affected convent musical life.

This book is structured into five chapters. Chapter 1 maps the seventeen convents under consideration, located inside (or very close to) the city walls of sixteenth-century Barcelona, and their history. It discusses the methodological challenges involved in approaching musical activities through the thick reading of a variety of archival documents, and analyses the socio-economic and cultural context of the nuns and their relationships to music. Several of these nunneries were inhabited by noblewomen, who lived in separate houses with their own servants and slaves within the convent premises, which had an impact on the functions of convent musical life. Chapter 2 describes the networks which configured the musical cartography of the city and the place occupied by convents in this complex system. Due to the scarcity and geographical dispersion of the musical sources belonging to sixteenth-century convents, it is necessary to approach the musical repertory performed by (and for) these nuns through the comparison of the preserved sources with later pieces from Catalonia and Castile, such as villancicos, *tonos*, and other polyphonic genres performed, for instance, during ceremonial professions of vows. Chapter 3 shows how the high social status of the nuns in most convents played an important role in the connections between convents, music, and political life. This chapter theorises about the 'inside-outside' spatial dichotomy in terms of nunneries in order to assess how nuns, from their own cloistered spaces, were able to exhibit and exteriorise the urban status of the institution through music. Chapter 4 argues that one of the reasons for the importance of convents in the urban soundscape was their use as spaces where, through liturgical music, it was possible to establish a connection with the celestial realm. The belief in music as a means to relieve the suffering of the souls in Purgatory and the identification of nuns' voices as those of angels were connected to popular and official religiosity both before and after the Council of Trent. Comparative analysis of a diversity of archival sources is needed to assess the extent to which music was present in the Masses and Offices celebrated in urban convents and their impact on the aural experience of the citizens. Finally, Chapter 5 addresses processes of musical-cultural exchange, arguing that religious orders were an important means of disseminating music and musical discourse across geographical boundaries. The study of the religious orders facilitates a preliminary analysis of the musical and liturgical networks connecting Barcelona to other European cities and also to the New World. It appears that these networks not only served to disseminate musical artefacts and musical discourse, but also to transmit oral traditions in music.

Due to their length, appendices are presented online. They include an outline of the records of inquiries into the lineage of Santa Maria de Jonqueres nuns, tables showing the development of the collection of chant books belonging to the convents of Santa Maria de Jonqueres and Sant Antoni i Santa Clara, lists of printed lyrics of villancicos sung during ceremonial professions of vows by chapel musicians from outside the convents, original language transcription of selected documents such as the wills of Santa Maria de Jonqueres nuns which act as evidence, for instance, of individual book ownership and legacies between women, the references to music and the convents under study in the *Dietaris de la Generalitat de Catalunya* between the fifteenth and mid-seventeenth centuries, and a list of archival documents. The complete information provided by most of the archival documents analysed in this study has been incorporated into an online database which is a product of the URBANMUSICS project.[9] This database allows the reader to connect each document to the people, urban spaces, music genres, or religious orders mentioned. Moreover, this platform makes available to researchers a rich body of material which will hopefully fuel further study from a variety of disciplines in the future. This technological tool, together with an online application which presents the locations of these nunneries on a current map of the city, and links these locations to archival documents and images, complements and illustrates this study.[10]

Notes

1 See, for instance, Marín 2002 on Jaca, and Ruiz Jiménez 2019 about Granada, or Bejarano 2019 on Seville, among others. For a review of the studies on 'urban soundscapes' in the sixteenth century, see Fenlon 2018.
2 Truax 2001 [1984]: 66. See, among others, Knighton 2017a, 2017b, 2017c; and Knighton and Mazuela-Anguita 2015, 2017, 2018.
3 For general studies on Catalan convents and monasteries, see Pladevall 1974 (particularly pp. 194–235); and Zaragoza i Pascual 1997, which provides information on 425 institutions.
4 Garí *et al.* 2014. The CLAUSTRA platform is accessible at <http://www.ub.edu/claustra/>.
5 See, for example, Zaragoza Gómez 2016 and Gras Casanovas 2013c, among others.
6 In the field of art history, these methodological challenges have been raised in the case of the Barcelona nunnery of Santa Maria de Valldonzella by Albacete i Gascón and Güell i Baró 2014.
7 Amelang 1990: 191: 'la religión puso a disposición de las mujeres un vocabulario rico y expresivo, y sirvió como sistema de comunicación social, en el que, por diversas razones, las mujeres se distinguieron como participantes especialmente eficaces' [translations are the author's].
8 Monson 2002: 1. On the impact of the Council of Trent in Catalonia, see Kamen 1993. Regarding how the Counter-Reformation affected Spanish music, see, among others, Roldán 2015.
9 URBANMUSICS database, <http://urbanmusics.com>.
10 *Urban Convents and Music Networks in Early Modern Barcelona*, <http://arcg.is/14e55P>.

1 Mapping convents' sound in the city

At least seventeen female convent institutions that were located inside or very close to the city walls were active in sixteenth-century Barcelona (Table 1.1). Most of their buildings have disappeared and it is necessary to consult contemporary artistic evidence, as well as later drawings, engravings, and photographs, to ascertain details of their location and appearance.[1] The earliest institutions, such as the Benedictine convents of Sant Pere de les Puel·les and Sant Antoni i Santa Clara, the Cistercian Santa Maria de Valldonzella and the convent of Santa Maria de Jonqueres, belonging to the Order of Santiago, were located in strategic points close to the gates of the city wall (Figures 1.1 and 1.2). In fact, the eleven bastions of the city wall which protected Barcelona in the seventeenth century included three named after these convents: Santa Clara, Jonqueres, and Sant Pere (Figure 1.3). The convents of Santa Teresa, Santa Maria de Montsió, Santa Maria Magdalena, Beates de Santo Domingo, and Trinitat were around the cathedral, close to the male religious houses, in the space occupied by the medieval city. The area located on the west side of Les Rambles expanded as a consequence of the foundations of female convents, such as Santa Maria de Jerusalem, Nostra Senyora de la Misericordia, Santa Elisabet, Montalegre, Mare de Déu dels Àngels, Nostra Senyora de la Victòria, Les Jerònimes, and Santa Margarida la Reial, which were located further away from the cathedral surroundings. The surviving itineraries of sixteenth-century processions in Barcelona suggest that the western nunneries were considered to be second-ranked in comparison with male institutions on the east side of Les Rambles (Puentes-Blanco 2018: 453) and recent studies in the field of ancient history have shown the importance of gender in the cartography of a city, as a category to plan and design the spaces and to rethink the city and its networks (Martínez López and Ubric Rabaneda 2017). Moreover, the relevance of gender in the definition of early modern routes and spaces has already been addressed from interdisciplinary perspectives, resulting in the nuancing of the traditional gendering of space through the dichotomy between private and public, and the analysis of how gender influenced the experience of space (Wiesner-Hanks 2015).

Barcelonan convents formed part of a network of religious and civic institutions and musical activity functioned both as a link between these different centres and as a shared means of displaying social status. Music might act as an outlet of

DOI: 10.4324/9781003292371-2

Table 1.1. Urban nunneries active in sixteenth-century Barcelona

		Religious order	Foundation date	Sixteenth-century location
1	Monestir de Santa Maria de Valldonzella	Cistercian (*bernardas*)	1237. Moved to its sixteenth-century location in 1269	Creu Coberta, current Valldonzella Street
2	Monestir de Les Jerònimes (also known as Santa Margarida or Sant Maties)	Jeronymite (beguines between 1425 and 1475)	1475	Corner of Sant Antoni and Bisbe Laguarda Streets, space now occupied by the church of the Carme (convent currently located on 7 Mercè Rodoreda Street)
3	Monestir de Santa Margarida la Reial	Capuchin Poor Clare	1599	Carme Street (corner of Riera Alta Street)
4	Monestir de Nostra Senyora de la Victòria	Augustinian	1576	Carme Street (current Milà y Fontanals school)
5	Monestir de Santa Maria de Montalegre	Augustinian Canonesses (from 1256)	1362. Community abolished in 1593	Montalegre Street (from 1802 it was the Casa de la Caridad and currently it is the Centre de Cultura Contemporània de Barcelona)
6	Monestir de la Mare de Déu dels Àngels	Dominican	Moved from the Villa de Caldes to Peu de la Creu in 1497. Inside the city from 1561. Moved to Pedralbes in 1906	Dels Àngels Square, next to the Museu d'Art Contemporani de Barcelona (from 1562). Currently located at the convent of Sant Domènec (2 Mare de Déu del Roser Avenue, Sant Cugat del Vallès)
7	Monestir de Santa Elisabet	Poor Clare	1564	Elisabets Street. From 2007 these nuns have formed part of Santa Clara convent in Huesca (7 Santa Clara Square)
8	Casa de Nostra Senyora de la Misericordia [Charity]	Franciscan Third Order	1583	6 Elisabets Street (space currently occupied by the bookshop La Central del Raval)
9	Monestir de Santa Maria de Jerusalem	Poor Clare (from 1494)	1453	Gardunya Square. Moved to Vallvidrera (Passatge Mare de Déu de l'Estrella) in 1970

(*Continued*)

Table 1.1. (Continued)

	Religious order	Foundation date	Sixteenth-century location
10 Convent de la Trinitat	Trinitarian	1492. Transferred to Trinitarian monks in 1529	Ferran Street
11 Monestir de Santa Teresa (also known as Puríssima Concepció)	Discalced Carmelite	1588. First church began to be built in 1601 (inaugurated in 1608)	Vila de Madrid Square
12 Monestir de Santa Maria de Montsió (also known as Sant Pere Màrtir)	Dominican	1351	Santa Anna Square (Portal de l'Àngel Avenue, corner of Montsió Street). The *Liceu* was founded in this space in 1835. Convent currently located on Església Street, Esplugues de Llobregat (in the province of Barcelona)
13 Monestir de Santa Maria de Jonqueres	Order of Santiago	1212. Inside the city walls from 1300	Jonqueres Street
14 Monestir de Santa Maria Magdalena	Augustinian (from 1500)	1372	Riera de Sant Joan Street (this street disappeared with the opening of Vía Laietana). Currently located on 5 Vallmajor Street
15 Beates de Santo Domingo	Dominican	1532	Beates Square
16 Monestir de Sant Pere de les Puel·les	Benedictine	10th century	1 Lluís el Piadós Street. The church of the former convent remains as a parish church. The convent is today located on 31 Dolors Monserdà Street
17 Monestir de Sant Antoni i Santa Clara	Poor Clare; Benedictine (from 1513)	1236	Ciutadella Park (space currently occupied by the secondary school IES Verdaguer and the Ciutadella chapel). The convent is today located on Sant Benet de Montserrat (Marganell, Barcelona)

8 *Mapping convents' sound in the city*

Figure 1.1. Location of the female convents active in sixteenth-century Barcelona. Map of sixteenth-century Barcelona (copy) [Markers are the author's]. AHCB, Fons Gràfics, Reg. 2980

competition between the city's ecclesiastical institutions, as is demonstrated by the disputes between churches such as Santa Maria del Mar or Santa Maria del Pi and the cathedral regarding the performance of polyphony. These references to polyphonic performances in Barcelonan churches, including those in nunneries, emphasise the need to reconsider the cathedral's supposedly exclusive right to freely perform polyphony in Barcelona, which led to confrontations between the chapel masters of Barcelonan ecclesiastical institutions and that of the cathedral in the second half of the sixteenth century. According to Josep Maria Gregori, the cathedral chapel master only granted licences for polyphonic performances to the city's ecclesiastical institutions on specific religious feasts. For instance, Antoni Salvat, the chapel master of the cathedral between 1517 and 1529, issued a licence for particular singers to perform polyphony at the convent of Sant Pere on 16 February 1526.[2] According to the 1579 testimony of Joan Borgunyó, a chapel master, at the time of Jaume Caçador—Bishop of Barcelona between 1546 and 1561—some obsequies were celebrated with a polyphonic Mass at the same convent, and it was the vicar general who provided the book of polyphony used in the performance.[3] Thus, both the spatial distribution of Barcelonan nunneries and their contribution to the musical networks operating in the city were closely connected to urban hierarchies of power.

Barcelonan nunneries belonged to three categories in the sixteenth century, depending on their religious order: those who had taken a vow of poverty, such as Franciscans, Augustinians, Dominicans, Trinitarians, and Discalced Carmelites;

10 *Mapping convents' sound in the city*

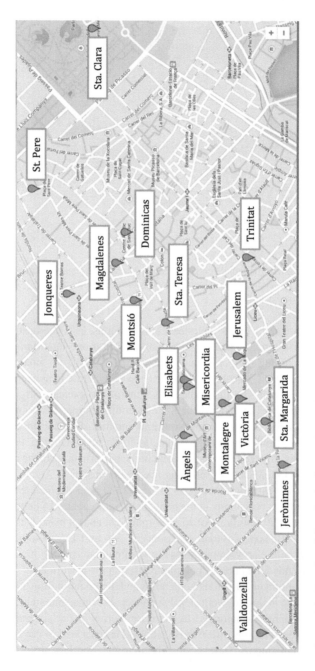

Figure 1.2. Female religious institutions active in sixteenth-century Barcelona on the current map of Barcelona city centre

Figure 1.3. Drawing (watercolour and graphite pencil on paper) of the bastion of Jonqueres (close to the convent of Santa Maria de Jonqueres) at the city wall of Barcelona (1825), by Adolphe Hedwige Alphonse Delamare (Paris, 1793–1861), Barcelona, Museu Nacional d'Art de Catalunya, depósito de la Generalitat de Catalunya, Col·lecció Nacional d'Art, 2017. © Museu Nacional d'Art de Catalunya, Barcelona, 2022

those who lived a monastic life, including Jeronymites, Benedictines, and Cistercians (*bernardas*); and those belonging to military orders, such as the Order of Santiago.[4] Different religious orders drew on music in a variety of ways, and the differences between them were more pronounced in the case of male institutions (Table 1.2). The important role played by music in Franciscan hagiography, art, theology, philosophy, and prayer is well known (Loewen 2013; Estévez 2021), as well as the emphasis on singing among the Jeronymite male monastic institutions.[5] The importance of music in Jeronymite male communities is reflected in the history of the order written by José de Sigüenza in 1600. Sigüenza's account includes a chapter on the training of novices which indicates the strong emphasis Jeronymite choirs placed on singing with extreme unity, solemnity, and heartfelt modesty; it ascribes superiority to the singing of Toledo Cathedral, which served as a point of imitation for Jeronymite choirs, while another chapter recounts the excellent musical skills of Bernardino de Aguilar, a friar at the (male) convent of Sant Jeroni de la Murtra in Barcelona, who died singing a psalm.[6] However, specific information on Jeronymite nuns' music is lacking. Likewise, the Benedictine order favoured music as a means of adding solemnity to the liturgical celebrations, and Zaragoza i Pascual (2003) identified forty-two Benedictine friar musicians in the sixteenth century, twenty-seven of them related to the abbey of Montserrat; by

12   *Mapping convents' sound in the city*

Table 1.2. Main male religious houses active in sixteenth-century Barcelona city

	Religious order	Foundation
Convent de Sant Agustí Vell	Augustinian	1309
Col·legi i convent de Sant Guillem d'Aquitània	Augustinian	1587
Convent de Sant Antoni Abat	Antonian	First stone in 1430
Monestir de Sant Pau del Camp	Benedictine	
Monestir de Santa Anna	Canónigos del Santo Sepulcro / Canons regular	1145
Monestir de Santa Eulàlia del Camp	Canons regular	1155
Canónica de la Catedral de Barcelona	Canons regular / Secular canons	
Convent de Montcalvari	Capuchin	1580 (church consecration)
Convent de Santa Madrona	Capuchin	
Convent de la Mare de Déu del Carme	Discalced Carmelite	1291–1292
Col·legi i convent de Sant Àngel	Discalced Carmelite	1593 (church consecration)
Convent de Sant Josep	Discalced Carmelite	1586
Priorat de Santa Maria de Natzaret	Cistercian	Early fourteenth century
Convent de Santa Caterina	Dominican	1219
Convent de Sant Francesc / Sant Nicolau de Bari	Franciscan	Early thirteenth century
Convent de Jesús	Franciscan	First stone in 1427
Encomienda de Sant Joan de Jerusalem	Hospitalarian	Early thirteenth century
Convent de la Mercè	Mercedarian	Fifteenth century
Capella Reial	Mercedarian	Ceded to the Mercedarian order in 1423
Convent de Sant Francesc de Paula	Minims	1573

contrast, there is once again a paucity of information about the music of female Benedictine houses in Barcelona. The evidence analysed in this book suggests that overriding issues of gender had a greater bearing on musical practices in female religious houses than the diversity of religious orders. Yet despite the increasing restrictions on nuns' musical activity beyond a simple declamation of the Divine Office over the course of the century, nuns managed to contribute to the soundscape of the city from their own spaces.

Urban nunneries

The Benedictine nunnery of Sant Pere de les Puel·les was the earliest female convent in the whole county of Barcelona and is considered the most important nunnery of the city in the Middle Ages. Located adjacent to the city walls, near the gate used by travellers coming from Girona, this convent dates back to the first half of the tenth century and was founded by the counts Sunyer and Riquida. Its church was consecrated in 945 (Pladevall 1974: 202) and torn down in 985 by Almansor's troops, thereafter being restored by Count Borrell II and inhabited by the daughters of the Catalan nobility (Diago 1603: 51r, 80v–81r, 83v; Alcalá 1998: 109). A new church was consecrated in 1147, which still survives today as a parish church, albeit with some gothic and Renaissance modifications (Crispí 2020; Figure 1.4). The convent's function as a parish church meant that its offerings of religious worship were deeply integrated into the daily life of Barcelona citizens.[7] The abbess of Sant Pere held considerable authority over urban life within the parish limits;[8] for instance, documents from the convent include mandates to expel women of immoral life from houses within the parish.[9] In 1835 the nuns were expelled, and the convent became a prison. It was collapsed in 1837 and some pieces of the original Romanic low cloister from the late twelfth century are preserved at the Museu Nacional d'Art de Catalunya (Figure 1.5). The community moved the current convent in Sarrià in 1879, where its archive is preserved (Pladevall 1974: 202).

The convent of Sant Antoni i Santa Clara was the first Poor Clare community in Catalonia. The foundation of this convent has been studied in the field of medieval history by Núria Jornet (see Jornet 2002, 2005, and 2007). The presence of a mendicant order in a medieval city was a symbol of urban status, in some ways equivalent to having a train station in the nineteenth century (Freed 1977; Loewen

Figure 1.4. The parish church of the convent of Sant Pere de les Puel·les as it survives today. Photograph by the author

14 *Mapping convents' sound in the city*

Figure 1.5. Pieces from the low cloister of the convent of Sant Pere de les Puel·les (after 1187). Barcelona, Museu Nacional d'Art de Catalunya, depósito de la Generalitat de Catalunya, Col·lecció Nacional d'Art, 1879. © Museu Nacional d'Art de Catalunya, Barcelona, 2022

2013: 44). By the time of Saint Francis's death in the 1220s, there were at least fifteen Franciscan foundations in the Iberian Peninsula, rising to at least sixteenth monasteries and many other convents for Poor Clare nuns by the end of the century (Loewen 2013: 197). The Barcelonan convent of Sant Antoni was founded in 1236[10] and located outside the city wall, at the current park of the Ciutadella, close to the Portal de Mar (Gate of the Sea) or of Sant Daniel—for this reason, the convent was also known as convent of Sant Daniel (Figure 1.6). The convent's boundaries were marked out by the Rec Comtal, an irrigation channel which existed until the nineteenth century. The medieval building was torn down in 1713, and its site is now occupied by a secondary school (IES Verdaguer, housed in the former governor's palace) and the Ciutadella chapel.[11] The cloister of this convent was considered the most architecturally distinguished in Barcelona (Diago 1603: 282v). The process of changing from the Poor Clare order to the Benedictine one finished in 1513 (Jornet 2012). The community moved to the Palau Reial in 1936, and then to the convent of Santa Cecília in Montserrat. In 1952 the community merged with the Benedictine convent of Sant Benet in Mataró and both communities founded the new community of Sant Benet de Montserrat, which resides in the current convent of Sant Benet de Montserrat (Margarell, Barcelona) from 1954.

Fourteen nuns of the Sant Antoni convent participated in the foundation of the Poor Clare convent of Santa Maria de Pedralbes, one of the main nunneries outside the city. This convent has not been included in this study on account of its very distant location from the city walls, aligning it more readily with more rural and feudal contexts than the urban institutions discussed here. It was founded

Mapping convents' sound in the city 15

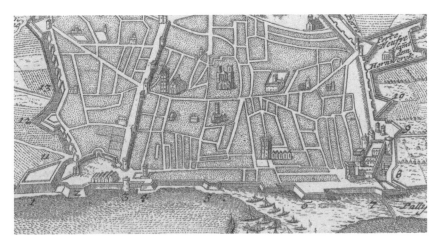

Figure 1.6. Location of the convent of Sant Antoni i Santa Clara adjacent to the gate of Sant Daniel (no. 9). Detail from: Johann Stridbeck (1666–1714), 'Barcelona, die Haupt Statt des Fürstenthums Catalonien' (1714), in *Curioses Staats und Kriegs Theatrum* (Augsburg: Johann Stridbeck, 1714). Barcelona, Institut Cartogràfic i Geològic de Catalunya. Creative Commons

by Elisenda de Montcada (1292–1364), who was the widow of King James II of Aragon, in 1327.[12] The connection between convents and aristocracy is also evident in the case of the convent of Santa Maria de Valldonzella, which was founded by Bishop Berenguer de Palau in 1237. In 1269 the community moved to a new building located outside the city walls, near the gate of Sant Antoni, at a place known as the Creu Coberta (Figure 1.7).[13] The convent, which was

Figure 1.7. Detail from: Jean Boisseau, *Nouvelle description de la fameuse ville de Barcelone cappitalle de la province de Catalogne* (Paris: chez Lou. Boissevin a la rue St Iaques a limage Ste Geneviesve, 164[5]). The location of the convent of Valldonzella is marked with 'V'. Barcelona, Institut Cartogràfic i Geològic de Catalunya. Creative Commons

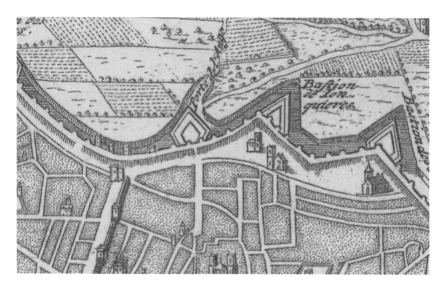

Figure 1.8. Location of the convent of Santa Maria de Jonqueres. Detail from: Johann Stridbeck (1666–1714), 'Barcelona, die Haupt Statt des Fürstenthums Catalonien' (1714), in *Curioses Staats und Kriegs Theatrum* (Augsburg: Johann Stridbeck, 1714). Barcelona, Institut Cartogràfic i Geològic de Catalunya. Creative Commons

demolished in 1651 during the war of *Els Segadors*, was a place of retirement for monarchs, including John I and Martin I of Aragon, and also served as a residence for sovereigns when they visited Barcelona. It was traditional for the monarchs to reside in Valldonzella, outside the city walls, the night before formal entry was made into the city.[14]

Bishop Berenguer de Palau was additionally responsible for the foundation of the important nunnery of Santa Maria de Jonqueres in Sant Vicenç de Jonqueres, near Sabadell (Barcelona) in 1214.[15] This community was formed around Maria de Terrassa, who was the first prioress of the nunnery. Originally under the Order of Saint Benedict, in 1234 the convent was acquired by the Order de Santiago, one of the military orders established in the Kingdom of León in the twelfth century to fight against the Muslim presence there and elsewhere (Lomax 1965; Mutgé 2001). The community moved to the Molí d'en Carbonell (Clot) in 1270, and to its final location inside the walls of Barcelona in 1300 (Figures 1.8 to 1.11). The Barcelonan building began to be constructed in 1293,[16] and the convent premises were limited by Jonqueres Street, Via Laietana, and Urquinaona Square. Although the community dispersed in 1808 when French troops turned the convent into a military hospital, the church and the cloister remained and were translated stone by stone to Aragó Street in 1868, as part of the Basilic of the Puríssima Concepció.[17] The historian Mercè Costa i Paretas has published prolifically on the history of the convent of Santa Maria de Jonqueres, and her work challenges the

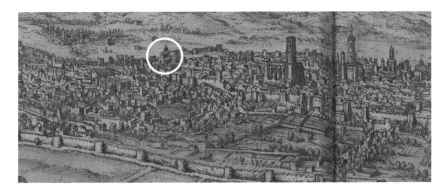

Figure 1.9. Location of the convent of Santa Maria de Jonqueres. Detail from: Georg Braun (1541–1622) and Joris Hoefnagel (1542–1601), *Barcino, quae vulgo Barcelona dicitur, urbis est apud Hispanos celeberrima* ([s.l.]: [s.n.], 1572). BNE, R/22249(1) PL. 6. Public Domain

Figure 1.10. The convent of Santa Maria de Jonqueres in its original situation, in a drawing by Francesc Soler Rovirosa (1864). AHCB, Fons Gràfics, Reg. 01047

statement included in Antoni Pladevall's study on Catalan convents and monasteries, according to which the convent of Jonqueres 'never was a convent with a very brilliant life'.[18]

Founded in 1347 with a bequest left by the princess Maria of Aragon, daughter of King James II, the convent of Santa Maria de Montsió is the oldest community

Figure 1.11. Drawing (watercolour and graphite pencil on paper) of the convent of Santa Maria de Jonqueres on 2 September 1827, by Adolphe Hedwige Alphonse Delamare (Paris, 1793–1861), when the building turned into a military hospital (from 1810). Barcelona, Museu Nacional d'Art de Catalunya, depósito de la Generalitat de Catalunya, Col·lecció Nacional d'Art, 2017. © Museu Nacional d'Art de Catalunya, Barcelona, 2022

of Dominican nuns in Barcelona. The clergymen attending on the Montsió nuns were the Dominican friars of the convent of Santa Caterina, and the mortal remains of the founder Maria of Aragon were translated from Santa Caterina to the cloister of Montsió in 1549.[19] The history of this nunnery from its foundation to the mid-sixteenth century has been studied in depth by María Soledad Hernández Cabrera.[20] In 1371 the king granted permission to build the new convent at the Raval, in the Gardunya Square.[21] This building, known as *casa d'En Porta*, was very close to the male Carmelite convent of Sant Josep, which would be founded in 1586 in a walled area at Les Rambles,[22] and also to houses for repentant women and brothels (Hernández 1997: 36). In 1423 the community moved to Santa Anna Square, close to the convent of Santa Maria Magdalena, changing its name from Sant Pere Màrtir to Santa Maria de Montsió.[23] The convent was bombarded in 1714, and, in addition to several military occupations, this space was also the place where the *liceu* of music and declamation was founded (Angelón 1870: 154; Alcalá 1994: 259). Finally, when the ruined building was returned to the nuns in 1875, the church and cloister of the convent were moved to the Rambla de Catalunya-Rosselló, where the community built a new convent in 1882 (Carreras i Candi [1908–1918?]: 475–476). In 1950 the community moved to Esplugues de Llobregat (in the province of Barcelona).

In 1487, the Montsió nuns had already expressed their disagreement with the foundation of a second Dominican convent, that of the Mare de Déu dels Àngels (Gras 2013b: 119; Paulí 1941b), which was at first located outside the urban centre, near the city walls and the sea in a place named Villa de Caldes. It was in 1497 when the community passed from being *beatas* to being nuns and the new convent was settled in a hermitage also outside the city walls (Peu de la Creu), which had previously been inhabited by the Poor Clare nuns of Santa Elisabet.[24] On 19 March 1562 the community moved to a location inside the city walls, at Dels Àngels Square, with the approval of Guillem Caçador (1510–1570), Bishop of Barcelona, who was away from the city attending the Council of Trent (Saurí and Matas 1849: 121). The building of the convent church began on 3 April 1562 and was finished on 23 February 1566. The translation of the most holy sacrament to the new building was a very solemn event involving the participation of the bishop of Tortosa, while the consecration of the church on 1 May 1566 was celebrated by Guillem Caçador himself (Paulí 1941b: 21). Writing in 1603, Francisco Diago described the convent as 'very religious and with a great number of nuns'.[25] The community currently resides in Sant Cugat del Vallès (in the province of Barcelona). It became custom that every pilgrim who entered or left Barcelona visited this convent (Vilarrúbia and Jové 1990: 35, no. 22). These nuns went out to found convents in Vic and Manresa, and four of them were commissioned by Bishop Joan Dimas Loris to improve the religious life of the Barcelonan convent of Santa Maria Magdalena, between 19 June 1586 and 13 April 1595 (Paulí 1941b: 22).

In 1365, the *Consell de Cent* (Barcelona's city council) promoted the establishment of a convent for repentant women. They first occupied a building in the parish of Santa Maria del Mar, and, afterwards, the community was settled in a chapel at the Riera de Sant Joan (Figure 1.12).[26] The convent was founded on 4 September 1372 under the Augustinian rule, and, subsequently, a community of Augustinian Canonesses nuns from Terrassa took over the convent.[27] It was confirmed in 1535 and was known as Santa Maria Magdalena or Les Magdalenes. The building was converted into a prison in the seventeenth century and demolished in 1877 (Hernández 1997: 36). Then, the community moved to the Torre Sarjalet in Gràcia and, in 1880, to a space between València and Muntaner Streets. The new convent was burned in the *Setmana Tràgica*—a violent episode between the Spanish army and the republicans of Barcelona and other Catalan cities during the week of 25 July 1909—and a new convent was inaugurated in 1911 in Vallmajor.

It was in the early modern period when ecclesiastical or private institutions emerged with the purpose of helping prostitutes. The houses for repentant women proliferated especially from the seventeenth century, linked to the royal decree which prohibited the existence of *mancebías*. In her study of the house for repentant women of Magdalena de San Jerónimo and the convent of San Felipe de la Penitencia in Valladolid, Margarita Torremocha explains how the sins of the flesh become a more pressing issue as a consequence of the regulation of marriage and pre-marital sexual

Figure 1.12. The convent of Santa Maria Magdalena in a drawing by Eduard Gràcia (1910–1915). AHCB, Fons Gràfics, Reg. 01667

relations stipulated by the Council of Trent (Torremocha 2014: 17–23). The municipal authorities managed the *mancebías*, whose organisation was delegated to confraternities, which organised prostitution. In the case of Barcelona, in addition to the convent of Santa Maria Magdalena, another convent for repentant women was founded in the sixteenth century, namely that of Nostra Senyora de la Victòria. It was formed by a community of repentant women who, with the help of charitable sponsors, bought a house at Carme Street in 1576. The life of this institution was quite short, as the community was disbanded in the mid-seventeenth century as a consequence of the plague.[28] It was also quite short the life of the convent of the Trinitat, which was created in 1492 as part of a church founded around 1394 for recent Jewish converts. The nunnery, which was constituted of three nuns and the abbess, was transferred to monks in 1529.[29] The church was also the seat of a confraternity, of which King John II of Aragon himself became a member (Diago 1603: fols. 313v–314r).

Close to the convent of Nostra Senyora de la Victòria and also under the Order of Saint Augustine was the convent of Santa Maria de Montalegre. Its origin was a community of Canonesses which was settled in Tiana (El Maresme) in 1265.[30] In the fourteenth century they moved to the Raval,[31] where their new church was inaugurated with a solemn Mass on 22 November 1362.[32] Other communities from both the convent of Santa Magdalena i Santa Margarida in Castellbisbal and the convent of Sant Joan de l'Erm in Sant Just Desvern joined the convent of Montalegre in 1438 and 1468 respectively (Zaragoza i Pascual 1997: 147). As this nunnery did not accept the enclosure prescriptions that followed the Council of Trent, the admission of novices was prohibited,[33] and the convent was abolished in 1593, when it was turned into a Tridentine Seminary, also named Montalegre.[34] Between 1802 and 1957 the building was a charity house, and the Centre de Cultura Contemporània de Barcelona currently occupies the convent historic site.[35] The male Augustinian house in the city, named Sant Agustí Vell, was founded in 1309 and was deeply embedded into Barcelona's cultural life—for example, its chapel of Our Lady of the Piety was very important for the devotion of Barcelonan citizens.[36] By order of Pope Alexander IV in 1256, the Augustinian friars, following the example of the Franciscan and Dominican orders, 'abandoned contemplative life and adopted an active life, preaching, teaching and healing souls'; competitivity resulted from the overlapping of activities developed by parish clergy and friars, who enjoyed the favour of aristocracy and popes.[37] This shows the different ways of imbrication of female and male Augustinian institutions into urban life.

Also on the west side of Les Rambles was the convent of Santa Maria de Jerusalem, founded by a widow named Rafaela Pagès upon her return from a pilgrimage to Jerusalem in 1462;[38] this was done with the assistance of a young widow from Pisa called Antonina who accompanied her to Barcelona (Diago 1603: fols. 311v–312r). From 1475 the community occupied the *casa d'En Porta*, the building which had belonged to the Dominican nuns of Montsió between 1371 and 1423.[39] When the Dominican nuns moved to Santa Anna Square, some houses were built, which were to be inhabited by 'sinful' women. In the late fifteenth century, after Rafaela's death, Antonina brought four nuns from the convent of the Trinitat in Valencia with the purpose of establishing the Poor Clare order in the convent: Aldonça de Corella, as the abbess, Eleonor Vildig, as the vicar, Elisabet Alpicart, and Gerónima de Peñarroja. They were welcomed by the Barcelonan nuns in processions singing the *Te Deum laudamus* (Marca 1764: 268–269). Queen Joana of Aragon (1425–1468) played an important role in the foundation of the convent, and this monarchical patronage and oversight was continued by Ferdinand the Catholic and Charles V. For instance, Ferdinand asked the *consellers* in a 1495 document that the nuns behave with the due honesty, as sometimes, thinking that nobody was able to see them from outside the convent, they were naked inside the cloister and visible from the surrounding houses (Carreras i Candi [1908–1918?]: 480). Such accounts tally with observations by María Soledad Hernández Cabrera which characterise this convent as the occasional subject of inappropriate attention, or, to use her wording, as 'a dark object of desire' (Hernández 1997: 37). Concerns over public morality were more pronounced in urban contexts than in rural communities. In her essay on pastoral visitations in Barcelona in the early fourteenth century, Lucía Conte Aguilar indicates that in both the countryside and the city sexual transgressions were denounced using verbs such as *fornicatur* and *adulteratur publice*; however, in the city there are also 'references to prostitution, pimping, and the organisation of festivities presented as orgies, including music, drinks, gambling, and sex'.[40] The convent of Jerusalem was overthrown in the 1868 revolution, and in 1970 the community moved to a new building in Vallvidrera.

The importance attributed to the education of girls is reflected in the establishment of the convent of the Beates de Santo Domingo in 1532: located in the square of the same name, this institution was founded by Sor Joana Morell with the purpose of instructing girls from poor families (Pi 1854: 523). These girls received free embroidering and sewing lessons and were taught 'tasks appropriated for their sex' (Saurí and Matas 1849: 523). Its church, dedicated to Our Lady of the Rosary, was not finished until 1803. The relationship between convents and charity houses where girls were educated is also revealed in the case of the charity house of the Misericordia, instituted in 1583 by commission of the *consellers* of the city as a way of removing the poor from the public view.[41] It was founded by Diego Pérez de Valdivia (Baeza, Jaén, 1524-Barcelona, 1589), a Franciscan preacher and theology professor first at the University of Baeza and, from 1578, at Barcelona University (see Chapter 4). The Franciscan order had a history of working to promote religious activity centred upon the Immaculate Conception of the Virgin Mary; initially this was for purely devotional purposes, but by the end of the sixteenth century this focus came to serve a charitable function (García Oro 1988). The charity house of the Misericordia was structured into three spaces: a hospice for disadvantaged people—mainly poor girls—, the college of Sant Guillem d'Aquitània, and the chapel of Nostra Senyora de la Misericordia. The Franciscan Third Order convent of the Misericordia remained until the end of the Spanish Civil War. It has been stated that the house was sometimes inhabited by up to 700 girls (Angelón 1870: 154). In his study of the musical life in Santiago de Chile, Alejandro Vera argues that 'one of the functions that the nunneries fulfilled in the colonial period was the education of women', so that convent communities included 'little girls and young women who entered the convent to learn various topics, either with the eventual goal of becoming nuns or returning to the outside world' (Vera 2020: 104).

Derived from a previous *beaterio* (community house) founded by Brígida Terré in 1426,[42] the Jeronymite nunnery of Barcelona was founded under the name of Santa Margarida in 1475, following approval from Pope Sixtus IV.[43] The convent was protected by the queen of Sicily and in 1484 the community moved to a site at the Padró Square previously occupied by the hospital of Sant Maties, thereafter acquiring this name.[44] During the *Setmana Tràgica* in 1909 the building was burned, and the community moved to Sarrià (Iradier Street), before moving to Sant Gervasi (Mercè Rodoreda Street) in 1984 where it remains. The current church of the Carme was built in the space occupied by this nunnery in the sixteenth century (Figure 1.13).

Likewise, the convent of Santa Elisabet has its origin in a community of *beatas* under the Franciscan Third Order, which in 1553 was joined by Juana Fornés, a widow, who became the head of the community. This community obtained a licence to acquire a building in *d'en Borra* Street (former name of Elisabets Street) in 1554.[45] The celebrations of the constitution of the convent and the profession of the nuns were presided over by Philip II and his court in 1564 (Marca 1764: 352–353; see Chapter 3).

In the same post-Tridentine context, the Discalced Carmelite convent of Santa Teresa was founded by Estefania de Rocabertí in 1589.[46] It was located on Mare de Déu Street on the corner with Canuda Street until the Spanish Civic war.[47] Finally, within the chronological limits of this study, the convent of Santa

Mapping convents' sound in the city 23

Figure 1.13. Current church of the Carme in Barcelona, built in the space previously occupied by the Jeronymite nunnery. Photograph by the author

Margarida la Reial, which was named in honour of Queen Margherita of Austria, was established by Sor Àngela Serafina Prat (1543–1608) in 1599 (Figure 1.14).[48] The founder translated into Catalan the constitutions of the Capuchin nuns of Naples and Milan. She professed on 7 April 1602 and, already being the abbess, she received the profession of the first novices in a ceremony presided by Bishop Alfons Coloma on 12 August (Serra de Manresa 2003). This convent founded several daughter houses, establishing the Capuchin foundations of Girona, Valencia (1609), Saragossa (1613), Manresa (1638), Palma de Mallorca (1664), and Mataró (1741). It remained closed between 1835 and 1846 and again between 1869 and 1877, and the community was settled in a new convent in Camp de Galvany (Sant Gervasi) in 1881. The new building was destroyed during the *Setmana Tràgica* in 1909 and another convent was constructed in Sarrià in 1910, from which the community was expelled in 1936. A new seat was inaugurated in 1956 and overthrown in 1989. The convent is currently located on Pomaret Street.

Sources for the study of convent music

Having explained that most of these institutions and their buildings suffered damage, decline, and destruction as a consequence of centuries of wars and military occupations, it is hardly surprising that sixteenth-century documentation related to these convents has been unequally preserved and most of the known surviving

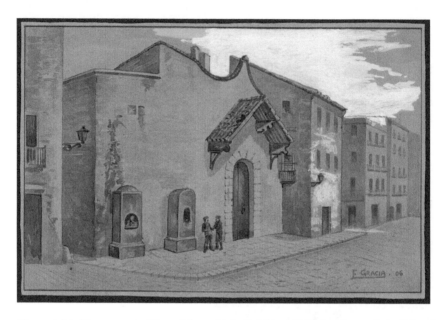

Figure 1.14. The convent of Santa Margarida la Reial in a 1906 drawing made by Eduard Gràcia. AHCB, Fons Gràfics, Reg. 01662

documents are scattered over different archives and libraries in and outside Barcelona. The archives of most of the convents considered in this study have disappeared. For instance, the archive of the convent of Santa Maria Magdalena suffered a fire on 13 June 1690, so that there is no information about these 'virtuous nuns',[49] while the archive of the convent of Santa Margarida la Reial was destroyed during the *Setmana Tràgica*. Likewise, no archival documents belonging to the convent of the Beates de Santo Domingo, the charity house of the Misericordia or the convent of Nostra Senyora de la Victòria have been found.

In the case of the convent of Sant Pere, there is a convent archive (AMSP) held by the community in their current premises in the Barcelona neighbourhood of Sarrià (Anglí Street). This collection, together with the archives of both the convent of Sant Antoni i Santa Clara in Barcelona and the convent of Sant Daniel in Girona, forms part of the Service of Archives of the Catalan Federation of Benedictine Nuns (*Servei d'Arxius de la Federació Catalana de Monges Benedictines*), headed by Irene Brugués. In the preparation of this study it was possible to consult the extant chant books, and also sixteenth-century documents such as books of foundations (*llibres de fundacions*), account books (*llibres d'abadesses*), payment notes (*llibres d'albarans*), sacristy books, books of works (*llibres d'obres*), and notarial books, as they include references to expenses and contracts related to music and musicians.[50] Moreover, there are three books of visitations dating from the sixteenth century which contain, among other information, records of the visitations to the convent church and its chapels ordered by the abbess, including references to the musical practices of the priests and the books located in the church. Research undertaken in this archive for the present study had to contend with the substantial body of material, to which public access is limited. These remarkably extensive archival documents relating to accounting or notarial transactions list thousands of payments which are overwhelmingly concerned with non-musical matters; however, the small number of references to musicians discovered therein, newly presented in the course of this study, offer tantalising snapshots of the cultural life of this convent.

The archive of the convent of Sant Antoni also forms part of this Service of Archives, and the documental collection, entitled *Fons del Monestir de Santa Clara de Barcelona*, is currently preserved at the convent of Sant Benet de Montserrat. This archive has been studied by the already mentioned Núria Jornet. Although limited to the medieval period, her publications have served as a starting point to localise sixteenth-century archival documents of musical interest. For example, she mentions a chronicle preserved in the convent archive, entitled 'Llibre de les coses dignes de memoria del present monestir de Santa Clara' and written by Sebastià Roger from 1 May 1599 onwards.[51] A scribe from Ripoll (Girona), Roger was charged with ordering the convent archive, according to an agreement between him and the abbess Francisca Monmany in 1597.[52] Several visits were made to this archive, initially focused on the musical sources. The large-format plainchant books to be used in the choir are dated from 1600 onwards, although there are some undated books and fragments, as well as a plainchant book printed in 1552. The collection also includes small-format handwritten books probably used individually by the nuns in processions—most of them dating from the eighteenth century—and a few sixteenth-century music books (see Chapter 2). Moreover, this archive contains other sixteenth-century sources of musical interest such as account and notarial books, chronicles, books of anniversaries, and ceremony books. Of particular interest is the 1598 book on the different professions in the convent and their obligations also written down by the already mentioned Sebastià Roger.[53] Documents from Sant Antoni i Santa Clara convent are also scattered over the AHPB (six notarial books between 1443 and 1505), the AHCB (inventory of 1624 and manuscript drafts), the ACA (fourteen parchments between 1429 and 1599, and an account book), the BC (a Rule of Sant Benet and eighteenth-century *censales*, that is, contractual documents), and the Archivo General de Simancas (Valladolid).[54]

The archive of the convent of Santa Maria de Montsió, known as *Archivo de las Dominicas de Montesión*, is preserved in the convent's new premises in the town of Esplugues de Llobregat. María Soledad Hernández, who analysed the configuration of this nunnery through documents preserved in the convent archive, listed a total of 216 manuscripts from the fifteenth to the sixteenth centuries (Hernández 1997). Among them, an undated manuscript entitled *Páginas Históricas del Real Monasterio de Montesión* offers particular interest on account of its atypically high proportion of references to music-related transactions. Other documents from this convent are preserved at the AHPB,[55] the ADB,[56] the AHCB, the ACA, the Institut Municipal d'Historia de Barcelona, and the Biblioteca de Catalunya (mainly legal documents from a later period).

An important collection of documents from this nunnery is currently preserved at the ACA, as the disentailment of 1835 resulted in the translation of remaining monastic and convent documents and libraries to the library of the University of Barcelona and to the ACA (Miquel 1949). During the Liberal Triennium (1820–1823) it was stipulated by a Royal Decree that Catalan monastic libraries and archives would be transferred to the ACA. These were returned to the monastic institutions in 1824, but many were subsequently lost or damaged in the burning of churches and convents in 1835. The intervention of the ACA saved some archives, but, although it was stipulated that the archives of abolished convents passed to the ACA (Royal Decree of 30 January 1836), most documents were claimed by the offices of the Public Credit, an organism in charge of managing the State's debt. Consequently, the ACA only preserves some collections and in a partial way. For instance, with respect to the convent of the Trinitat, there is an inventory dating from 1529 to 1542—the convent only having been transferred to the friars in 1529—and other archival documents which refer to the time when the convent was inhabited by monks.[57]

A body of documents that had passed to the library of the University of Barcelona in the nineteenth century—mixed with the monastic libraries deposited there—was incorporated into the ACA in 1943 (*Orden de la Dirección General de Archivos y Bibliotecas* of 16 March 1942).[58] This includes the documentary collection of the convent of Santa Maria de Jonqueres. It comprises around 125 files and volumes from the broad sixteenth century, containing, among other types of documents, notarial books,[59] anniversary books, a book of nuns' wills (*desapropis*), ceremonial books,[60] a manuscript history of the convent by Joan Baptista Fontanet, who was a priest of Barcelona Cathedral and former hebdomad—*hebdomedari* or *domer* (Catalan) and *hebdomadario* (Spanish), meaning 'weekly', refers to a benefice holder who was appointed on a weekly basis to sing Mass—of the convent (Fontanet 1686),[61] and books of visitations which have been particularly interesting from a musicological perspective (Figure 1.15).[62]

In the late fifteenth century, the Catholic Monarchs became administrators of the Order of Santiago and visitors—usually a knight of the Order and a clergyman—were periodically sent to inspect the nuns.[63] These pastoral visitations were similar in nature to the diocesan visitations conducted by bishops; they were a frequent occurrence of the sixteenth century, more generally a major period of ecclesiastical reform which was well underway before the Council of Trent. It was customary for these visitors to review every aspect of convent life, examining the archive and the accounts, questioning the nuns and making an inventory of the convent's belongings. These inspections generated documents, which included the names and duties of the nuns, inventories of the items in the church and the choir—including the collection of chant books—descriptions of the liturgical use of the community, and indications of the aspects that, according to the visitors, needed to be changed. Twenty visitations carried out between 1481 and 1628 have been examined in preparation of this study (Table 1.3). The visitations analysed were carried out in May and November 1481, 1495, 1499, 1501, 1504, 1509, 1512, 1515, 1529, 1538, 1549, 1556, 1560–1561, 1566, 1573, 1576, 1597, 1605,

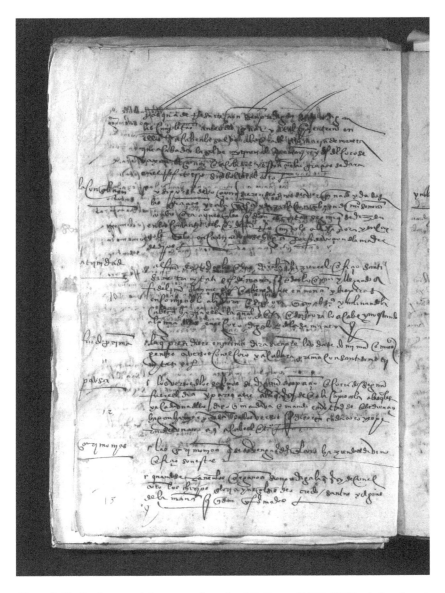

Figure 1.15. Book containing records of visitations (1536–1726), belonging to the convent of Santa Maria de Jonqueres. ACA,ORM, Monacales-Universidad,Volúmenes,169, fol. 2v (visitation of 1538)

and 1628. Thereafter, the next visitation was not carried out until 1719, while the final such investigation dates from 1819, when the convent ceased to exist.[64]

The *Dietaris de la Generalitat de Catalunya 1411-1713*, also preserved in the ACA, are a compilation of the handwritten notes made by the official chroniclers of the Palau de la Generalitat on the events occurred in Barcelona throughout

28 Mapping convents' sound in the city

Table 1.3. Records of the visitations to the convent of Santa Maria de Jonqueres

Year of visitation	Records of the visitation
1401	
1480	
1481, 22 May	'Libro de visitas antiguas' (1495–1529), ACA,ORM,Monacales-Universidad,Volúmenes,167, fols. 45–50 (copy made in 1495) 'Libro de copias de las visitas generales' (1495–1789), ACA,ORM,Monacales-Universidad,Volúmenes,168 'Protocolo sexto del notario Bartolomé Costa' (1477–1483), ACA,ORM,Monacales-Universidad,Volúmenes,180, fols. 107r–118v
1481, 2 October	'Libro de visitas antiguas' (vol. 167), fols. 1–2 'Libro de copias de las visitas generales' (vol. 168) 'Protocolo sexto del notario Bartolomé Costa' (vol. 180), fols. 127v–130v
1493	
1495, 29 June	'Libro de visitas antiguas' (vol. 167), fols. 3–16 AHN, códice 1114, fols. 21–37 Serra Álvarez 1966: 250-251
1498–1499	'Libro de visitas antiguas' (vol. 167), fols. 17–24 AHN, códice 1115, fols. 39–56 Serra Álvarez 1966: 260
1501	'Libro de visitas antiguas' (vol. 167), fols. 25–32
1504	'Libro de visitas antiguas' (vol. 167), fols. 33–44
1509	'Libro de visitas antiguas' (vol. 167), fols. 51–63, 71–74
1512	'Libro de visitas antiguas' (vol. 167), fols. 67–70
1515, March	'Libro de visitas antiguas' (vol. 167), fols. 75–82
1529	'Libro de visitas antiguas' (vol. 167), fols. 64–66
1538	'Libro de visitas hechas por diferentes visitadores' (1538–1726), ACA,ORM,Monacales-Universidad,Volúmenes,169, fols. 1r–7r
1549	'Libro de visitas hechas por diferentes visitadores' (vol. 169), fols. 21v–26v
1556	'Libro de visitas hechas por diferentes visitadores' (vol. 169), fols. 27r–30r
1560, July (orders confirmed in March 1561)	'Libro de visitas hechas por diferentes visitadores' (vol. 169), fols. 31r–52v 'Libro de copias de las visitas generales' (vol. 168)
1566	'Libro de visitas hechas por diferentes visitadores' (vol. 169), fols. 53r–57r
1573	'Libro de visitas hechas por diferentes visitadores' (vol. 169), fols. 57v–60v
1576	'Libro de visitas hechas por diferentes visitadores' (vol. 169), fols. 61r–66v
1597	'Libro de visitas hechas por diferentes visitadores' (vol. 169), fols. 67r–77v
1605	'Libro de visitas hechas por diferentes visitadores' (vol. 169), fols. 78r–129v
1628	'Libro de visitas hechas por diferentes visitadores' (vol. 169), fols. 130r–177v 'Libro de visitas' (1628–1790), ACA,ORM,Monacales-Universidad,Volúmenes,170
1719	'Libro de visitas' (vol. 170), fols. 180r and ff.
1819	

more than three centuries. Edited in modern times as a ten-volume collection (Cases *et al.* 1994), they are a rich source on the integration of convents in the cultural, political, and musical life of the city. In the preparation of the present monograph, the relevant passages pertaining to convents have been considered from the first six volumes of this collection, corresponding to the period between 1411 and 1656 (Appendix 4.2). Additionally, the so-called *Dietari of the Antich Consell Barceloní*, a series of forty-nine volumes where descriptions of the expenses of the municipal government were registered, has been published in twenty-eight volumes corresponding to the years between 1390 and 1839 (*Manual de novells ardits...*). The references to nunneries in the long sixteenth century that are included in these chronicles have also been analysed, as well as those contained in the *Rúbriques de Bruniquer*, a compilation of provisions and events between 1249 and 1713 preserved at the AHCB; the task was initiated by the notary Gilabert Bruniquer i Riera (1561–1642) at the request of the city councillors and the documents have also been published in five volumes (*Ceremonial dels magnífichs consellers ...*).

Scattered documents of Barcelonan nunneries are preserved at the AHN in Madrid, including bundles of documents accounting for the lineage of the nuns of Santa Maria de Jonqueres (*expedientes de pruebas de sangre*) (Figure 1.16). These sources offer rich details to contextualise the background of these nuns, as well as the names and social status of their ancestors and relatives. From 1549 onwards, the visitors imposed the previous investigation of the lineage of the prospective nuns before they were admitted to the convent, as they were not allowed to be *moriscas* or *conversas*.[65] These reports were required for prospective nuns of the military orders—Santiago, Calatrava, and Alcántara. These consisted in detailed investigations, asking witnesses who were reliable and usually elderly, in order to prove that no ancestor had been related to Jews, Moorish or people condemned by the Inquisition.[66] Seventy-six files related to nuns who entered the convent in the sixteenth and seventeenth centuries have been consulted for this study.[67] These documents are valuable as they allow us to establish connections between the nuns and their social context. For instance, one of the witnesses who most frequently participated in the investigations was Joseph de Bellafilla, who is also mentioned by Francisco Civil in his study on seventeenth-century organists from Girona as 'very learned in the art of music'.[68] The systematic information on the prospective nuns and their lineage and the people who surrounded the family and acted as witnesses in the inquiry provides a panoramic on the context of the nuns of a particular Barcelonan convent, and can be useful for carrying out further research in other disciplines.[69]

The research was carried out by a knight of the Order of Santiago and typically involved the questioning of a number of witnesses. Research took place in the hometown of the girl, and also in the towns of origin of her parents and grandparents. Elderly witnesses were often called on the basis they were more likely to have known a prospective postulant's ancestors. Witnesses were often knights, honourable citizens, and clergymen, and thus the great majority were male. These files firstly include a royal letter of declaration which explained that a particular

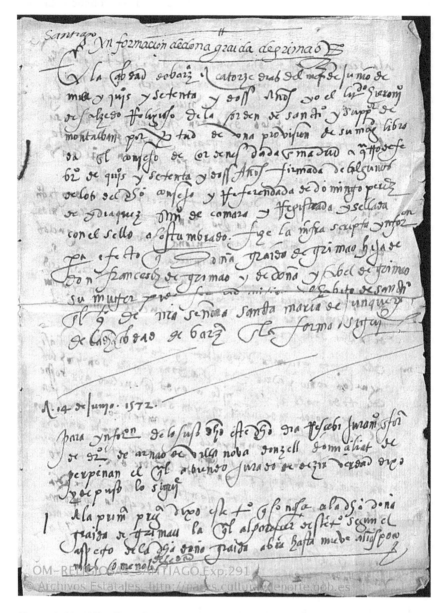

Figure 1.16. 1572 file of the inquiry into the blood purity of Agraïda Grimau (d.1614), choir director of Santa Maria de Jonqueres convent. AHN, OM-RELIGIOSAS_SANTIAGO,Exp.291

girl intended to enter the convent and ordered an inquiry into the purity of her lineage. Thereafter these files include a list of the questions to be asked of witnesses, usually focused on the girl's family history, and which are followed by the witnesses' answers. The names, ages, and positions of the witnesses are specified together with their responses. The last part of the file used to be an approbation of the admission of the girl in the light of the information provided by the inquiry. In addition to this, documents of Santa Maria de Jonqueres convent are also scattered in the BC and the AHPB, among other institutions (Bassegoda 1993; Costa 1979).

The inventory of sixteenth-century documents at the AHPB was analysed in preparation for this study, in order to track the notaries associated with convents and confraternities.[70] The type of document that appears most frequently is the *capbreu*, that is a legal document which recorded the incomes and privileges that belonged to a person (such as a nun) or institution (a convent) as a result of land ownership. For example, there is a scattering of documents of this type from the convent of Montalegre at the AHPB.[71] However, convent documents with musical references are rarely found at this archive, beyond those including agreements between confraternities and convents with respect to the celebration of liturgical ceremonies.

At the ADB, there is a section of 'clergy and nuns'.[72] As it was reported that this does not contain documents which originated directly from convents, this research focused on more general documents where details about nunneries could be found, such as both the indexes of the *Index Regestorum comunium* and the records of pastoral visitations carried out in the sixteenth century. The documents are licenses, mandates, briefs, indulgences, reports of prioresses' elections, and records of instauration of confraternities in convent churches, among other documentation related to sixteenth-century Barcelonan convents, as well as records of sixteenth-century pastoral visitations to the convents of Sant Pere, Les Jerònimes, and Santa Maria Magdalena (which do not contain references to music).[73] With regard to the Jeronymite nunnery, there are books of visitations also at the monastery of El Escorial.

In the case of Santa Elisabet nunnery, Antonio Paulí (1968) pointed out that he was able to consult the 'saved archive of the convent'.[74] With regard to the convent of Santa Maria de Valldonzella, no complete 'archive' survives, and Paulí (1972) mentioned the 'old archive of Valldonzella (disappeared)' in addition to some other documents scattered at the AHPB and the archive of Barcelona Cathedral.[75] Musical references in the study of Antoni Albacete i Gascón and Margarida Güell i Baró (2013: 111) about this convent provide clues on the documents to consult. Moreover, chronicles, poetry sources, and the *Dietaris* offer a glimpse of the musical life of this nunnery and its relationship to the urban soundscape.

Archives of particular religious orders, such as the Arxiu dels Caputxins de Catalunya i Balears—which contains a collection named 'Convents' including documents from 1578 to 1936—the Arxiu dels Carmelites Descalços de Catalunya i Balears—which preserves documents from Santa Teresa nunnery studied by Mercè Gras—and the Arxiu Històric of Franciscans of Catalonia, are also available.[76] Most of the convent documents that are preserved at the library of Barcelona University and the BC date from the eighteenth century. For example,

32 *Mapping convents' sound in the city*

there are lyrics of villancicos printed in the late seventeenth and eighteenth centuries which demonstrate the participation of choirs (*capillas de música* or 'music chapels') from other religious centres of the city, such the cathedral, the Palau de la Comtessa or the church of Santa Maria del Pi in the ceremonial of the convents on the occasion of nuns' professions. This raises questions about what happened in this regard in the sixteenth century. Beyond some plainchant books, almost no 'music' sources belonging to sixteenth-century Barcelonan convents survive. Sixteenth-century books of polyphony preserved at the BC are not related to the convents of the city. For instance, one of the phylograms in the paper of *E-Bbc 587* is almost identical to that found in a 1596 document from the convent of Els Àngels (Puentes-Blanco 2018: 131–132), but the book has no direct relationship to the convent.[77]

It is clear that nuns had to learn how to sing the Divine Office; however, we have no evidence of nuns who acted as 'composers' and, with the exception of a few choir masters and organists, we cannot identify nun musicians in sixteenth-century Barcelonan convents. Thus, the scarcity and dispersion of sources for the study of musical life in the nunneries active in sixteenth-century Barcelona lead us to a close reading of 'non-musical' archival documentation to find indirect references to convent musical activity, in which nuns participated not only as performers but also as promoters and organisers.

Nuns' social environment and musical background

In the sixteenth century, Barcelonan convents such as those of Sant Pere, Santa Clara, Santa Maria de Jonqueres, Els Àngels, Les Jerònimes, Santa Maria de Jerusalem, Santa Maria Magalena, or Santa Teresa were inhabited by noblewoman or members of high-status families. Elizabeth Lehfdelt has studied the mechanisms by which laywomen 'were "converted" into nuns' in early modern Europe and how 'religious rules, convent architecture, male ecclesiastical oversight, material culture, the rhythms of daily life within the convent, and other factors' shaped these conversions, arguing that these were 'uneven or incomplete' resulting a blurring between sacred and secular worlds.[78] In the Spanish context, Ángela Atienza has pointed out that the rules of female convents 'allow us to see the order, but not the disorder or the disordered' as 'life, the daily practice, flows between rules'.[79] She has also carried out a biographical review on nuns' resistance to reformation and enclosing from the time of the Catholic Monarchs to the seventeenth century (Atienza 2018a,b). In the Barcelonan context, noblewomen who became nuns did not make a community life and even had slaves working for them—we have references to slaves in the nunneries of Santa Maria de Jonqueres, Valldonzella, Santa Clara, and Pedralbes in Barcelona,[80] and the presence of slaves and servants in convents has also been reported for other cities of the Iberian Peninsula and the New World.[81] One wonders if some of these servants and slaves had musical skills and contributed to the musical life of the convent, as there are references to members of the Spanish nobility owning male slave musicians or else female servants with musical skills or who were provided with musical training by their patrons and patronesses in the early modern period for their entertainment.[82]

The convent of Santa Maria de Jonqueres was one of the 'fashionable' convents in Barcelona. Although it first housed the daughters and wives of knights of the Order, noblewomen in general came to predominate, and this institution has been described by the historian Mercè Costa i Paretas as more 'a luxury guesthouse' than a 'strict convent'.[83] This was the only convent discussed here that was ruled by a military order and, according to Mercè Costa, its occupants should be considered more as aristocratic ladies who had taken vows, rather than nuns (Costa 2005, 2008). They lived in noble apartments within the convent boundary organised by families (Costa 1973a: 107, b; 2000: 297). Costa has studied the daily life of these nuns: at 6.30am they went to the choir and, after having breakfast and offering morning greetings to the prioress, nuns were able to devote themselves to their own occupations or to go back to their own houses; likewise, after celebrating the Office at 2pm, they were free until dinner time (Costa 1974: 264). These nuns were allowed to get married and had slaves working for them. The number of slaves, generally Slavic (mainly Russian) or Asiatic, was considerable, and they were acquired by the nuns directly through a solicitor (Gelaberto 1994: 335; Costa 2000: 299). According to Costa, there is evidence of the existence of slaves in the convent between 1368 and 1541, and she identifies forty female slaves and two references to male slaves (Costa 2000: 297–298).

The nuns of Santa Maria de Jonqueres were free to maintain their social lives by entering and exiting the cloister, revealing an attitude which considered enclosure as contrary to their lifestyle. From the late fifteenth century onwards, the visitors of the Order of Santiago attempted to impose enclosure on them and encourage behaviour befitting nuns instead of laywomen.[84] In 1538 they were ordered to wear a veil and were forbidden to wear coloured clothes or ornaments on their apparel.[85] Although it had already been ordered in the visitation of 1495 (Serra Álvarez 1966: 294–298), in 1560 the nuns were forbidden to talk through the windows that led to the streets and to ride with people who did not belong to their family, while the number of excursions they were permitted was also regulated. It was also ordered that the convent be fitted with locked lattice windows. However, the nuns put up considerable resistance to such reforms, which is detailed in the *Dietaris*: on 26 December 1560, it is recorded that 'Pedro Morejón, visitor of this convent, has done some aggravating thing to these nuns'; on 9 January 1561 the city councillors 'decided to send an ambassador to the King given that the visitor of Jonqueres wanted to impose cloistered life'; on 3 February 1561, the windows of the convent began to be walled by order of the visitors Morejón and Días; and, finally, on 4 March Morejón asked five nuns to leave the convent.[86] However, it has been said that all these rules hardly modified these nuns' lifestyle until their exclaustration by the French troops in 1808 (Gelaberto 1994: 336–337). Isabel Serra (1966: 17) considered that there was a scarcity of vocations in this convent in the sixteenth and seventeenth centuries, mainly motivated by the reformations fuelled by the Catholic Monarchs to restrict the nuns' freedoms. In contrast, Mercè Costa (1974: 307) assessed that the number of nuns increased in the sixteenth century, reaching more than forty in 1557, and visitors limited the number of nuns to forty in 1560.[87]

A similar negotiation between religious and secular lives was found at the Benedictine convent of the city. Around 1602, the visitor of the convents of Sant Pere and Santa Clara (and also of the convent of Sant Daniel in Girona) indicated the following:

> [The nuns] do not have an established novitiate time or a deadline to profess, even though they reach the age of sixteen [without having done so]. Those who enter the convent at an early age do not take the black veil soon, but they extend the profession until the twenty-five years old and some of them until the thirty years old. All of them still hope to be married and for this reason they attempt to look beautiful, dressing elegantly, some of them using cosmetics and colours [...], and flirt, talking to secular knights freely at parlours with no one listening to them, although they are twenty years old. They are treated in everything as secular young girls, without any type of devotion or retreat.[88]

In 1604 a brief was sent from the Roman curia to the bishop criticising the convents of Sant Pere and Santa Clara and ordering that they be subjected to disciplinary action by their ordinary, the bishop, and adopt a more rigorous religious life. However, according to the *Dietaris*, this would have discouraged knights' daughters from entering these convents, which would cause great harm throughout the principality, and the city deputies concluded that if the pope had been aware of this danger, he would not have issued such a brief.[89] Sebastià Roger's 1598 book on the different professions in the convent of Santa Clara contains a section on the 'chambers at the convent', including the surnames of the families of nuns who lived in each 'house'.[90] According to the constitutions of the Benedictine convents approved in Barcelona in 1615, novices were required to have professed by the age of sixteen, as it was prejudicial for the cloistered life to wait more.[91] Novices had to go to the room of the nun in charge of teaching them at least twice a week to receive instruction on aspects of liturgical ceremony in divine worship, and seven-year-old novices who were able to read the Christian doctrine were allowed to receive the habit.[92] As late as the eighteenth century the nuns lived in private houses inside the convent premises, as in the case of Santa Maria de Jonqueres convent. Likewise, the Poor Clare nuns of Pedralbes did not make a community life, although they had to attend the religious offices.

The convent of Santa Maria de Jerusalem was also inhabited by Barcelonan noblewomen and was a highly regarded nunnery. According to Francesco della Marca (1764: 274), there were sixty-three nuns in 1542 and seventy-two in 1560.[93] He included information of several nuns, such as Juana Moliner (d.1547), from Lleida, who was admitted as choir nun; Isabel Dusay from Barcelona (d.1548), an instructor for novices and abbess for fourteen years; Magdalena Rovira (Barcelona, 1531–1619), a noblewoman who also acted as an instructor for novices; Mathea Castellví (d.1600), from Vilafranca del Penedès (in the province of

Barcelona); and Juana Figuerola, among others.[94] The lack of sources makes it difficult to identify the nuns of the convent of Montalegre. The prioresses in the sixteenth century who had been identified are Violant Despalau (1501–1510) and Blanca Castellarnau (1593) (Zaragoza i Pascual 1997: 147). Documents also survive relating to Leonor Torta, who is mentioned as the convent prioress in a document related to the construction of the convent organ in 1520.[95] Writing in 1699, José Massot observed that many virtuous nuns had flourished in this convent, but their lives went unrecorded because of the lack of attention by his predecessors (Massot 1699: 135).

The convent of Santa Elisabet was inhabited by high-status women. The *beatas* living in *d'en Borra* Street with Juana Fornés were Juana Bravo (d.1572), Violant Jordana, Ana Genloch, Catalina Algasia, Catalina Roca, Juana Serafina, Elena González (from Perpignan, d.1596), Isabel de Mella, and Clara Monells (from Vic, elected abbess three times, d.1612) (Marca 1764: 351; Paulí 1968: 14). The charity work of the *beatas* once they become nuns was carried out by the Sisters of the Third Order of Penance, who belonged to important Barcelonan noble families.[96] Juana Fornés was appointed abbess, but she died eleven days later, being followed in the position by Juana Bravo (who had been the vicar) for two years. Thereafter, no remaining nuns fulfilled the conditions to be abbess, and three nuns were brought from the Poor Clare convent of Perpignan to stay for three years in the Barcelonan convent: Àngela Guimerà as abbess, Dionisa Pol as instructor for novices, and Luisa de Terreros as *tornera* (the nun who works the revolving window of the convent).[97]

Although the convent of Santa Maria Magdalena was initially inhabited by repentant women, by 1500 they were no longer received in this nunnery—they instead passed to Nuestra Senyora de la Victòria—and women of higher social status entered the convent (Paulí 1942). Likewise, the community of the convent of Jeronymite nuns was initially formed by beguines, who were named *rescluses* in Catalonia. These beguines were named *terreres* after their founder Brígida Terré (d.1471), and they carried out a series of care tasks; they were related first to the hospital of Santa Margarida and subsequently to that of Sant Maties (Botinas *et al*. 2002: 84–92). However, when the Jeronymite convent was founded in 1475, the community exclusively included noblewomen who lived in separate houses with their servants within the convent limits. By 1495 the community had grown significantly,[98] and throughout the first half of the sixteenth century the nuns resisted attempts to make their enclosure stricter, having been warned with regard to this issue by Bishop Jaume Caçador in 1551 (Botinas *et al*. 2002: 90–91). An order of Philip II given in Madrid on 10 December 1586 mentions that the king had given these nuns 3,000 *lliures* in 1563 to finance the works carried out in the building to improve enclosing.[99]

According to the city chroniclers, two nuns of the convent of Els Àngels toured Catalonia searching for alms in order to build their convent in 1515.[100] In 1534, the seven-year-old Jerónima de Rocabertí y de Soler was received at the nunnery and, according to Mercè Gras, completely changed this Dominican community (Gras 2013b: 118). Again, this convent was inhabited by high-status Barcelonan women, with some belonging to the noble families of Rocabertí, Setantí, and Sorribes.[101] On 25 November 1576, the *Consell de Cent* attempted 'to avoid the infractions that must have been happening at the convent by building walls even more insurmountable'; however, it has been asserted by Verònica Zaragoza that 'the attempts to isolate these nuns were not enough to break their links to the outside world, as the community projected a strong social influence across the city'.[102] Likewise, Santa Teresa convent was patronised by the family of Estefania de Rocabertí (b.1528), a noblewoman who is considered the first Catalan Discalced Carmelite nun, and her association with the convent would have enhanced its reputation through her family's prestige and social influence (Gras 2013a). Thus, Barcelonan convents were places where different sectors of Barcelonan society met, facilitating exchanges between religious and secular life. Musical activities served as one such conduit between convents and their urban surroundings.

The book compiled by the archivist Sebastià Roger in 1598 on the Santa Clara convent indicates that the position of main singer (*cantora*) had been present in this nunnery from time immemorial. This position, as well as those of abbess, prioress, treasurer, *pastrinyera*—in charge of the convent oven—and *cellerera*—responsible for the convent cellar—was a position held for life.[103] Chapter 10 is devoted to the position of singer:

> The charge and profession of singer is also a life-time position, or it can last as long as the abbess wants. It is not biennial, as this is a charge granted by ability and not by the order hierarchy. This is a profession that can be served by any nun who already has another profession. And in this way, today, in 1599, Belloc has this charge, and she is also *cellerera* and *obrera*. It is the charge of the singer to make preparations for the anniversaries of the convent and other particular anniversaries in honour of certain people. She distributes the alms, which she receives from the procurator, among the nuns. It must be noted that, until today, the abbess received and additional half stipend more than the black veiled nuns and the choristers, who received the same quantity for the anniversaries, except for the anniversary of the marchionesses [?], celebrated on [gap] July when half the stipend more is given to the black veiled nuns than to other […]. On Fridays, she sets the table and […] she has also the charge of selecting the nuns in the choir who have to say lessons […]. She also has de charge of asking the procurator to bring firewood after gathering information about which nuns need it […]. She also has the charge of asking the procurator to buy the bouquets for Saint Clare's feast day, which use to be three vases, and she distributed them among all the nuns and minor officials of the house.[104]

The same book devotes a chapter to 'the nuns, from entering the convent to death' in which it is observed that the girls who entered the convent were allowed to sing in the choir together with the choristers when it was not an important day, in order to practice.[105] In the case of the convent of Pedralbes, one can obtain a glimpse of the high cultural level of these nuns and the role of music in their lives through the studies of Anna Castellano i Tresserra and Cristina Sanjust i Latorre, among others in the fields of medieval and art history, which include details of musical interest that have been extracted from the conventual archive documentation, such as ordinations on the celebration of the Mass, inventories, and account books.[106] For example, Castellano emphasises the importance of singing and reading in this community (Castellano *et al.* 2001: 167), while Sanjust (2008: 427) argues that the church was the space for music, while the rest of the convent was a place for silence. Castellano (1996: 512) draws a distinction between those who sang, typically the senior nuns who were allowed to hold a charge in the convent, and those who prayed. Sanjust indicates that the orders of service for the community's Masses specify who had to sing each prayer, indicating an alternation between female and male choirs, between plainchant and polyphony,[107] although no documentary references to nuns who were able to play musical instruments have been found (Castellano 1996: 560). However, references to organs and their maintenance and construction from 1364 to the twentieth century have been extracted from the convent documentation.[108]

The presence of nun singers at the convent of Santa Maria de Valldonzella dated from the time of its foundation. According to Montserrat Obiols, the foundation of Cistercian convents in Catalonia followed a well-established procedure: two qualified Cistercian nuns were sent from the mother house to the new convent in order to prepare the space and the community. One of them would be the abbess of the newly founded convent and the other was typically a nun who was skilful in music, singing, calligraphy, and copy of manuscripts, and used to act as the *cantatrice* (singer) of the new convent, being in charge of teaching the chant for the different liturgical rituals and later would promote to the position of prioress or abbess.[109] The mother house in this case was the convent of Santa Maria de Vallbona, which had a school where young women from the nobility were trained, and also a scriptorium where disciplines such as literature, drawing, liturgy, calligraphy, embroidery, and knitting were cultivated (Piquer 1957: 24–27; Obiols 2005: 205–206). The convent's charter of foundation included the signature of 'Francisce cantricis', as well as those of the abbess, who was Berenguela de Cervera, the prioress, and the sacristan (Anglès 1988: 57). The importance attributed to the position of *cantatrice* provides evidence of the weight of musical culture in these Cistercian convents.[110]

The positions of *precentrix* and *subprecentrix* are documented in Valldonzella for the first time on 10 June 1434 and are equivalent to the cathedral positions of *chantre* (precentor) and *sochantre* (succentor) (Albacete and Güell 2013: 76). According to the articles relating to these positions in the convent's charter, in addition to direct the singing of the community, the *precentrix* was responsible for keeping the books used in the choir.[111] The charter also established the position of organist who was in charge of accompanying the choir.[112] The convent was supervised by the visitors from the Cistercian monastery of Pedra, who wrote a 'letter of visitation' on aspects such as enclosure and nuns' behaviour. These letters were kept by the *cantora* of the convent, who had to read them to the other nuns (Obiols 2005: 278).

Caterina Boïl de Boixadors is documented as the *cantora* of the convent from 1474,[113] and by 1476 she is named in conjunction with Isabel Carreira, the *subcatora* (Casas i Homs 1967). Boïl occupied the position of abbess at least from 1478 until the time of her death on 28 December 1503, being replaced by Serena de Vallseca, elected on 4 January 1504.[114] Caterina Boïl was a noblewoman, the daughter of Joan Boïl de Boixadors, Lord Constable of the castle of Montoliu and citizen of Tarragona.[115] Her high social and economic status is demonstrated by the fact that she had a slave named Joan, whom she had inherited from her brother Pere, Joan Boïl's successor as Constable of the castle of Montoliu, and to whom she freed on 3 April 1477, when he reached the age of 30 (Madurell 1976: 24, 27).

Caterina Boïl had been highly praised for her musical skills and her sensibility to courtly traditions by the Barcelonan notary Antoni Vallmanya in a poem entitled *Sort* (1458).[116] Vallmanya also wrote several poems which referred to Valldonzella, including one entitled 'In praise of the Valldonzella nuns' (*En lahor de les monges de Valldonzella*). Barbara R. Woshingsky (2016) has studied how nuns in French convents represented objects of desire in male-authored narrative and, through literary analysis, explores the place of convents in the early modern imagination. Vallmanya's poetry acts as evidence of the musical and literary culture of these nuns, who maintained their noble way of living inside the cloister, and his participation in poetry sessions that took place in the choir area of the convent testifies to the closeness of his connection to their musical culture.[117] Following this period, the cultural activity in Valldonzella is poorly documented until the late eighteenth century, at which time the Baron of Maldá began visits to the convent and wrote descriptions of the festivities and ceremonies with music celebrated there.[118] Visitations records show that in the 1540s the convent had more than forty nuns (Paulí 1972: 57). After the definite imposition of enclosure by a papal bull of Paul V on 22 October 1611, the nuns complied on 7 December 1612, according to the *Dietaris*, celebrating 'a festivity with much music' which was attended by the city councillors.[119]

Evidence also survives for the musical backgrounds of nuns in the convent of Santa Maria de Jonqueres. Of the seventy-six files from inquiries into the lineage of sixteenth- and seventeenth-century nuns of Santa Maria de Jonqueres that were consulted for this study, only one includes any mention of music, namely the 1578 lineage report on Angelina de Lupià, from Perpignan (Table 1.4).[120] Fernando de Villanova, a seventy-seven-year-old knight who acted as witness in the research, testified that she was highly virtuous and that she was also being taught how to sing 'and do other good exercises'. Another seven-year-old girl from Perpignan, named Magdalena Armengol y Prado, was reported to 'enthusiastic about literature and her private devotion'.[121] These files also provide substantial evidence of the widely established tradition of nuns taking charge of the training and promotion of their nieces when they entered the convent at an early age (see Chapter 2).

Until at least 1576 these nuns had their own liturgy, which differed from that established by the Order of Santiago, at which point the Roman liturgy was imposed on the convent following the Council of Trent (see Chapter 5). Therefore,

Table 1.4. Contents of the report from the investigation into Angelina de Lupià's lineage in 1578

Section	Relevant information
Philip II's letter on 5 February 1578	
Angelina's genealogy	Parents: Lluís de Lupià and Violant Saragossa Cabeça Paternal grandparents: Francesc de Lupià and Àngela Sancha Maternal grandparents: Diego Çaragoça and Constança Viver
Research report (started on 12 March 1578) including testimonies of seven witnesses:	
• Diego Gonçalo, a 60-year-old canon of La Real	
• Diego Bodet Garcia, a 50-year-old canon of the church of Saint-Jean	'To the fifth question he responded that he knows that all the daughters of Francesc Lupià are very reserved and virtuous and of good customs as their mother is highly principled and very kind and therefore brings up her daughters with much modesty'.[a]
• Fernando Vallaro, an 18-year-old knight	
• Juan Girau, a 17-year-old knight	'She must be 12 years old'.
• Fernando de Villanova, a 77-year-old knight	'To answer the fifth question, he said that Ms Angelina is very reserved and virtuous, and that she has a very good understanding and customs, as she is the daughter of such an illustrious lady, and that she has been taught how to sing and do other good exercises for many days'.[b]
• Luis Paulet, a 76-year-old citizen	
• Francisco Julián, a 70-year-old farmer	

[a] 'A la quinta pregunta dixo que todas las hijas de don Francisco Lupia sabe que son muy recoxidas i virtuosas i de buenas costunbres porque la madre es muy principal de mucha bondad i ansi cria las hijas con muncho recoximiento' (s. fol.).
[b] 'A la quinta pregunta dixo que sabe que la dicha doña angelina es muy recoxida i virtuosa i de buen entendimiento i costumbres como hija de señora tan principal i que a muchos dias que le enseñan a cantar i a otros exerçiçios buenos' (s. fol.).

the main objectives of the sixteenth-century visitations were to adapt the particular liturgical practice of this convent first to the rules of the Order and later to the Roman liturgy, and to prevent the access of men—in particular musicians—to the convent. These visitation records offer evidence relating to an organist named Guiomar de Saiol (see Chapter 2), and two choir directors in the late sixteenth and early seventeenth centuries: Agraïda Grimau (d.1614) and her younger sister Eugènia (d.1636) (Mazuela-Anguita 2015b). Agraïda professed on 17 November 1586, and is mentioned among the nuns who were present in the records of the visitation of 1597.[122] In the 1605 visitation she is referred to as the '*capiscola* who leads the choir', together with the sacristan Helena de Montsuar, the nuns in charge of baking Margarida de Guimerà and the *portera* Isabel de Marimon.[123] In this visitation, the nuns reported the visitors that it was customary for there to be forty nuns in the convent, but at that time there were only eighteen professed nuns and five choristers. Agraïda Grimau lived in one of the noble houses inside the convent with Maria d'Erill i Cardona and her younger sister Eugènia Grimau, who is referred to as choir director in 1628.[124] In 1608 Agraïda was the secretary of the convent chapter,[125] according to the lineage file of her nieces Anna Maria Sentmenat (1594–1668) and Casilda Sentmenat (1596–1669), who were the daughters of Anna de la Nuça, Agraïda's cousin, who had also professed in the convent in 1577.[126] Agraïda acted as the convent prioress between 1609—elected on 31 May and confirmed on 11 October—and 1612.

Using a variety of archival documents, it is possible to compose a genealogy of these nuns; for instance, Agraïda mentioned in her will the names of her siblings.[127] The lineage of Agraïda was investigated between 14 and 19 June 1572 in order to confirm the 'cleanness' of her blood, and the inquiry was carried out by Jerónimo de Salcedo of the Order of Santiago.[128] In 1578 the same investigation was extended for her twelve-year-old sister Isabel.[129] The linage investigation shows that Agraïda, Isabel, and Eugènia were the daughters of Francesc de Grimau and Isabel de Lupià, both from Perpignan, and Francesc himself appears as a witness in eight other lineage investigations. Agraïda's paternal parents were Jaume/Diego Vidal Grimau and Àngela de Vives,[130] and the maternal grandparents were Francesc de Lupià, royal procurator of the village of Perpignan, and Àngela de Lupià/Sancha, who was the daughter of Mossèn Sancho.[131] One wonders if the aforementioned Angelina de Lupià, the prospective nun of Jonqueres who was being taught how to sing in 1578, was a relative of Agraïda. Agraïda was reported by the witnesses to be around nine years old according to her appearance, and her ancestors were said to have always lived as upright people who subsisted on their rental incomes without having any other office. The lineage inquiry's information was revised and approved on 28 August 1572 (see Appendix 1).

Agraïda's will—dated 2 August 1614, the day before her death—named all her siblings as executors.[132] She requested that she be buried in Santa Paula chapel at the church of the convent, where her father's sister, Àngela Grimau (d.1601), had also been laid to rest.[133] She left 100 *lliures* to her brother Joan to pay for her burial, with the remainder to be devoted to the celebration of Masses for the relief of her soul. Among her belongings was a harp, to be inherited by the convent, and a clavichord (*manacort*), which she bequeathed to Montserrat Puig.[134] Although the particular relationship between Grimau and Puig is unknown, the latter is also mentioned in Eugènia Grimau's will, where it is indicated that Puig was a priest and benefice holder at Barcelona Cathedral.[135] These bequests give rise to the possibility that there was a musical relationship between Puig and the two sisters. In any case, this reflects Agraïda's contacts with other musical centres and her integration in urban musical life. After bequeathing other goods to particular people, Agraïda appointed Eugènia the heir of her remaining belongings.

Ownership of musical instruments among Barcelonan women is scarcely recorded in written sources. Madurell offers one rare example in the inventory of Elisabet Farrera (previously named Balle) of 1591, which includes three good 'violas', one of nine strings, the second of eleven strings, and the third bowed.[136] It is not clear the provenance of Agraïda's musical instruments, although the will suggests that these were at her father's house and not the convent. The harp and the clavichord may have served for her musical training during childhood, or could have been a legacy of her aunt Àngela Grimau, who named Agraïda and Eugènia as her principal heirs and numbered them among her executors in her will of 12 April 1595. Agraïda was obliged to share the bequest with Eugènia, although she was entitled to choose which goods were to constitute her part, while Eugènia was to take whatever was left over.[137] The tradition of legacies between aunts and nieces and that of aunts in charge of nieces' education was well established in convents, as the case of Jonqueres makes clear. Agraïda was probably under the care of her aunt Àngela, while she took care of her cousin's daughters Anna and Casilda.

The research into Anna and Casilda's lineage was very detailed. It took place in May 1606 and was focused on the maternal line (de la Nuça or de Lanuza), as this surname did not have a good reputation in Aragon. The witnesses indicated that the girls' mother had been chorister (*escolana*) and then nun in the convent of Santa Maria de Jonqueres. This was confirmed by the administrator of the convent Ginés de Mora. The chapter secretary of the convent, Agraïda Grimau, showed him a book of records where her profession was registered in 1577. The king's letter from 23 March 1572 permitting this entrance was also inspected, as were the baptism certificates of both girls. Jaume Calcer, a knight of the Order of Santiago, was interviewed in Perpignan. While he claimed not to know the girls directly, he testified that two daughters of Galceran de Sentmenat and Anna de la Nuça who were between ten and twelve years old were in Barcelona at the house of their father's sisters, who were in charge of their education. This surely referred to Agraïda and Eugènia Grimau, as in 1628 the visitors reported that Casilda Sentmenat and Eugènia Grimau lived in the same house.[138]

The permeability of the cloister (the ability for professed nuns to move freely in and out convents) and the rich cultural life in Barcelonan nunneries over the sixteenth century is also evident in the case of the convent of Santa Maria de Montsió. According to Hernández, in the meeting celebrated in 1502, seventeen nuns signed, although they may have been a half of the total of nuns at the convent at that moment.[139] Throughout the sixteenth century the convent had not been strictly enclosed, and nuns enjoyed a rich cultural life, singing, playing musical instruments and receiving singing lessons:

> it seems clear that, in late fifteenth and throughout the sixteenth century, laymen and women continued to enter and leave through the door of Montsió

and that the cloister was permeable. Meanwhile the nuns enjoyed a rich cultural life: they read, wrote, sang, played string instruments and even had singing teachers, all this despite increased strictures to the contrary, as is clearly shown in the 1461 statutes (*ordenacions*) drawn up by Marcial de Auro Bello, general of the Dominican Order.[140]

Hernández (1997: 73) explains that the position of singing and string instrument master is documented in the Montsió convent, although no names are provided. Generally, girls were admitted after being eleven years old, and they had a novice teacher who taught them psalmody, the Divine Office, and the basics of convent life (Hernández 1997: 77, 89). She also explains that the *escolanes* (choristers) were in charge of singing in the choir (Hernández 1997: 75). One of the offices in the convent which remains today in Dominican convents is that of *hebdomadaria* (hebdomad), in charge of preparing what to read and sing (Hernández 1997: 70).

In the case of the convent of Els Àngels, Mercè Gras (2013b) refers to a few cases of late-seventeenth- and eighteenth-century musical nuns who were granted with a dowry reduction because of their skills; however, there is no mention of sixteenth-century nun musicians in Gras's studies. She also explains that one of the duties of choristers was to blow the organ bellows and this was considered quite burdensome, so a 1707 agreement freed the nuns from this task for four years after their profession of vows (Gras 2013b: 127–128). A laywoman connected with the Rocabertí family, Anna de Cardona i Pinós, is documented as having excelled in her musical skills. Anna, a Barcelonan noblewoman who has been identified as Joan de Cardona-Rocarbertí's wife and the Count of Quirra's aunt, was praised for her musicianship in a poem by the Sardinian Antonio Lo Frasso and was reported to have sung sonnets and glosses accompanying herself with the harp (Mazuela-Anguita 2018b: 198). There is, however, no explicit evidence for musical links between this noblewoman and the convent of Els Àngels.

Hipòlita de Rocabertí (Barcelona, 1551–1624), a Dominican nun from the convent of Els Àngels, was sent together with other three nuns of the same convent by Bishop Joan Dimas Loris to reform the convent of Santa Maria Magdalena for the period 1586–1591. She acted as the novices' master for five years and reported on her experience in *De los sagrados huessos de Christo señor nuestro* (1679). Her account included a description of her close relationship with a nun who was skilful in singing:

> Later we received many novices again. One of the oldest of the black-veiled nuns loved me so much, as if we were mother and daughter. We shared confidences and spent some nights in the choir. Although she was old, she had a very nice voice and sang some things about sweet Jesus, and I contemplated.[141]

Massot, who devoted an extensive section to this convent and to the nuns from important families who entered in it,[142] identified this nun as Francisca de la Cerda (d.1593), the king's cousin and daughter of the ambassador of Rome (Massot 1699: 140–142). Torremocha's study on a convent in Valladolid for repentant women also gives some insight into the presence of music in these institutions. For instance, at the pious house of the Aprobación in Valladolid, musicians were hired to sing the Miserere during the celebrations of the feast of Saint Mary Magdalene on 22 July (Torremocha 2014: 75).

Writing in the mid-nineteenth century, Manuel Saurí and José Matas indicated that the convent of Santa Teresa had 'the reputation for having the best voices for divine worship'.[143] A commemorative book in the convent archive which served to preserve the memory of deceased nuns includes compliments for Beatriu de l'Encarnació de Borgó i Roger (1600–1637), who occupied the position of choir director, and distinguished herself for her performances at the clavichord, the spinet, and the guitar, and who supposedly remarkable voice is described as clear and delicate.[144] Writing in 1739, the historian Anastasio de Santa Teresa, indicated that this nun 'had a very clear, mellifluous, and corpulent voice, with which she governed the choir and made less burdensome the Divine Offices'.[145] Similarly, at the convent of Santa Margarida la Reial, there is some evidence from later periods for nuns with musical skills celebrating secular festivities in the convent. According to her autobiography, Marta Noguera (1774–1830) sang *folias* and love romances while accompanying herself with the guitar and the psaltery.[146] Pi i Arimon (1854: 527) mentions the relation of the Marquise of Montesclaros to this convent. The 1649 biography of the founder Sor Àngela Serafina Prat, written by Iván Pablo Fons and revised by Miguel Torbavi, which was dedicated to Anna of Austria, dowager Queen of France, includes references to singing at the convent. According to the biography, Àngela Serafina gave much importance to devotional singing, reprimanding faults in the choir and leading by example (Fons and Torbavi 1649: fol. 131v). Singing accompanied her even on her deathbed:

> Cheerfully she sent for a nun who was able to sing a very devotional romance on the birth of Jesus and begged her to sing, as she loved listening to her. While the nun was singing, she was so pleased that, even being so exhausted that almost was unable to move, she sat up on the bed lightly, with no help, and said: 'I want to help you sing'. Both continued to sing with tender devotion. The other nuns, fearing she would become tired, wanted to stop her singing, offering to take her part, but she would not accept, adding: 'I know about a soul which the baby Jesus has on his heart'. This was referring to herself.[147]

Moreover, she made her daughter Bárbara develop musical skills to help her enter a convent, and thus avoid paying a dowry:

> But when there were difficulties—which always are involved in holy works— regarding the payment of the dowry, as she had no money, she was anxious that there should be founded in Barcelona a Capuchin convent which might welcome daughters of honourable parents without a dowry. But this did not

discourage her, and she decided that the girl should learn how to sing and play the organ, as she already was able to read [...]. Through study she soon became very skilful in both things. With this, gates opened to the Franciscan convents in Lleida and Montblanc, which offered to receive her only for her ability and virtue, but problems arose as always, as God wanted her in the Franciscan convent of Santa Isabel in Barcelona.[148]

Finally, Bárbara entered the convent of Santa Elisabet and was required to pay a fee of 200 *escudos*, as 'the ability in singing and playing the organ was useless for this religious convent, where the Divine Offices were celebrated and sung with more devotion and skill'.[149] This indicates that the convent of Santa Elisabet, apparently, did not give priority and favourable treatment to prospective nuns who were skilful in music. Batlle (1710), Antonio Boer (1735), and Francesco della Marca (1764) include biographies of some nuns of Santa Elisabet, such as Juana Serafina, one of the founders, who was born in Tunisia and was educated in the Islamic faith. She was taken as a slave in 1535 by Mathias Moncayo, a knight from the Kingdom of Aragon (Marca 1764). His wife was jealous of the slave and ceded her to Anna de Cardona, countess of Aytona and Juan de Montcada's wife. Another sixteenth-century nun was Petronilla Palau, who was born to a rich Barcelonan family. Her father wanted her to enter the convent of the Jeronymites, but she asked instead to enter the convent of Santa Elisabet, as she wanted 'to live in poverty and humility'. According to Marca, Juana Bravo, first vicar and then abbess, was rigorous in her enforcement of the rules of enclosure and did not allow nuns to talk in the parlour, only sometimes to their parents, but standing up and veiling their faces (Marca 1764: 354). Antonio Boer, in his biography of Ana Mitjans (abbess between 1576 and 1582), introduces the question of the appropriateness of singing, a highly valued practice among Franciscan orders who appreciated it for its devotional possibilities, but one which also required the presence of men from outside the convent. There was a division of opinions between the nuns, and Mitjans believed that singing compromised conventual life too greatly:

> Mitjans's opinion was that singing must not be allowed, arguing that singing compromised the perfection of life. On the occasion of singing, there would be much distraction among nuns, as they would have to go to the grilles and parlours; and as no one is born knowing how to sing, it would be needed the presence of men to teach the nuns, which would endanger perfection.[150]

Boer adds that the nuns ceded to the reasons provided by Mitjans and that even the music books of the convent were disregarded (Boer 1735: 59–60).

This chapter has mapped Barcelonan convents amid urban spaces, exploring the social history of conventual life in their civic context. It has introduced the scattered and incomplete sources which inform this study of music in female religious houses, and in so doing has already revealed the first glimpses of the rich artistic life therein. The convent's *torno* (revolving window), considered by Elizabeth Lehfdelt to be the place where 'the cloister intersected with the outside world' (Lehfeldt 2015: 205), can be taken as a metaphor for the way in which music transcended the boundaries of religious enclosure presented in this chapter. Hereafter, this study demonstrates the way music functioned as a *torno*, facilitating contact between nuns and their urban surroundings.

Notes

1. This graphic material is preserved at the Arxiu Fotogràfic de Barcelona, the ANC, the AHCB, the Reial Acadèmia Catalana de Belles Arts de Sant Jordi, or the Arxiu Gavín of the convent of Les Avellanes, which includes a collection of photographs of more than 26,000 religious buildings in Catalonia. The online project *Barcelona entre muralles* <http://www.barcelonaentremuralles.com/> includes a map entitled 'La Barcelona dels Àustries (segles XVI–XVII)' with photographs of some of the convents explored in this book. The altarpieces of some convents in late seventeenth century have been studied by Roig 1990.
2. Gregori 1991: 106–107, 124 [*Quadern amb la relació de diversos testimonis sobre la preheminència del mestre de cant de la Seu* (1579), fol. 3v]. Although it is focused on the seventeenth and eighteenth centuries, César Alcalá's study of music in Catalonia (Alcalá 1994) contains a few references to the sixteenth century and chapters on the music chapels in Barcelona.
3. Gregori 1991: 110, 122 [*Quadern amb la relació de diversos testimonis sobre la preheminència del mestre de cant de la Seu* (1579), fol. 2v].
4. On the women of the Order of Santiago in the medieval period, see Echániz 1992.
5. Sigüenza 1907–1909 [1600]: vol. 1, 262–263, book 2, chapter 26 (on male novices' training); Noone 1998; Vicente 2010.
6. Sigüenza 1907–1909 [1600]: vol. 1, 262–263 (book 2, chapter 26), 490 (book 4, chapter 27). Aguilar is also mentioned in Vicente 2010: 851. It must be observed that 'convent' refers to both male and female religious houses in Spanish and Catalan.
7. On civic religion and Barcelona convents in the early modern period, see Zamora 2018.
8. For lists of sixteenth-century abbesses at this convent, see Paulí 1945; and Zaragoza i Pascual 1997. The profession letters of these nuns between the late seventeenth century and the nineteenth century were the subject of Miriam Palomba's project 'Les cartes de professió del monestir de Sant Pere de les Puel·les de Barcelona: des de finals del segle XVII fins al segle XIX. Una lectura dels llibres comptables', funded by the Generalitat de Catalunya.
9. See, for example, AMSP, Llibres de visites, no. 1 (1572), fol. 4v.
10. Saurí and Matas 1849: 120–121 indicate 1233; Zaragoza i Pascual 1997 gives a date of 1237.
11. Saurí and Matas 1849: 120–121; Pi 1854: 533; Zaragoza i Pascual 1997; Carreras i Candi [1908–1918?]: 345; Peñarroja 2007: 217, 240; Jornet 2007: 91.
12. Anna Castellano i Tresserra has studied the medieval history of this convent in depth (Castellano 1996 and 1998) and its relation to the Montcada family (Castellano *et al.* 2001), while Cristina Sanjust i Latorre devoted her PhD dissertation to the construction of the convent following its foundation to the sixteenth century (Sanjust 2008). See also *Ceremonial dels magnífichs consellers…*, vol. 3, p. 70.
13. It was close to the current Espanya Square, between Calàbria and Borrell Streets. On this convent, see, among others, Albacete and Güell 2013 and 2014; *Diccionari d'Història Eclesiàstica de Catalunya*, vol. 3, p. 624; Diago 1603: fol. 292r-v; Saurí

and Matas 1849: 121; Pi 1854: 518; Casas i Homs 1967; Paulí 1972; Duran 1972–1975; Madurell 1976; Zaragoza i Pascual 1997: 236–237; and Vallmanya 2007: 32–80.
14 Diago 1603: fol. 292v. See also Raventós 2006; Chamorro 2013 and 2017; and Chapter 3.
15 Anglès (1988: 55) mentions this foundation in a section on Catalan singers from the tenth to the thirteenth centuries.
16 Lomax 1965: 82. On the history of the Barcelonan building, see Costa 1973. See also Peñarroja 2007: 199, 206, 214; Vilarrúbia and Jové 1990: 100, no. 266; Zaragoza i Pascual 1997: 124–126; and Saurí and Matas 1849: 120.
17 For a nineteenth-century description of the church, see Garriga 1899: 27. See also Zaragoza i Pascual 1997: 124–126 (here it is indicated that the translation took place in 1869); Saurí and Matas 1849: 120; Vilarrúbia and Jové 1990: 100, no. 266; and Altés 1990. On the Basilic of the Concepció, inaugurated on 15 August 1871, see Bassegoda 1997.
18 Pladevall 1974: 210: 'No fou mai cap monestir de vida molt brillant'.
19 *Ceremonial dels magnífichs consellers...*, vol. 3, p. 70.
20 Hernández 1997 and 2002. See also Diago 1603: fol. 303r–v (who dates the foundation in 1451) and Paulí 1952.
21 *Ceremonial dels magnífichs consellers...*, vol. 3, p. 74.
22 On the contribution of the Discalced Carmelite friars to Catalan culture, see Arnall i Juan 1986. About the library of this convent, see Arnall 1976. The three catalogues preserved at Barcelona University library (MS 1259, 1360, and 1361) indicate that the library included 2,000 books from the foundation of the convent to 1665, whereafter it reached the 5,573 books as a result of a donation from the canon José Jerónimo Besora.
23 Peñarroja (2007: 195) indicates the precise location of the convent. See also Saurí and Matas 1849: 122 (he dates the foundation in 1351).
24 Pi 1854: 522; *Ceremonial dels magnífichs consellers...*, vol. 3, p. 81. On the conversion of *beaterios* into convents in early modern Spain, see Atienza 2007 and Canabal 2016.
25 Diago 1603: fol. 311v: 'Es muy religioso y de mucho numero de religiosas'.
26 Paulí 1942; Diago 1603: fol. 312r–v; Carreras i Candi [1908–1918?]: 476; Saurí and Matas 1849; Pi 1854: 521.
27 *Ceremonial dels magnífichs consellers...*, vol. 3, p. 72.
28 Pi 1854: 517; and Paulí 1942.
29 See 'Trinitaris', in *Diccionari d'Història Eclesiàstica de Catalunya*, vol. 3, p. 586; Pi 1854: 351; Alcalá 1994: 36; and *Ceremonial dels magnífichs consellers...*, vol. 3, p. 86.
30 On female communities of Canonesses, see López de la Plaza 2020.
31 Masabeu 2004; *Diccionari d'Història Eclesiàstica de Catalunya*, p. 653; Pi 1854: 535; Zaragoza i Pascual 1997: 147; Diago 1603: fol. 286r; Massot 1699: 135.
32 *Ceremonial dels magnífichs consellers...*, vol. 3, p. 71.
33 On the difficulties of Barcelonan nuns when total enclosure was commanded by the Council of Trent, see Bada 1970.
34 *Ceremonial dels magnífichs consellers...*, vol. 3, p. 69.
35 In this charity house folk songs were collected in the context of the 'folkloric missions' commissioned by the Instituto Español de Musicología between 1944 and 1960. See *Fondo de Música Tradicional IMF-CSIC*, ed. Emilio Ros-Fábregas <https://musicatradicional.eu/>.
36 On the history of this convent, see Martí 1980. About the convent in the fourteenth century, see Mutgé 1998. On the community's move to a new building, see Armanyà [1751]. With regard to its library at the end of the seventeenth and the eighteenth centuries, see Casas Nadal 1998. This study alludes to the lack of information about the

medieval and Renaissance library of the convent (Casas Nadal 1998: 215). The BC preserves handwritten documents on the convent, dated in the late seventeenth and eighteenth centuries.
37 Mutgé 1998: 508: 'a partir del mandato expedido por el papa Alejandro IV en 1256, los Agustinos, siguiendo el ejemplo de las otras Ordenes Mendicantes, como Franciscanos y Dominicos, dejaron de lado la vida contemplativa del ermitaño que hasta entonces habían practicado y adoptaron la vida activa de la predicación, enseñanza y la cura de almas. El hecho de que la misión principal de estos frailes y la del clero parroquial fuera similar; esto es, la cura espiritual de sus contemporáneos; y que unos y otros buscaran las mismas recompensas materiales, forzosamente hubo de traer como consecuencia una rivalidad entre ambos grupos [...]. Además, los frailes contaron con el favor de reyes y papas, hecho que decepcionó a los párrocos'.
38 Marca (1764: 267) asserted that the convent was founded in 1453.
39 Marca 1764: 263–264. See also Saurí and Matas 1849: 121; Pi 1854: 521; López 1919; and Peñarroja 2007: 244.
40 Conte 2003: 98: 'El que realment sobta en el cas de la gran ciutat és que els problemes de moralitat pública semblen més presents que al camp. En un i altre àmbit hi ha la transgressió sexual típica que es denuncia amb els verbs *fornicatur* i *adulteratur publice*, però criden l'atenció a ciutat les referències a la prostitució, el proxenetisme, i l'organització de festes que es presenten com orgies, amb música, begudes, joc i sexe'.
41 See Cebrián 2007 on the house of the Misericordia in Valencia, founded in 1670 following the examples of Barcelona and Zaragoza (1669). See also Pi 1854: 532.
42 Botinas *et al.* 2002: 84–92. See also Saurí and Matas 1849: 121 (they date the foundation in 1418); Zaragoza i Pascual 1997: 38–39.
43 It was the queen Violant of Aragon who started the Jeronymite order in Catalonia, founding the convent of Vall d'Hebrón. See Sigüenza 1907–1909 [1600], book 1, chapter 21. On this convent, see, among others, *Diccionari d'Història Eclesiàstica de Catalunya*, vol. 2, p. 420; Paulí 1941a; and Zaragoza i Pascual 1997: 38–39.
44 *Ceremonial dels magnífichs consellers...*, vol. 3, p. 78.
45 Paulí 1968: 13. See also Diago 1603: fol. 314r-v; Pi 1854: 523; Vilarrúbia and Jové 1990: 83, no. 184 (they dated the foundation in 1544).
46 Gras 2013. See also Diago 1603: fol. 315v; Pi 1854: 526; and Saurí and Matas 1849 (they dated the foundation in 1580).
47 Vilarrúbia 1990: 195, no. 597.
48 On this convent, see Serra de Manresa 2002 and 2003; Diago 1603: fol. 318r; Pi 1854: 527; Saurí and Matas 1849; Vilarrúbia and Jové 1990: 65, no. 122; and Chamorro 2013: 315.
49 Massot 1699: 136. Paulí (1942) dates the fire on 14 June. Later documents on the convent are preserved at the BC.
50 Irene Brugués refers to the existence of 77 account books between 1501 and 1600, 29 notarial books from 1501 to 1662, 8 sacristy books, 7 books of works (*llibres d'obres*), and 3 books of payment notes from the sixteenth century. See Appendix 5 for a list of archival documents. Notarial books usually only include a list of documents and not the content of those documents. According to the archivist, the nuns themselves preserved their own notarial documents.
51 'Llibre de les coses dignes de memoria del monestir de S. Clara de Barcelona' (1599–1895), AMSBM, box 8, no. 742.
52 'Llibre de les coses dignes de memoria...', p. 52.
53 'Llibre dels càrrecs i oficis' (MS, 1598), AMSBM, box 12, no. 743.
54 Simancas, Archivo General de Simancas, Secretaría de la Sección Gracia y Justicia (Monjas), legajo 294.
55 An example is the 'Capbreu del monestir de Santa Maria de Montsió de Barcelona' (1601–1611), AHPB, 535/64.

56 ADB, Registro de Comunes, vols. 22, 29, 36, 43, 53, 57, 59; Registro de Gracias, vols. 2, 5, 6, 26, 40, among other documents.
57 'Barcelona, convento de Santíssima Trinitat. Inventario de las cosas que este Monasterio tiene, así en muebles como raíces'. ACA,ORM,Monacales-Universidad,Volúmenes,15; 'Memorial dels qui pagan vuy al beneficial de la Santa Trinitat en lo monestir de la Santa Trinitat de Barcelona, que obté vuy mossèn Miquel Terça y se tenen de capbrevar' (1570), AHPB, 378/74; 'Confessions fan per lo beneficiat del benefici de la Santíssima Trinitat instituït en lo altar major de la capella de la Santíssima Trinitat' (1607), AHPB, 1549/25. Likewise, references to the convent in the *Dietaris* date from the seventeenth century.
58 In addition to the typed inventories available in paper at the archive, see Torra 1995 and 2002.
59 The notaries of the convent in the sixteenth century include Luis Jorba el Mayor (1500–1519; ACA,ORM,Monacales-Universidad,Volúmenes,184 to 186) and Luis Jorba el Menor (1564–1593; ACA,ORM,Monacales-Universidad,Volúmenes,187 to 188).
60 For example, there is a seventeenth-century book on the way in which nuns had to be welcome when they professed: 'Forma per a rebre les freyles quant alguna vol fer professio', ACA,ORM,Monacales-Universidad,Volúmenes,392.
61 The AHCB preserved a list of prioresses of the convent from its foundation to 1686 extracted from Fontanet's text: 'Priorologi de Santa Maria de Jonqueres' (1686), AHCB, 02.01/1M-0054.
62 These books have been used as source in historical studies of the convent by Serra Álvarez 1966; Altés 1990; and Costa 1974 and 2005, among others.
63 Printed rules of the order of Santiago contain sections devoted to the visitors; see, for instance, *Regla dela orden dela caualleria de señor Santiago del espada* (Toledo, 1529), fol. 81r.
64 Lists of visitations and visitors can be found in Fontanet 1686: fols. 7v–17v; and Costa 2005: 75–77.
65 'Libro de visitas hechas por diferentes visitadores' (vol. 169), visitation of 1549, fol. 24r. See also Costa 1974: 258.
66 Similar inquiries were also usual in other religious orders such as the Benedictine. See *Constituciones para los monasterios de religiosas de la Congregacion Benedictina...* (Barcelona, 1615), p. 10.
67 See Appendix 1. For a catalogue of these files concerning nuns of the orders of Santiago, Calatrava, and Alcántara, see Pérez Castañeda and Couto de León 1980.
68 Civil 1972–1973: 119. Bellafilla went from Barcelona to Girona to opine about the organ built there by Josep Bordons (agreement on 29 April 1591).
69 The URBANMUSICS database provides the complete information extracted from these documents at the AHN; see <https://urbanmusics.com>.
70 This archive publishes the journals *Estudis històrics i documents dels arxius de protocols* (1980–2011) and its precedent *Estudios históricos y documentos de los archivos de protocolos* (1955–1979).
71 See, for instance, the 'Capbreu del monestir de la Verge Maria de Montalegre, del bisbat de Barchinona' (1558–1560), AHPB, 378/36.
72 *Guía de los archivos de la Iglesia en España*, p. 89.
73 For the sixteenth century, see ADB, Registro de Comunes, vol. 26, which includes Latin records of the 1499 visitations to both Sant Pere (fol. 221) and Santa Maria Magdalena (fol. 225). Vol. 28 contains the records of visitations to Sant Pere in 1504 (fol. 113), 1513 (fol. 205) and 1520 (fol. 308), the Jeronymite convent in 1513 (fol. 197), and Santa Maria Magdalena in 1513 (fol. 201) and 1520 (fol. 309). Vol. 31 includes records of the 1510 visit to Sant Pere in 1510 (fol. 117) and Santa Maria Magdalena (fol. 121). Vol. 37 includes records of visitations in 1549 and 1554 to the Jeronymite convent (fols. 114, 140). Vol. 38 contains records of the visits to Sant Pere

in 1579 (fol. 37), 1554 (fol. 1). Vol. 64 (1551–1576) includes records of visitations to the Jeronymite convent. Vol. 69 contains records of the 1587 visitation to Sant Pere (fol. 1). On pastoral visitations in Barcelona in early fourteenth century, see Conte 2003: vol. 2, 87–106. See also Cárcel and Trenchs 1979–1980, and Cárcel 1999.
74 Paulí 1968: 'Archivo salvado del Monasterio'.
75 For transcriptions of documents of the thirteenth and fourteenth centuries from the 'Arxiu de Valldonzella', see Mas 1902.
76 *Guía de los archivos de la Iglesia en España*, p. 108. It includes documents from male religious houses such as Sant Francesc (thirteenth to nineteenth-century manuscripts), and the convent of Jesús (eighteenth-century manuscripts).
77 Visitations to the convent of Els Àngels in late fifteenth century are cited by Tarsicio de Azacona (1967). Ignatius of Loyola visited and reformed female convents such as that of Els Àngels. One wonders if his visitations were registered and what he stipulated about musical practice. Paulí (1941b) has also described the archive of the convent in passing. Some documents are at the AHPB. See, for instance, 'Primus liber negociorum et actorum monasterii Beata Marie Angelorum et Pedis Crucis, ordinis Sancti Dominici de observancia, presentis civitatis Barcinone' (1587–1588), AHPB, 438/7.
78 Lehfdelt 2017. On the increasing influence of aristocratic culture on conventual spaces in Naples through changes in conventual architecture after the Council of Trent, see Hills 2004.
79 Atienza 2012: 447–448: 'En definitiva, las reglas nos permiten ver el orden, pero no el desorden ni lo desordenado. Ofrecen una sola imagen, pero congelada, y suspendida en el tiempo. Sin vida. [...] La vida, la práctica cotidiana, discurre entre reglas'.
80 Costa 2000; Jornet 2007: 248; Castellano 1998: 293.
81 In the case of convents in Santiago de Chile, Alejandro Vera (2020: 104) also mentions that communities were not composed entirely of nuns, but also of their servants and slaves.
82 On the ensemble compounded by six slaves from the New World belonging to Juan Alonso de Guzmán (1502–1558), sixth Duke of Medina Sidonia, see Gómez Fernández 2017: 169–180. About the slave musicians owned by Ana de Mendoza (1540–1592), Princess of Eboli, see Schwartz 2001: 440; and Mazuela-Anguita 2018c: 25. On female servants recruited by nobility because of their musical skills, see Mazuela-Anguita 2013. About the slave Juan de Vera (*fl.*1575–1617), who belonged to canon Antonio de Vera and served as singer at Puebla Cathedral, see Morales Abril 2010.
83 Costa 1973a: 102: 'un pensionat de luxe que no un convent estricte'. On these nuns, see, in addition to Mercè Costa's studies, Garriga 1899; *Diccionari d'Història Eclesiàstica de Catalunya*, vol. 2, p. 434; Ibáñez 1966 and 1981; Serra Álvarez 1966; Solsona 1984; and Carreres 1988, among others. Printed Rules of the order of Santiago contain sections on the wives and daughters of the knights; see *Regla dela orden dela caualleria de señor Santiago del espada* (Toledo, 1529), fol. 10v.
84 'Protocolo sexto del notario Bartolomé Costa', fol. 129v (visitation of November 1481).
85 'Libro de copias de las visitas generales', pp. 95–96 (visitation of 1538).
86 See Appendix 4.2; and *Ceremonial dels magnífichs consellers...*, vol. 2, p. 188 (9 January 1561) and vol. 3, p. 88 (7 February 1561).
87 According to Costa (1974: 306), the convent was inhabited by 181 nuns and choristers in the sixteenth century, while there were 131 in the fifteenth century and 230 in the seventeenth century. Serra Álvarez (1966: 17) indicates that there were 21 professed nuns and 12 novices and choristers in 1495, and that there were 23 professed nuns and 16 novices and choristers in 1499. For a list of prioresses, see Zaragoza i Pascual 1997. On the type of prioress elections, see Costa 1980.
88 'Ordenaciones del visitador de las monjas benedictinas de Cataluña para los monasterios de Sant Pere de les Puelles, Santa Clara de Barcelona y Sant Daniel de Gerona',

Madrid, Archivo del Ministerio de Asuntos Exteriores de Madrid, Fondo Santa Sede, leg. 48, fols. 182r–183 bis v. Transcribed in Zaragoza i Pascual 1976–1977: 201: 'No tienen determinado tiempo de noviciado ni para hazer professión aunque lleguen a los dieziséis años las que entran de poca edad no [...] toman el velo negro luego, antes bien alargan la professión hasta [los] veynte y cinco años y algunas dellas hasta treynta y todas ellas con [esperanza] de que podran ser casadas y por esta razón procuran ser vistas [como] hermosas, visten curiosamente algunas con afeytes colores y otras [...] y que festean, hablan con cavalleros seglares con libertad en los locutorios sin escucha alguna aunque sean de veynte años y en todo se tra[tan como don]zellas seglares sin ningún género de devoción ni recogimiento'.

89 Appendix 4.2. See also *Ceremonial dels magníﬁchs consellers...*, vol. 3, p. 151.
90 'Llibre dels càrrecs i oﬁcis', p. 47. See also Zaragoza i Pascual 1997; and Jornet 2007: 223–224. Darna Galobart (2014) studies the coat of arms included in profession letters of these nuns between the sixteenth and the twentieth centuries.
91 *Constituciones para los monasterios de religiosas de la Congregacion Benedictina...* (Barcelona, 1615), p. 11.
92 *Constituciones para los monasterios de religiosas de la Congregacion Benedictina...* (Barcelona, 1615), p. 7.
93 See also *Diccionari d'Història Eclesiàstica de Catalunya*, vol. 3, p. 390. For a list of sixteenth-century abbesses, see Paulí 1970.
94 See also Batlle 1710: vol. 2, fols. 92–107 for biographies of nuns of Santa Maria de Jerusalem.
95 Madurell 1949: 205. See Chapter 2.
96 Marca 1764: 352. On female health assistance in eighteenth-century Granada, see Arias and López-Guadalupe 2015.
97 For a list of abbesses, see Paulí 1968: 59.
98 For the names of the nuns and novices in that period, see Vergés 1987: 28. Some prioresses in the sixteenth century are not identified because of the destruction of the archive during the *Setmana Tràgica*. For lists of prioresses, see Paulí 1941a; Vergés 1987; and Zaragoza i Pascual 1997.
99 'Felipe I el Prudente. Diversorum 19', ACA,CANCILLERÍA,Registros,NÚM.4314 (1585–1587), fol. 200v.
100 *Ceremonial dels magníﬁchs consellers...*, vol. 3, p. 84. See also Paulí 1941b: 14.
101 For a list of prioresses in the sixteenth century (until 1549 the names are unknown), see Paulí 1941b.
102 Zaragoza Gómez 2012: 243: 'evitar las infracciones que se debían de dar al monasterio, con la construcción de muros que fuesen aun más infranqueables. No obstante, los intentos de aislar las religiosas de los Ángeles no fueron suficientes para romper los vínculos de estas mujeres con el exterior, puesto que la comunidad tenía una cierta proyección social en la ciudad de Barcelona'.
103 'Llibre dels càrrecs i oﬁcis', p. 5.
104 'Llibre dels càrrecs i oﬁcis', pp. 39–40 (chapter 10, 'Del offici de la Cantora'): 'Lo carrec y offici de cantora es tanbe carrec o de vida od e tant temps com plau a la Rnt Abadessa no es biennal per que es carrec ques dona per habilitat y no per grau de habit. E es offici que lo pot seruir qualseuol senyora monga que tinga altre offisi // E axi vuy en 1599 Regeix dit offisi la señora belloc la qual es cellerera y obrera // Lo carrec de la cantora es fer celebrar los aniuersaris de Conuent y altres particulars de persones certes y ella reparteix la charitat entre totes les señores monges la qual reb de ma del procurador y lin fa rebuda es de notar que fins avuy de tots los aniuersaris la Rnt abadessa reb la mitat major charitat que les señores vel negrades y escholanes totes les quals reben ygual charitat en los aniuersaris si no es ab lo aniuersari de les marqueses [?] ques fa a [hueco] de juliol e lo qual se dona la mitat mes charitat a les velnegrades que a les altres [...] // En los diuendres aperella la taula [...] // E mes te carrec de senyalar en la taula del cor les

señores monges que tenen dir lliçons [...] // E mes te carrec de fer portar lenya ço es auisar al procurador quen fassa prouisio informantso ab les señores monges quina delles ne vol y quanta la qual prouisio se fa destin per hauer ne mes barato y aquesta lenya // mes te carrec dita cantora de fer comprar al procurador los rahims per al dia de santa clara que de ordinari son tres barralons los quals parteix a totes les señores monges y als oficials menors de la casa'.

105 'Llibre dels càrrecs i oficis', p. 20 (chapter 4, 'de les monges desde la otorgation fins a la mort')'.

106 This convent archive is being digitised in a project headed by Jordi Rifé, and has therefore been inaccessible to researchers in recent years. An inventory of this archive can be found in Castellano 1996.

107 Sanjust 2008: n. 1883; AMP, sèrie lligalls, Institucions 136, fol. 4v. The inventories included, for instance, a 'missal ab nota' (Sanjust 2008: 448; AMP, sèrie lligalls, Inventari, 137).

108 Sanjust 2008: 429–431. The first reference to 'some organs' (*uns organs*) is found in AMP, Lligalls, Inventaris, 137. References to the reparation and constructions of the organs date from 1410 (AMP, Llibre de comptes, 84, fols. 34v–35), 1450–1452 (AMP, Llibre de comptes, 94), 18 November 1490 (AMP, Llibre de comptes, 103, fol. 154v), 1517 (Anzizu 1897), 25 November 1521 (AMP, Llibre de comptes, 116, fol. 62r), 1626, 1895 (AMP, *Dietari d'arxiu*), 1927 (Sanahuja 1959: 822), 1728 (AMP, Llibre de comptes, 178, fol. 90), 1753 (AMP, Llibre de comptes, 192, fol. 60v), 1754 (AMP, Llibre de comptes, 192, fol. 61), 1756 (AMP, Llibre de comptes, 194, fol. 64v), 1759 (AMP, Llibre de comptes, 197, fol. 55), 1760, 1761 (AMP, Llibre de comptes, 198, fol. 59), 1777 (Anzizu 1897), 1782 (AMP, Llibre de comptes, 213, fol. 52).

109 Obiols 2005: 127, 204. Obiols mentioned the case of Cecília de Cartellà, singer at the convent of Santa Maria de Valldaura in 1302, who became sub-prioress in 1311, prioress in 1314, and abbess between 1315 and 1340. Then she became the abbess of the new convent of Santa Maria de Montbenet until 1345.

110 On Cistercian convents in Portugal in the post-Tridentine period, see the studies of Antónia Fialho Conde, such as Conde 2013 and 2019, Conde and Silva 2015, and Conde and Lalanda 2015.

111 *Constituciones en forma de capítulos y artículos* (1947), chapter XXVIII, articles 218 to 239; cited in Albacete and Güell 2013: 76.

112 *Constituciones en forma de capítulos y artículos* (1947), chapter XXIX, article 240; cited in Albacete and Güell 2013: 76.

113 Vallmanya 2007: 218, n. 71. See also Madurell 1976: 63–65.

114 Paulí 1972: 50, 153; Zaragoza i Pascual 1997; and Vallmanya 2007: 218, n. 71.

115 For a genealogic tree of the Boïl family, see *Gran enciclopèdia catalana*, vol. 3, p. 663.

116 Vallmanya, 2007: 71, 217–218; Briz, 1867: 280: 'Clarament viu ab forma cortesana / é gest estar semblant una deéssa / d'art musical mostra ser capitana / axí canta como sentit de mestressa / é ab cant mòlt fi é manera artizada / passa un lay molt gloriós d'oir / lo sentit seu basta per discernir / tot cas d'amor axí n' be stilada / molt afrontada / e ben gosada / lo seu nom es Na Boyl Caterina / de totes mes gentil é que Lavina'. On the depiction of woman singers in the poetry of the count of Villamedina, see Castillo Bejarano 2020.

117 Auferil 1986; Vallmanya 2007: 31, 71; and Albacete and Güell 2013: 111.

118 Albacete and Güell 2013: 111–112. See also Bertran 2017.

119 See Appendix 4.2 and *Ceremonial dels magnífichs consellers...*, vol. 3, p. 154.

120 'Expediente de pruebas de Ángela de Lupiá Zaragoza Sancha y Vives, natural de Perpiñán, para el ingreso como religiosa en el Convento Santa María de Junqueras de la Orden de Santiago' (1578), AHN, OM-RELIGIOSAS_SANTIAGO, Exp.375.

121 'Expediente de pruebas de Magdalena Armengol, natural de Perpiñán, para el ingreso como religiosa en el Convento Santa María de Junqueras de Barcelona de la Orden

de Santiago' (1592), AHN, OM-RELIGIOSAS_SANTIAGO, Exp.50, report of Galceran de Armengol (44 years old, Magdalena's godfather): 'y en lo que toca a las costumbres que es una muchacha muy bien acondicionada dada a recogimiento y aficionada a letras y a devoción desde su edad que es niña'.

122 'Libro de profesas' (1582–1787), ACA,ORM,Monacales-Universidad,Volúmenes,164; 'Libro de visitas hechas por diferentes visitadores', fol. 68v.

123 'Libro de visitas hechas por diferentes visitadores', fol. 86r.

124 'Libro de visitas hechas por diferentes visitadores', fol. 132v. According to the records of this visitation, they lived at the house belonging to the families Pujades, Ballester, Grimau, Pinós, togheter with Maria d'Erill i Cardona (see also Costa 1973a: 112); 'Libro de visitas hechas por diferentes visitadores', fols. 102v (visitation of 1605), 132v (visitation of 1628). See also Costa 2005: 24.

125 This charge was created following the prescriptions of the visitors of 1556 (vol. 168, fol. 27). They ordered that one the nuns be appointed secretary and that she would transcribe on a book the chapter agreements.

126 'Expediente de pruebas de Ana de y Casilda Sentmenat de Lanuza de Oms y de Grimau, naturales de Barcelona, para el ingreso como religiosas en el Convento Santa María de Junqueras de la Orden de Santiago' (1608), AHN, OM-RELIGIOSAS_ SANTIAGO,Exp.649.

127 For a genealogic tree of Agraïda Grimau, see Mazuela-Anguita 2015b: 49.

128 'Expediente de pruebas de Graida de Grimau de Lupiá Vives y Sancha, natural de Barcelona, para el ingreso como religiosa en el Convento Santa María de Junqueras de la Orden de Santiago' (1572), AHN, OM-RELIGIOSAS_SANTIAGO,Exp.291. See Figure 1.16.

129 'Expediente de pruebas de Isabel Grimau de Lupiá de Vives y Sancha, natural de Perpiñán, para el ingreso como religiosa en el Convento Santa María de Junqueras de la Orden de Santiago' (1578), AHN, OM-RELIGIOSAS_SANTIAGO,Exp.292.

130 She was named by the witness as 'Fulana' de Vives and was known as 'señora Grimalda' and the witnesses did not know her name, although one of them mentioned that she was the lord of Alana's daughter. Her name, Àngela, is provided by the file of Isabel de Grimau. Likewise, in Agraïda's file her grandfather is referred to as Jaume, while in that Isabel is referred to as Diego.

131 Although *mossèn* is currently an ecclesiastical title denoting membership of the priesthood, in the sixteenth century it was a title of medieval origin used in the Crown of Aragon to refer to knights, honourable citizens, and other socially distinguished people.

132 'Libro de desapropio (testamento)' (1411–1741), ACA,ORM,Monacales-Universidad,Volúmenes,241 , fols. 237v–238r, fol. 237v.

133 'Libro de desapropio (testamento)', fols. 226v–227r.

134 'Libro de desapropio (testamento)', fol. 238r: 'Item deix y llegue al present monestir de nostra senyora de Jonqueres la arpa. Item deix y llegue a mossen monserrat Puig preuere lo manacort'. See also Costa 1974: 272; and 2005. For a photograph of a clavicord from the seventeenth or eighteenth centuries at Pedralbes convent, see Castellano et al. 2001: 169.

135 'Libro de desapropio (testamento)', fols. 270r–272r, fol. 270v. A student named Montserrat Puig, who was training as a chaplain in Sant Boi in 1608, is referred to in Codina 1993: 141. Likewise, a priest named Montserrat Puig Cabrer is mentioned in a 1616 notarial document (Camós and Marquès 1988: 138).

136 Madurell 1949: 220.

137 'Libro de desapropio (testamento)', fols. 226v–227r.

138 'Libro de visitas hechas por diferentes visitadores' (vol. 169), fol. 141r.

139 Hernández 1997: 79; 2002: 37, n. 19. For a list or prioresses and sub-prioresses, see Hernández 1997: 67; and Paulí 1952: 133–136.

140 Hernández 2002: 28: 'pero parece claro que a finales del siglo XV y a lo largo del XVI mujeres y hombres laicos seguían entrando y saliendo por la Puerta de Montesión y

que la clausura era permeable. Las monjas, por otro lado, tienen una rica vida cultural, leen, escriben, cantan, tocan instrumentos de cuerda o incluso tienen profesores de canto, todo ello a pesar del endurecimiento de las prescripciones en contra, de las que son clara muestra las "Ordenacions" de 1461 redactadas por Marcial de Auro Bello, general de la orden de los Predicadores'. These ordinations are preserved in the convent archive (ADM, Plec, 7 - doc. 5), according to Hernández. See also Hernández 1997: 106.

141 Lorea 1679: 124; Massot 1699: 138–139: 'Despues recibimos muchas Novicias de nuevo. Vna de las mas ancianas de Velo Negro, puso en mi tanto amor, que ella, y yo nos tratavamos como madre, e hija; las dos haziamos nuestros secretos, en velar algunas noches en el Coro, y aunque vieja, tenia muy linda voz, y cantava algunas cosas del dulce Jesvs, y yo contemplava'.

142 Massot 1699: 136–154. He based on Diago 1603: fol. 312r–v.

143 Saurí and Matas 1849: 122: 'Este convento tiene fama de tener las mejores voces, para el canto divino'.

144 *Libro en que se escriben los elogios de las religiosas que han muerto en este convento de la Purísima Concepción [...] de Barcelona, desde su fundación [...] de 1588*, Barcelona, Arxiu dels Carmelites Descalços de Catalunya i Balears. Cited in Gras 2015: 'El llibre d'elogis de religioses difuntes no s'està d'alabar el virtuosisme musical de la noble Beatriu de l'Encarnació, de Borbó i Roger (1600–1637), que es distingia en la interpretació de 'música de manacor o espinete y guitarra, y lo mejor la voz, que yo en los días de mi vida he ohido de mejor y gargantilla más clara y delicada […]. Aquesta formació musical li va proporcionar la qualificació necessària per dirigir el cor conventual'. See also Gras 2013c.

145 Santa Teresa 1739: 553: 'Tenía muy clara y meliflua y corpulenta voz, con la que governava el coro, y hazía menos gravosos los oficios divinos'. Cited in Gras 2015.

146 Noguera's autobiography was published in 1911. See Noguera 1911: 32, 62–63, cited in Serra de Manresa 2003: 192–193, n. 33: 'Me vas donar en èsta casa a tot art de festèj y compliments de mos divertiments, ab tanta sutilèsa y práctica, que no hi havia qui me vencés ni passés al devant; que a tots guanyava y vencia […] Aprenguí a cantar ab gran primor follies y romançors de amor; y per acompañarme en lo primor de la vèu y tòns de lo que cantava, vas apèndre ab gran afició el tocar el salteri y sonar la guitarrà'.

147 Fons and Torbavi 1649: fol. 167v: 'Entrava ya la vigilia del regozijado parte de la virgen, y Nacimiento del Salvador, y con èl, se acercava el feliz transito de la Madre Serafina, según del cielo le avian significado, quando alegre mandò llamar una Religiosa, que sabia cantar un romance muy devoto del Nacimiento del Niño Iesus, y la rogò lo cantasse, porque gustava de oirle sumamente. Mientras cantava la Religiosa, se alegrò y recreò, tan por estremo la devotissima Madre, que estando casi acabada que no se podia menear, con gran ligereza, sin ayuda de nadie se assentò en la cama, y dixo: yo os quiero ayudar a cantar. Prosiguieron las dos con devota ternura. Las otras Religiosas, temiendo no se fatigasse, quisieron atajar el canto, ofreciendole a suplir sus vezes, pero no quiso, añadiendo: yo se una alma que tiene al niño Iesus, sobre su coraçon. Que en su estilo, fue dezir ella misma'.

148 Fons and Torbavi 1649: fols. 50r–v: 'Pero luego assomaron dificultades, (que son compañeras de obras santas) para la execucion, de donde sacaria dote, la que no tenia una blanca. Aqui le recrecieron las ansias de ver Convento de Capuchinas en Barcelona, donde pudiessen recoger sin dote hijas de padres honrados. Mas no acovardò esto à Serafina, antes resuelue que la niña aprenda de canto, y de tañer organo, ya que sabia leer, para que supliesse la habilidad, lo que no podia su facultad. Estudiòlo, y en breve fallò muy habil en ambas cosas. Con esto se abriò la puerta al Convento de Franciscanas de Lerida, y al de Monblanch de la misma Orden Serafica, donde ofrecieron recibirla con gran voluntad à titulo solo de su habilidad, y virtud; pero quando venian a la execucion, salian siempre estorvos, porque nuestro Señor la

queria en Barcelona en el Convento de santa Isabel de la Orden del Serafico Padre san Francisco'.

149 Fons and Torbavi 1649: 51r: 'porque nuestro Señor la queria en Barcelona en el Convento de santa Isabel de la Orden del Serafico Padre san Francisco: pidiòlo a la Abadessa, y al Provincial, vieron la donzella, aggradaronse della, y mas por ser hija de tan santa madre; pero dizenla; que atento la pobreza de su Conveto era necessario para ayuda de costa una lismosna de docientos escudos: porque la habilidad del canto, y organo, era inutil para aquel Religioso Convento, donde con mas devocion que artificio se cantan, y celebran los Divinos oficios'.

150 Boer 1735: 57–59: 'Para probarla assi [a Ana Mitjans], permitió el Señor alguna question en el Convento de Santa Isabel. Se moviò en este Real Monasterio una dificultad, ò que fuesse para purificar mas estas almas perfetas, lo permitiera la Providencia Divina; ò que fuesse astucia diabólica, para sembrar cizaña, embidioso de que se cogiera el grano selecto de tanta caridad en el campo de tanta virtud. Y fuè, que se dividiò el Convento en diferentes opiniones, sobre si el Oficio Divino se havia de celebrar con Canto, ò sin él. Fueron los dictamenes opuestos, sin que por esto dexàran de estar en un mismo espíritu unidos los corazones. Todas tenían un santo fin que era la gloria de Dios: por que las del dictamen de haverse de usar el Canto, dezian: que era justo seguir à la Religion del Serafin Francisco, en donde con tanta edificación se canta, que parece en esta habilidad ser sin segunda; y porque cantarse à coros con acorde armonía, elevava mas los animos à la Gloria. Esforçava este partido, que se usàra del Canto llano, porque un San Gregorio havia puesto en forma este Canto, que por esso se llama Gregoriano. Es verdad, que Pio IV estava determinado quitar la musica de la Iglesia, y fuè propuesto al S. Concilio Tridentino; pero se determinò: que se permitiera con la composición grave, y dulce. De San Carlos Borromeo se lee, que la musica disponía, y elevava assi su espíritu, que después de haver oído su suavidad, subia à Dios con mas fervor. Si la musica compuesta, como pide el lugar mueve tanto à devoción, que por esso la llaman quinto Elemento; porque concuerda los quatro naturales, que tenemos en el cuerpo, sino en su sér, por lo menos en su virtud, como disputan los Filosofos; es cierto, que el cantar à coros, se debe poner en practica; yà porque, como la voz se fragua en el corazón, el esfuerzo mayor, con que èl canta, serpa porque sale de mas encendida oficina; y con aquella emulación con que alternativamente se alaba à Dios cantando, se imitan las alabanzas del Cielo; que por esso cada passo persuade la Escritura Sagrada, que se alabe al Señor cantando, para conformarse con su Gloria en el Mundo.No hemos de hazer question aquí, de si es mejor, que se diga el Oficio con solfa, ò sin ella. Vemos, que uno, y otro se usa en la Santa Iglesia, y que tantas Religiones Sagradas, movidas del espíritu de su santa humildad, no cantan, ni rezan assi. Pero siguiendo el hilo de nuestra historia, hubo por esso una santa contienda. La V. Mitjans era del sentir, que no se havia de cantar, y para esta resolución, dava por razon, que embarazava la perfeccion de vivir. Dezia: que por ocasión del Canto, avria mucho distrímiento en las Religiosas, porque habían de ir à rexas, y locutorios; y como nadie nace enseñado en este Mundo, era preciso haver de venir à enseñar hombres, y con la misma enseñanza, poner la pefeccion en contingencia Si no està encerrado, ò oculto el trigo en la tierra, que estuvo trabajada, no se puede esperar cosecha; y si las Religiosas, dezia, nos enterramos en vida para crecer en bendiciones de Dios, no las abundarà su Divina Magestad'.

2 Music as a commodity
Music, convents, and the economy of the city

Nunneries often became centres of cultural activity embedded in the social and economic life of the city. For instance, the archive of Sant Pere convent preserves a 1577 decree according to which Christian doctrine had to be taught to the general public at the convent church every Sunday, which reflects the imbrication of the convent in ordinary citizens' everyday life.[1] Nuns were also economic actors within the city: account books of the same convent include records of the pittances received by black-veiled nuns and choristers on the occasion of important feast days: 3 *sous* for nuns and 1 *sou* and 6 *diners* for choristers on Our Lady's feast day (15 August), and 5 *sous* for nuns and 2 *sous* and 6 *diners* for choristers on Saint Andrew's feast day (30 November).[2] At the major convents in Barcelona, nuns themselves sang, but clergymen were also paid for singing at the most solemn events celebrated there, and these were usually attended by city councillors, nobility, and royal representatives. Organ-builders and organists also formed part of the musical networks that linked the nunneries to the city economically, and a further musical link was the commissioning and repair of plainchant books used in the choir. Therefore, treating music as a commodity allows a fuller description of the networks which configured the musical cartography of the city and the place occupied by convents in this complex system. Nunneries participated in the economy of the city through musical exchanges, and these were two-way processes, which also demonstrates the porosity of the urban cloister in this period.

Singers, organ-builders, organists, and music teachers

Convent churches usually had a community of priests who sang Masses and Divine Offices. For instance, during the reign of Queen Elisenda, there was a permanent community of four priests in Pedralbes church, and each was paid 100 *sous* per year (Castellano 1996: 79). They had the obligation to celebrate two Masses daily, which were sung only by the men. It was the abbess's duty to organise the activity of these priests (Castellano 1996: 87, 126, 326, 555). The account books of the convent of Sant Pere de les Puel·les include annual payments to priests and chaplains who performed the first and second Vespers and the Compline daily, as well as the deacon (a clergyman in charge of singing the

Gospel) and sub-deacon (a clergyman in charge of singing the Epistle) who participated in the Mass on the Feast of Saint Peter, the patron saint of the convent. Similar payments were made on Saint John the Baptist's feast day (Table 2.1).[3] Saint Peter's feast day celebrations at Sant Pere convent were attended by royalty and nobility, so that this feast acquired a political nuance, as Chapter 3 explores.

Moreover, records of annual payments to the community of priests of Sant Pere convent for their contribution to liturgical celebrations such as anniversaries are included in the account books of the convent, usually in a section entitled 'details about responsories and ordinary salaries'. For example, the priest and bookseller Salvador Cabessa paid 1 *lliura* and 15 *sous* to the community of priests for anniversaries, according to an account book of 1530–1531.[4] The bookseller Mossèn Romeu, procurator of the chaplains' anniversaries, received 2 *lliures*, 6 *sous*, and 6 *diners* corresponding to the year 1541–1542.[5]

Details on the daily musical practices of the male singers at Sant Pere convent church are scattered across different document types. For instance, in a book that includes records of the visitation of the abbess Anna Desbosch to the convent church on 16 November 1572, prescriptions referring to the apparel and behaviour of the benefice-holders while singing Masses and Offices are recorded.[6] The priests' behaviour in the church was also cautioned by Abbess Elisabet de Vilalba on 9 July 1587; according to her, they spoke with profanity among them, breaking the peace of the sacred place, and giving a bad example to those who entered the church.[7] It is interesting that the collection of documents of the ADB includes a 1487 edict against the 'blasphemers' who entered nunneries with no licence to play dice.[8] On 10 April 1584 the abbess Violant Despès ordered that, in order to avoid confusion regarding the time of sung Mass, which was celebrated daily at the convent church by clergymen, Mass had to be celebrated on feast days at the same time as on Sundays; on the Quaresma days, it should be celebrated after the homily.[9] The books of visitations of the convent even provide a picture of the members of the community of priests in 1582 (Table 2.2).

At the Dominican convent of Montsió, the hebdomad, who was appointed according to a weekly rota, used to be a Dominican friar from the male convent of Santa Caterina. His function was to assist in the celebration of the Office. According to Hernández (1997: 83), some of these hebdomads were seen as scandalous and disordered, and it seems that they worked with the *hebdomadaria*, that is the nun in charge of organising what to read and sing. Therefore, there was constant contact between nuns and clergymen for musical reasons and convent churches must have been a place of overlap between convent and urban lives.

A principal altar server or acolyte was also employed by female convents to carry out musical functions. He was called *escolà*, translated into Spanish as *monaguillo*, and not as *escolano* (choir boy), since the altar server was an adult appointed by the nun sacristan and the abbess; both nuns supervised the *escolà*'s functions. For instance, the obligations of the *escolà* at the convent of Sant Pere de les Puel·les listed on 23 August 1587 included paying the altar boys, sweeping the church and the choir, changing the holy water, folding the chaplains' clothes, ringing bells following detailed prescriptions, and continuously assisting clergymen

Table 2.1. Extraordinary payments to priests for the celebration of solemn Offices and Masses at the church of Sant Pere de les Puel·les convent[a]

Year	Festivity	Celebration	Payment
1525	Saint Peter	First and second Vespers	19 *sous*
1526	Saint Peter	First and second Vespers	18 *sous* 4 *diners*
1527	Saint Peter	First and second Vespers	1 *lliura*
1528	Saint Peter	First and second Vespers	16 *sous*
1529	Saint Peter	First and second Vespers	18 *sous* 6
1530	Saint Peter	First and second Vespers	14 *sous*
1531	Saint Peter	First and second Vespers	16 *sous* 2 *diners* [3 *diners* for each chaplain, 6 *diners* for each hebdomad (*domer*) and succentor (*capiscol*)]
1532	Saint Peter	First and second Vespers	16 *sous* 8 *diners* [6 *diners* for each hebdomad and the 4 succentors, and 3 *diners* for the other benefice-holders]
1533	Saint Peter	First and second Vespers	16 *sous* 5 *diners*
1534	Saint Peter	First and second Vespers	19 *sous* 3 *diners*
1537	Saint Peter	First and second Vespers	17 *sous* 8 *diners*
1538	Saint Peter	First and second Vespers	16 *sous* 1 *diner*
1549	Saint Peter	First and second Vespers, second Compline, and Mass	23 *sous* 10 *diners* [3 *diners* per chaplain, 12 per hebdomad and succentor] 6 *sous* for the priest, deacon, and sub-deacon who celebrated the Mass
1550	Saint Peter	First and second Vespers, second Compline, and Mass	25 *sous* 1 *diner* [3 *diners* per chaplain, 12 *diners* per hebdomad and succentor] 6 *sous* for the priest, deacon, and sub-deacon who celebrated the Mass
1552	Saint Peter and Nativity	First and second Vespers, second Compline, and Mass on the Feast of Saint Peter First and second Vespers and Compline on Nativity's feast day	1 *lliura* 7 *sous* 6 *sous* for the priest, deacon, and sub-deacon who celebrated the Mass 1 *lliura* 5 *sous* (Nativity)
1555	Saint John the Baptist	First and second Vespers and second Compline	1 *lliure* 8 *sous*
1556	Saint John the Baptist	First and second Vespers and second Compline	1 *lliure* 8 sous
1557	Saint John the Baptist	First and second Vespers, second Compline, and Mass	1 *lliure* 8 *sous* 3 [3 *diners* per priest and choir boys] per Hour, 12 per hebdomad and succentor] 6 *sous* per that who celebrated the Mass, deacon and sub-deacon

(*Continued*)

58 *Music as a commodity*

Table 2.1. (Continued)

Year	Festivity	Celebration	Payment
1558	Saint John the Baptist	First and second Vespers, second Compline, and Mass	1 *lliure* 4 *sous* [3 *diners* per chaplain] per Hour, 12 per hebdomad and succentor] 6 *sous* per that who celebrated the Mass, deacon and sub-deacon
1559	Saint John the Baptist	First and second Vespers, first Compline, and Mass	1 *lliure* 9 *sous* 3 *diners* [3 *diners* per chaplain] 6 *sous* for the Mass [2 *sous* per man (celebrant, deacon and sub-deacon)]
1560	Saint John the Baptist	First and second Vespers and Compline	1 *lliure* 13 *sous* 3 *diners* [3 diners per chaplain] 6 *sous* for the Mass [2 *sous* per man (celebrant, deacon and sub-deacon)]

[a] AMSP, Llibres d'abadesses, no. 188 (1525–1527), fols. 31r, 32v; no. 191 (1527–1529), fols. 31r, 32r; no. 193 (1529–1531), fols. 25, 27r; no. 195 (1531–1533), fols. 38v, 39v; no. 197 (1533–1535), fols. 34v, 35r; no. 199 (1537–1539), fols. 37r, 38r; no. 205 (1549–1551), s. fol.; no. 209 (1551–1553), s. fol.; no. 212 (1555–1557); no. 214 (1557–1559); no. 215 (1559–1561).

Table 2.2. Members of the community of priests at the convent of Sant Pere de les Puel·les in 1582. AMSP, Llibres de visites, no. 1, fol. 9r

Bartolomeu Vilanovo	Major hebdomad
Pere Gonser	Minor hebdomad
Joannes Porn	Benefice-holder
Paulo Pi	Benefice-holder
Joannes Sala	Benefice-holder
Jacobus Roca	Benefice-holder
Joannes Riba	Benefice-holder
Jacobus Burguera	Benefice-holder
Andreas Miguel	Benefice-holder
Francisco Segols	Benefice-holder
Pere Forroll	Benefice-holder
Antonio [?] Corens	Benefice-holder
Joannes Giberga	Benefice-holder
Berengarius Genoves	Benefice-holder
Joseph Llavaneres	Benefice-holder
Bartolomeu Riba	Benefice-holder

and nuns in the performance of liturgical celebrations.[10] The *escolà* was also in charge of collecting the payments for burials and *albats*—liturgical celebrations in honour of children who had died at an early age (see Chapter 4)—and of letting the sacristan nun know the address of the deceased person. He had to sleep near the organ because of his continuous assistance at sacraments such as the Extreme

Unction.[11] Among his obligations, he was paid 40 *sous* specifically for working the organ bellows.[12] Notarial books provide the names of men who served as *escolà* at Sant Pere convent, such as Antich Mimo, a Barcelonan clergyman who accepted the position in the late 1570s;[13] Nicolau Ribafort, a student from Cardedeu (Barcelona), who played the same role a decade later;[14] or Franciscus Prats who, as the convent *escolà*, carried out an inventory on 8 November 1596 which includes three books 'for saying the responsories and Matins to the nuns'.[15]

Besides clergymen and altar servers, organ-builders and organists also formed part of the music networks that linked the convent to the city. According to Maricarmen Gómez, Gabriel Picanyes, an organ-builder from Barcelona, used the organ placed at Santa Eulàlia chapel in Barcelona Cathedral around 1455 as a model to build that of Santa Maria de Jonqueres nunnery.[16] This was one of the three organs at the Cathedral in the fifteenth century, and has been described by Josep Maria Gregori as the smallest of the three, which was rebuilt by Picanyes in 1464 (Gregori 1987: 260–261; 2017: 45). In the sixteenth century a new organ was built in the convent, located over Sant Francesc chapel. On 29 September 1521 a proof of payment was signed by Joan Ferrando, an organ-builder and organist from Girona who had also worked on the organ of Santa Maria del Mar church in 1519 and on that of the church of the Mercè in Barcelona (a proof of payment existing from 1510). The procurator of Jonqueres convent stipulated the payment of 12 *lliures* for the repair of the church organ.[17] It would be repaired again by Antoni Boscà in 1730 and its doors were painted in 1762, while the bellows were repaired by Josep Boscà in 1784.[18] According to Costa (1974: 278), there was also a portative organ in the convent from 1716. Other people from outside the convent of Santa Maria de Jonqueres who entered the church for musical reasons were the *manxaires*, in charge of working the organ bellows. Costa (1974: 278) identified some of those serving in this nunnery in the seventeenth century: Josep Ramis (1625), Ramon Coromines (1630), and Silvestre Perallada (1633).

Likewise, on 24 February 1520 Miquel Serdanya received 6 *ducados* from Eleonor Torta, prioress of the convent of Montalegre, for rebuilding the convent church organ.[19] This reputed organ-builder also worked on the organ of Santa Maria del Mar in 1518, the organ of the monastery of Sant Cugat del Vallès (documented in 1523), the organ of the church of Sant Cugat del Rec in Barcelona (documented in 1526), that of the church of Jesús also in the city of Barcelona (he died before completing this work), and that of the parish church of San Baudilio de Llobregat in the province of Barcelona (Baldelló 1946: 196, 217–218). One of the account books from the convent of Sant Pere in the 1530s shows that 11 *sous* were given to Mossèn Soler, an organ-builder, on the understanding that he would give the money to an Augustinian friar who had given the homily on Sant Peter's feast day.[20] We do not know the relationship between the convent and this organ-builder, but it is notable that this organ-builder from outside the convent was being entrusted with this transaction.

Subsequently, organ-builders from other countries settled in Barcelona. In 1576, the organ-builders Pedro Arrabasa and Josep Bordons were employed to improve the organ register and bellows at Sant Pere convent;[21] then Pere Alberch

Vila, the organist at Barcelona Cathedral and an important composer, was invited to test the instrument.[22] These organ-builders were paid 110 *lliures* for their work, which had to be done by Eastern Sunday in 1577. Pedro Arrabasa had previously contributed to the building of the organ of Santa Maria del Pi in 1540 and to the reparation of the cathedral organ in 1551 (Baldelló 1946: 201, 203, 220–221). Josep Bordons belonged to an important family of organ-builders based in Solsona (Lleida). He was the son of Pierre Bordons, a French organ-builder, and built the organ of Sant Joan Cathedral in Perpignan. He would also launch the building of a new organ at Girona Cathedral, which was agreed on 29 April 1591 (Civil 1972–1973: 118). In Barcelona, he had contributed to the reparation of the organs of Santa Maria del Mar in 1576, Sant Miquel church in 1558, and the parish church of Sants Just i Pastor in 1581, among others (Baldelló 1946: 221). In January 1579, Arrabasa and Bordons received 25 *lliures* for repairing and tuning the organ of the male convent of Sant Josep and, in October, Arrabasa was paid 8 *sous* for tuning the same instrument.[23]

Twenty years after the agreement between Josep Bordons and the nunnery of Sant Pere, the same organ-builder agreed with the prioress of the Jeronymite nunnery the building of a new organ in the convent church. The agreement, signed on 11 June 1596, indicates that the prioress would pay 150 *lliures* and that the work would be done in six months. The organ would have forty-two keys, including the 'flats' (*bemolls*), and a windchest and soundboard (*salmer*) fitted with six ranks of pipes: the first was to be a set of wooden flute pipes intended for intoning and accompanying psalms; the second, a 4' octave, was to be rank of case pipes displayed on the front of the instrument (likely to be from the diapason or principal family, and louder than the 8'); the third would be a *quinzena*, a fifteenth or rank of 2' pitch; the fourth was to be a mixture comprising a *dizinovena* and *vintidozena*, or a nineteenth (1 1/3') and twenty-second (1'); the fifth was to be a *sinbalet* (a second mixture for which no pitches were given, but likely to be higher still).[24] According to Vergés, the large organ of the Jeronymite convent was then renewed on 24 March 1695, while there was also another smaller organ, considered to be redundant by 1693, so a new one was acquired (Figure 2.1).[25] There are also agreements and contracts for the construction of organs in convent churches in a later period. For instance, Joan Garcia built an organ in Santa Elisabet nunnery in 1688 (he was also the builder of the large organ of Montserrat abbey in 1702).[26]

Account book and notarial documents provide information on organists hired by these convents. At the convent of Santa Clara, in 1440, a Franciscan friar was in charge of playing the organ, being paid 55 *sous* per year. According to late-sixteenth- and early-seventeenth-century convent documents, the organist was selected by the abbess,[27] and his salary was at that time 10 *lliures*.[28] A notarial book from Sant Pere convent includes information on Pere Armendia who, as the organist of this nunnery church, asked for a salary increase in 1589.[29] Complaining about the low salary he received, despite the long hours he worked, Armendia petitioned the abbess to be paid the same amount as other benefice-holders for funeral ceremonies, even those he was absent for. He also demanded that he should receive a comparable salary to organists at other Barcelona churches at the

Figure 2.1. Barcelona Jeronymite nunnery in an 1868 drawing by Francesc Soler Rovirosa. AHCB, Fons Gràfics, Reg. 01054

time. The abbess considered Armendia's request to be fair and ordered that the salary increase be granted to him.[30]

Previous studies about the Sant Pere organ were based on notarial documents (Paulí 1945; Alcalá 1998) and, consequently, the first historical reference to the organ in Sant Pere convent was believed to be the 1576 contract with Pere Arrabasa and Josep Bordons, and it was not known if there were organists other than Armendia in the sixteenth century (Alcalá 1998: 116). However, account books of this nunnery include details of previously unknown organists hired by the convent earlier in that century (Table 2.3). Missing and overlapping years are presumably due to incomplete documentation. Sant Pere's interaction with the musical economy of Barcelona was not restricted to paying organists for its sacred ceremonies. The convent collected rent from its land and dwellings, including from musical people such as Anthony Mordenayrs (a *violer*, that is a luthier),[31] Domingo Blanch (*sonador de organos, organista*), and Miquel Artís (*organer, organista*).[32] Blanch and Artís were also employed by the convent as organists (the former in the late fifteenth century, the latter in the early sixteenth)—and thus experienced both directions of the two-way financial and musical flows around the convent.

Organists were not always confined to the church. There is evidence of organists entering the cloister in order to teach music to the nuns and play the organ located in the nuns' choir. For instance, in 1538 visitors from the Order of Santiago required that the two youngest girl choristers of the nunnery of Santa Maria de Jonqueres should learn how to play the organ. The purpose of this request was to save the organist's salary and 'other inconveniences':

Table 2.3. Organists hired by the convent of Sant Pere de les Puel·les in the sixteenth century according to the account books

Organist	Period	Annual salary	Source
Domingo Blanch	1487–1488	3 *lliures* 6 *sous*	AMSP, Llibres d'abadesses, no. 231 (1486–1487), fols. 70r, 136r
Mossèn Cammsa. [Camarasa?]	1503–1504	3 *lliures* 6 *sous*	AMSP, Llibres d'abadesses, no. 172 (1503–1504), fol. 29r
Mossèn Miquel Artís/Abril	1511–1516	3 *lliures* 6 *sous*	AMSP, Llibres d'abadesses, no. 176 (1511–1513), fols. 35v, 36v; no. 177 (1513–1516), fols. 26v, 28r
Mossèn Nicolau Alm	1515–1516	3 *lliures* 6 *sous*	AMSP, Llibres d'abadesses, no. 179 (1515–1516), fol. 40r–v
Mossèn Jo[an] Martí, a priest	1528–1529	3 *lliures* 8 *sous*	AMSP, Llibres d'abadesses, no. 182 (1528–1529), fol. 32r; no. 193 (1529–1531), fols. 28v, 29r
Mossèn Vicens Comes, a priest	1526–1533	3 *lliures* 6 *sous* / 7 *lliures*	AMSP, Llibres d'abadesses, no. 188 (1525–1527), fol. 34r–v; no. 191 (1527–1529), fol. 34r–v; no. 195 (1531–1533), fols. 33r, 34r; no. 209 (1551–1553), s. fol.; Llibres d'albarans, E-10 (1532–1533), fols. 36r–v, 37r, 38r
Mossèn Pere Col, a priest	1533–1535	3 *lliures* 6 *sous*	AMSP, Llibres d'abadesses, no. 197 (1533–1535), fols. 38r, 39r, 39v
Ramira Lorenç	1537	1 *lliura* 13 *sous* (for playing on Saint John the Baptist's feast day)	AMSP, Llibres d'abadesses, no. 199 (1537–1539), fol. 40v; Llibres d'albarans, E-11 (1537–1539), fol. 62r
Joan Rabasa	1537–1539	3 *lliures* 6 *sous*	AMSP, Llibres d'abadesses, no. 199 (1537–1539), fols. 42r, 43r; E-11 (1537–1539), fols. 65v, 67r
Joan Astor	1549–1552	7 *lliures*	AMSP, Llibres d'abadesses, no. 205 (1549–1551), s. fol.; no. 209 (1551–1553), s. fol.; Llibres d'albarans, E-17 (1551–1553), fol. 8r
Mossèn Vicens	1555–1556	7 *lliures*	AMSP, Llibres d'abadesses, no. 212 (1555–1557)
Francesc Nin, a clergyman	1557–1559	7 *lliures*	AMSP, Llibres d'abadesses, no. 214 (1557–1559), s. fol.; no. 215 (1559–1561)

[the visitors] ordered the prioress that the two least senior choristers who displayed best musical talent had to be taught how to play the organ, with the purpose that, from this moment onwards, they can play the organ during the Hours, avoiding the salary paid to the organist and other inconveniences that can follow it.[33]

Guiomar de Saiol (d.1560) must have specialised in this task, since in 1549 she was provided with a teacher to complete her learning process, so that she would be able to teach other girls. In this way, the convent avoided the necessity for male organists to enter the choir:

> in order to avoid the entry of male organists into the choir, they [visitors] ordered Guiomar de Saiol [d.1560], a nun of that religious order [Order of Santiago], to finish her organ apprenticeship. For this reason, she had to be provided with a teacher at the expense of the convent. This teacher had to complete her learning process; in this way, and once she has been taught, she will be able to teach other girls, so that there will always be a nun who can play the organs.[34]

In her monograph about this nunnery, Costa includes a list of organists (Table 2.4), which makes it evident that the convent did not hire male organists in the sixteenth century. This gap coincides with the visitors' order. Later, a singing teacher appeared in the records in 1675, and a *solfa* teacher, in charge of teaching the singing of the lamentations to the nuns, was recorded in 1780 (Costa 1974 and 2005). Likewise, there are records of a payment of 21 *lliures* and 11 *diners* to the organist of the convent of Santa Maria de Jonqueres in June 1662,[35] and Manuel Altabàs, a clergyman from La Bisbal, has been identified as the organist of the convent from 1781 onwards (Marquès 1999: 111).

Table 2.4. Organists hired at the convent of Santa Maria de Jonqueres between the fifteenth and the seventeenth centuries

Organists	Date
Verger, a friar, and Gaspar, a student	1436
Guillem Bello, a student	1437
Dalmau Ginebret, a scribe (he was paid 66 *sous*)	1454
Joan Cellers	1625
Pere Moreta	1683
Miquel Valls	1687–1689
Flavià Mingalla	1687
Francesc Badia	1690–1699
Pau Miser and Ramon Vinyals	1697

(source: Costa 1974: 278; 2005: 54)

Guiomar de Saiol belonged to a high-status Catalan family and lived in one of the houses inside the convent premises which was shared by the families Saiol and Sentmenat (Costa 1973a: 118). She had a young slave named Helena, part of the 1541 legacy of her cousin, Luisa de Gualbes.[36] This suggests that she was not a 'hired' nun musician—as Colleen Baade (2005) describes this type of nuns—but a high-class woman who had received musical training. She died on 11 November 1560, and, in the visitation initiated at the end of that same year, the visitors ordered that girls who were most able to be organists should have preference in receiving the habit. Other attributes being equal, the choice had to be made in favour of a girl who displayed greater musical talent:

> Furthermore, it is a great inconvenience the non-existence of a nun at the convent who can play the organ, since a man had to enter the choir where the nuns are in order to play the organ, and the entry of a man into the choir for any reason is not desirable. Therefore, we order the admission of any unmarried woman who has the qualities to receive the habit in our Order according to the rules and is also a musician and can play the organ as needed to celebrate the Mass and the Hours. As stipulated, she would have to pay 150 *lliures*. If two or more young women applied for entering the convent at the same time, the most skilful and best musicians should be selected. She will have to teach one or two choristers, so that the convent never lacks who can play the organ.[37]

Again, they alleged that the entry of a man to the convent's choir was undesirable.[38] In 1549, the visitors had forbidden the nuns of Santa Maria de Jonqueres to ask the prioress for permission to go outside the convent and attend the public feasts celebrated in the city;[39] and in 1560 nuns were warned by the visitors not to attend dance parties.[40] Such instructions clearly indicate that these things did occur, and all this illustrates the two-way flow between the convent and the city for musical purposes: nuns went out to attend dance parties, while male musicians entered the convent to teach the nuns.

It seems that this suspicion of male music teachers was a constant through the centuries in both convents and the domestic milieu.[41] For instance, the 1461 ordinances of Montsió convent already prohibited nuns from being taught to sing by a (either lay or religious) man, and also from playing string instruments through the grille or at the door.[42] One hundred years later, in 1563, a letter was sent to the nuns by the provincial prior of the Dominicans in Aragón, in which he still prohibited singing or organ playing lessons if they were not taught by the nuns themselves. Moreover, the small windows of the organ which looked towards the church were ordered to be closed.[43]

Therefore, the references in the books of visitations to Guiomar de Saiol and organ practice in the convent of Santa Maria de Jonqueres both result from the controversy around enclosure and the visitors' wish to break the musical links between the cloister and the outside world, and in particular the entering of organists, singers, and music teachers into the nuns' spaces.

Chant books, scribal activity, music repertoire, and printers

A variety of sources, such as inventories, account books, and the music books themselves, show that a further link—made for musical purposes—between convents and the economy of the city was the commissioning and repair of chant books. The possession of music books varied considerably between convents. For instance, according to the constitutions of the Order, the Capuchin Poor Clare convent of Santa Margarida la Reial should have possessed only four books to be used in the choir:

> The choir has to be humble, modest, poor, but also bright and joyful. It will only have some benches around a lectern which will be high enough, with only four books: a psalter for singing, a breviary for saying the lessons, a martyrology, and a Roman missal.[44]

On the other hand, the collection of plainchant books of Pedralbes convent, which is preserved today in the convent museum, is formed of ten volumes of graduals and antiphonaries created during the period when Maria of Aragon—King Ferdinand the Catholic's daughter—and then Teresa de Cardona were abbesses (1514–1520 and 1521–1529, respectively); they were the result of religious reforms promoted by the Catholic monarchs and Cardinal Cisneros, and the collection has received attention from different academic disciplines.[45] According to the history of the convent written by Sor Eulàlia Anzizu (1868–1916), between 1521 and 1529 eight chant books and one Santa Regla were inscribed on parchment, with illuminated initials and miniatures created by Mestre Joan Gonçal.[46] Further music books are recorded in the convent's inventories.[47]

As with Pedralbes convent, a collection of chant books is preserved today at the archive of Sant Pere convent. Furthermore, account books include details about the reparation of the books, and inventories provide further information on the collection of music books belonging to this nunnery. For instance, among the 'ordinary expenses' at the convent of Sant Pere for the biennium 1503–1504 is the payment of 10 *sous* for the reparation of chant books.[48] On 13 December 1552 a handwritten and illuminated book of hours and a manuscript breviary, both on parchment, are recorded in an inventory included in a notarial book.[49] According to an inventory of the choir carried out in 1585–1586, there were two wooden lecterns and a cabinet where a diversity of books was preserved, among them an ancient dominical.[50] In a cabinet at the sacristy there were two Roman missals, a large manuscript copy (on parchment) of a book for Compline which was quite worn, an old missal worn by frequent use, three books handwritten on parchment with black covers used by nuns and hebdomads for the celebration of Matins, and a deteriorated ordinary. In the lower drawer there were an epistoler and two old handwritten missals—two of them on parchment and one on paper.[51] At the chapel and high altar there were two missals—one was described as Roman and the other as 'old' (*vell*).[52] Among the books included in an inventory (c.1591) of Sant Pere convent is a *llibret de cant* (that is, a singer's book) 'on parchment

66 *Music as a commodity*

Table 2.5. Earliest handwritten chant books preserved in the convent of Sant Pere de les Puel·les

	Date	Type
Col·lecció de cantorals, no. 1	1598	Gradual
Col·lecció de cantorals, no. 2	1599	Antiphonary
Col·lecció de cantorals, no. 3	Not dated	Miscellaneous volume (5 fragments of graduals and antiphonaries)
Col·lecció de cantorals, no. 4	16th century	Antiphonary
Col·lecció de cantorals, no. 6	Not dated	Miscellaneous volume (4 fragments of antiphonaries)
Col·lecció de cantorals, no. 11	1430 and others	Miscellaneous volume (5 fragments of graduals and antiphonaries)
Col·lecció de cantorals, no. 12	Corrected in 1630	Antiphonary

with the incipit *O sacrum convivium,* in deteriorated condition, lacking in some booklets, with black covers and two locks'.[53] This book, which starts with the Corpus Christi antiphon *O sacrum convivium,* is also listed in the inventory made by the *escolà* on 12 December 1592, in which a new missal is added to the previous books.[54]

Table 2.5 presents a list of the earliest handwritten plainchant books preserved today in the convent of Sant Pere de les Puel·les. These books are written on parchment and bound in leather-covered boards with metallic ornaments and locks; they include beautifully illuminated initials. These books show signs of use which provide information on the musical practices of the convent; others contain vestiges of the relationships between the convent and other religious institutions of the city. The oldest chant book preserved in the convent is no. 11, which bears the date 11 June 1430 (Figure 2.2).[55] This is confirmed by a note on the initial cover sheet: 'it was finished in 1430' (*acabat l'any 1430*). However, an examination of bibliographical detail demonstrates that this book is composed of excerpts from different chant books bound together, and the 1430 date corresponds only to the first, which begins with the psalm *De profundis clamavi ad te*. There is a folio numbering in the bottom-right corner with pencil; fol. 27r is blank and on fol. 27v another fragment starts with a setting of the Credo (Figure 2.3). Likewise, fol. 31r is blank, and on fol. 31v a new excerpt starts, with pieces for Saint Benedict's feast day (Figure 2.4). This excerpt has independent folio numbering in the top-right corner from 1 to 16. On fol. 47r a further excerpt begins with pieces for Matins from the *Commune Confessoris*. It is incomplete, and its sheets were initially smaller and were completed with paper to reach the same size as the rest of the book. On fol. 57r a further excerpt starts with two Magnificat for San José Cupertino's feast day.

Plainchant book no. 6, with no date, is a large-format antiphonary comprising excerpts of different books. The first foliation goes from 1 to 196 and this part, starting with the antiphon *Salve crux pretiosa,* is quite similar to the sixteenth-century plainchant books of the convent regarding the initials and type of

Music as a commodity 67

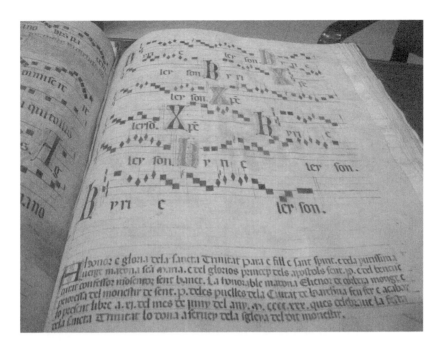

Figure 2.2. AMSP, Col·lecció de cantorals, no. 11, fol. 21r. Photograph by the author

Figure 2.3. AMSP, Col·lecció de cantorals, no. 11, fol. 27v. Photograph by the author

Figure 2.4. AMSP, Col·lecció de cantorals, no. 11, fol. 31v. Photograph by the author

Figure 2.5. AMSP, Col·lecció de cantorals, no. 6, fol. XLIr. Photograph by the author

lettering. The second excerpt starts with the antiphon *Hoc est praeceptum meum*, and the foliation here goes from I to XXXV. The third part has no foliation and comprises six folios, beginning with a Magnificat for Saint Jacob's feast day. Finally, there is an excerpt starting with fol. XLI and the antiphon *Iacob autem genuit* (Figure 2.5).

Music as a commodity 69

Figure 2.6. Sixteenth-century antiphonary belonging to the convent of Sant Pere de les Puel·les. It shows interesting signs of use. On the left margin: 'lo segon es de la scolana que li toca la llamentacio' ('the second is for the choir girl in charge of performing the lamentation'). AMSP, Col·lecció de cantorals, no. 4, fol. 3v. Photograph by the author

Plainchant book no. 4 includes handwritten notes indicating how the different parts of musical pieces were distributed among the nuns and choristers who formed two choirs (Figure 2.6).[56] In another hand there are notes on the mode, usually indicating that 'the eighth tone will be performed with natural G'.

Fragments of folia from older books were used to line the inside cover of book no. 3 (with no date), which is bound in boards. This book comprises fragments of different books (see Table 2.6). Plainchant book no. 12 contains a note indicating that it was amended in 1630, and the initial of the first antiphon is beautifully illuminated with a depiction of the Epiphany.

Book no. 1 includes the handwritten addition of accidentals, texts, lines to divide the *melismata*, or indications of the tone of a piece. It also has parchment patches covering musical excerpts, in particular *melismata*. Similar signs of use are found in book no. 2. A note at the end of book no. 1 points out that, in accordance with the decrees of the Council of Trent, the Roman liturgy began to be practised in the convent on the first Sunday of Advent in 1597,[57] rather later than in some other institutions in Barcelona, such as the convent of Santa Maria de Jonqueres, where the Roman liturgy had been imposed in 1576. For this reason, the nuns of Sant Pere must have commissioned a new gradual and an antiphonary that were completed in 1598 and 1599, respectively. The gradual (book no. 1) was valued at 96 *lliures* 5 *sous* and 8 *diners*, and the antiphonary (book. no. 2)

Table 2.6. Excerpts bound together in chant book no. 3 of the convent of Sant Pere de les Puel·les

1	Gradual excerpt	The lettering size is bigger than in chant book nos. 1 and 2 The illumination of the initials is also different Signs of use: addition of accidentals and time measures in blue pen	Music of the Mass (Kyrie, Gloria, Credo, Sanctus, Agnus Dei)
2	Antiphonary excerpt	The first folio number is LXVI Music is written on black 4-line staff (while chant book nos. 1 and 2 used red 5-line staffs) One of the lines (the second or the third) is red-coloured and, in some systems, the third or fourth line is in yellow Illuminated initials are smaller Some folia are missing or disordered: the numbering jumps from fol. 68 to 94, from fol. 106 to 124, and from 124 to 134; from fol. 135 it jumps to fol. 127 and from 127 to 120, which is the last folio of the excerpt	Music of the Divine Office
3	Antiphonary excerpt	Red 5-line staff, bigger lettering size in comparison with previous excerpt Beautifully illuminated initials	It starts with the title 'Officium Purissimae Conception. Ad primas vesp. Aña'
4	Requiem Mass excerpt	Folios numbered from 1 to 18 Beautifully illuminated large format initials	Requiem Mass
5	*Officium Defunctorum*	Red 5-line staff Illuminated initials	It starts with 'Qui Lazarum resuscitasti a monumento foetidum' It includes *Responsoria Defunctorum*, *Officium Defunctorum Ad Vesper*, and 'In Dedicatione Ecclesia Ad Vesper Añ'

costs 73 *lliures* and 12 *sous*. The introduction of the Roman liturgy at the convent of Sant Pere is also shown by the purchase of a copy of the *Graduale Romanum De Tempore, et Sanctis, Ad ritum Missalis, ex decreto sacrosancti Concilij Tridentini restituti, Pii Quinti Pontificis Maximi iussu editi, Et Clementis viij. auctoritate recogniti*, printed in Venice in 1618—a good indication of the convent's participation in the international circulation of music books. An inscription in the gradual of the convent of Sant Pere provides a detailed breakdown of the price and indicates that it was written by Jeroni Clarí, a priest at the parish church of Santa Maria del Mar, at the request of Aldonça de Olvia and Isabel de Oliver, prioress and sacristan of the convent, respectively.[58] The antiphonary (book no. 2), with very similar physical features, was probably written by the same scribe,[59] as well as two chant books belonging to the also Benedictine convent of Sant Antoni i Santa Clara.

A few administrative documents related to Jeroni Clarí are preserved, detailing the social networks of this scribe and his importance in Barcelona cultural life. In 1571 he already held the benefice of Nostra Senyora de les Neus i Sant Sever at the parish church of Santa Maria del Mar, a position that he still held in 1598 when he wrote down the book for Sant Pere nunnery.[60] He studied at the school of Pere Joan Nunyes (1522/1529–1602), a Valencian humanist, established in Barcelona from 1575. Two discourses in Latin—*De laudibus philosophiae* (written on 30 June 1583) and *De laudibus L. Aemilii Pauli*—and a discourse in Greek written by him as scholarly exercises are included in a manuscript entitled *Orationes discipulorum Petri Ioannis Nunnesii*, which is preserved at the library of Barcelona University.[61] In the discourse in Greek, which is a panegyric to Alexander the Great of Macedonia, Clarí mentioned his young age and inexperience. Moreover, three proofs of payments (*àpoca*) signed by Jeroni Clarí in 1574 are preserved at the archive of Barcelona Cathedral: the first for writing psalters—including initials—for the cathedral hebdomads; the second for writing two hymn fascicles (*quaderns d'Hymnes*); and the third, a payment of 14 *lliures* and 8 *sous*, for writing eight hymn fascicles for a major psalter.[62] Therefore, this case study provides us with a glimpse of the distribution and scribal networks for music books, in which Barcelona convents actively participated. The books of Sant Pere nunnery are still used to perform music in concerts and workshops organised by the convent.[63]

The plainchant books to be used in the choir belonging to the convent of Santa Clara—the other Benedictine convent active in sixteenth-century Barcelona—follow the Roman liturgy and seem to be related to those of Sant Pere convent. Ten large books and some single sheets and chant book excerpts are preserved in the convent archive (the earliest single sheet is dated to the seventeenth century). The first book is entitled *Dominical de Misses comensant lo diumenge primer del Aduent fins al dissapte del diumenge de Rams* (with folios numbered from 1 to 241) and the second, dated 1600, is entitled *Secunda pars Missarum dominicalium dominica palmarum vsque ad Aduentum Et etiam, Kyrie, Gl[or]ia in Excelsis Creo Sanctus e Agnus 1600*. The latter starts with the processional antiphon *Asperges me* and is numbered from folios 1 to 270. Following this section, other undated fragments without foliation appear. On the last page, one of these fragments includes a decorated initial depicting a harlequin and a vihuela player (Figure 2.7).[64] The date of this unusually secular image is not known, nor whether it is connected to vihuela-playing in Santa Clara nunnery or to wooing of nuns. References to vihuela-playing in convents outside Barcelona have been found by other studies: as part, for instance, of plays in Castile convents (see Chapter 5), or the education of young women in the New World. According to Imelda Cano, in Santiago de Chile young women who entered convents to be educated were

72 *Music as a commodity*

Figure 2.7. Detail from: Kyrie in plainchant book no. 2 (1600) from the convent of Sant Antoni i Santa Clara. AMSBM, Cantoral no. 2. This detail is on the last page and forms part of a fragment with no date. Photograph by the author

taught, among other disciplines, 'vocal and instrumental music, especially guitar and vihuela'.[65] These two plainchant books appear to be the result of the instauration of the Roman liturgy at Santa Clara nunnery and might well have been also inscribed by Jeroni Clarí. This shows the connections between these female convents and professionals from other institutions in the city.

Plainchant book no. 5 from Santa Clara convent dates from 1750, while book no. 3, which is a Sanctorale starting with the Introit *Dominus secus mare Galilaeae*, contains a table dated 1754 (fol. 224). On the first folio there is an initial similar to that of book no. 6 (a beautifully illuminated antiphonary starting with the antiphon *Propheta magnus surrexit*). Book nos. 4 and 7 are similar to those from Sant Pere convent: book no. 4 starts with an index of antiphons, while book no. 7 starts with the hymn *Conditor alme* and its folios are numbered on the versus of the sheet to fol. 155. Book nos. 8 to 10 contain different excerpts bound together. Book no. 8 starts with the antiphon for Vespers on Saint Gertrudis's feast day, and book no. 9 begins with the antiphon *Sacerdos in aeternum*. Book no. 10 contains a variety of fragments (both printed and manuscript) of different sizes; one of them is entitled *Añae et missae quae ad novissima Sanctorum Ecclesiae Universae Officia Spectant Accurate Dispositae*, inscribed by Joan Tovella i Fauli in Barcelona in 1797.[66]

In addition to these plainchant books used in the choir, there are other handwritten plainchant books with no date,[67] and also printed sixteenth- and seventeenth-century music books in the library of the convent of Santa Clara. For example, the convent library currently preserves copies of *Contenta in hoc volumine Passio Domini Nostri Iesu Christi secundum quattuor Evangelistas* (Saragossa: Bartolomé de Nájera, 1552), which contains the Passions in Gregorian chant and signs of use, the plainchant handbook by Juan Francisco Cervera entitled *Arte y suma de canto llano* (Valencia: Pedro Patricio Mey, 1595), and the *Liber psalmorum cum aliquot canticis ecclesiasticis. Litaniae. Hymni ecclesiastici, omnia diligenter reposita* (Paris: Guillaume de la Nouë, 1582).[68] Copies of other books printed in Paris, Rome, and Valladolid in the seventeenth century also form part of the convent library.[69] Even this considerable collection of music books is not comparable in size with the impressive book collection of the male convent of Santa Caterina, now located in the rare books section (*Fons Antic*) of Barcelona University library—founded in 1820 as a result of the ecclesiastical confiscation and uncatalogued until recently—which includes several early modern music treatises, such as Giorgio Valla's *De expetendis et fugiendis rebus* (Venice, 1501), Enríquez de Valderrábano's *Silva de sirenas* (Valladolid, 1547), Marin Mersenne's *Quaestiones celeberrimae in Genesim* (Paris, 1623), and Andrés Lorente's *El porqué de la música* (Alcalá de Henares, 1672).[70]

However, inventories provide evidence of other music books existing at Santa Clara nunnery during the sixteenth century. For instance, a single sheet inserted in a 1600 book contains records of bills (*albarans*) from 1567, including 'an old book of antiphons left for Marianna Meca'.[71] Likewise, a 1422 inventory of the sacristy of the convent includes a series of books which are presented in Table 2.7.[72] The 'libre per metre les fadrines al cant' should be highlighted, as it may refer to a book used by *fadrines*, that is, unmarried and unordained women, to learn how to sing. We do not know if these single women were novices. Likewise, the inventory includes two small-format books for the training of infants (*libres prims en que aprenen les infantes*) and a book explicitly used by female singers (*libre per les cantores*).

Analysing the inventories of books preserved in the choir of Santa Clara convent provides evidence of the development of the collection over the sixteenth century. I have analysed and compared the inventories of books located in the convent choir made in 1534, 1544, 1546, 1561, 1565, 1567, 1575, 1579, 1581, and 1585 (see Appendix 2.2).[73] The first inventory includes, among other items, two large *leccionarios* and one small (according to the inventory 1544, this small *leccionario* was known as *Llibre Vermell*, that is 'red book'); nine missals 'with parts for the singers', four Sanctorales, four *Aspiciens* (responsories), four *Locutus*, nine psalters, an antiphonary, a book of *versets*, and three small books with the Offices for the dead (one of them made by 'Gualbes'). From 1561 'a new book which combines Sanctorale and Dominical' (*mes un llibre nou que es Sanctoral y Dominical tot junt*) is recorded, and the antiphonary is described as 'a booklet on parchment which serves to say the antiphons'. Moreover, from 1561 it is specified that there were two *capitolers*, one with the old Office and the other with the new Office (*dos Capitolers, la hu del offici vell y l'altre del offici nou*), probably referring to the instauration of the Roman liturgy. The inventories

Table 2.7. Books included in a 1422 inventory of the convent of Sant Antoni i Santa Clara. 'Memorial de desapropis i càrrecs', AMSBM, box 15, no. 640/20 (1422), fol. 7v

Quantity	Original description
2	liçoners grans
8	officiers missals
9	psaltiris entre nous e vells
15	santorals
4	responsers dominicals: dos locutus e quatre aspiciens
3	ordiinaris: la hu en pla [in the vernacular?] e dos en lati
1	libre de Vicis e Virtuts
1	libre de Santa Paula
1	Breviari
2	libres en que dien de Morts
4	libres de or[açi]ones
1	Flos Santorum en pla
1	libre dels Sants Pares
1	libre al qual dien Monsoneguer
1	libre en que scriuen les defunctes
2	libres prims en que aprenen les infantes
1	Datari en que anuncien la luna
2	capitolers: lo hu nou e l'altre vell
1	libre per les cantores
1	libre per metre les fadrines [single women?] al cant
1	breviari fermat en lo capitol
1	altre breviari a la porta del reffetori
1	Diornal a la porta del torn
1	altre Flos Santorum qui serveix a legir al reffetor
1	libre dels Evangelis qui serveix en quaresma
1	Biblia
2	Retgles
1	Deus Dicit

of 1544 and 1546 contain a book for the choristers' training (*hi un libre en que aprenen les escolanes*). Only the last inventory (1585) explicitly refers to books containing the Roman liturgy (for example, *altre libre nou ab titol de Santoral i Misal Romà*).

A handwritten processional that had belonged to the convent of Sant Antoni i Santa Clara is currently preserved at the BC (Ms. 1458). This book, which is presented in a quarto format and is composed of fifty-four parchment folios, contains plainchant pieces for funerals, Purification feast, and Palm Sunday, in addition to the hymn *Te Deum laudamus* and the antiphon *O sacrum convivium* (Figure 2.8). The rubrics are written in Catalan, and the book has been dated to the fifteenth (Janini 1980: vol. 2, 455) or the sixteenth century (Olivar 1983: 132). The rubrics

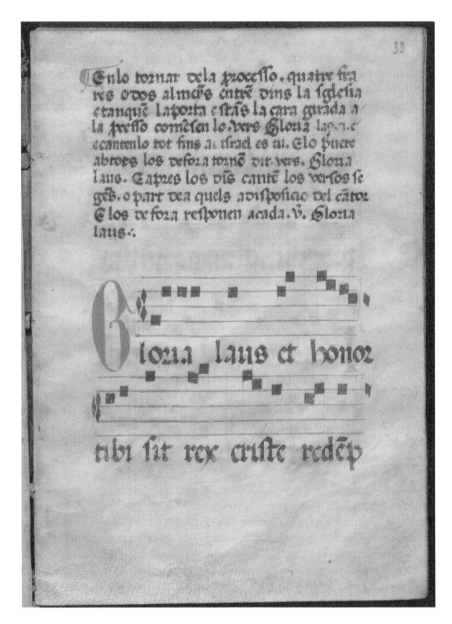

Figure 2.8. Rubric and beginning of the hymn *Gloria, laus et honor* included in a processional which belonged to the nunnery of Sant Antoni i Santa Clara in Barcelona. BC, Ms. 1458, fol. 33r. Public Domain

refer to the participation of several men—the presbyter and his ministers, the deacon, the male singer (*cantor*), the choir, and the friars (*frares*)—in liturgical ceremonies and processions, but there are no indications of nuns' musical role in these ceremonies. In contrast, another fifteenth-century processional preserved at the BC (Ms. 865) might have been created for these nuns. This seventy-one-folio book on parchment was copied to be used in an unidentified Poor Clare nunnery, which might well have been the convent of Sant Antoni i Santa Clara in Barcelona.[74] In this manuscript the participation of the nuns in the ceremonial singing is reflected in the rubrics, written in Latin (Figure 2.9). The book includes the ritual and chants of nuns' professions of vows (fols. 1r–13r) and burials (*Ad sepeliendum sorores vel seculars*, fols. 13r–31v), several psalms, the processional antiphon *Lumen ad revelationem gentium* (fols. 46–57r), the ritual of Palm Sunday procession (fols. 57v–69r), and the *Seven Joys of the Virgin* (fols. 69v–71v).[75]

Personal handwritten plainchant books, as a kind of notebook to be taken to processions, are a further type of music book preserved in the convent of Santa Clara, where processions were usually celebrated inside the cloister (see Chapter 3). The nature of these books seems to be different from that of the two books preserved at the BC, as these notebooks were created for a particular nun's individual use. The booklets from Santa Clara convent have no date indication, although they can be dated approximately by identifying their owners, who were nuns in the eighteenth and nineteenth centuries (Table 2.8). However, the use of these individual notebooks can be extrapolated to earlier periods. Figure 2.10 depicts books very similar to those preserved in Santa Clara convent.

At the ADB there is a very similar plainchant notebook which contains indications of the owner and the dates of copying (Figure 2.11). According to the archive staff, this paper book in quarto format with handwritten music notation appeared shortly before my visit to the archive among a variety of unrelated documents. This was copied for the use of Maria Dominga Pinós, a Capuchin Barcelonan nun, and is very neatly written.[76] It is not known if it was copied by a professional or by a nun. It is named *libreta* (notebook) in the table of contents, and, as indicated in the notebook itself, the copying begun on 1 September 1795 and finished on 15 September 1796.[77] The book is formed from different types of paper, containing a variety of watermarks. The pages are numbered to 150 and, at the end of the book, sixty-seven pages were added. The notebook contains mainly Masses. The table of contents is not complete. It describes up to page 139, but there were additional pages inserted with a Mass for the sick (*Missa pro infirmis*, p. 142) and a Mass for pregnant women (*Missa pro Mulieribus Pregnantibus*, p. 144). Therefore, in contrast with the notebooks from the Sant Antoni nunnery, it is not a book to be used specifically in processions.

Although no sixteenth-century books similar to this are preserved today, other sources indicate that handwritten plainchant notebooks for singing specifically in cloister processions were already being used in the sixteenth century and that they formed part of a tradition of legacies between women, and in particular between aunt and niece. The wills of Santa Maria de Jonqueres nuns demonstrate this

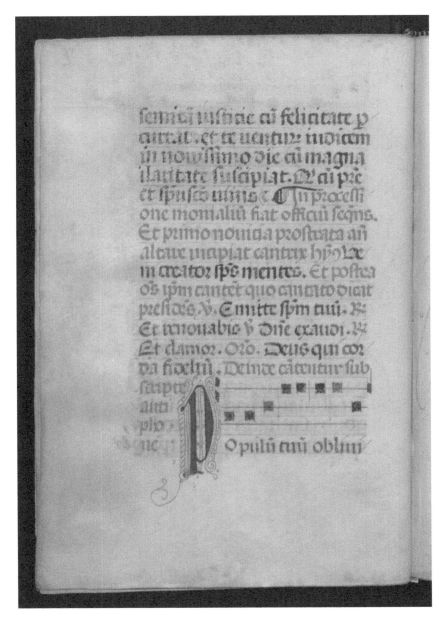

Figure 2.9. Rubric and beginning of the antiphon *Populum tuum obliviscere*, included in a processional copied for the use of an unidentified Poor Clare nunnery which might be that of Sant Antoni i Santa Clara in Barcelona. BC, Ms. 865, fol. 6v. Public Domain

78 *Music as a commodity*

Table 2.8. Handwritten plainchant books for processions belonging to individual nuns that are preserved in the archive of the convent of Sant Antoni i Santa Clara

Signature	Date	Contents	Owner	Physical description and use
BMSCB 160				Handwritten plainchant book
BMSCB 161	[18th century]	Office for Saint Clare and other saints	'Ad usum Dona Maria Francesca Planella'; 'Es de Dona Maria Francisca Sans'[a]	71 manuscript pages, 103 blank pages, 18 cm
BMSCB 162	[18th century]	Office for Palm Sunday, various saints and feasts	'Es de Dona Maria St. Joan y de Planella, Religiosa de Sta. Clara de Barcelona'[b]	66 manuscript pages with music notation, 9 staff paper pages, 17.5 cm. It includes the drawing of a dove
BMSCB 163	[19th century]	Office for Palm Sunday, various saints and feasts	'Es per us de Apolonia Tarragó, Religiosa Benita. Del Monestir de S. Antón y Sta. Clara de Barcelona'[c]	64 manuscript pages with music notation, 5 staff paper pages, 8 blank pages, 22 cm. It includes the drawing of a dove. At the beginning: 'Diumenge de Rams: a la **Professó** se Cantan las Seguents Añas' p. 22: 'Despues entre la **Procession** a la Iglesia, cantando el siguiente Respons[a] Ingrediente'
BMSCB 164	[19th century]	Office for the feast of the Purification, other feasts and saints	'Ad ussum D[a] **Maria Rosa Aguiló**. Benedictina de Sta. Clara' (printed note)[d]	69 manuscript pages with musical notation (2 inks), 4 blank pages, 20 cm fols. 15v–16r: 'En lo tornat de la **professo**, quatra religiosas, o dos al menos entran dins la Iglesia tancant la porta, y tenint la cara girada à la **professo** comensen lo V. Gloria laus &c. y cantenlo tot com se segueix, y lo Sacerdot ab las demes Religiosas de fora tornen a repetir lo dit V. Gloria laus. y despues los de dins canten los versos despues seguents o part de aquells a disposicio de la cantora. y los qu estan fora responen cada V. lo sobre dit V'.

BMSCB 165	[18th century]	Office for Palm Sunday, various saints and feasts	'Es de mi Sra. Dña. **Maria Theresa Cortada y Brú**'e	77 pp. with notation, 6 blank pages, 18 cm
BMSCB 166		Office for Palm Sunday, various saints and feasts		63 pages with notation, 22 cm
BMSCB 167	1783	*Processionarii, five libelli ad pompam rogationum, à Fr. Joanne Pujató Reg Ord. B.V.M. de Mercede scripti pro Regali Monasterio Sancti Cucuphatis Vallen nullius Diaecesis an. 1783*	Note: 'Joan Nogués preuere'	Oblong
BMSCB 168		Office for Saint Peter and Saint Paul and Office for Saint Torcuato		22 pages with notation, 22 blank pages, 25 cm
BMSCB 169	1750		'**Francisca Sentmanat, et de Oms**, Filia Sancti Patris Nostri Benedicti Iesus'	The person who sings each part is indicated: 'Incipit Sacerdo', 'Ministri respondent', 'Totus Chorus', 'Duo Cantores in medio', 'Primus chorus', 'Secundus Chorus' On the last page the following is indicated: 'Scripsit Frater Franciscus a Sancto Antonio de Padua, Ordinis Excalceatorum Sancti Patris Nostri Augustini, In Conventu Sancta Monica, Civitatis Barcinonensis, Anno Millessimo Septingentessimo Quinquagessimo Iussu Dominae Francisca Sentmanat, et de Oms, Filia Sancti Patris Nostri Benedicti Iesus'

(*Continued*)

80 *Music as a commodity*

Table 2.8. (Continued)

Signature	Date	Contents	Owner	Physical description and use
BMSCB 170	[18th century]	Office for Palm Sunday, various saints and feasts	**Francisca de Sentmanat i de Oms**[f]	It includes an engraving 'En lo tornat de la professo. Quatre Religiosas, o dos, al menos entre dins la Iglesia tancan la porta i tenint la cara girada a la professo comensant lo v. Gloria laus etc. y cantenlo tot fins a Israel es tu. I lo Sacerdot ab las demes religiosas de fora tornen a rrepetir lo dit v. Gloria laus. y despues los de dins canten los versos despues seguents o part de aquells a disposisicio de la cantora y los que estan fora responen a quisu v. lo sobre dit'

[a] Darna (2014: 181) refers to a Maria Francisca Planella who professed vows in 1729 (AMSBM, Carp. 100, Carta de Profesión 121.9).
[b] A Maria Sant Ioan, who professed vows in 1710, is mentioned by Darna (2014: 178) (AMSBM, Carp. 100, Carta de profesión 116.4).
[c] According to the list of nuns of the convent, Apolonia Tarragó i Puigibet entered the convent with a dowry of 1,000 *lliures* on 14 May 1825 being 29 years old. She professed vows on 16 June 1826 and died on 10 September 1855. She was a chorister.
[d] Darna (2014: 197) refers to a Maria Rosa Aguiló who was abbess from 11 May 1855 to 1876. A portrait of her is preserved at the convent archive. According to the list of nuns of the convent, 'M. Rosa Aguiló i Aloi' was a chorister who entered the convent with a dowry of 500 *lliures* on 24 October 1832 being 20 years old, professed vows on 27 October 1833, and died on 17 October 1876.
[e] In the list of nuns between 1718 and 1952 Maria Teresa Cortada i Bru is included as sub-prioress and minor singer (*cantora menor*), entering the convent on 31 May 1725, professing vows on 10 June 1725, and dying on 11 December 1768. Vinyolas (1913: 150) refers to 'Doña Teresa Cortada y Brú', who commissioned a new silver lamp for the convent on 15 October 1757, according to the 'Llibre de les coses dignes de memoria...', fols. 63 and 118.
[f] Francisca de Sentmanat was the daughter of the viceroy of Perú, the Marquis of Castelldosrius (Barcelona, 1651–Lima, 1710). She occupied the positions of prioress, nurse, minor singer, and second archivist at the convent. She entered the convent on 2 July 1719, professed on 23 February 1721, and died on 4 December 1775.

Music as a commodity 81

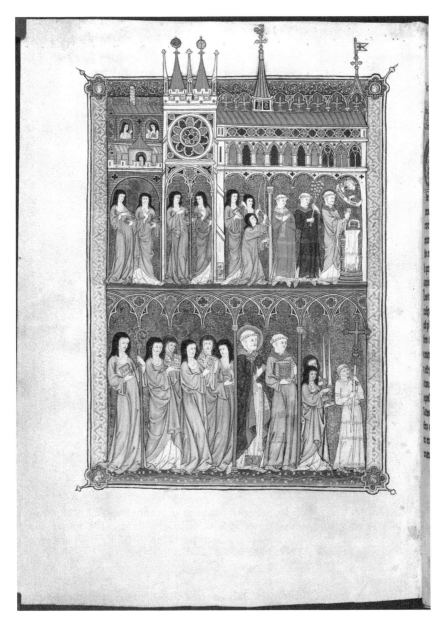

Figure 2.10. 'Nuns in Procession', in *Collection of moral tracts* (MS, c.1290), probably commissioned by the Cistercian nunnery of Notre-Dame-la-Royale at Maubuisson in France. London, British Library, Yates Thompson MS 11. Public Domain

82 *Music as a commodity*

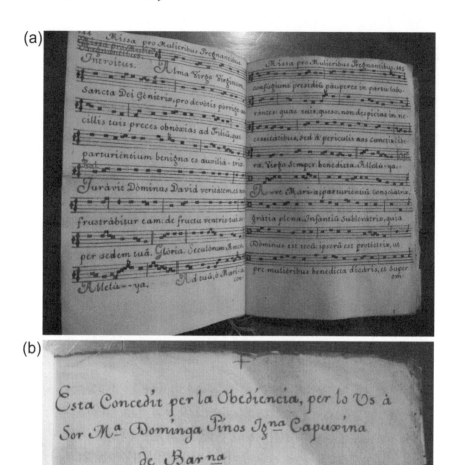

Figure 2.11. Missa pro Mulieribus Pregnantibus and annotation about the book owner in a plainchant notebook used by Sor Maria Dominga Pinós, a Capuchin nun in Barcelona. ADB, Jurisdicción Castrense 14, pp. 144–145, and blank sheet at the beginning. Photograph by the author

tradition in the sixteenth century, and it seems that the custom of bequeathing books to nieces was less common in the seventeenth century or it was simply not recorded (Table 2.9 and Appendix 4.1). Thus, this type of book offers an opportunity to study the distribution of musical artefacts among women.

These wills, together with the later books preserved at Santa Clara convent, demonstrate that the tradition of having personal plainchant notebooks for singing in cloister processions lasted several centuries. This begs the question of whether the books were written by the nuns themselves, which would suggest that they

Table 2.9. Legacies of procession plainchant notebooks recorded in wills of Santa Maria de Jonqueres convent. 'Libro de desapropio (testamento)' (1411–1741), ACA,ORM,Monacales-Universidad,Volúmenes,241

Will date	Nun	Legacy	Recipient
25 September 1457	Margarita de Monmany	Some procession booklets (*vns coerns de proffesso*) (fol. 49r)	To the nuns of her lineage
11 October 1468	Costanç Descros	One procession booklet with velvet covers (*hun libret de proffesso ab cubertes de vellut*)	To Rosa
	Isabel de Gualbes	Some small procession and preces booklets (*coherns petits de proffessons e de preses a na Isabel lulla*); some large booklets (fol. 71v)	To Isabel Lulla (the small booklets) To all the nuns (*en seruey de totes*) (the large booklets)
25 December 1491	Elionor de Vilanova, sub-prioress	Some procession booklets (*huns coherns de professo*) (fol. 88r)	To her niece Joana de Vilanova
25 August 1497	Leonor Gualbes, sub-prioress and sacristan	8 small procession booklets (*vuy cuerns de professons petits*) (fol. 98r)	
18 July 1501 (her death date)	Elizabet de Sentmenat	Some procession booklets (*huns coerns de profeso*) (fol. 104r)	To her nieces Aldonça and Joana de Vilanova (*de lurvida apres sia de las fillas del dit nabot meu*)
1 June 1515	Yolant Llull (see Costa 1984)	2 procession booklets, one of them including the Office for the dead (*dos coerns de professo en la hu es notat lo offici de morts*) (fol. 120r)	
15 November 1527	Violant Desllor, sub-prioress	A procession booklet which is well bounded (*un cuern de professo ben cornats e ligats*) (fol. 131r)	
12 mayo 1530 (her death date)	Joana de Gilabert	Some procession booklets	To her niece
21 June 1531	Joana de Vilanova, prioress	Some small procession booklets on parchment (*vns coerns de pregami de professo petit*) (fol. 150r)	

(*Continued*)

84 *Music as a commodity*

Table 2.9. (Continued)

Will date	Nun	Legacy	Recipient
5 June 1541 (the date of her death)	Luisa de Gualbes	2 handwritten booklets for processions (*vn libre ab cubertes vermelles ab un ballouerts de Canto*; *dos cuerns de cant de ma per professons*) (fol. 163v)	
25 December 1560 (the date of her death). Will on 12 December 1549	Isabel Miquela	Some parchment procession booklets (*uns coernets de pregami de profasso*) (fol. 167v)	To her nephew
24 January 1555	Isabel de Monmany, sub-prioress	Some procession booklets (*E mes reste vn breuiari de pergami y vn salptiri de pergami y vns cuerns de professons y altres de mostrar de cant en la casa hon esta en lo pati dalt en dret dels archs es de linatge de monmany*) (fol. 177r)	To the nuns of her lineage
24 October 1556 (the date of her death)	Anna Marqueta	Some procession booklets with silver locks (*uns quers de profasso ab los tancados de plata*) (fol. 185v)	

had the ability to do so, or if they asked someone else to write the music for them. For instance, in addition to the procession notebooks, according to her 1497 will, Leonor Gualbes possessed eight small procession notebooks. In addition to this, she had two breviaries, one small and the other larger and old, and two books of hours (one new and the other old), and she indicated that she had written the small breviary herself. Perhaps she also wrote the music books? Luisa de Guabes's 1541 will specifies that her procession notebooks were for singing and that they were handwritten, but she does not indicate who copied the music. She also had, among other volumes, a plainchant book with red covers. Isabel de Gualbes left to Constança Lull 'the book with which she [Constança Llull] had learned'.[78] This may indicate that Gualbes taught Lull (music?).[79] According to her will of 1555, Isabel de Monmany had some procession notebooks and, in addition to those, other notebooks which showed how to sing; all these books had to be preserved in the house of the nuns of her family.

In the case of the convent of Santa Maria de Jonqueres, no sixteenth-century plainchant books to be used in the choir are preserved today. However, the collection of chant books and also the spaces devoted to making music at this nunnery were described in detail by visitors of the Order of Santiago, while taking inventory of all the items of the convent. In the centre of the choir there was a big iron candelabra and a lectern with drawers at its base where the books to be used in the choir were kept.[80] Forty seats for the nuns were placed around the choir, while novices and choristers sat on low benches. The choir's floor was covered by rugs. On the left of the choir there was an image of the Virgin and Child. On the right, on a small tribune, there was a medium-size organ with doors on which were pictures of Saint James and Saint Mary Magdalene.[81] In front of the choir and the organ there was a wooden grille. In 1495 the visitors ordered it to be made higher, presumably to hide the nuns.[82] They did not obey this command, since this order was reiterated by subsequent visitors.[83] There are no references to acoustic jars to improve the sound of singing in sixteenth-century Barcelona convent churches.[84]

Through the books of visitations, it is also possible to examine the development of the collection of choir books. It has been said that the quantity of books belonging to Santa Maria de Jonqueres nunnery was quite limited (Serra Álvarez 1966: 125). The number of liturgical books inventoried ranges from thirteen to twenty-five over the course of the sixteenth century (see Appendix 2.1 and a summary in Table 2.10). Even though the visitors provided few details of the books in their inventories, the comparison between them makes analysis of the development of the collection of chant books possible. The visitors usually specified the genre of the books and whether they included music. Until 1509 it was specified that all the books inventoried were manuscript written on parchment. However, the inventories failed to indicate whether the music books contained polyphony or plainchant, and—after 1509—whether they were printed or handwritten. Sometimes the year of creation of the book is indicated; for instance, the inventory carried out in 1509 includes a two-volume dominical and 'other new chant book' made after the last pastoral visitation—that is after 1504.

Since the nuns of Santa Maria de Jonqueres followed their own liturgical practice until 1576 (see Chapter 5), they also had their own liturgical books such as the manuscript *Responsorium Sanctorale*, dating from 1504 and written by Miquel Vallès, a clergyman from Tarragona. This included annotations for singing in the choir (Costa 2005: 34). The receipt of delivery of an *euangelister ab solfa de cant pla* (a Book of the Gospels containing plainchant notation) to the prioress on 3 September 1455 is preserved.[85] The nuns inscribed music books themselves as well: in the fourteenth century, Isabel Llull 'wrote' (copied?) a dominical plainchant book, assuming herself the cost of the materials;[86] this book was bequeathed to the convent and is included in the inventories of the visitors. It is described as being in 'very good' condition still in the inventory of 1509.[87]

In 1515 the visitors, sent by Ferdinand the Catholic, made reference to the need for all the convents of the Order of Santiago to acquire the breviary that the king had ordered to be printed (no copies of this book are known).[88] Instead of using the Order's breviary, the prioress Caterina Durall signed a contract on 22 October 1520 with the Barcelona bookseller Joan Trinxer to print 500 breviaries

86 *Music as a commodity*

Table 2.10. Some of the plainchant books to be used in the choir belonging to the convent of Santa Maria de Jonqueres, according to inventories included in visitation books

1495	1498	1509	1560–1561	1605	1628
dominical de canto	dominical de canto	libro dominical de missa de muy gentil letra	dominical dende el principio del adviento hasta el fin del viernes santo de antifonas himnos y responsos puntados	dominical de canturia de pergamino grande que comiença desde la dominica del conuento hasta las visperas de pasqua de resurrection del officio de visperas y maytines	dominical de canturia de pergamino grande que comiença desde la dominica primera de aduiento asta las bisperas de pasqua de resurrection
dominical de canto de la resureçion	dominical de canto de la resureçion		cuerpo de libro de la misma suerte [dominical] dende el sabado de pascua hasta la postrera dominica antes del adviento que entramos sirven todo el año para visperas y maytines	dominical de canturia que comiensa de las visperas de pasqua de resurrection asta el aduiento a donde estan las maytinas y horas del dia	dominical de canturia que comiença de las bisperas de pasqua de resurrection asta el aduiento a donde estan las maytinas y horas del dia
dominical y santoral	dominical y santoral	dos officerios de canto el uno dominical y el otro santoral	otro libro en dos cuerpos de liciones de maytines dominical para todo el año un dominical ofiçerio de misas en dos cuerpos para todo el año	dos dominicales en dos cuerpos llibro de las chalendas y euangelios de dominical de santos y proffessias y la regla de san augustin	dos dominicales en dos cuerpos

Music as a commodity 87

dominical de canto de Isabel Llull *dominical de canto de Isabel Llull* *dominical de canto muy bueno [...] que scriuio una Isabel lullo freyla del dicho monesterio*

dominical y festivial de canto

containing the nunnery's local liturgy and following an original sample provided by the nuns.[89] These copies would be sold to current and prospective nuns of Santa Maria de Jonqueres. Altés (1990: 59) points out that, according to Antonio Odriozola, a breviary preserved at the Biblioteca Pública Episcopal in Barcelona might be an incomplete copy of the breviary from Santa Maria de Jonqueres nunnery (see Figure 2.12). In 1556 the visitors found that the nuns still did not follow the breviary of the Order and they required the prioress to go to the monastery of Uclés to obtain a copy of the new missal of the Order of Santiago.[90] In the visitations carried out in 1560–1561 and again in 1566, the instruction to collect and use missals and breviaries of the Order was reiterated.[91] Moreover, in 1566 the visitors prohibited nuns from praying or singing by heart,[92] which demonstrates that the convent's local liturgical use was deeply rooted and this is probably the reason why the collection of chant books at the convent seems to be limited (see Chapter 5). After the implementation of the Roman liturgy at the convent in 1576, visitors often specified for every book in particular whether it followed the Roman liturgy.[93] Books containing the old liturgical use of the nunnery were still preserved in the seventeenth century, although the visitors indicated that these books were no longer used.

In her book about women and music in sixteenth-century Ferrara, Laurie Stras analyses the connection between the *Motetes Voci Pari* of the 1540s and Scotto's *Voci Pari Colletion* of 1563 to the convent of Corpus Domini. She points out that in the 1580s composers in the North of Italy started to publish arrangements for equal voices of various Offices and Masses, so that the repertory available to nuns was increased. For instance, Paolo Isnardi, the cathedral chapel master, produced books which might show the music available for the convents of the city. Likewise, Stras studies the relationship between convent repertory and that performed in courtly spaces in Ferrara. In the case of Barcelona, one of the difficulties in the research into the contribution of convents to the musical life of the city is the identification of the repertory performed by Barcelona nuns in the sixteenth century, beyond that preserved in liturgical chant books. Sixteenth-century polyphonic books belonging to Barcelona convents have not been preserved. However, archival documents include references to polyphonic singing in Barcelona convents. Likewise, polyphonic music books are included in inventories of Barcelonan women.[94]

Given the scarcity and dispersion of the musical sources belonging to sixteenth-century Barcelona convents, it is necessary to approach the musical repertory performed by these nuns through the study of later polyphonic pieces performed, for instance, during professions of vows. As one kind of music repertory produced by the convent, villancicos were sung at the ceremonies of profession of particular nuns who entered the major convents of the city, such as those of Sant Pere, Santa Elisabet, Santa Maria de Valldonzella, or Santa Clara. Printed lyrics of these villancicos provide information, on the title page, about the identity of the performers and the nun who professed. The villancicos were usually performed by chapel choirs (*capillas*) from other Barcelonan musical centres such as the cathedral, the parish churches of Santa Maria del Pi or Santa Maria del Mar, and the chapel of Our Lady of the Palau (Table 2.11 and Appendix 3). Singers from these

Figure 2.12. [Breviary from the convent of Santa Maria de Jonqueres (Lyon: Bernard Lescuyer, 1521)], Common of the Saints, fol. 1r. Barcelona, Biblioteca Pública Episcopal, Res. 264-13 Bre. Image from: Altés 1990: 61

90 *Music as a commodity*

Table 2.11. Participation of external chapel musicians (*capillas*) in the singing of villancicos on the occasion of nuns' professions at sixteenth-century Barcelona convents

Date of profession	Nun	Convent	Performers
18 May 1681	Felicia Callar, Raimunda Tord, and Teresa de Solanell	Valldonzella	Cathedral chapel under Lluís Vicenç Gargallo (1635–1682)
23 April 1687	Inés Fluvia i de Aguilar and Clemencia Foix i de Pi	Valldonzella	Our Lady of the Palau chapel under Felip Olivelles (1657–1702)
1688	Maria Àngela de Sant Josep ('en el siglo doña Maria Àngela Martí i de Vilanova')	Santa Teresa	Cathedral chapel under Joan Barter (1648–1706)
22 February 1693	Zeferina Berenguer de Castell-Germà i Areny	Santa Teresa	Our Lady of the Palau chapel under Felip Olivelles
12 February 1696	Catalina and Gertrudis Piñatelli/Pignatelli i Aymerich, daughters of the marquises of San Vicente	Sant Pere	Our Lady of the Palau chapel under Felip Olivelles (1657–1702)
26 April 1696	Teresa Abarca y Velasco, daughter of the Count and Countess de la Rosa	Sant Pere	Our Lady of the Palau chapel under Felip Olivelles
11 June 1696	Cecilia Oliver i de Miralles	Sant Pere	Our Lady of the Palau chapel under Felip Olivelles
1697	Teresa de Crist (Espanyol i Ardenuy)	Santa Teresa	Cathedral chapel under Francesc Valls (1671–1747)
6 May 1698	Maria Flora Carcer i de Martí	Jerònimes	Our Lady of the Palau chapel under Felip Olivelles
[1700]	Maria Josefa de Vilallonga i Ialpi	Sant Pere	Cathedral chapel under Francesc Valls
17 November 1700	Isabel Piñatelli/Pignatelli i Aymerich, daughter of the marquises of San Vicente	Sant Antoni i Santa Clara	Our Lady of the Palau chapel under Tomàs Milans (1672–1742)
8 August 1701	Inés de Rius i de Falguera	Jerònimes	Cathedral chapel under Francesc Valls
20 August 1703	Josefa and Antonia de Berardo i Morera	Jerònimes	Cathedral chapel under Francesc Valls
17 December 1703	Francesca de Lentorn i de Civilla	Montsió	Cathedral chapel under Francesc Valls
16 June 1704	Teresa and Maria Agustina de Vega i Copons	Sant Pere	Our Lady of the Palau Chapel under Tomàs Milans
22 June 1705	Teresa Mollar i Mitjans	Santa Elisabet	Santa Maria del Mar chapel under Lluís Serra (c.1680–1758)
29 June 1706	[It is not indicated if the villancicos were created on the occasion of a profession.]	Sant Pere	Cathedral chapel under Francesc Valls

Music as a commodity 91

Date	Name	Convent	Chapel
12 August 1706	Maria Inés Riera i Vidal	Santa Elisabet	Santa Maria del Mar chapel under Lluís Serra (c.1680–1758)
30 January 1707	Maria Rosa Serra i Postius	Santa Elisabet	Santa Maria del Mar chapel under Lluís Serra
January 1708	Maria Agustina Cavaller y Ratés	Santa Elisabet	Santa Maria del Mar chapel under Lluís Serra
18 January 1708	Gerònima Llaurador i de Vilana-Perlas	Santa Elisabet	Cathedral chapel under Francesc Valls
16 April 1708	Maria Clara Albià i Fayet	Jerusalem	Santa Maria del Mar chapel under Lluís Serra
22 April 1708	Ana Queralt Reart i de Xatmar	Jerusalem	Our Lady of the Palau chapel under Tomàs Milans
3 October 1708	Maria Orosia Pou i Çanou	Santa Elisabet	Cathedral chapel under Francesc Valls
12 October 1709	Augustina Bassols i Rafart	Santa Elisabet	Cathedral chapel under Francesc Valls
21 November 1709	Emanuela de Cruillas i Zarriera	Sant Pere	Cathedral chapel under Francesc Valls
29 December 1709	Magdalena de Ferran i Fivaller and Maria Antonia de Copons i Cordelles	Sant Pere	Our Lady of the Palau chapel under Tomàs Milans
5 May 1711	Arcàngela Rossinès i Fontllonga	Àngels	Santa Maria del Mar chapel under Lluís Serra
28 June 1711	Teresa de Cartellà Fons i Sebastida	Santa Teresa	Our Lady of the Palau chapel under Thomàs Milàns
17 June 1715	Francesca Gaetana Amat i de Iunyent	Sant Pere	Our Lady of the Palau chapel under Josep Picanyol (1700–1771)
24 June 1715	Gerònima de Cors i Pinyana	Montsió	Our Lady of the Palau chapel under Josep Picanyol
28 June 1716	Francesca Rossinès i Fontllonga	Àngels	Santa Maria del Mar chapel under Jaume Caselles (1690–1764)
4 October 1717	Francesca Gaetana Amat i de Iunyent	Sant Pere	Our Lady of the Palau under Josep Picanyol
3 March 1727	Maria Ignacia de Santa Teresa and Isabel de la Madre de Dios (sisters)	Santa Teresa	Santa Maria del Mar chapel under Jaume Caselles
14 December 1728	Josefa Martí i Baseya	Santa Elisabet	Our Lady of the Palau chapel under Bernat Tria (d.1754)
26 June 1729	Maria Gertrudis Mollar i Roig	Santa Elisabet	Santa Maria del Mar chapel under Jaume Casellas (1690–1764)
3 August 1730	Maria Magdalena de Berart i de Ramon, Francesca de Magarola i de Reart, and Francesca de Boixò i de Francolí	Valldonzella	Our Lady of the Palau chapel under Bernat Tria

(*Continued*)

92 *Music as a commodity*

Table 2.11. (Continued)

Date of profession	Nun	Convent	Performers
4 November 1730	Teresa de Jesús ('en el siglo doña Teresa Marí i de Vilana')	Santa Teresa	Cathedral chapel under Josep Picanyol
31 July 1731	Maria Àngela Martí i Baseya	Santa Elisabet	Our Lady of the Palau chapel under Bernat Tria
25 November 1731	Maria Madrona Surià	Santa Margarida	Santa Maria del Mar chapel under Jaume Caselles
21 September 1732	Jacinta Seguí i Rovira	Jerusalem	Santa Maria del Pi chapel under Pau Llinàs (1680–1749)
5 January 1733	Maria Fontana i Cotxet	Jerusalem	Cathedral chapel under Josep Picanyol
19 April 1733	Maria de Llinàs i de Lapeyra	Magdalenes	Santa Maria del Mar chapel under Jaume Caselles
1 July 1733	Teresa de Sans i Montrodon and Ignacia de Fivaller i de Rub	Sant Pere	Cathedral chapel under Josep Picanyol
25 October 1733	Maria Francesca Llauder i Duran	Jerusalem	Santa Maria del Mar chapel under Jaume Caselles
5 May 1734	Esperança Mollar i Roig	Santa Elisabet	Santa Maria del Mar chapel under Salvador Figueres (d.1759)
12 May 1734	Maria Ignacia de Bergadá i de Taraval	Santa Teresa	Cathedral chapel under Josep Picanyol
19 December 1734	Maria Gracia de la Santíssima Trinitat	Santa Elisabet	Santa Maria del Mar chapel under Salvador Figueres
24 January 1736	Antonia Martí i Baseya	Jerusalem	Our Lady of the Palau chapel under Bernat Tria
8 April 1736	Maria Teresa Llauder i Duran	Santa Teresa	Santa Maria del Mar chapel under Salvador Figueres
11 June 1736	Josefa del Santíssim Sacrament ('en el siglo Josepha Cortés y Dalmau')		Santa Maria del Mar chapel under Salvador Figueres
2 June 1741	Maria Anna de Graell i de Anglassell	Sant Antoni i Santa Clara	Our Lady of the Palau chapel under Bernat Tria
3 June 1742	Eulàlia Francesca Martorell i Reyt	Jerusalem	Our Lady of the Palau chapel under Bernat Tria
10 October 1742	Anna Maria Nin i Steva	Santa Elisabet	Our Lady of the Palau chapel under Bernat Tria
23 April 1743	Maria Antonia and Maria Josefa de Magarola i Clariana	Sant Pere	Santa Maria del Pi chapel under Pau Llinàs (c.1680–1749)

Music as a commodity 93

26 October 1743	Eulàlia de Crist ('en el siglo Eulalia Piferrer y Pou')	Santa Teresa	Our Lady of the Palau chapel under Bernat Tria
8 May 1746	Maria Josefa de Tort i de Llar, Maria Teresa de Sabater i de Oriol, Maria Gertrudis de Magarola i de Reart, Maria Teresa de Moixò i de Francolí, and Maria Victòria de Foxà i de Mora	Valldonzella	Our Lady of the Palau chapel under Bernat Tria
1747	Eulàlia del Cor de Jesús ('en el siglo Eulalia Compte y Reyón')	Santa Teresa	Our Lady of the Palau chapel under Bernat Tria
15 October 1748	Maria Ignacia Piñatelli/Pignatelli i de Rubí	Sant Antoni i Santa Clara	Cathedral chapel under Josep Pujol (*fl*.1734–1798)
21 October 1749	Maria Francesca de Sentmenat y de Bach, daughter of the Marquises of Castelldosrius	Sant Antoni i Santa Clara	Our Lady of the Palau under Bernardo Tria
30 March 1750	Teresa Maria Gispert i Illa	Jerusalem	Santa Maria del Mar chapel under Pau Montserrat (d.1759)
6 October 1750	Esperança de Jesús Maria ('en el siglo Esperança Cots')	Santa Teresa	Santa Maria del Mar chapel under Pau Montserrat
25 January 1752	Maria Bàrbara de Pascalí i Sanpere ('en el siglo Maria Madalena de Pascalí i Sanpera')	Àngels	Our Lady of the Palau chapel under Bernat Tria
23 April 1753	Maria Gertrudis Cabanyes i Boet	Jerusalem	Our Lady of the Palau chapel under Bernat Tria
7 February 1754	Marianna de Sala i de Pujades	Sant Pere	Cathedral chapel under Josep Pujol
16 July 1761	Maria Ignacia and Maria Eulàlia de Moxò i de Ninot	Valldonzella	Our Lady of the Palau chapel under Josep Duran
29 December 1765	Maria Teresa Sociats i Guitart	Jerusalem	Cathedral chapel under Josep Pujol
1767	Teresa Grases i Cortés	Santa Teresa	Santa Maria del Mar chapel under Pere Antoni Monlleó (1720–1792)
1769	Maria Ignacia de Sant Josep	Santa Teresa	Cathedral chapel under Josep Pujol
1769	Maria Benita Lacóma i Martí	Jerusalem	Cathedral chapel under Josep Pujol
16 January 1770	Cayetana Dolcet i Baliart	Jerusalem	Cathedral chapel under Josep Pujol
29 June 1772	Maria Josefa Esquís i Prats	Jerusalem	Cathedral chapel under Josep Pujol
1782	Maria Bàrbara de Sant Joan de la Creu ('en el siglo Maria Antonia Viver y Sors')	Santa Teresa	Cathedral chapel under Francesc Queralt (1740–1825)
1798	Teresa del Cor de Jesús ('en el siglo Bruguera y Pallós')	Santa Teresa	Cathedral chapel under Francesc Queralt

institutions visited the convents to carry out these performances under the direction of chapel masters such as Luis Vicente Gargallo (c.1636–Barcelona, 1682), Francesc Valls (c.1671–1747)—composer of the controversial *Missa Scala aretina*—Josep Picanyol (d.1769), or Josep Pujol (*fl*.1734–1798) from the cathedral; Felip Olivelles (d.1702), Tomàs Milans (1672–1742), the same Josep Picanyol, Bernat Tria, and Josep Duran (Cadaqués, c.1730–Barcelona, 1802) from the chapel of Our Lady of the Palau; Lluís Serra (Barcelona, 1680–Zaragoza, 1758), Salvador Figueres (d.1759), Jaume Caselles Genovart (Valls, Tarragona, c.1690–Toledo, 1764), and Pau Monserrat from the parish church of Santa Maria del Mar; and Pau Llinàs (c.1680–1749) from Santa Maria del Pi parish church.[95]

The earliest preserved example of a villancico lyric booklet was printed in 1681 and indicates the villancicos performed by the cathedral choir (*capilla*) under Lluís Vicenç Gargallo during the profession ceremony for three nuns—Felicia Callar, Raimunda Tord and Teresa de Solanell—at the convent of Valldonzella. This date is in keeping with similar materials from other places, since the earliest texts analysed by Andrea Bombi in his study of the cultivation of the villancico in Valencian convents date from around the same period, while Janet Hathaway has studied a corpus of villancicos for nuns' professions at the Discalced convent in Madrid between 1670 and 1698.[96] It is unknown whether this tradition also can be extrapolated backwards to the sixteenth century or whether it was more related to the solemnity of the Baroque aesthetic of the ceremonial. According to Juan Ruiz Jiménez, who has compiled information of villancicos composed for the profession of nuns in a variety of cities in Europe and the New World, the earliest printed lyrics to be sung during a nun's profession of vows to be preserved are a series of *chanzonetas* and romances composed for the profession of Francisca de Córdoba y Ribera, the daughter of Alonso Fernández de Córdoba, fifth Marquis of Priego, at the convent of Santa Clara in Montilla (Córdoba) in July 1634.[97] Yet in any case, as Chapter 3 will show, nuns reportedly sung villancicos on special occasions in the sixteenth century.

The printed lyrics of villancicos performed by external *capillas* in Barcelona convents usually include three villancicos (the 1681 print contains four), following a refrain-verse structure. The profession villancico aimed to instruct and 'can be considered a "sermon in music" for its message, tropes and images, and for its realization in (musical) performance' (Hathaway 2007: 227, n. 33). However, both this musical repertory and the subsequent printing of lyrics were undoubtedly a means of exhibiting social status. For instance, the title page of the villancicos sung in 1700 by Our Lady of the Palau chapel choir directed by Tomàs Milans at the convent of Santa Clara indicates that the occasion was the profession of the 'illustrious lady' Isabel Piñatelli i Aymerich, daughter of the Marquis of San Vicente. Moreover, the lyrics of the villancicos usually mention the name of the nun who was professing vows and praised her.

In his study of Valencia, Andrea Bombi (2007) states that villancicos were performed by convent chapel choirs only in the convents of Santa María Magdalena and Santa Catalina de Siena, since they had important chapel choirs; however, in other cases, chapel choirs from outside were hired, as also occurred in Barcelona.

Taking as his main source four Valencian *cancioneros* (songbooks), Bombi points out that 'only two villancicos to be sung on the day of the entry of nuns into a convent are preserved in the four cancioneros' (Bombi 2007: 180), although other genres for these occasions are also included. This contrasts with Barcelona convents, where the villancicos, which required a considerable chapel choir, were the genre par excellence in the celebration of nuns' vow-takings. This might be related to the high status of the nuns who lived in most of the Barcelona convents. Bombi mentions that 'the degree of ceremony is related to the level which a noble family could afford in order to solemnify the entry of one of their members into a convent'. He points out that, in Valencia, 'normally such events took place with less ostentation and were sometimes even quite intimate'. This meant that 'nun singers could themselves perform the works for the feast of their vow-taking' and 'young girls might sing at the vow-taking of a relative' (Bombi 2007: 157). In the case of Barcelona, these printed lyrics of villancicos suggest that the ceremonial associated with nuns' professions were less intimate and more ostentatious (see Chapter 3).

We do not know if the nuns sang or otherwise contributed to the performance of these villancicos, joining the male singers. However, one composition whose notation has survived may suggest the participation of nuns in the singing of profession villancicos. Francesc Valls, chapel master in Barcelona Cathedral, probably composed the villancicos sang during professions of vows at the convents of Sant Pere (1700 and 1709), the Jeronymite nuns (1701 and 1703), Santa Maria de Montsió (1703), and Santa Elisabet (1708 and 1709). A *tono* entitled 'Deidades del abismo' for two tiples and accompaniment composed by him to be sung for a profession of vows is preserved at the Biblioteca de Catalunya (Figure 2.13).[98] However, the use of two tiples does not necessarily imply nuns, as these parts might have been sung by boys or countertenors. Likewise, at the Biblioteca de Catalunya, the 16 *particelles* of a villancico for two choirs (CT/SCTB), two violins, two oboes, two horns, and three continuo instruments composed by Josep Pujol 'for a veil', that is, a nun's veiling, in 1740 is preserved under the title 'Angélicos giros' (Figure 2.14). The lyrics demonstrate that the nun who professed must have been named Gerònima and belonged to the Dominican order (*Qual victima pura Geronima emprende siguiendo a Domingo*). *Tonos*, villancicos, and other works by Lluís Vicenç Gargallo, Felip Olivelles, Tomàs Milans, Bernat Tria, and Josep Duran, among other chapel masters, are also preserved in Catalan archives, although none of them is explicitly related to professions of vows. Even though it is impossible to confirm whether these villancicos were performed by the nuns, they certainly were performed for the nuns, and constitute further evidence of the relevance of nunneries as institutions that promoted music creation in the city.

Different convents used the same workshops for the printing of villancico lyrics booklets; for example, it seems that villancicos from Sant Pere and Sant Antoni were printed in the same printing workshops, such as those of Figueró and Giralt (Figure 2.15). Publishers played an important role in the musical culture of any city,[99] and further examples of women's invisibility in music history occur with

96 *Music as a commodity*

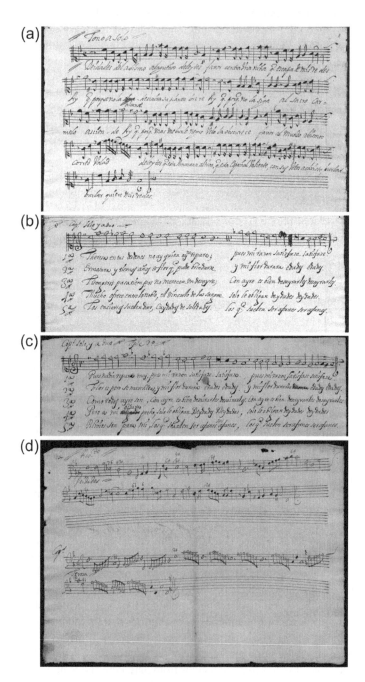

Figure 2.13. Francesc Valls (c.1671–1747), 'Deidades del abismo', *tono* for two tiples and accompaniment to be sung during a profession of vows. BC, M 1686/26. Public Domain

Music as a commodity 97

Figure 2.14. First folio of the first alto part of the profession of vows villancico 'Angélicos giros' (1740) by Josep Pujol. BC, M 1470/19. Public Domain

women who worked as printers. While there was a printing workshop in the male convent of Santa Caterina itself, with considerable activity in the last decades of the sixteenth century—for example, the Malo and the Cormellas families of printers, both from Aragon, worked there—there is no evidence of printing activity in sixteenth-century Barcelona nunneries. Generally, clues of women's presence in the printing industry emerge only when the head of both the household and the workshop died and his widow took charge of the business. The ordinances of the guild of booksellers in Barcelona stipulated that widows were allowed to be in charge of the printing workshop of their late husbands only until they married again (Peña 1997: 45–46; see also Madurell 1972: 195–196). However, even in such circumstances, women's names hardly ever appeared in colophons, since the works that were produced during this time were signed 'the widow of'. The association between woman printers and widowhood might suggest that women's involvement in printing was provisional; however, since printing workshops were family businesses usually located within the printer's household, women were very probably working in them during their husbands' lives, even though they are rarely documented as doing so. As a consequence, the few cases in which there is evidence to relate woman printers and music books may be just the visible trace of years of invisible work (Mazuela-Anguita 2012a: 435–439; Noone 2020). In Barcelona, one example is Bartomeva Riera, mother of the Barcelona bookseller Miquel Riera, who in 1524 owned five 'small chant manuals from Saragossa' (*art*

98 *Music as a commodity*

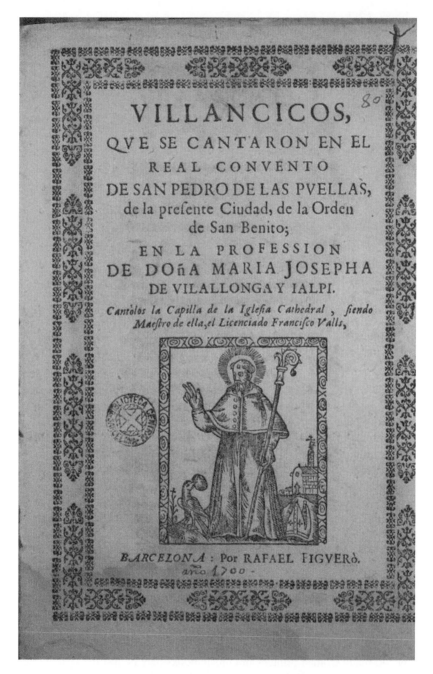

Figure 2.15. Title page of the printed lyrics of the villancicos sung at the convent of Sant Pere de les Puel·les for the profession of Maria Josefa de Vilallonga i Ialpi. BC, F.Bon. 9484. Public Domain

de cant de Saragosa, petit), probably copies of Gonzalo Martínez de Bizcargui's *Arte de canto llano et contrapunto et canto de organo* (Saragossa, 1508), and six 'small chant manuals in French' (*art de cant, petit, en frances*) (Madurell 1968: 208; Ros-Fábregas 2001–2002: 36).

Table 2.12 presents a list of woman printers and booksellers in sixteenth-century Barcelona.[100] Some of these printers were involved in the publication of books which circulated through Barcelona convents, such as collections of devotional verse in songbooks which were frequently aimed at women as a kind of 'pious musical entertainment'. One example is the music published by María Velasco, widow of Hubert Gotart, who had printed Nicasio Zurita's *Motectorum* (1584) and Joan Brudieu's *De los madrigales del muy reverendo Juan Brudieu, maestro de capilla de la Santa Iglesia de la Seo de Urgel, a cuatro voces* (1585).[101] As Hubert Gotart's widow, she printed a songbook entitled *Cancionero de Nuestra Señora: en el qual ay muy buenos romances, canciones y villancicos: aora nueuamente añadido* in 1591 (see Chapter 5). In January of that year, she married Sebastián de Cormellas, who was her employee (Pontón 2015: 17), and who became a member of the confraternity of booksellers in 1595.

Confraternities and guilds

Confraternities and guilds constitute a further musical link between convents and the city, and their relationships demonstrate the porosity of the early modern urban cloister. As in other countries, confraternities and guilds also made use of convents' spaces such as chapels and altars and their devotional practices called for music of various kinds including nuns' singing and playing the convent organ.[102] In medieval and early modern Barcelona, in addition to the religious confraternities, there were many guild confraternities (*gremis*), that is, associations formed by lay artisanal people, usually of middling status, that joined together to carry out devotional and charitable activities. For instance, in Barcelona there were confraternities of wool makers (*paraires*),[103] second-hand clothe sellers (*pellers*),[104] makers of brushes to card the wool (*carders*, established at the parish church of Sant Cugat del Rec and who celebrated a solemn procession with music on the Octave of the Corpus Christi),[105] master builders and millstone makers (*mestres d'obra i molers*),[106] wine-skin makers (*boreriorum*),[107] and even musicians, among many other examples (Baldelló 1928). Each guild had a meeting place, either in a house situated on the streets and squares of the city, or in the church where they had a dedicated chapel or altar and where they celebrated the annual feast day of their patron saint.

Margarita Tintó pointed out that, in the Middle Ages, popular festivities were not numerous, so people waited with enthusiasm for the feast of the patron saint of each guild.[108] These festivities enjoyed the support of the city council and included the presence of music in the streets as well as processions between the guild house and the chapel used by the guild for the celebration of liturgical ceremonies. Most of these chapels belonged to nunneries. For instance, the guild of ropemakers practised their religious ceremonies at a modest chapel in the church of the old convent of Els Àngels outside the city walls (Paulí 1941b: 13).

Table 2.12. Female printers and booksellers in sixteenth-century Barcelona

Bartomeva Riera	Mother of the Barcelonan bookseller Miquel Riera. In 1524 she had five 'small chant manuals from Saragossa' (*art de cant de Saragosa, petit*), probably copies of the *Arte de canto llano et contrapunto et canto de organo* (Saragossa, 1508) by Gonzalo Martínez de Bizcargui, and six 'small chant manuals in French' (*art de cant, petit, en frances*) (Madurell 1968: 208; Ros-Fábregas 2001–2002: 36).
María Velasco, Gotart's widow	Hubert Gotart was a printer from Savoy who was active in Barcelona between 1581 and 1590 (Madurell 1972; Delgado 1996: 292–294; Establés 2018: 483).
Widow of Juan Carlos Amorós	Active between 1551 and 1554. Carlos Amorós got married three times: with Margarita, Eulàlia and, in 1542, with Gracia Nunyes (Millares 1982; Delgado 1996: 31). Amorós had printed the *Missale secundum consuetudinem fratrum beate Marie de Mercede Redemptionis captiuorum* (Barcelona: Per Iohanem Luschner et Karolum Amoros, 1507), including music notation.
Eulàlia, widow of Pere Montpezat	Active between 1571 and 1576. Eulàlia and Pere married in 1531. She was the widow of Pere Puig and printed four books as 'Viuda Montpezat' or 'Viuda Montpezada'. In 1573 she printed *Cobles ara nouament fetes sobre la presa dels sexanta bandolers* (Barcelona: en casa de la viuda Mompesada, 1573) and other similar *pliegos* (Delgado 1996: 472–475; Establés 2018: 260–261).
Elena, widow of Llorenç Deu	Active between 1647 and 1650. She appears as 'Viuda Deu' or 'Elena Deu'. Llorenç Deu had printed Joan Carles Amat's *Guitarra española* (1639) (Delgado 1996: 181–182; Establés 2018: 249).
Maria Dexen, widow of Pedro Juan Dexen	Active between 1647 and 1649 (Delgado 1996: 182–183; Establés 2018: 357).
Elisabet Dulach, widow of Pere Lacavalleria	Active in 1646. She only made one printing, as her son took charge of the workshop (Delgado 1996: 363–364; Establés 2018: 245).
Widow of Jaime Matevad	Active between 1644 and 1650. She appears as 'Viuda Matevad' or 'Viuda Mathevada'. Jaime Matevad was printer of the City and of the University and had a bookshop (Delgado 1996: 443–444).
Catalina Matevad (d.1675)	Active between 1652 and 1675. She was printer of the Consell de Cent. She was Sebastiá Matevad's and Paula Umbert's daughter and Jaime Matevad's sister (Delgado 1996: 443; Pizarro 2003:143; Establés 2018: 370–371).
Paula Matevad, widow of Sebastiá Matevad	Active between 1645 and 1651. He printed Amat's *Guitarra española* (1640). On her husband, see Delgado 1996: 444–445.
Elisabet Tomasa	Active in 1627. According to Delgado (1996: 675), she might have been the widow of Antonio Thomas (see also Establés 2018: 249–250).

Music as a commodity 101

As Luis Robledo (2006: 491) writes of Madrid, these organisations allowed people of medium status to participate in urban events and festivities, contributing to the creation of an urban music network, since music chapels performed for the different confraternities in convent churches throughout the year. Andrea Puentes-Blanco (2018: 472–563) has studied the musical activity and repertoire associated with the Marian confraternities of the Rosary and the Conception in Barcelona, the former established at the male convent of Santa Caterina and the latter at the cathedral. The male convent of Sant Francesc was the seat of the confraternity of Saint Nicholas and, at the ACA, there are several sixteenth-century books belonging to the convent containing inventories, lists of members, or accounts, among other information about the confraternity.[109] Likewise, the Carmelite male convent of Sant Josep was the seat of the confraternity of Our Lady of the Carmen.[110] The 1606 ordinances of this confraternity stipulated the celebration of a solemn *trentenari* in honour of dead past members on the day following the second Sunday of May, at eight o'clock in the morning. Commemorations or 'anniversaries' had to be celebrated on the day after a member's death. On the second Sunday of every month a solemn Office and the Vespers had to be sung specifically in polyphony.[111]

Although studies of convents in other cities mention the participation of these institutions in processions and other public ceremonies organised by confraternities (see Chapter 3), it is significant that they refer neither to confraternities being established within specific convents nor to the close connection between citizens and convents' musical ceremonies through membership in a confraternity. Since Barcelona's nunneries were the seat of numerous confraternities, documents generated by these organisations form part of the convent archives (Table 2.13). Confraternities' books of proceedings often include references to agreements with convents for the celebration of specific feasts with music, and nuns were themselves members of confraternities, as is reflected in their wills (Appendix 4.1). The musical connections between confraternities and convents are evident in the links between the convent of the Jeronymite nuns and the confraternity of Barcelona booksellers. When founded on 31 January 1553, this confraternity needed a church or chapel where the annual feast day of their patron saint, Saint Jerome, could be celebrated. On 17 May, the confraternity signed an agreement with Caterina Rodés, the prioress of the Jeronymite nunnery, according to which her nuns were obliged to celebrate, every year, a solemn Office at the high altar with priest, deacon, sub-deacon, organ, and homily on the feast day of Saint Jerome in the presence of the members of the confraternity. They also had to celebrate the first and second Vespers that day in the same way and decorate the church. Likewise, the following day a solemn 'anniversary' in memory of the deceased members of the confraternity had to be celebrated. The confraternity covered the expenses of these services and also provided candles:

> [the nuns of the Jeronymite convent] promise the honourable booksellers that they will celebrate at the main altar a solemn Mass with priest, deacon, subdeacon, organ, and sermon on the feast day of the glorious Saint Jerome; they will

Table 2.13. Examples of confraternities instituted in Barcelona nunneries

Convent	Related confraternities
Convent of Els Àngels	Guild confraternity of ropemakers (*corders*). Patron saint: Saint Francis
	Guild confraternity of grain-weighers (*mesurers*). Patron saint: the Most Holy Trinity
	Confraternity of the Most Sweet Name of Jesus (*Dulcissim Nom de Iesus*)[a]
Convent of Les Jerònimes	Guild confraternity of booksellers (*llibreters*). Patron saint: Saint Jerome (1553)
	Confraternity of the Holy Land (*Terra Santa*) (1618)
Convent of Santa Maria de Jerusalem	Confraternity of the Saint Guardian Angel (*Sant Àngel Custodi*) (1532)[b]
Convent of Santa Maria de Montsió	Confraternity of the Rosary (*Roser*) (1488)
	Guild confraternity of municipal rod-bearers (*verguers*) and gatekeepers (*porters*). Patron Saint: Saint Cristopher (1524)
	Confraternity of Saint Apolonia (1534)
Convent of Sant Pere de les Puel·les	Guild confraternity of cloth dyers (*tintorers*) (sixteenth century). Patron saint: Saint Maurice
	Confraternity of Saint Magí Martyr (1580)
	Guild confraternity of market gardeners (*hortelans*). Patron saints: Saint Abdon and Saint Sennen
	Guild confraternity of tailors (*sastres*). Patron saint: Saint Homobonus
Convent of Sant Antoni i Santa Clara	Confraternity of Our Lady (*Nostra Senyora*)
	Guild confraternity of sailors (*mariners*). Patron saint: Sant Elm
	Guild confraternity of fishermen (*pescadors*). Patron saint: Saint Peter
	Guild confraternity of carpenters (*fusters*). Patron saint: Saint John the Baptist

[a] *Als Illustres reuerendissims egregis, spectables, nobles [...], los administradors de la Confraria del Dulcissim Nom de Iesus, fundada en lo Monestir dels Angels de la ciutat de Barcelona, [...] certifica Confraria del Dolcíssim Nom de Jesús (Barcelona, Catalunya)* [Barcelona?: s.n., 1596?]. Campruví and Anglès 1743: fol. 96v.
[b] Marca 1764: 271.

adorn the church with drapery and greenery to the best of their ability and use the best vestments, baldachin, and ornaments required for the feast; they will do the same for first and second Vespers of the feast day; they promise that they will not celebrate Vespers and Mass until the honourable booksellers, or at least the majority of them, are present in the church of the nunnery.[112]

These ceremonies had an impact on urban daily life and were often attended by the city councillors (Vergés 1987: 42–44; González Sugrañes 1915–1918:

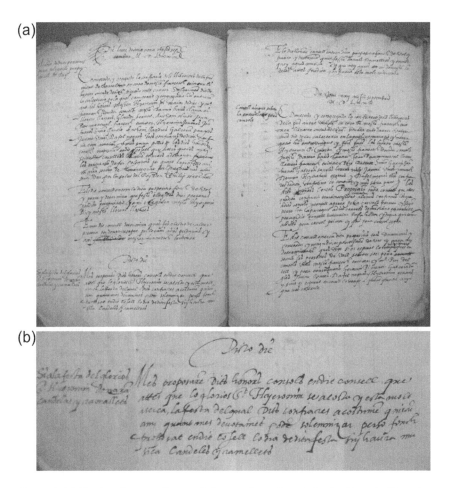

Figure 2.16. Book of proceedings of the confraternity of booksellers in Barcelona (1579–1583). 'Llibre d'actes de la confraria de Sant Jeroni dels llibreters de Barcelona'. AHPB, 409/88. Photograph by the author

109–109). According to a book of proceedings from the booksellers' confraternity, the arrangements for the feast day of Saint Jerome included music, candles, and flowers, as was the custom for many of the confraternities (Figure 2.16).[113] This document also indicates that the ceremony took place, as did the confraternity's regular meetings, at the nunnery. The proceedings also include the lists of books submitted for examination.[114] In the 1560s, the prioress Caterina Rodés was succeeded by Violant de Guardiola, who was probably related to Joan Guardiola (d.1561), a major Barcelonan bookseller and one of the founding members of the confraternity. He is well known in the musicological context for the unusually high proportion of international musical repertory listed in the inventories of his bookshop.[115]

The confraternities founded at Sant Pere nunnery might represent a further case study to analyse the contact between convents and city inhabitants, not only through their musical activities within its walls, but also through donations made by members, and their wish—expressed in their wills—to be buried there. The statutes of the confraternity of Saint Magí Martyr—whose feast day is 19 August—were submitted for the approval of the bishop of Barcelona on 19 April 1580. The confraternity was founded by two major figures (*prohoms*)—Bartolomé Vilanova and Pere Guancer—both hebdomads of the convent church, together with twenty members of the church's community of benefice-holders, and two Barcelona citizens: Serapi de Sorribes, then a young member of the militia (*donzell*), and Bartolomé Soldevila, a wool-carder (*paraire*).[116] Brígida Millàs (1576–1581), who was the abbess at that time, was placed in charge of the administration of the confraternity. On 30 August 1581 the confraternity obtained a number of spiritual graces: full indulgence for its members on their death, and other indulgences for those who visited the Sant Magí chapel on the patronal feast day and attended the ceremonies celebrated in his honour or participated in the suffrages (*sufragios*) held in memory of deceased members for the relief of their souls in Purgatory. In 1595 these graces were extended by Pope Clement VIII. Unsurprisingly, the documentation preserved at the convent contains records of monthly payments for weekly masses (on Wednesdays) in honour of confraternity members. This confraternity left Sant Pere nunnery in 1596 and moved to the church of Sant Sebastià, where it still resides today.

The Barcelona cloth dyers guild, also based at the convent of Sant Pere, endowed an annual celebration of a sung Mass with organ in honour of their patron saint Saint Maurice on 27 October 1578 (Figure 2.17).[117] However, in that year the money allocated to the organ was spent on repairing, rather than playing, the organ.[118] The account books of Sant Pere convent detail that a confraternity of tailors paid in 1523, among other occasions, for an anniversary to commemorate Antoni Pla, one of the members, and his wife, including a said Mass and also a high sung Mass.[119] The books of visitations of Sant Pere convent also make reference to a confraternity of market gardeners which, in 1587, had founded the celebration of a said mass every Sunday at the high altar of Our Lady as well as three anniversaries each year.[120]

Other convents were also associated with the ceremonies and musical activities of confraternities. For example, the confraternity of the Rosary was founded at the convent of Montsió in 1488.[121] The Rosary feast in May was solemnly celebrated at the Dominican convent, including the playing of trumpets and drums through the streets.[122] Later, when Pope Gregory XIV (1590–1591) dedicated the month of October to the Virgin of the Rosary, the confraternity celebrated the 'Rosary month' with singing and processions (Paulí 1952: 60). Àngela Pujades (c.1491–1549), a nun of Montsió, headed the confraternity of the Rosary between 1521 and 1547 and drew up statutes for it (Adiazola 2007). A further example is that of the confraternity of Saint Christopher whose members comprised the municipal rod-bearers (*verguers*) and gatekeepers (*porters*). They signed an agreement with the convent and its prioress, Caterina Amat, in 1524 (Figure 2.18).[123] One of

Figure 2.17. Saint Maurice, patron saint of the cloth dyers guild in Barcelona. Copy of a sixteenth-century image preserved in Barcelona, Gremi de Tintoreres y Bugaders. enciclopedia.cat

the clauses of these statutes concerned the celebration of a solemn Mass on Sant Christopher's feast day, with organist (*sonador del orga*), as well as the celebration of Requiem Masses and commemorations for the deceased members of the confraternity and their relatives. Another confraternity, that of Saint Apolonia (for protection against the toothache), was founded at Montsió on 29 January 1534. The lyrics of *goigs* (devotional songs in the vernacular similar to the Italian *lauda*) in honour of Saint Apolonia and other saints associated with the convent were often printed for distribution among those present at the celebration, and some are still preserved today.[124] These poetic texts, usually in Catalan, were sung by the community in the context of religious celebrations, such as a Mass or a procession. Most were sung to popular tunes that circulated as part of oral tradition.

The convent of Sant Antoni i Santa Clara was home to the confraternity of Our Lady. According to José García Oro's studies of confraternities devoted to the Immaculate Conception, their original aim was essentially devotional, but by the late sixteenth century their activities in social welfare had become increasingly important (García Oro 1988). Music formed an intrinsic part of their devotions; for example, the statutes of the confraternity of the Most Pure Conception in Burgos include detailed information about the feast of Our Lady, Saint Anne, and Saint Francis held at the Franciscan convent, including the celebration of

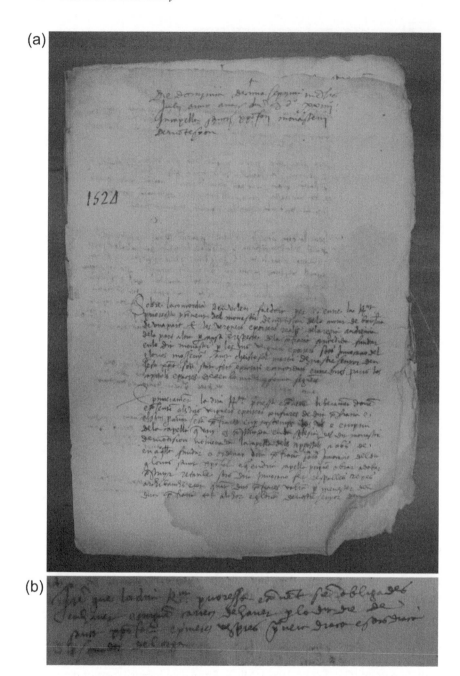

Figure 2.18. Agreement between the convent of Santa Maria de Montsió and the confraternity of *verguers* and *porters* in 1524. Barcelona, AHP, 278/43. Photograph by the author

Masses and processions throughout the city, and the participation of instrumentalists (García Oro 1988: 464–465). Several receipts of the confraternity of Our Lady, dated between 1502 and 1526, are preserved in the archive of Sant Antoni nunnery.[125] On the first Sunday of every month it was customary to celebrate a sung Mass, with a procession and a responsory for the deceased members of the confraternity. Requiem Masses were also celebrated in honour of its members. Every Sunday, after the main Mass celebrated in the convent church, the Marian antiphon *Conceptio Tua Dei genitrix* was to be sung.

A confraternity of sailors, also based at Sant Antoni convent, celebrated the eve of the feast of their patron saint Sant Elm with Vespers sung by the nuns. The nuns then sang a solemn Mass on the feast day itself, and an anniversary on the following day, and the confraternity paid 1 *sou* to each nun who participated. According to a book of 1598 belonging to the convent, this tradition dated back at least to 1461.[126] These events acquired a major profile thanks to the attendance of city councillors and wealthy merchants. The guild confraternity of carpenters, dedicated to Saint John the Baptist, was also established at this nunnery, and its celebrations also included the singing of Masses by the nuns.[127] Similarly, the confraternity of fishermen organised ceremonies at the same nunnery:

> The confraternity of fishermen has its chapel and altar dedicated to Saint Peter at the church of this convent, where they organise celebrations on the following days: the feast of Saint Peter, Our Lady of August, the feast of Saint Andrew, and the Virgin of Hope. The Masses are sung by the nuns on the occasion of the feast days of Saint Peter and Saint Andrew, when Vespers are also sung. Organ, minstrels, and a sermon are customarily included. For each Mass, the confraternity pays 15 *sous* and a further *sou* for the nun responsible for pumping the organ bellows.[128]

Thus, female convents active in sixteenth-century Barcelona were places for encounter, integration, and interaction between different sectors of Barcelona society, and played an essential role in the musical networks operating in the city. Music contributed to the porosity of the cloister, since the musical life of these convents was necessarily related to the city through musicians (singers, teachers, organists), the circulation of music books, and the particular kind of musical patronage involved in liturgical foundations both by collectives such as confraternities and guilds and by a broad cross-section of individual citizens. Previous research on rural music networks around the nearby area of Perpignan, in the historical county of Roussillon, allows comparison between rural and urban networks for the distribution of musical artefacts and the circulation of musicians (Mazuela-Anguita 2016c). As the following chapters will show, the urban musical networks in which nunneries were embedded were related to the notion of music as a symbol of political power and social status (Chapter 3) and, above all, as a means of reaching heaven (Chapter 4), and these notions functioned similarly in a rural context.

Notes

1. AMSP, Manuals de notaris, no. 61 (27 October 1576 to 6 November 1580).
2. AMSP, Llibres d'abadesses, no. 188 (1 May 1525 to 30 April 1527), fol. 41r (1525–1526); Llibres d'abadesses, no. 191 (1527–1529); Llibres d'abadesses, no. 193 (1 May 1529 to 30 April 1531), fol. 34r; Llibres d'abadesses, no. 195 (1531–1533), fol. 52r.
3. I have analysed details of annual payments between 1503 and 1561 recorded in AMSP, Llibres d'abadesses, no. 171 (1501–1503), 172 (1503–1504), fols. 21v, 23v; 176 (1511–1513), fol. 27v, 28r; 177 (1513–1516), fol. 21r; 179 (1515–1516), 182 (1519–1520), fol. 29r, 29v; 188 (1525–1527), 191 (1527–1529), 182 (1528–1530), 193 (1529–1531), 195 (1531–1533), 197 (1533–1535), 199 (1537–1539), 205 (1549–1551), 209 (1551–1553), 212 (1555–1557), 214 (1557–1559), and 215 (1559–1561).
4. AMSP, Llibres d'abadesses, no. 194 (1530-1531), 'Dades de responsions y selaris', fol. 57r. Other example is found in Llibre d'abadesses no. 198 (1537), s. fol., 'dates de responsions y salaris ordinaris'.
5. AMSP, Llibres d'abadesses, no. 201 (1540–1542), s. fol.; no. 201 (1540–1542), s. fol.
6. AMSP, Llibres de visites, no. 1 (1572), fol. [1]v.
7. AMSP, Llibres de visites, no. 1, fols. 9v–10r.
8. ADB, Registro de Comunes, vol. 59, fol. 119.
9. AMSP, Llibres de visites, no. 1, fol. 9r–v.
10. AMSP, Llibres de visites, no. 2, fol. 50r–v (23 August 1587). Receipts of payments to the *escolà* for ringing the bells are included in AMSP, Llibres de sagristia, no. 2 (1532–1535).
11. A later book of visitations is quite detailed in its descriptions of the *escolà*'s functions. See AMSP, Llibres de visites, no. 4 (1670-1672), fols. 7v–8r.
12. AMSP, Llibres de visites, no. 2, fol. 50r-v (23 August 1587): '[…] y tambe lo manxar al orga per los quals treballs del orga los obrers li donen quoranta sous'.
13. AMSP, Manuals de notaris, no. 61 (27 October 1576 to 6 November 1580), fol. 47r.
14. AMSP, Manuals de notaris, no. 63 (10 November 1586 to 1 June 1591), fol. 67r.
15. AMSP, Manuals de notaris, no. 64 (1591–1597), fol. 121r: 'Item tres llibres per a dir los responsos y las matinas a las senyoras monyas'.
16. Gómez Muntané 2001: 311–312. This payment letter is mentioned in Baldelló 1946: 208. However, this was signed by Jaime Mathoses, rector of the parish church of Claramunt on 15 March 1455. It is not mentioned that Mathoses was the procurator of Jonqueres convent. See also Ausseil 1970: 29; and Gregori, 1987: 257.
17. Baldelló 1946: 196, 218; Madurell 1949: 205. The document is in AHPB, Juan Lunes, leg. 1 (1519-1521).
18. 'Comptes donats per los Procuradors del Real Monastir de Junqueres, desde 1 de Juny de 1740' (to 1764) ACA,ORM,Monacales-Hacienda,Volúmenes,362, s. fol. Account book (from 1780), ACA,ORM,Monacales-Hacienda,Volúmenes,365, s. fol. See also Costa 1973a: 100.
19. Madurell 1949: 205. His source is AHPB, Pedro Saragossa, leg. 8 (1519–1520).
20. AMSP, Llibres d'abadesses, no. 197 (1533–1535), fol. 37v.
21. AHPB, Pedro Martí Tost, leg. 1 (19 August 1576), cited in Baldelló 1946: 220–221. See also Paulí 1945: 83–84; and Alcalá 1998: 111.
22. On Pere Alberch Vila as a link between the Cathedrals of Barcelona and Girona, see Gregori 1985–1986.
23. 'Barcelona, convento del Carme. Libro de gasto' (1575–1581). ACA,ORM,Monacales-Hacienda,Volúmenes,1971 [January 1579 and October 1579]. The same account book also refers to the purchase of a clavichord (*monacort*) for the convent which cost 36 *sous* in July 1576.
24. Madurell 1949: 209. His source is AHPB, Francisco Pujó, leg. 3, protocolo 13 (1596).

Music as a commodity 109

25 Vergés 1987: 29–30. His source is the *Calendario de actas* of the convent archive, fol. 68v.
26 Madurell 1951: 215. Proof of payment on 26 February 1688, AHPB, Francisco Falgueras, leg. 5, manual 12 (1688), fol. 29v.
27 'Llibre dels càrrecs i oficis', p. 104 (ch. 39, 'Del orgue').
28 'Llibre de les coses dignes de memoria…'.
29 AMSP, Manuals de notaris, no. 63, fol. 66r. See also Alcalá 1998: 116.
30 AMSP, Manuals de notaris, no. 63, fol. 67v.
31 AMSP, Llibres d'abadesses, no. 175 (1507–1508), fol. 3v.
32 Domingo Blanch is mentioned in AMSP, Llibres d'abadesses, no. 171 (1501–1503), fol. 11v; no. 174 (1504–1505), fol. 11v; no. 175 (1507–1508), fol. 11v; and no. 183, fol. [8]r. Miquel Artís is mentioned in AMSP, Llibres d'abadesses, no. 171 (1501–1503), fol. 25r; no. 174 (1504–1505), fol. 25v; no. 175 (1507–1508), fols. 7v, 29r, and 31r; no. 187 (1523–1524), fol. 3v; no. 189 (1525–1526), fol. [3]v; no. 192 (1529–1530), s. fol.; and no. 194 (1530–1531).
33 'Libro de visitas hechas por diferentes visitadores' (1536–1726), ACA,ORM,Monacales-Universidad,Volúmenes,169, fol. 4v (records of the visitation to the convent of Santa Maria de Jonqueres in 1538: '[…] item dixo que mandava e mando a la dicha priora que de las escolanas que ay en la casa de menos tiempo haga muestra de tañer horganos a dos dellas las que le paresciere tenga mas abilidad para que estas y las que ellas […] de alli adelante puedan tañer a las oras los organos y se escuse el salario que se da al organista y otros inconvenientes que se pueden seguir […]'.
34 ACA,ORM,Monacales-Universidad,Volúmenes,169 (records of the visitation to the convent of Santa Maria de Jonqueres in 1538), fol. 25r–v: 'Otrosi mandaron que por evitar costa y entrada de hombre horganista al choro que acabe de aprender a tañer los horganos guiomar de sayol religiosa de la dicha horden y que para ello se busque un maestro a costa del dicho monesterio para que le acabe de mostrar porque ansi enseñada ella muestre despues a otras para que siempre aya religiosa que sepa tañer los horganos'. See also Costa 1974: 278.
35 'Barcelona, convento de Santa Maria de Jonqueres. Libro de cuentas', ACA,ORM,Monacales-Universidad,Volúmenes,381, s. fol. ('Polizas pagades per lo mes de Juny 1662').
36 'Libro de desapropio (testamento)', fol. 165r. See also Costa 2000: 307; and 2005: 62. In her will, Guiomar mentioned the goods that she had received from her cousin, including a breviary, a psalter, and other books, and asked that these were returned to Lluïsa. She also indicates that she wanted to be buried without any solemnity ('vull ser soterrada en lo vas como y sens pompa'); see 'Libro de desapropio (testamento)', fols. 191r–192v. At the archive there is also a 'Capbreu dels violaris y altres rendes de la senyora Guiomar de Sayol, monja del monestir de Jonqueres', ACA,ORM,Monacales-Universidad,Legajos,10,3.
37 ACA,ORM,Monacales-Universidad,Volúmenes,169, fol. 41v (visitation of 1560–1561): 'otrosy por quanto es grand ynconbenyente no aver religiosa en la casa que sepa tocar el organo porque a de subir un hombre al choro a tañella donde estan las religiosas cosa que no paresçe bien que entre un hombre por ninguna causa por tanto mandamos que qualquyer doncella en quyen concurran las calidades para recebyr el abyso de nuestra orden conforme a los establecymyentos della que fuere musyca de organo e tañere lo necesario en el para oficiar la mysa y oras que le pydiere que pagando las ciento y cynquenta libras que esta mandado que se paguen de entrada le de la priora que al presente es y por tiempo fuere el abizo y dende agora madamos que syn otra consulta ny replica la admyta y reciba por religiosa de la casa y sy recuryeren en un mesmo tiempo dos y mas doncellas a pedyr el dicho abizo por la razon susodicha en tal caso la mas abil y mejor musica sea preferida a las otras y aquella se recyba y despues y este en el monasterio la pryora le mande que enseñe, una u dos escolanas porque nunca falte qyen sepa tañer en la casa el

organo'; fol. 43r: 'pero que por la neçecsidad grande que ay de recebyr una doncella que sepa tañer el organo la priora que al presente es y por tyempo fuere segund y como arriba le esta mandado lo recyba e otorgue con [...] en ella las calydades y condiciones en el capitulo [...] destos nuestros mandatos contemplados so pena que si la tal priora otorgare ny consintiere otorgar otra alguna doncella contra el tenor deste nuestro mandato sea de nyngun valor y efeto la tal recepción ecomo sy no hubiesen otorgado la tal doncella'. See also Costa 1974: 208; and Mazuela-Anguita 2015b and 2018a.

38 ACA,ORM,Monacales-Universidad,Volúmenes,169, fol. 49r (visitation of 1560–1561): 'mandamos a la priora que no permyta ny de lugar a que suban cantores al choro'.

39 ACA,ORM,Monacales-Universidad,Volúmenes,169, fol. 26r (visitation of 1549): 'yr a ver fiestas publicas de la çibdad o fuera della'.

40 ACA,ORM,Monacales-Universidad,Volúmenes,169, fols. 40v–41r (visitation of 1560–1561): '[...] otrosi mandamos que sy alguna freyla o escolana dandole lyçençia la priora para yr a casa de sus padres o hermanos o tios por los cabsos contenydos en el capitulo antes deste a la yda o a la venyda se fuere a pasear por la maryna o ver fiestas bayles y regozyjos que en la cybdad se hagan la dicha priora hecha su ynformaçion e averiguando ser verdad la de penytençia de medio año segund y como lo manda la regla de nuestra orden'. See also Costa 1974: 266.

41 Mazuela-Anguita 2013: 24. In the case of eighteenth-century England, see Leppert 1993.

42 Hernández 1997: 73, 107. These eleven-item ordinances, preserved on parchment at the archive of the convent of Montsió (ADM, Plec. 7°, doc. 5), are transcribed by Hernández (1997: vol. 2, 58).

43 This 1563 document is preserved at the convent archive (ADM Plec 9°, doc) and is transcribed by Hernández (1997: vol. 2, 66–67).

44 *Regla Primera de la Gloriosa Madre Santa Clara...* (1693), p. 191: 'El Choro há de ser humilde, llano, pobre: pero claro, y alegre, y solo tenga unos bancos al derredor, havrá em èl um facistol de competente altura, donde major pareciere, com solo quatro libros, um Psalterio para cantar, um Breviario grande para decir las Lecciones, um Martyrologio, y Missal Romano'.

45 Castellano et al. 2001: 170–174; Sanjust 2008. On the miniatures of these books, see Bohigas 1958–1961; and Planas 2004 and 2013.

46 Anzizu 1897: 139. Anzizu includes and inventory of the convent belongings made when the founder Queen, Elisenda de Moncada (1292–1364), died, which includes some books (no music books) and an organ (Anzizu 1897: 82–83).

47 For an inventory of the convent belongings—including books and organs—at the time of the queen's death, see Anzizu 1897. Castellano (1996: 735) mentions a *Llibre de Privilegis* of 1325 with covers containing musical notation.

48 AMSP, Llibres d'abadesses, no. 172 (1503–1504), fol. 28v ('per que hauia feto lligar los libres del cor').

49 AMSP, Manuals de notaris, no. 54 (1548–1554).

50 AMSP, Llibres de visites, no. 2 (1585–1586), fol. 42r-v; no. 4 (1670–1672), fol. 69v.

51 AMSP, Llibres de visites, no. 2 (1585–1586), fols. 4r, 11r–v. The three books to say Matins and responses are also registered in the inventory of the *escolà* Francesc Prats on 8 November 1596; see AMSP, Manuals de notaris, no. 64 (1591–1597), fol. 121r.

52 AMSP, Llibres de visites, no. 2 (1585–1586), fol. 11v.

53 AMSP, Manuals de notaris, no. 63 (1586–1591), fol. 68r–v.

54 AMSP, Manuals de notaris, no. 64 (1591–1597), fol. 51r.

55 AMSP, Col·lecció de cantorals, no. 11, fol. 21r: 'Al honor e gloria de la sancta trinitat para e fill e sant spirit e de la purissima uerge madona sancta maria e del glorios princep dels apostols sent p[ere] e del beneuenturat confessor monsenyor sent banet la honorable madona Elienor de corbera monge e prioressa del monestir de sent p[ere]

de les puelles de la Ciutat de barch[elo]na feu fet e acabat lo present libre a xi del mes de juny del any m.cccc.xxx. ques celebraue la feta de la sancta trinitat lo dona a seruey de la sglesya del dit monestir'.

56 Notes on AMSP, Col·lecció de cantorals, no. 4, fol. 2v: 'Las llamentacions son del cor a ont es lo fi lo primer respons de las fineras'; fol. 3v: 'Lo segons es de la scolana que li toca la llamentacio'; fol. 5r: 'Lo terceres de las priora y dela mayor de son cor'; fol. 7v: 'son del cor a ont es lo fi an de resaruar dos de las mayors per los tractats'; fol. 9v: 'Lo diu la señora abbadesa a la mayor del seu cor'; fol. 14r: 'las cabiscolas'; fol. 20r: 'las llamentacions son a ont no es lo fi'; fol. 24r: 'los tractats son del cor a ont es lo fi'; fol. 35r: 'las llamentacions son del cor a ont es lo fi'; fol. 38v: 'las tractas son del cor a ont no es lo fi'; 'Los responsos son del cor a ont es lo fi'.

57 Notes on AMSP, Col·lecció de cantorals, no. 1 (1598), last folio (after the index): 'A la hor de nostre señor rey Jesu Christ sia e de madona Sancta Maria e del Benauenturat Sant Pere e del glorios Sant Benet patro del present nostre monestir de Sant Pere de les Puelles de Barcelona se comensa de Officiar lo offici nou Roma lo primer Diumenge del Aduent del Any 1597 gouernant la Santa Igleisa Catholica papa Clement octau y los Regnes de Spaña lo Rey don Phelip segon y lo present Monestir la Ilustrisimo y molt Rnt. señora Magdalena de Oluia Abadessa de dit monestir'.

58 Notes on chant book no. 1 (1598), last folio (after the index): 'Fonch fet lo present libre de Missas axi del propi dels sants com del comun, per orde y voluntad de les illustrisimas señores Aldonça de Oluia priora y Isabel de Oliuer Secristana de dit monestir sonch escrit y apuntat per mi hieronim clari pre[vere] benef[iciat] en sancta Mari[a] de la mar y occupe dit libre xxxiiii quaderns y vi fulas de escriptura y se a pagat per quadern j ll[iures] 16 s[ous] que summen Lxii ll[iures] xi s[ous]. Mes an entrat en dit libre xi dozenas y viii pergaminins a rao de xxxx sous dozena valen xxiii ll[iures] vi s[ous] viii diners. m. per la enquadernacio de dit libre. v ll[iiures] m. los bolons y gafets ii ll[iures] m. vn vadel per cobrir dit li. i ll[iures] xviii s[ous] m. per les posts i ll[iures] que suma x ll[iures] les quales tres partides poçades en vna suma val dit libre. Lxxxxvi ll[iures] viii. diners. Fonch acabat lany 1598'.

59 Notes on chant book no. 2 (1599), first folio: 'Lo present libre de añes que comense lo primer diumenge del Aduent y dure fins al Dimecres Sant foch fet è lany 1599 esset abadessa la illustre doña Magdalena de Oluia y Priora la señora Aldonsa de Oluia. Coste entre pergamins y enquadernar scriure y notar setanta tres lliures y doze sous dich lxxiii ll[iures] xii s[ous] en lo mes de Abril se acaba en lany de la nativitad de nostre señor MDLXXXXIX'.

60 'Venda d'un censal de pensió de 5 ll[iures] 17 s[ous] i preu de 117 ll[iures], feta per Esperança, vídua de Bartomeu Armengol, i d'altres, de Cervera, a Jeroni Clarí, detentor del benefici de Nostra Senyora de les Neus i Sant Sever de Santa Maria del Mar. Notari: Antic Servat, de Barcelona (Barcelona, 26 de maig de 1571)'. In 'Documentació diversa', BC, Fons històric de l'Hospital de la Santa Creu, AH 1088/2.

61 '[Discursos dels deixebles de Pere Joan Nunyes]', Barcelona, Universitat de Barcelona, Biblioteca de Reserva, 07 Ms 105. The three texts are as follows: 'Oratio de laudibus L. Aemilii Paulli conscripta et habita publice a Hieronymo Clarino apud Petrum Johannem Nunnesium' (fols. 135–144v), 'Oratio [En alfabet grec: perì ton enkomíon tes filosofias] a Hyeronymo Clari elaborata publiceque habita pridie kalendas julii anno MDLXXXXIII' (fols. 248r–254v); and '[En alfabet grec: Klarinou peri tou Alexandrou makedónos lógos eta didaskalou Nounnesiou]' (fols. 207r–210v). For a study of Clarí's Greek discourse and other by Jeroni García included in the same manuscript, see Flores 1980.

62 Mas 1916: 451: 'Apoca firmada per Jeroni Clarí, P[re]b[e]re, beneficiat de Santa María del Mar, per escriure Psaltiris per los senyors domers y, a més, les capitals (1574)'; 'Més per dit Clarí qui escrigué dos quaderns d'Hymnes (1574)'; 'Més àpoca feta per Clarí, de 14 lliures, 8 sous, per vuyt quaderns d'Hymnes per Saltiri major (1574). (Arx. Cat., Albarans d'Obra, 1573–1575, fs. 35 a 48)'.

63 Examples are the concerts of the female choir Auditexaudi, founded in 2012.
64 Mas 1914 refers to some book illustrators mentioned in documentation from Barcelona cathedral, although they are not documented as related to the illustration of music books for the cathedral. For the second half of the sixteenth century, the names listed are Joan Bru, Llorens Regner, Andreu Spinosa, Tomàs Bonamich, Baltasar Barbarà, and Simón Fallcó.
65 Cano Roldán 1981: 312; cited in Vera 2020: 104.
66 In the same year, the same scribe created an antiphonary (*Antifonae V&r a 1 die mensis Maii, Iunii & Iulii*) preserved in Girona Cathedral with call number GiC_LLC-34.
67 See, for instance, 'Llibre manuscrit de cant' (55-folio MS), AMSBM, BMSCB 266.
68 AMSBM, BMSCB 198, 155, and 171, respectively.
69 *Directorium chori: ad usum omnium ecclesiarum cathedalium et collegiatarum, a Ioanne Gvdetto olim editum et nuper ad novam romani breviarii correctionem ex precepto Clementis VIII, impressam restitutum et plurimis in locis auctum et emendatum* (Rome: Apud Andream Pheum, 1615), AMSBM, BMSCB 138; *Antiphonale benedictino-romanum sive cantus diurni monastici Pauli V.P.M. authoritate recogniti pro omnibus sub Regula S.P. Benedicti militantibus. Tali ordine dispositum ut etiam inserviat omnibus breviarium romanum recitantibus. Cui addita sunt omnia quae communiter cantantur in Matutinis cum Officio, Missa et Sepultura defunctorum* (Paris: Ex Officina Nivelliana. Sumptibus Sebastiani Cramoisy, via Iacobeae sub Ciconiis, 1616), AMSBM, BMSCB 140; *Processionarium: Iuxta ritum Monasticum Pauli V iussu aeditum. Capituli Generalis anno 1621* (Valladolid: Ex officina Ioannis Baptistae Vatessi, 1623), AMSBM, BMSCB 11.
70 On the Italian books at the library of Santa Caterina convent and on the configuration of the collection from the medieval period and the vias through which the books were acquired, see Casas Nadal 2002. The convent library was praised by Jeroni Pujades; see Pujades 1975–1976.
71 'Llibre de records', AMSBM, box 8, no. 672 ('un llibre vell antiphones dexat a dona marianna meca en 77 fol. 9').
72 'Memorial de desapropis i càrrecs', AMSBM, box 15, no. 640/20 (1422), fol. 7v.
73 AMSBM, box 22, no. 23 (1534), no. 10 (1544), no. 25 (1546), no. 26B (1561), no. 27 (1565), no. 28 (1567), no. 29 (1575), no. 30 (1579), no. 31 (1581), and no. 32 (1585).
74 Donovan 1958: 201; Bohigas 1960-1967; Janini 1980: vol. 2, 436; Gudayol *et al.* 2017: 158-159.
75 A similar book related to an unidentified convent in Mallorca is preserved at the BC with call number M 903. It is a sixteenth-century 180-folio manuscript on parchment which contains antiphons and responsories for processions, and also some pieces for other uses (Donovan 1958: 201; Huglo 1999: 296–298; Gudayol *et al.* 2017: 227–228).
76 The first sheet is blank as a cover and on the following sheet the following annotation appears: 'Esta Concedit per la Obediencia, per lo Us à Sor Mª Dominga Pinos Ig^{na} Capuxina de Bar^{na}'.
77 'Taula de la l. y Present Llibreta Comensada als Primers de setembre de 1795 y acabada als 15 de setembre de 1796'.
78 'Libro de desapropio (testamento)', fol. 75v: 'Item leix a na Constaça lulla aquell libre en que ha apres'.
79 A note on the copy of the plainchant handbook *Modo de rezar las horas canonicas* (Valladolid, 1614) by Dámaso Artufel preserved at the BC (R(2)-8-484) indicates that this belonged to Sor Maria Benita Bassecourt i Briás, a nun of the convent of Els Àngels in the eighteenth century ('Es per us de Sor Maria Benita Bassecourt').
80 The lectern of Santa Maria de Jonqueres convent was built between 1511 and 1513, and would be replaced by a new one in 1721 (Costa 1973a: 100).
81 'Libro de visites antigues, 1495–1515?', ACA,ORM,Monacales-Universidad, Volúmenes,167, fol. 23. See also Serra Álvarez 1966: 250–251. For later descriptions of

the choir, see the records of the visitations of 1560–1561 (fol. 36r), 1597 (fol. 72v), 1605 (fol. 99v), and 1628 (fol. 137v) in ACA,ORM,Monacales-Universidad,Volúmenes,169.
82 'Libro de visites antigues, 1495–1515?', ACA,ORM,Monacales-Universidad,Volúmenes,167, fol. 23. See also Serra Álvarez 1966: 251.
83 'Libro de visites antigues, 1495–1515?', ACA,ORM,Monacales-Universidad,Volúmenes,167, s. fol. (visitation of 1499): 'non lo cunplieron, mandaron los dichos señores vesitadores que las alçen, segund e la manera que primeramente les fue mandado'; s. fol. (visitation of 1501): 'Paresçio por el libro de la visitaçion pasada que fue mandado a la dicha priora e sopriora del dicho monesterio por los dichos visitadores pasados que alçasen las rexas de la delantera del choro e las de los organos dos palmos en alto mas de lo que estauan lo qual no fue conplido'; s. fol. (visitation of 1504): 'Otrosi parecio por el libro de la visitacion pasada que fue mandado a la dicha priora e sopriora del dicho monesterio e por todos los visitadores pasados que alzasen las rexas de la delantera del coro e la de los organos dos palmos en alto mas de lo que son e hallaron que en las rexas del coro se hauia complido ell dicho mandamiento y que solamiente quedaua la rexas de los organos mandaron a la dicha priora e sobpriora en virtut e obediencia que de aqui al dia de sant Johan en junio deste presente anyo fagan la dicha rexa'.
84 For a compilation of more than 250 churches with acoustic jars from the ninth century onwards throughout Europe, see Kottmann 2015. I am grateful to Jirki Thibaut for this reference.
85 'Protocolo segundo del notario Bartolomé Costa' (1455–1458), ACA,ORM,Monacales-Universidad,Volúmenes,176, fol. 27v. Madurell 1968: 206: 'Item un *Apistoler* ab solfa de cant pla'.
86 'Libro de visitas antiguas', fol. 26 (visitation of 1495). See also Serra Álvarez 1966: 63, 127, 260.
87 'Libro de visitas antiguas', s. fol. (visitation of 1509). Serra Álvarez 1966: 63.
88 'Libro de visitas antiguas', s. fol. (visitation of 1515).
89 Madurell 1955: 621–623, doc. 356. His source is AHPB, Joan Lunes, 1519–1521, leg. 1, caja III. See also Altés 1990: 61.
90 'Libro de visitas hechas por diferentes visitadores', fol. 27v (visitation of 1556).
91 'Libro de visitas hechas por diferentes visitadores', fol. 50v (visitation of 1560–1561).
92 'Libro de visitas hechas por diferentes visitadores', fol. 54r (visitation of 1566): 'Ytem mandaron que antes de començar el ofiçio de misa cantada y de bisperas solemnes las cantoras que stubieren diputadas por semanas tengan siempre registrado lo que se a de cantar y dezir en el dicho coro y en ninguna manera se diga ni reze cosa alguna de cabeça aunque se sepa y lo mesmo haga la semanera que hiziera el ofiçio y para questo se haga con horden como conbiene al ofiçio divino la capiscola tenga cargo de [...] edomedaria y cantoras el sabado de cada semana que scriban la semana que se siguiese'.
93 'Libro de visitas hechas por diferentes visitadores', fol. 61v (visitation of 1576).
94 For the will and inventory of Joana Folch de Cardona, Duchess of Cardona and of Segorbe, see Madurell 1968: 217. This inventory (2 October 1608) includes three polyphony books containing music by Morales and Josquin ('Item tres libres de cant d'orga de Morales y de Jusquin'). The document is preserved in AHPB, Gaspar Montserrat Xemallau, leg. 3. For more inventories of Barcelonan women including music books, see Madurell 1956, which contains the inventory of Angelina, widow of Guillem de Santcliment, a Barcelonan knight, on 27 July 1472 ('Item, quatre cuerns en que ha dues passies notades de cant, alguns Evangelis e altres coses a punt de cant'), and that of Stephani Naves, on 18 March 1562 (on the latter, see also Kamen 1993: 378).
95 On Pau Llinàs, see Badal 2017.
96 Bombi 2007; Hathaway 2005: 141–155. On the sacred villancico in early eighteenth century, see Torrente 1997.

97 *Romances y chançonetas que se cantaron en la profession de [...] Doña Francisca de Cordova, y Ribera hija de los [...]Marqueses de Priego [...]* (Montilla: [s.n.], 1634). See Ruiz 2020.
98 The dedicatee of this piece has been identified as Teresa Espanyol Ardenuy (born in 1677), who was a nun at Santa Teresa convent; see Gras 2021. The lyrics of the villancicos were published in 1697 (see Appendix 3).
99 For a study of the music publishing trade in Leipzig from the sixteenth century, see Keym and Schmitz 2016.
100 On the organisation of work in the city of Barcelona, see Bonaissie 1975; and Solà 2009.
101 Pedrell and Anglès 1921; Bernadó 2001; Gregori 2004. The book was dedicated to the duke of Saboya on the occasion of his visit to Barcelona when he was to marry Catalina of Austria in Saragossa on 11 March 1585. Some verses of the printer praising the author are included in fol. 4r.
102 On music and confraternities in Italy, see O'Regan 2011 and 2013. See also Kisby 2001: 178. About music and confraternities in seventeenth-century Madrid, see Robledo 2006. About confraternities in Castilian Dominican nunneries in the late medieval period, see Pérez Vidal 2015: 248. On music and Iberian confraternities, see Knighton 2020. About the close connection between the Barcelona confraternities and conventual ceremonies in the sixteenth century, see Mazuela-Anguita 2020.
103 'Libre... dels actes e contractes e altres coses fahents per lo offici e confraria dels parayres de la ciutat de Barchinona, 1517, febrer, 12 – 1545, gener, 17', AHPB, 310/1; 'Plec de documentació relativa a la confraria dels paraires de Barcelona', AHPB, 450/1.
104 'Capbreu de la confraria dels pellers' (1566–1604), AHPB, 359/37, fols. 4–17; 'Capbreu de la confraria dels Paellers tret en lo any MDCXXXXII, 1566, maig, 17 – 1557, maig, 24', AHPB, 259/37.
105 'Llibre de negocis de la confraria dels carders de Barcelona, 1549–1559', AHPB, 410/3, fols. 21v–22v: 'aniran en la professo que los dits obrers faran quant se recondira los sant sagrament y aquella seguiran ab dita lluminaria per totes aquelles parts per les quals dits obrers determinaran fer aquell e per los gastos que dits obrers faran en dita professo ansi per los capellans y musica, e totes altres cosas que dits obrers fer volran per veneratio del sant sagrament e de dita professo donaran y paragaran a dits brers lo dit dia o lo sendema ques sera feta dita professo sinqueanta sous moneda barcelonesa, e per solemne ques faça dita professo dits Promens e confrares no volen esser obligats en mes de dits sinquanta sous'.
106 'Llibre d'inventaries de la confraria de mestres d'obra i molers de Barcelona' [1592], AHPB, 535/67.
107 'Liber confrarie boteriorum sub invocacione Sanctorum Georgii, Laurencii et Joannis baptiste presentis civitatis Barcinone, 1563–1575', AHPB, 414/3; 'Liber confrarie boteriorum sub invocaciones Sanctorum Georgii, Laurencii et Joannis Baptista, presentis civitatis Barcinone 1586, març, 13 – 1592, setembre, 13', AHPB, 414/3.
108 Tintó 2003: 899. On Barcelonan guilds, see also González Sugrañes 1915-1918; and Darna 2000–2001.
109 ACA,ORM,Monacales-Hacienda,Volúmenes,2343 (1547–1548) (account book and 1562 inventory of goods belonging to the confraternity); 2344 (1594) (book of confraternity members); 2345 (1650) (book of administration); 2346 (1626) (*Liber contractuum sancti Nicholai episcopi*); 2347 (1621) (book of administration); 2349 (1633) (book of administration); 2350 (1629) (book of administration); 2351 (1447) (book of confraternity members); 2352 (1632–1633) (visit of the *mayoral* Jaume Damians); 2353 (1602–1603) (book of *albaranes*); 2355 (seventeenth century) (book of *débitos*).
110 'Barcelona, convento del Carme. Libro de ordenanzas y deliberaciones de la cofradía y hermandad de Nuestra Señora del Carmen' (1606–1681), ACA,ORM,Monacales-Universidad,Volúmenes,74; 'Barcelona, convento del Carme. Cofradía del Carmen.

Documentación variada' (1682), ACA,ORM,Monacales-Hacienda,Volúmenes,1999; 'Barcelona, convento del Carme. Cofradía del Carmen. Insaculaciones de cargos' (1660), ACA,ORM,Monacales-Hacienda,Volúmenes,1996.
111 'Barcelona, convento del Carme. Libro de ordenanzas y deliberaciones de la cofradía y hermandad de Nuestra Señora del Carmen' (1606–1681), ACA,ORM,Monacales-Universidad,Volúmenes,74, ch. 9 and 32 of the ordinations of 1606.
112 Agreement between the convent of the Jeronymite nuns and the confraternity of Barcelona booksellers on 17th May 1553. 'Capitulacio feta per y entre la Rt. Priora y convent de les hieronimes de una part y la confraria dels honorables libraters de la part altra, en poder den francescus mulnell notari de Barcelona de dits monestir y confraria a xvii de maig del any MDLIII', in 'Liber Confratrie sancti Hieronimi bibliopolarum Barchinone, Barcelona', AHPB, Notaries Francisco Mulnell and Pedro Mambla. Transcribed in Paulí 1941a: 60–61: '[the nuns of the Jeronymite convent] prometent a dits honorables libraters que elles lo dia o festa de dit glorios Sanct Hieronim faran y celebraran en lo dit altar maior solemne offici ab prevere diaca sotdiaca orgue e sermo e empaliaran y enramaran la dita Iglesia com millor y mes solemnament poran servitse dels millors vestiments palit y altres ornaments a la celebratio de dita festa necessaris que elles tindran E lo mateix faran y servaran a las primeres y segones vespres de dita festivitat Les quals vespres e offici prometen que no diran ni celebraran lo dit dia y vigilia fins a tant los dits honorables libraters eo la major part de aquells sien presents en la sglesia de dit Monestir'.
113 'Llibre d'actes de la confraria de Sant Jeroni dels llibreters de Barcelona' (1 October 1579 to 20 December 1583), AHPB, 409/88. References to music arrangements at the convent for the confraternity's patron saint feast are found in fols. 2v, 3r, 8v, and 12r.
114 AHPB, 409/88, fols. 1v, 2r, 4r, and 7v.
115 Madurell 1968: 211–212; Peña 1994: vol. 2, 316; Ros-Fábregas 2001–2002: 23–24, no. 47.
116 AMSP, Llibres de visites, no. 2, fol. 49v; no. 4, fol. 74r. On 23 August 1587 it is stated that the confraternity of Saint Magí had been founded at Sant Pere convent seven years before (AMSP, Llibres de visites, no. 2, fol. 40v).
117 'Fundació de un ofici solemne per la festivitat de Sant Maurici, eo lo primer Diumenge seguent a ella', AMSP, Manuals de notaris, no. 61 (1576–1580), fols. 62v–63v.
118 AMSP, Manuals de notaris, no. 61, fol. 84r–v. Part of this document is cited in Alcalá 1998: 111.
119 AMSP, Llibres d'abadesses, no. 185, fol. [2]v.
120 AMSP, Llibres de de visites, no. 2, fol. 48r (22 August 1587), fol. 48v; Llibres de de visites, no. 4 (1670-72), fol. 75r-v.
121 On this confraternity, see 'Registre de llicencies de la confraria de Santa Maria del Roser' ([1574]–1590), AHPB, 418/59.
122 Paulí 1952: 57; and Hernández 1997: 114. Hernández takes as her source ADM, *Páginas históricas*.
123 Plec de documentació (1524), AHPB, 278/43; Paulí 1952: 63–64; and Hernández 1997: 115.
124 Paulí 1952: 61–65; Hernández 1997: 114. *Goigs de la gloriosa verge, y Martyr Santa Polonia, ques cantan en la sua Capella, fundada en la Iglesia de las Religiosas de Monte-Syon, de la Ciudad de Barcelona* (Barcelona: Joan Piferrer, [c.1740]). Other goigs linked to the convent are *Goigs del Glorios Sant Nicasi Bisbe y Martyr advocat contra la peste: Los quals se cantan en lo Monestir de Religiosas Dominicas de Mo[n]tesion de Barcelona, que està la sua Santa Reliquia* (Barcelona: En casa Antoni Lacavalleria, 1651).
125 AMSBM, box 19, no. 374 (1502).
126 'Llibre dels càrrecs i oficis', ch. 31 ('de les confraries fundades en la iglesia del present monestir o que tenen costum venir hi en cert dia'), p. 88. See also a single sheets paged 147–148.

116 *Music as a commodity*

127 'Llibre dels càrrecs i oficis', ch. 33 ('De la confraria de san joan dels fusters'), p. 90. For a later period, see the book of the confraternity of Sant Peter Apostle at the convent of Sant Antoni (1675), ACA,ORM,Monacales-Hacienda,Volúmenes,2124; and the list of members of this confraternity (1679) ACA,ORM,Monacales-Hacienda,Volúmenes,2130. On the confraternity and guild of carpenters, see also 'Llibre de Concells de la Confraria dels fusters' (1583), AHCB, Gremis, Fusters, 37/2.
128 'Llibre dels càrrecs i oficis', ch. 32 ('de la confraria dels pescadors'), p. 89: 'La confraria dels pescadors tenen son capella y altar de sant pere en la iglesia del present monestir en lo qual fan festa en los dias seguents // lo dia de sant pere // lo dia de nostra señora de agost // lo dia de san Andreu // y lo dia de la verge maria de sperança // los offisis son cantats per les señores monges // en les festes de sant pere y san Andreu y ha primes vespres // soly hauer orgue juglars y sermo // per cada hu de dits officis donen de charitat quinze sous y un sou per la menxadora'.

3 Music as a symbol of political power and social status

In the collective imagination, music was associated with both high status and institutions of power, such as the Crown and the church hierarchy, since it was heavily associated with royal and ecclesiastical projections of power and authority in the early modern period (Peters 2012; Cummings 2012: 9–10). The following excerpt from a panegyric for Queen Isabel of Castile (1451–1504), written by the royal chronicler Andrés Bernáldez (1450–1513), reflects the importance of music for the exhibition of power and political stability:

> Who can tell of the greatness and harmony of her court, […] the singers and harmonic music in the ceremonial of divine worship, the solemnity of Masses and Hours that were continuously sung at her palace; […] the multitude of poets, troubadours, and musicians of all kinds.[1]

Throughout the modern period cities become 'theatres of ceremony' (Fenlon 2018: 210), and urban spaces were places where power was negotiated through rituals and events in which music played an essential, solemnifying role.

Convents played an important part in the political life of a city, as Janet K. Page has showed in the case of eighteenth-century Vienna (Page 2014). Likewise, Laurie Stras observes that Ferrarese convents functioned as a type of politicised civic service and that 'throughout the 1590s there are increasing references to the nuns of Ferrara becoming involved in civic display for the benefit of visitors' (Stras 2018: 53). According to Stras, bishops were less worried about liturgical reform than about keeping a good relationship with the civic authorities, and the musical reputation of convents was directly related to the capacity of a city to arrange major ceremonies and events (Stras 2018: 318). Musical networks were thus associated with politics and power, and female convents contributed to the political life of the city of Barcelona and its ceremonial; this overlap of music, power, and religious life was thus embedded in the expectations and perceptions of the public.

The involvement of convents in the political life of Barcelona is illustrated by their constant appearance in the city's *Dietaris* (Appendix 4.2). The high social status of the nuns of most convents—inhabited by female members of the Catalan nobility such as those of Santa Maria de Jonqueres and Sant Pere

DOI: 10.4324/9781003292371-4

de les Pue·les—played an important role in the connections between convents, music, and political life. Convents functioned as a setting for prominent social exchanges between nuns and laywomen, and the latter used convent spaces to display social status through the commissioning of devotional musical celebrations (see Chapter 4). This chapter assesses the role of convents in the political life of the city, considering their relationship to government institutions, royalty, the church hierarchy, and the nobility, not only through the musical contribution made by convents to civic ceremonies and occasions, but also through the participation of political elites in the liturgical and political life of convents, in which music played a major part.

The musical activities organised inside the cloister acquired a political tone through the attendance of the city councillors, visiting monarchs, and members of the nobility. Likewise, music might be performed around convent buildings in ways which actively sought to project sound towards the outside world, such as the highest windows of the building, allowing nuns to participate in urban ceremonies on the occasion of beatification, canonisations, royal entries, and a variety of processions. More rarely, music was performed directly outside the convent space. In light of these unusual circumstances surrounding the reciprocal relationship between female religious houses and political culture, useful comparisons can be drawn between male monastic institutions and nunneries to assess the influence of gender and enclosure on the role played by convents in urban music networks. This chapter therefore focuses on this inside-outside dichotomy, offering examples to illustrate the different strategies used by Barcelonan nunneries in order to reach their urban surroundings through music.

Politics within the cloister: Music and civic status

Silvia Evangelisti draws on both the evidence presented by Kathryn Burns (1999) regarding the musical life in convents of colonial Cuzco and the picture *The Nuns' Parlour at San Zaccaria* (c.1745–1750; Venice, Fondazione Musei Civici) by Francesco Guardi (1712–1793) to conclude that 'parlours were not the silent and austere spaces that the authorities would have liked them to be'. Indeed, she argues that 'well after Trent, nuns played harps and guitars in the parlour, sang profane songs, or even danced in their habits in front of the visitors, who did the same on the other side of the windows' (Evangelisti 2007: 51). In Lima, the singing of the Tenebrae responsories during Holy Week by the nuns of the convent of La Encarnación was annually attended by the viceroy, and Juan Antonio Suardo reported in the *Diario de Lima* on 'a concert' performed by these nuns for the viceroy and his wife on 21 November 1631:

> their Excellencies having taken their seats near to the door which was half-open, the approximately thirty nuns behind it began to sing and play a variety of instruments and afterwards they brought out many drinking fountains with delicious, exquisitely scented refreshments, which entertained the Count and Countess until eight o'clock in the evening.[2]

In the case of sixteenth-century Barcelona, archival documentation indicates that the convents inhabited by the daughters of the Catalan nobility celebrated festivities with music—for instance, on their patron saint's feast day or on the occasion of professions—which were attended not only by the city's social and political elite, but also by visiting monarchs. For instance, at the convent of Els Àngels, liturgical ceremonies served as an occasion for the encounter between nuns and their families, 'reinforcing family links and exhibiting public support'.[3] Likewise, writing in 1617, Antonio Juan García de Caralps pointed out that the convent of Santa Maria de Jonqueres was a place for encounters between knights of the Order of Santiago and for the celebration of festivities:

> All these nuns are of very noble and famous blood. They enjoyed the privilege of being able to marry once, without leaving the Cross of the Sword, which they wear not only on the cloak, but also on the dress. At this convent, all the knights of the Order of Santiago meet on some occasions to celebrate their festivities, confess, and take communion, wearing their habits and white coats, with much devotion.[4]

The account books of the convent of Santa Maria de Jonqueres reflect the fact that the feast of Saint James (25 July) was celebrated with much solemnity, with the knights of the Order of Santiago and members of the nobility in attendance. As early as in 1436, payments to the priests who sang the Vespers on the vigils are recorded, as well as expenses relating to the hiring of two *tenoristes*—skilful singers who performed the lowest parts of polyphony and sometimes acted also as choir directors—who had taught 'new works' for the Office to the nuns.[5]

In the same way that the feast of Saint James was an important event at the convent of Santa Maria de Jonqueres, the celebration of the feast of Saint Peter (29 June) was a significant ceremonial occasion at the convent of Sant Pere, attended by the city councillors and visiting monarchs. Numerous references to payments to singers on this feast are recorded in the convent's account books.[6] Evidence of the role of music in enhancing the ceremony of this occasion can be seen when Philip III and his wife Margaret of Austria stayed in Barcelona on the feast day of Saint Peter in 1599, and were invited to preside over the liturgical events celebrated at the convent of Sant Pere. The nuns welcomed them at the door of the cloister and accompanied them to the high choir stalls while singing the hymn *Te Deum laudamus*. Then a solemn Mass was celebrated, enhanced by the nuns' singing:

> King Philip III and his most august wife Margaret of Austria were in Barcelona on the festivity of Saint Peter Apostle, the titular of the church and convent [of Sant Pere] and, according to custom, as members of the royalty, they were invited to preside the liturgical ceremonies.
> Displaying their patronage to the convent, the monarchs accepted the invitation, arriving at eleven o'clock in the morning at the outer door of the royal convent. They were received by the community of priests wearing surplices.

At the cloister door, the abbess, who bore the staff and wore a stole, and the nuns were waiting and accompanied the monarchs through the main stairs to the high choir, singing the *Te Deum*. When the retinue arrived in the choir, the abbess offered the holy water to the monarchs, who sat the munificent seats prepared for that occasion.

A solemn Mass took place the altar of Saint Peter, celebrated by the Abbot who was the president of the Benedictine order. This ceremony involved an unprecedent pomp, which was complemented by the nuns' singing.[7]

Likewise, on Saint Peter's day in 1603, it was the dukes of Savoy who attended the ceremonies in Sant Pere (Paulí 1945: 87–89). The city councillors also attended important festivities in convents, such as those on Saint Peter's day at the convent of Sant Pere or the Offices of the feast of the Name of Jesus at the convent of Els Àngels, as referred to in the *Dietaris*, for instance, on 18 January 1568 and 13 January 1572 (see Appendix 4.2). Moreover, they were invited by the prioress of Els Àngels to attend the feast of Saint Joseph's feast day on 19 March 1563,[8] and also to attend the Offices organised by the merchant class (*estament mercantívol*) in the same convent on 24 April 1622 (Appendix 4.2). The representatives of the church (*diputats*) and the military and royal judges (*oïdors*) went to the convent of Montsió to attend the Office and homily on occasion of the festivity of the *Quinze Graons* (referring to the 'fifteen steps' leading up to the temple in ancient Jerusalem) on 17 November 1560 (Appendix 4.2). On the feast day of Saint Clare (12 August), the city councillors attended the Offices at the Sant Antoni i Santa Clara convent, occupying the high seats of the choir next to the abbess (Carreras i Candi [1908–1918?]: 565). The book in which all the festivities of the convent throughout the year are recorded includes a detailed description of the ceremonies for this feast day and its Octave: Matins and Prime were sung and the church was cleaned and adorned; 'the councillors come on this day to listen to the Office in the choir of the nuns'.[9] Likewise, on the feast day of Saint Jerome (30 September), they went to the convent of the Jeronymite nuns.

In addition to the celebration of patronal festivals, another important event in the calendar of a convent of a wider civic significance was the election of abbess or prioress, which reached beyond the confines of the nunnery. Such occasions were political affairs which were relevant to the city as a whole and which were solemnised with the singing of the *Te Deum* (Casas i Homs 1967: 68). At the convent of Santa Maria de Jonqueres, the position of prioress was an appointment for life and there were several forms of election: the vote of all the professed nuns, the delegation of the responsibility of the selection to other people, or else the divine inspiration of one of the nuns who felt favoured and proclaimed herself as prioress (Costa 1980; Ibáñez 1981). One notable example of an appointment being decided by an election occurred in 1557, when a vote was held among several of the nuns and Guillem Caçador, who was a canon in that period, acted as the director of the process (Costa 1980: 161).

City councillors also participated in the obsequies (funeral rites) of abbesses and prioresses, whose deaths would trigger the election process described above.

The funeral rites and burial of Elisabet de Malla, prioress of the Santa Maria de Jonqueres nunnery who was entombed in her convent church on 6 March 1534, are described in detail by the city chroniclers: her body was brought from the choir area—which the city councillors were permitted to access—to the church, where the archbishop presided over the singing of the funeral Office. The councillors gathered with the nuns to initiate the process of election of a new prioress.[10] Likewise, on 16 November 1545, the council attended the burial of the abbess of the convent of Santa Clara, which was sung by the friars of the convent of Sant Pau.[11]

The death of abbess Joana de Palau (1539–1562) at the convent of Sant Pere was reported in the *Dietaris* on 12 February 1562, and on 16 February the abbess's nephews went to the consistory court to invite the councillors to attend her burial at the convent on the following day. Consequently, on 17 February, the *Dietaris* record the attendance of the deputies and account judges (*oïdors de comptes*), who were accompanied by many officials from the Deputation house, the General house, and the *Casa de la Bolla* (where the taxes related to the textile trade were collected), forming a large delegation dressed in mourning robes (*gramallas*) (Appendix 4.2). Likewise, according to the *Dietaris*, six chaplains went to the consistory on 6 February 1576 to invite the deputies on behalf of the convent of Santa Clara to attend the burial of Francesca de Argençola, the abbess of the convent, who had died two days before and was to be buried the following day.

A book of 1594 containing the 'ceremonies for the dead abbess' at the Santa Clara convent refers to the burial of Isabel Vilallonga, appointed abbess there in April 1585 and who died on 20 June 1594. On the day of her burial a homily was preached, with the city councillors attending the Mass from the high altar.[12] After the Mass and the *absolta*—a responsory in honour of the dead—twelve chaplains entered to carry the abbess, and twelve friars also came in to head the procession; the nuns remained silent without service books. The procession proceeded through the cloister slowly, reciting the psalm *In exitu Israel* devoutly, and some chaplains entered the parlour to sing an *absolta*. The practice of singing responsories at nuns' burials was also customary in other countries. For example, Miriam Wendling's analysis of convents' Sisterbooks—collections of texts originated in German-speaking Europe in the fourteenth century, which record episodes, often mystical, from the lives and deaths of members of Dominican convents—has shown them to contain references to communities processing with the bodies of deceased nuns while singing the responsory *Libera me* (Wendling 2020).

A book which posthumously records the lives of Discalced Carmelite nuns includes the story of the burial of Dionísia Meca de Vilana (1592–1636), who professed as Teresa de Jesús.[13] This account not only shows the simplicity of this religious Order's liturgical celebrations and the impact of the Council of Trent on the musical practices of convents, but also illustrates how music could be a source of controversy between ecclesiastical authorities and the families of nuns. In this case, the family insisted that her burial be celebrated at the Discalced Carmelite convent in Barcelona with much solemnity and presence of professional musicians; however, when the nunnery's prioress consulted with the Carmelite prior, he refused on the basis that it would set a precedent for others. Nevertheless, when he arrived in the church to celebrate the Office, he found the church crowded with important people and noticed that his directions had not been followed. He eventually relented and consented to the participation of a choir, but forbade them from playing the organ, arguing that this was not appropriate in a Discalced nun's burial. When he was beginning the Office, he realised that the organ was to be played. Yet, the account records that the organ malfunctioned and had to be abandoned, which the account attributes to God's displeasure at excess in the burials of Discalced nuns and friars, suggesting it was a result of divine providence. Upon completion of the burial process, the organ worked once more.

The profession of vows by nuns offered another important event in the convent's calendar which was marked by musical performance, and which attracted civic interest and involved high-ranking members of society. For example, Miquel Garriga highlights the participation of a chapel choir in the entries and professions of nuns at Santa Maria de Jonqueres, and these were attended by the nuns' families, with some relatives belonging to the nobility. His description possibly refers to the cathedral choir, or a choir from another religious institution in the city, as reflected in the printed villancicos studied in Chapter 2:

> Their entries and professions in the same period were celebrated with great ostentation, with the attendance of relatives, godparents, and the most distinguished noble families. The chapel choir usually participated, and the altars were adorned with a variety of flowers and lights. All the attendants brought candles.[14]

The city chroniclers describe the attendance of the monarchs at the profession of twenty-eight nuns at the convent of Santa Clara in 1368, recounting the 'dignified festivities, celebrated with beautiful solemnity'.[15] Sixteenth-century documents from the archive of the convent of Santa Clara include details of the ceremony of the taking of the habit, which differs from the earlier ritual of nuns' professions as described in the fifteenth-century processional preserved at the BC (Ms. 865, fols. 1r–13r), which might have been created for these nuns. On the day when nuns donned the habit, the Office was celebrated at ten o'clock with music and a Mass of the Holy Spirit was performed; after *Et incarnatus* (a part of the Credo), the sacristan gave the priest the habit to be blessed:[16]

> The habit is always given at the main Office. It is the custom that the procurator of the convent celebrates the profession Mass, which is sung at the high altar. The godparents of the nun who take the habit go up to the door at the end of the stairs. And there they collect the nun and accompany her to the high altar where they listen to the Office. At the Offertory the nun gives a one-pound candle with a golden emblem to the nun sacristan. The godparents and the other people who are present offer what they want, and everything will belong to the nun. A said Mass was endowed many years ago, but a sung Office has long been celebrated […]. The abbess takes the nun by her

hand and leads her inside, where the other nuns are together holding candles and the singers are holding rods. They start to sing the antiphon *Veni sponsa Christi* and the abbess and the nun enter the choir and kneel before the altar of Our Lady in the middle of the choir. The *Salve Regina* is then sung, and they go down singing in procession to the room adjacent to the sepulchre which has the grille to the church. The godparents return to the church and the abbess, prioress, and treasurer dress the nun. The nuns perform *Veni Creator* with the organ according to the Breviary, along with the antiphon *Confessor Domini*; meanwhile, a nun—who has received the charge by the singer or by the hebdomad—says the prayer *Intercessio nos quaesumus, Domine* [...].

[During the profession ceremony] The nun kneels in the middle of the chapel bringing the profession letter and [...], after the singing, she is led to the altar where she signs the letter [...]. The nuns sing the *Veni Creator* and [...] the nun who is professing, on her knees, sings the verse three times: *Suspice me, Domine, secundum eloquium tuum, et vivam, / Et non confundas me ab expectatione mea*. The choir continues to sing the *Gloria Patri* and the Mass ends.[17]

In addition to the profession of vows, convents celebrated extraordinary festivities on the occasion of one-off visits of members of the royalty and the nobility. During their visits to Barcelona, the royal family visited several convents with the twofold purpose of attending the Offices and of supervising the instauration of the Tridentine reforms among the religious orders (Chamorro 2013: 314–315). In a manuscript history of the convent of Santa Maria de Jonqueres dated 1686, the hebdomad Joan Baptista Fontanet, reported on such events in a section entitled *Reyes, Reynas y Principes que Visitaron a esta Real casa* (Fontanet 1686: fols. 18r–v, 40r–41r; see also Mutgé 2001: 39). Table 3.1 outlines the details of royal visits to this nunnery in the sixteenth century—before this period, Costa (1974) describes

Table 3.1. Examples of royal visits to the convent of Santa Maria de Jonqueres in the sixteenth century

Date	Visitor	Nuns' music on the occasion
1529, 21 July	Charles V	
1539	Francisco de Borja, viceroy of Catalonia	
1582, 6 January	Maria of Austria	Nuns sang a polyphonic Mass with villancicos
1585, 14 June	Philip II with his wife and children	Nuns sang Vespers in polyphony
1599, 13 June	Philip III and Margaret of Austria	Nuns sang the *Te Deum laudamus* in polyphony alternating with organ playing, an Office of Compline, a villancico, and the *Sacris Solemnis*

the visits of the kings Jaume I, Pere II, Alfons III, Pere III, Alfons IV, and Ferran I to the convent. For example, on 6 January 1582, Maria of Austria, Philip II's sister, visited the convent of Santa Maria de Jonqueres, where she listened to a polyphonic Mass sung by the nuns themselves with villancicos (Fontanet 1686: fols. 18r, 40r; Costa 1974: 266–267). In 1585 Philip II went to this nunnery with his wife and children and listened to the Vespers sung to polyphony (Fontanet 1686: fols. 18r, 40v; Costa 1974: 267; and 2005: 45–46). On 14 May 1599 Philip III and Margaret of Austria, recently married in Valencia, arrived in Barcelona. On 13 June, they visited the convent of Santa Maria de Jonqueres and the arrival was celebrated with a performance of the *Te Deum laudamus* with alternation of organ playing and polyphonic singing. After a small meal, an Office of Compline was sung in polyphony at the low choir and, with the permission of the queen and king, the Marquis of Denia, the Duke of Nájera, the Marquis of Velada, and all the commanders of the Order of Santiago entered the convent. Compline was followed by exposition of the Blessed Sacrament, during which a villancico and the *Sacris Solemnis* were performed (Fontanet 1686: fols. 18r, 40v; Costa 1974: 267; and 2005: 45–46).

Later, on 12 July 1603, the Princes of Savoy also visited the convent of Santa Maria de Jonqueres and listened to a Mass from the high altar. The nuns played musical instruments and sang some motets and the psalm *Laudate Dominum omnes gentes* in counterpoint (Fontanet 1686: fols. 18r, 41r; see also Costa 1974). Likewise, a visit of the Queen of Hungary, Philip IV's sister, is reported on 24 February 1630 (Fontanet 1686: fol. 41r). A visit of Philip V and Mariana Luisa is also reported on 27 November 1701 as including the singing of the *Te Deum* at the chapter room, at a time when the church was partially derelict (Fontanet 1686: fol. 41r; Costa 1974: 267). Fontanet observed that almost all the viceroys of the principality visited the convent, especially Francisco de Borja (1510–1572), who also was a *trece* of the Order of Santiago (Fontanet 1686: fol. 18v). Juan of Austria, viceroy and general captain of the principality, also visited the convent on Saint James's day in 1653 (Fontanet 1686: fol. 18v).

During her visit to Barcelona in 1582, the empress Maria of Austria visited not only the convent of Santa Maria de Jonqueres but also the convent of Jerusalem after dinner on 16 January. Likewise, during their 1599 stay in Barcelona, Philip III and his wife visited several convents besides those of Santa Maria de Jonqueres and Sant Pere. They went to the convent of Els Àngels (Paulí 1941b: 25–26) and also that of Sant Antoni i Santa Clara on 23 June. A manuscript which gives an account of the latter contains a very detailed description of the event and remarks that the monarchs entered the choir accompanied by the Marquis of Denia and several ladies:

> and then the king sat on the abbess's seat with the queen sat beside him, while the ladies sat in the lower part far away. The abbess sat beside the king leaving a seat in between. The nuns were placed in the middle of the choir singing. The abbess asked the king if he wanted them to say Vespers or Compline, to which the king replied that the nuns should say Vespers, and thus they did.[18]

Music as a symbol of political power and social status 125

This royal visit of 1599, along with the others described above, can be seen as cultivating a hierarchy of status among religious houses, whereby the monarch's choice of which institution to visit accorded some with greater standing and approbation.

Male religious houses also formed part of this competing hierarchy, and archival documents can be shown to demonstrate the ways in which these male institutions, like the Dominican convent of Santa Caterina, accentuated their political and civic power through music. The *Dietaris* reflect the importance of the convent of Santa Caterina in the ceremonial of important Barcelonan festivities such as the Corpus Christi or the feast of Sant Jordi, while the annals of this convent are a three-volume manuscript which contains references to the repair of the organ, abundant information which relates the convent with its urban surroundings through confraternities—such as that of the Rosary—and political leaders, and descriptions of the festivities organised by the convent. According to these annals, during the 1599 visit of Philip III to Barcelona, the king wanted to listen to Vespers at Santa Caterina convent. The convent was prepared for the occasion and the king arrived accompanied by the queen, the archduke of Austria, and his wife Isabel, the king's sister. They were welcomed by the friars in procession, and two singers performed the *Te Deum laudamus* in alternation with the organ. This was because, according to the writer of the annals, 'the king explicitly did not want an outside choir [*capilla*] but our singing'. Moreover, the chronicler emphasises that this visit to the convent of Santa Caterina was the first time that the king had left the palace in Barcelona in order to listen to an Office.[19]

Likewise, the annals of the convent of Santa Caterina remark that during a visit of Philip II to Barcelona in 1584 to accompany his daughter Catalina—who had recently married the duke of Savoy and was to board a ship—the king's chaplain died and he was buried in the convent. The funeral rites included a procession in which the choir of the Chapel Royal participated and performed 'a very solemn absolution' at the convent church. The following day the royal music chapel returned to the convent to perform the Divine Office. The writer of the annals emphasises that these ceremonies were 'of great honour for the convent'.[20] Thus, the presence of the choir of the Chapel Royal at the convent of Santa Caterina was another expression of prestige for the institution in 1584, in addition to the status it gained when it was selected by Philip III as the first religious institution in which to hear the celebration of an Office during his 1599 stay in Barcelona.

Inside out: Convent music for external ceremonies

In addition to their role of accommodating public ceremonies, and thereby exerting political influence by hosting members of the nobility and civic dignitaries, female religious orders also contributed to public events which took place outside their buildings. Sometimes, convent music was projected beyond the limits of the cloister and reached the urban surroundings of the convent, most commonly on the occasion of extraordinary celebrations like beatification and canonisation feasts or royal entries. The festal ceremonies which surrounded the celebration of the cult of saints became increasingly defined by Counter-reformist culture. While on one level a city's celebration of a beatification or canonisation aligned it with the wider Catholic world, such occasions promoting particular saints also reinforced the power of the Church in that area, as well as the monarchy, and of local ecclesiastical and political institutions. It was not only necessary to hold these celebrations, but also to commemorate the ceremonies in the form of a written report or *relación*, commissioned by the organisers of the event as a kind of proto-newspaper, in order to reinforce its influence over time and possibly across a wider area. These *relaciones* can be seen as an exhibition of authority and power underpinned by their post-Tridentine context, in which music played an essential role. These texts, which tend towards idealisation and hyperbole (Ettinghausen *et al.* 1996; Pena 2001: 43; Knighton 2011: 27–31), present an additional challenge to musicologists, as their descriptions of music are brief, dominated by stylistic convention, and imply several possible meanings (Knighton 2017c); they are, nonetheless, acknowledged by Knighton to be worthy of some close reading in spite of their shortcomings (Knighton 2011: 29). While composers or specific musical works are hardly ever mentioned, the *relaciones* sometimes include the lyrics of the musical pieces performed. In the same way that archaeology of the senses attempts to recover the sensorial phenomena of the past (Hamilakis 2013), it is possible through contextualisation of the details of musicological interest provided by the *relaciones* to obtain information about the spaces where music was performed, the vocal and instrumental ensembles who participate, the impact of the music on the attendees, and the contribution of institutions such as convents to the soundscape of the celebration (Knighton and Mazuela-Anguita 2015; Mazuela-Anguita 2017a and 2019).

Music, both vocal and instrumental, as well as religious and secular, along with other sounds of bell ringing and rocket firing, was an essential element of urban ceremonies; since these sounds attracted people to the event, fostered feelings of public inclusion, and increased devotion. The *relaciones* afford us evidence of the use of music to symbolise as much the divine power—through vocal music that emulated the celestial choir—as ecclesiastical and political unity—by means of instrumental, heraldic music. It has been suggested before that sound is the component that serves best to measure the solemnity of an occasion, as the sounding elements intensify a ritual and transform it into a ceremony (Torres Fernández 2006: 128–132).

In 2015, on the occasion of the fifth centenary of the birth of Teresa of Ávila, I carried out a comparative analysis of the musical references included in several chronicles corresponding to the festivals for her beatification in October 1614 in eighty-five towns of the Iberian Peninsula (Mazuela-Anguita 2017a). The case of Saragossa—the capital of the Kingdom of Aragon, seat of both the archbishopric and the Inquisition tribunal, and characterised for having two cathedrals (La Seo and the Basilica of the Pilar) from the seventeenth century—offers a particularly strong illustration of the contribution of convents to the festive soundscape. Luis Díez de Aux (1562–c.1630), a poet who held municipal posts and was closely connected to the chapter and university, describes the events organised each day.

From the very beginning, his account emphasises the absolute integration of music at the different stages of the festivity, which had a well-established format in the Hispanic world (Díez de Aux 1615). The main feast day was 5 October and the most important celebrations, which included masses and offices, processions, masquerades, poetic competitions, parades, and knightly tournaments, began the day before and extended throughout the Octave of the feast.

The news of the beatification of Saint Teresa reached Saragossa on 27 May 1614, and it was celebrated not only at the two convents of Discalced Carmelites, but also at the city's other religious institutions by the ringing bells, setting light to rockets, 'singing hymns', and 'playing organs and several musical instruments'. The account reflects the subtle hierarchies and close networks established between the different ecclesiastical institutions of the city through sound, which contributed to enhance the Carmelite convents—both the female and the male—as the centre of the ceremonial celebrations. For instance, on the main feast day, the choir of the Basilica of the Pilar performed Vespers at the convent of Carmelite nuns, 'displaying its talent'; at the Carmelite friary, Vespers were sung by the choir of La Seo. Díez de Aux's account focused its praise on the second performance, providing significant details not only as to its impressive scale, but also of the urban spaces involved and the performance's impact on the audience:

> Here the psalms composed with the most extraordinary harmony could be heard; they were sung with incredible skill. There was a wide variety of both voices and music. The variations of the organ, the vocal ornaments, the sweetness of the small cornet, the melody of the *dulzainas*, the profundity of the dulcians, and the joyful fugue of the shawms charmed and caused admiration. There was much of this [music] and everything was extremely good. There were so many people—as much from the nobility and elite class as from the middle-class and workers—that the church, the square, and even part of the road were overcrowded and there was no room for even a single person.[21]

The account of Díez de Aux continues, explaining that, after Vespers, there was dancing at the friars' church: some boys got down from a triumphal float and, accompanied by six 'savages' (enslaved native Americans), danced very skilfully to the sound of harps and other instruments at the high altar. At the Carmelite nunnery 'harps, violones, and other instruments were played' by nuns and 'villancicos and divine motets were sung'; the sounds of 'concerted shawms' alternated with the military sounds of fifes and drums, while, at night, clarions alternated with trumpets and drums on the rooftop of the convent. Thereafter, 'tender and celestial Matins' were sung; Díez de Aux picks up on an established trope when he indicates that celestial choirs helped the earthly ones to sing gloriously. Therefore, the friars and nuns not only performed music, but also tried to add solemnity to the festivity with the best possible music, usually that of the choir of the main church of the city, or on occasion bringing famous choirs from other towns. For instance, Vicente Valeriola, a nobleman who had a sister at the Carmelite convent in Loeches, succeeded in bringing half of the Chapel Royal to that small town near Madrid, in order to 'imitate as much as possible the feast at the Court' (San José 1615: fols. 206v–207v). The *relación* of the beatification feast of Saint Teresa in Córdoba reports on the 'mystery' of the musicians who arrived at the Carmelite convent when the news of the beatification was celebrated, without notice, sent by the divine providence (Páez 1615: fols. 1r–v).

In Saragossa, the Carmelite convents, as the organisers of the celebration, were the principal contributors to the ceremonial soundscape; however, the nuns of the Poor Clare convents of Jerusalén and Santa Catalina were also distinguished for their music, which was projected to the city as a demonstration of their rejoicing. According to the account, they spent the night in the upper part of their convents singing 'motets and villancicos with celestial voices in concerted choirs' in a way that could be heard from some distance away. Díez de Aux emphasises the excellence of the voice of a nun at the convent of Santa Catalina, describing it as one of the most outstanding in Spain:

> These angels [nuns of all the convents in Saragossa], and above all others the exemplary nuns of [the convents of] Jerusalén and Santa Catalina, expressed their rejoicing in an incredible way. For most of that night—which seemed as bright as a day because of the illuminations—they stayed on the upper part of their famous convents singing motets and villancicos with celestial voices and concerted choirs as a demonstration of their and our rejoicing. They sang in such a way and there was such a calm inspired by heaven that night, that their melody could be heard from some distance away. Remarkably, one of the most outstanding voices, perhaps the best known in Spain today, sang at [the convent of] Saint Catalina as a soloist a *Veni sponsa Christi* in such a celestial way that it seemed impossible that her voice did not belong to an angel.[22]

The prior of the Carmelite house also wrote an account of the Saragossa festivities in which he recounts that the convents of Santa Catalina and Jerusalén competed against each other, and that more than eighty nuns played and sang that night (San José 1615: fols. 36v–44v). The competitive nature of these musical offerings shows how music offered an effective means to demonstrate status in urban settings. These expressions of competition also occurred outside Barcelona; Knighton argues that the singing of the calends on Christmas Eve in early modern Lima was most likely characterised by an element of competition between different convents (Knighton 2011: 26). Moreover, the *relaciones* recognise that the music of religious communities transcended the boundaries of enclosure as members of religious orders sang from windows, filling their urban surroundings with the sound of their music during important religious festivals. In the case of Saint Teresa's beatification celebrations in Saragossa, it is indicated that there was a variety of indoor and outdoor spaces for making music and that most of them were placed high up—platforms, towers, and the highest points of buildings. This suggests a wide reach for the sound of these musical offerings; for instance, the *relación* of the festivities in Valladolid highlighted the pleasurable sounds of trumpets and shawms playing on the rooftop of the Carmelite nunnery, noting that the sound reached the city with 'the harmony intact', even though the convent was located far from the urban centre (Ríos 1615: fol. 14v). The resulting absence of a visual component to the musical performances offered by nuns was thus one of these performances' defining features. The resulting experience for the listener of hearing sound emanate from these high places can be seen as having reinforced ideas of music forming a link between earth and heaven, as suggested by the persistent use of adjectives such as celestial or angelical to characterise nuns' singing, which caused emotion, tears, tenderness, and devotion (see Chapter 4).

In Barcelona, Josep Dalmau (1554–1633), royal councillor and protector of the Carmelite friary of Sant Josep, was the person in charge of writing a *relación* reporting on the celebration of the beatification of Saint Teresa there and in other Catalan urban centres (Dalmau 1615; Figure 3.1).[23] The book was dedicated to Luis Sans, Bishop of Barcelona, and reflects the role that the friary of Sant Josep occupied at the centre of these celebrations from the outset. However, the friary of the Mare de Déu del Carme, inhabited by Observant (*Calzados*) Carmelite friars, along with the Discalced Carmelite nunnery of Santa Teresa, also drew comment from Dalmau for the contribution they made to the soundscape of the festivities. This example therefore demonstrates the way in which male and female members of this same religious Order were brought together by the beatification of its principal saint, but it seems that there were hierarchies. News of the beatification had reached Barcelona on 31 May, and these three religious houses greeted the announcement with light displays, fireworks, and groups of musicians performing motets and madrigals; the *relación* notes the proximity of the sounds coming from these three buildings, giving the impression of a lively sonic exchange (Dalmau 1615: fol. 3r) (Figure 3.2).

The main festivities were announced on 2 October 1614 outside the church of the male convent of Sant Josep, where 'a big troop of wind-players, trumpets, and drums mounted on horseback' had gathered to herald the arrival of the knights 'each playing the music of their instruments'.[24] According to Dalmau, when the knights had collected the banners, they were to parade throughout the city from inside the church, the wind-bands and corps of trumpets and drums played again, and the royal crier made the announcement (Dalmau 1615: fol. 5r–v). The involvement of high-ranking members of society in enabling this ceremonial soundscape is also evident: the cost of the music was met by Gaspar Iofre, a knight of the Order of Saint John, who also is reported as dancing at the high altar of the friary church.

On the eve of the ceremony of beatification, the crowds gathered to listen to the different *coblas* (groups of instrumentalists) distributed around key parts of the city, all placed high up on towers or above gates:

> The whole crowd were entertained by six *coblas* of wind-players, which were spread around [the city]—some on the church of Sant Josep, others on the Mare de Déu del Carme, others on the church of the Discalced nuns, and others on the tower of the Pine [church of Santa Maria del Pi], on the Portaferrissa, and finally on the gate of the Boqueria—all of whom strove with great enthusiasm to play motets, madrigals, and battle pieces, each group responding to the other, to admirable musical effect.[25]

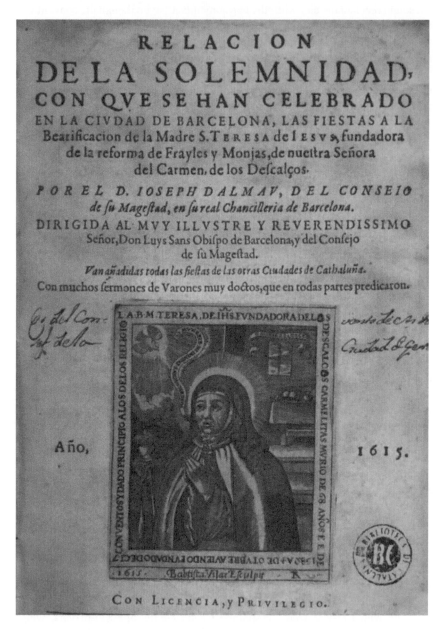

Figure 3.1. Josep Dalmau's *Relación de la solemnidad con que se han celebrado en la ciudad de Barcelona las fiestas a la beatificación de la madre S. Teresa de Jesús [...]* (Barcelona: Sebastià Matevad, 1615), title page. BC, 16-I-87. Public Domain

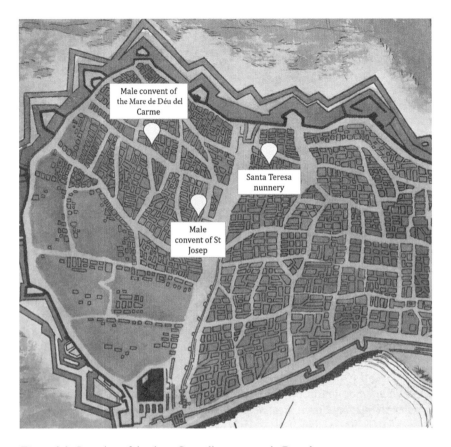

Figure 3.2. Location of the three Carmelite convents in Barcelona

The placing of several groups of musicians on platforms located at strategic points outside the monastic institutions allowed for antiphonal performance, emphasising the importance of these Carmelite religious houses in the context of this ceremonial. Dalmau devotes two complete chapters (12 and 13) to reporting the celebrations at the nunnery of Santa Teresa, underscoring the presence of music at the convent and the surrounding area during all the days the celebration lasted; in particular, minstrels performed music throughout the whole day, and the singing at the Offices included some polychoral music written for up to three choirs performing together (Dalmau 1615: fol. 19r). An artificial mountain designed to recreate a natural setting was built in the nunnery, on which there was an ensemble of minstrels whose playing 'livened up this festivity' (Dalmau 1615: fol. 13v). On the main feast day, however, the degree of solemnity at the nunnery decreased, as the Discalced Carmelite friars of Sant Josep assumed the limelight of the festivities on that Sunday:

> the Discalced Carmelite nuns, as Teresa of Jesus's daughters, celebrated the whole Octave at their church with great music and homily, except for the

first day, as it was the turn of the friars. They [the nuns] spent this first day with only one Mass, celebrated by three of the friars in the morning and sung by the nuns themselves, according to the ferial [ordinary, non-festal] tone. However, on Monday they were the centre of the feast, while the friars only celebrated one Mass in plainchant.[26]

Therefore, on the following Monday, the convent of Santa Teresa became the main focus of the festivity once more and the nuns used music to emphasise its prominent position in the ceremonial hierarchy:

> Once the Vespers were finished on the main feast day at the house of Discalced Carmelite friars (on which we reported above), the celebration stopped at the church of Sant Josep until the next Tuesday, and the celebration of the Compline took place at the church of the nuns of the same Order, starting in this way their festivity. Many people attended and the Office was sung in three choirs with all the solemnity. It was celebrated by the prior of Sant Josep with two assistants [...]. Once the Office of Compline was celebrated, flares were set off outside as they had been on the night of the vigil on the top part of the church and the convent. Many other nunneries and secular houses—particularly those located on the same street as the convent—did the same with a devotional purpose. At the convent street were the minstrels, trumpets, and drums of the municipality, playing different musics in turns. Many knights were at the street, making their best attempts at shooting rockets. So many people attended, and all the night passed as if it was a day. On Monday morning in the hours before the Office, the minstrels were in the church, playing different *mudanzas*, and all the figures which use to participate in the procession of the Corpus Christi came to the church [...] performing their respective dances to the sound of the same music. The Office was attended by the Viceroy, accompanied by his daughters, many ladies and knights, and the nobility of the city, with a high attendance from among the people, exceeding the church space. The Mass was celebrated by the prior of Sant Josep, with deacon, sub-deacon, and two assistants, with ornaments of very rich silver clothes. It was sung by the best voices of Barcelona in three choirs.[27]

This reference to polychoral performance is interesting because of the identification of polychoral practice and celestial music in this period (Robledo 2013). However, it is not indicated if the nuns contributed with their music to the ceremony on that day, and the 'best voices of Barcelona' presumably refers to the choir of the cathedral. The presence of singers from outside was undoubtedly a reflection of the solemnity of the occasion, while the nuns themselves sang 'with their ordinary tone' when the focus of the ceremonial was on another institution. Another sign of the demarcation of Santa Teresa convent as the key space on Monday was the presence of the wind-players of the municipality. Other nunneries of the city besides the convent of Santa Teresa contributed to the ceremonial, as in the case of Saragossa, but, in contrast, we do not have references to singing of nuns from non-Carmelite convents in Barcelona.

It would seem likely that the chapel master of Barcelona Cathedral, Joan Pau Pujol (1570–1626), composed some of the triple-choir works for the ceremonies.[28] Dalmau's *relación* includes the lyrics of eight villancicos sung at the friary of Sant Josep (Dalmau 1615: fols. 38r–41r) and specifies that most of them were written by Lope de Vega. At least in the case of the first one, Pujol might have composed the music, as a six-voice villancico with the same incipit ('Vistiose una vez Teresa') is recorded in his catalogue, although the music of this setting is no longer extant (Lambea 1999: vol. 2, 36–37). The lyrics of the first six villancicos compiled by Dalmau are also included under the heading 'Vilançicos de Lope de Bega para la fiesta de nuestra santa madre' in a manuscript at the library of Barcelona University, dated in the second half of the seventeenth century and possibly belonging to the friary of Sant Josep.[29] Likewise, the eight villancicos published by Dalmau are found in a manuscript at the BNE, which contains villancicos performed at Mexico Metropolitan Cathedral on Saint Peter's day in 1715, which shows the circulation of Barcelonan villancicos also in the New World.[30]

Not only nuns, but also women in general contributed with music to the beatification or canonisation ceremonial. For instance, in the *relación* of the earlier festivities celebrated in Barcelona on the occasion of the canonisation of Raimon de Penyafort (1180–1275) in 1601, a concluding section entitled *De las fiestas que las mugeres y los niños, han hecho à nuestro Santo* describes the involvement of women and children: the women, with 'music of several instruments', took flowers and candles to the sepulchre of the Saint, where they endowed a Mass in the saint's honour, while the children—even very young children—were taught polyphonic *goigs* to replace the secular and 'lascivious' songs they usually sang in the streets.[31] The *relación* subsequently describes how the children sang the newly devised devotional texts every evening before the shrine.[32] This passage is of particular interest in that it describes the involvement of women and children who were not nuns or choirboys, but who were able to contribute to the range of devotional music heard across the canonisation ceremonies.

While female and male religious houses shared the limelight at the festivities for the beatification of Saint Teresa, in the case of the celebrations on the occasion of the canonisation of Raimon de Penyafort in 1601, the Dominican male house of Santa Caterina was the sole host of the festivity, and no references to the musical participation of the Dominican nuns are found in the accounts.[33] The convent of Santa Caterina also celebrated every year the anniversary of the canonisation of Penyafort and, when reporting on the ceremonies held in 1612, the annals of the convent point out: 'the Mass was most solemn, sung in three choirs; the second Vespers and Compline were similar, so that music was listened to all day. I think that this [music] is a means of attracting many people'.[34] On other occasions the chronicler explained that it was the Duke of Cardona who covered the expenses of the music for the celebration of the Octave of the moving of Raimon de Penyafort, including musicians from the papal nunciature, the musical chapel of the parish church of Santa Maria, the choir of the cathedral, who sang in two choirs, and 'famous minstrels', so that this was the best festivity since the canonisation until then (Campruví and Anglès 1743: fol. 336v). Likewise, the chronicler commented on the arrangements made by Santa Catalina convent as the host of the beatification feasts of Saint Agnes of Montepulciano, herself a Dominican nun, on 20 April 1602. Rockets, gunpowder, drums, fifes, trumpets, and minstrels were considered necessary to imbue the vigil of the feast with the necessary solemnity; moreover, the chronicler emphasises the positive reception of the vigil by the population, 'with so much music at midday and at night, as it had never been seen before in Barcelona'.[35]

The Barcelonan festivities for the beatification of Penyafort in 1601 were marked with dozens of processions, and it was the male convent of Santa Caterina which served as the place of arrival. The processions entered the convent singing the hymn *Te Deum laudamus* and the friars would parade outside the convent to welcome the processions, accompanying them into the convent. It was reported that Santa Caterina was imitated by other religious institutions as regards the solemnity with which they celebrated festivities and processions, as it always had a massive influx of attendees (Campruví and Anglès 1743: fol. 88r).

Did nunneries contribute with music to these outside processions? The *Dietaris* point out that, for example, the nuns of Santa Maria de Jonqueres watched the main procession on 24 May 1601 from a corridor which was elevated above street level and with lattices windows:

> Before Jonqueres there was a beautiful altar with diverse portraits and silver and above the gate of that convent which looked to the square there was a corridor with lattices, where the nuns of that convent were to watch the procession.[36]

Another chronicle refers to this place from which the nuns watched the procession as a wooden platform (*cadafal*) and remarks that the nuns were sufficiently distanced to be removed from sight. The nuns of the convent of Santa Magdalena also watched the procession from a platform.[37] The grandeur of the ceremonial soundscape was enhanced by the placement of instrumentalists on wooden platforms which were built especially outside the convents of Santa Maria de Jonqueres and Montsió, although there is no evidence of the nuns themselves performing music.[38]

Likewise, on the occasion of the canonisation of Saint Hyacinth on 19 June 1594, which was also organised by the friary of Santa Caterina, a procession passed before the convents of Santa Maria Magdalena and Santa Maria de Jonqueres, and even entered the convent of Montsió.[39] The procession of *les cinc nafres* (five wounds of Christ) would also pass the Montsió convent, before proceeding to hospitals and convents (Bada 1970: 68), but no reference is made to any musical participation of the nuns in this case.

Some documentary evidence points towards nuns making musical contributions to the Barcelonan processions of rogations (*rogativas*). These processions involved visits to twenty-four parish churches, convents, and chapels of the city over a period of three days (Puentes-Blanco 2018: 370–376), and the importance of the institutions which were visited increased with each day. The first day saw visits to nunneries on the west side of Les Rambles, such as those of Capuchin, Jeronymite, and Carmelite nuns. On the second day the procession progressed to the Ribera neighbourhood, where the main houses of mendicant friars—such as those of Santa Caterina and Sant Agustí—were located; later in the day, the convents of Santa Maria Magdalena and Sant Pere were also visited. On the final day it was male institutions alone which received these processions, and typically those with a stronger association to the political life of the city. Inside some of the churches responsories and antiphons were sung: within the church of the convent of Santa Maria Magdalena a polyphonic antiphon used to be performed (Puentes-Blanco 2018: 373), while responsories were sung at the churches of the convents of Santa Teresa, the Jeronymite nuns, Santa Margarida, and Sant Pere, where it was sung by the community of the convent (Puentes-Blanco 2018: 375, n. 71). In thanksgiving for deliverance from time of plague, on 14 August 1589 the Jeronymite nuns vowed, among other things, to fast on the vigils of the feast day of Saint Roch, Saint Cristopher, and Saint Sebastian, and instituting a solemn Mass on these days, in addition to singing the devotion of the Seven Sorrows of the Virgin every Friday.[40]

The convent of Santa Clara also served as the destination for the processions seeking divine intervention in times of prolonged drought. For instance, on 7 April 1526, the cathedral canons and clergymen brought the body of the martyr Saint Severus in procession to the church of the convent of Santa Clara, where they celebrated a solemn Mass sung by the nuns.[41] On 30 January 1613, the body of Saint Severus was again brought in solemn procession from the cathedral to the convent church, with the participation of the bishop of Barcelona, all the clergy, the city councillors, and many confraternities.[42] The convent church was heavily ornamented with elaborate decorations on the occasion and the nuns sang a Mass from the choir. The records of the convent of Santa Clara even include documents describing the rules about the ordering of participants in the processions that arrived in the convent from the cathedral.[43] The cathedral processions which involved the city councillors in times of drought also visited other convents, such as those of Santa Maria de Jonqueres and Valldonzella.[44]

There is some documentary evidence for nuns making musical contributions to outside processions from inside the convent in the case of other cities. On the main feast day of the beatification feast of Ignatius of Loyola in Lima in July 1610, a procession was celebrated with the participation of the cathedral choir, who sang music with devotional lyrics addressed to Saint Ignatius before each altar; moreover, the nuns of the convent of La Concepción showed 'their affection and devotion to the Saint' by singing romances and lyrics during the two hour the procession was passing before the convent (Bravo 1610: fol. 5). The musical contribution of convents to urban processions was not restricted to beatification festivities, as the case of the nunnery of La Piedad in Guadalajara, founded by the noblewoman Brianda de Mendoza in 1524, demonstrates. Francisco Torres, alderman of the city, described an active musical life at this convent and reported

136 *Music as a symbol of political power and social status*

on the existence of an excellent choir formed by nuns who contributed with their singing to the city processions through the convent's upper lattice windows. He suggested that there were other choirs comprised solely of women in Guadalajara and equated the choir of La Piedad convent with that of the Chapel Royal in its musical skill, hinting at the possibility of joint performances between the two when the latter visited Guadalajara (Torres 1647: fols. 208v–209r; Mazuela-Anguita 2012a: 420–423). Therefore, Torres' account reflects the celebration of solemn urban festivities in which the nuns, even without leaving the convent, played a fundamental role from a sounding perspective.

The projection of music from the upper places of convents to the outdoors is similarly accounted for in an Italian example offered by Silvia Evangelisti, who reports on the nuns of Santa Maria degli Angeli in Siena. Evangelisti describes how, on the occasion of the Low Sunday procession in 1649, the nuns sang 'as loud as possible so that their voices could be heard outside' and that they organised an internal procession inside the cloister while 'the confraternities and other citizens followed the event and sang along from outside' (Evangelisti 2007: 122). Moreover, nuns from the adjacent convent of Santa Monaca also wanted to make their voices heard outside and, when the procession passed by the cloister wall on which they stood, the nuns sang a motet to the accompaniment of the organ. This example thus shows how the essential offerings of music made to urban processions were replicated in other Catholic countries, as well as emphasising the ability of nuns to perform from their cloistered spaces.

Furthermore, nuns celebrated processions inside the cloister (Figure 3.3) which might have imitated outside ceremonies. For instance, the city chroniclers recorded that on 18 September 1542 processions would be celebrated inside the convent to plead for divine assistance against the enemies of Christians, and that they would be organised as follows: on Tuesday, the procession would take place in the convent churches of Sant Pere, Valldonzella, Jerusalem, and Santa Maria Magdalena; on Thursday, the nuns of Santa Maria de Jonqueres, Els Àngels,

Figure 3.3. Circle of Giovanni Balducci, 'il Cosci' (c.1560-1631), *Procession of Nuns and Novices Honoring a Male Saint*, 166 x 412 mm. Chicago, Art Institute, The Leonora Hall Gurley Memorial Collection, 1982.269. Public Domain

Montsió, and Montalegre would celebrate processions; on Saturday, it would be the turn of the nunneries of Les Jerònimes and Santa Clara.[45]

The book on the convent of Santa Clara compiled by the archivist Sebastià Roger devotes a chapter to the processions which were held in the convent throughout the church's calendar.[46] Every Sunday a procession was celebrated in the cloister, and it is described as 'not solemn', meaning that the nuns only said the litany as they walked. The solemn processions took place on Palm Sunday, Our Lady in February, Saint Clare's feast day in August, and Saint Michael's feast day in September. At solemn processions, the prioress brought the cross, the abbess brought the gremial (a square cloth which a bishop wore over his lap) and the stole (*estola*), and the singers their rods (*bordons*).[47] The document clarifies that processions on Corpus Christi were to be suspended, as the nuns wanted to avoid the entrance of chaplains into the cloister.[48]

A book from the convent of Sant Pere for the period 1569–1603 describes the numerous occasions on which there were processions inside the convent and the ornaments, clothes, and sticks that had to be prepared for it.[49] Likewise, a ceremonial book from the convent of Santa Maria de Jonqueres refers to the particular pieces sung in the processions celebrated inside the convent all the Sundays of Advent, on Christmas, Epiphany, the Purification of Our Lady, Sunday of Lent, Palm Sunday, Easter Sunday, Saint Mark, the Ascension, Pentecost, Saint James, Our Lady of August, and All Saints (Figure 3.4). The guidelines for Palm Sunday's procession might serve as an example:

> After Sext, my lady the prioress and all the nuns will go down to the church grille in order to perform the ceremony of the Blessing of the Palms. The two minor choir directors will start with the antiphon that begins with *Hosanna* and all the choir together will proceed before. After the Epistle the same two choir directors will sing the responsory *In Monte Oliveti* and the choir will proceed before and the two choir directors will say the verse. Once the ceremony is finished, the chaplains will come to the grille and will open the door. My lady the prioress and all the other nuns will go to take their Palms and then all the servants. While the ceremony of taking the Palm is being performed, the two choir directors will sing the verse *Pueri Hebraeorum* […] and all the choir together will proceed before. Once the ceremony is finished, the chaplain will say a prayer and will say *Procedamus in pace*, and all the choir together will reply. The chaplains will enter and will do the procession. When going out the grille, the choir directors will sing *Cum ad propinquaret*. The procession will pass through the low cloister. When the procession returns to the grille door, the major choir director will enter the grille with the nuns she chooses. The door will be locked, and they will sing the verses and all the choir together will respond. The verses being finished, the chaplain will take the cross and will knock the door three times, and he will sing *Ingrediente Domino*. All the retinue will proceed singing the responsory and entering the grille. The two nuns who are most senior, one of each choir, will sing the verse. It should be noted that all the nuns who will go

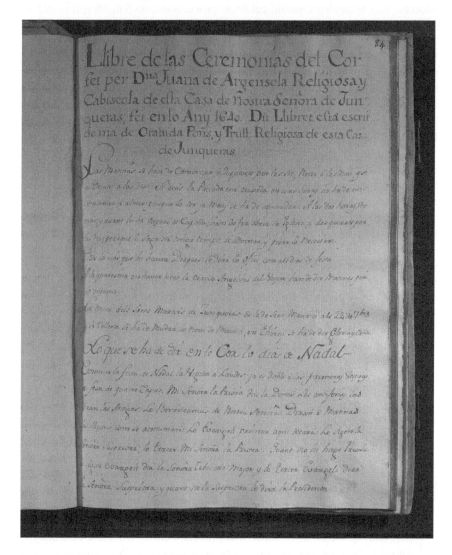

Figure 3.4. First page of the 'Llibre de las Ceremonias del Cor fet per Dona Juana de Argensola Religiosa y Cabiscola de esta Casa de nostra señora de Junqueras; fet en lo Any 1640', in *Libro de la fundación, traslado y visitas*, ACA,ORM,Monacales-Universidad,Volúmenes,244, fols. 84r–95v

to take the Palms and join to the procession will wear their skirt 'undone' and will not wear sleeves. The two choir directors will not proceed in the middle of the procession, but each of them in her place.[50]

Therefore, the book provides indications which allow us to reconstruct the itinerary of these processions: sometimes, the procession began at the choir, proceeded through the high cloister, and returned to the choir, whereas, on the most solemn occasions, such as Palm Sunday, the procession began at the choir, went to the low cloister, entered the church through the grille, and returned to the choir. The account shows that these processions involved contact between chaplains and nuns, as well as the joint musical performance, which leads to wonder if cloister procession not only imitated outside ceremonies but also exerted an influence on them. According to Pérez Vidal, nuns taking part in cloister processions in Castilian Dominican nunneries in the late medieval period 'seem to have had both inward and outward interaction, as they not only imitated urban liturgy inside the cloister but they had sometimes fostered the spreading of some devotions outside the walls, into the city' (Pérez Vidal 2015: 267). Further research is needed in order to assess the plausible influence of cloistered processions on outside events in sixteenth century Barcelona.

Outside: Nuns' music beyond the cloister?

On other occasions, convents might have been responsible for the performance of music outside their cloistered community buildings; however, gender was undoubtedly a determining factor in the ability of members of religious houses to make music in the outside world, and nuns did not enjoy the same degree of exposure as their male counterparts because of the strictness of female enclosure. An example of this greater mobility enjoyed by men can be seen in the visit of the polyphonic choir of the male convent of the Mare de Déu del Carme went to the friary of Santa Caterina to perform Compline for the feast of canonisation of Raimon de Penyafort in 1601:

> the ensemble of minstrels was there all day and at the appointed hour for Compline time the choir of the friars of the Mare de Déu del Carme came voluntarily and I had gone to ask them for that favour as they were reputed for singing.[51]

Likewise, friars performed music outside their house on the occasion of processions related to festivities such as beatification, canonisations, *autos de fe*, and royal entries. For example, at the procession of the Green Cross, which was celebrated on the vespers of an *auto de fe*, friars of the different convents of a city sang litanies continuously. The choir of the main church of the city or the Chapel Royal sang polyphony alternating with a choir formed by clergymen and friars who responded in plainchant. The annals of the friary of Santa Caterina indicate that all the religious orders participated in the Green Cross procession celebrated in Barcelona in September 1602 singing the hymn *Vexilla Regis*, while in the procession of the penitents, on the day of the *auto de fe*, the retinue of friars from Santa Caterina singing the Miserere *en tono* caused 'great terror' in the population.[52] The position of the religious orders in the retinue reflected a hierarchy, so it was sometimes a matter of dispute. The annals of Santa Caterina describe a procession celebrated on 8 January 1612 in which, according to custom, all the religious orders participated singing litanies. The choir director (*capiscol*) of the parish church of

140 *Music as a symbol of political power and social status*

Santa Maria del Mar asked both the vicar of choir of Santa Caterina and the author of the chronicle, who was a singer, to abandon their position in the retinue, which caused a conflict (Campruví and Anglès 1743: fol. 267v).

Although the friars left their convents in order to participate in urban festivities much more frequently than female communities, the nuns of the convent of Santa Maria de Jonqueres constitute a paradigmatic example as regards flexibility of enclosure. These nuns not only organised festivities with a musical component which were attended by members of the nobility, royalty, and knights of the Order of Santiago, but they also went out the convent in order to participate in festivities which involved musical performances. It is telling that still in 1549 the convent's visitors deemed it necessary to prohibit the nuns from asking the prioress's permission to leave the convent in order to attend public festivities in the city or outside the city and, again in 1560, the visitors warned the nuns on the prohibition on attending 'festivities, dances, and rejoicing' in Barcelona (see Chapter 2). Also, at the convent of Sant Pere, where the nuns had opposed to the enclosure imposed by the reformers of the Catholic Monarchs in 1493, it was still necessary in 1559 to prohibit the abbess from allowing the nuns to go out 'in order to attend festivities, markets, and make visits, which had been happening frequently and, in any case, they had to be accompanied by another nun appointed by the abbess'.[53]

The references to musical performances given by nuns outside the convent are very limited, especially after the Council of Trent. One of the clearest cases of the musical contribution of nunneries to the ceremonial and political life of the city through sound is that of the convent of Santa Maria de Valldonzella, located outside the walls of the city of Barcelona, very close to the gate of Sant Antoni (Figures 3.5 and 3.6). It served as a residence for royalty and aristocracy, who, before making their high-profile entries into the city were welcomed at the convent with music.[54] The case of

Figure 3.5. Location of the convent of Santa Maria de Valldonzella (number 19 on the map). Detail from: Johann Stridbeck (1666–1714), 'Barcelona, die Haupt Statt des Fürstenthums Catalonien', in *Curioses Staats und Kriegs Theatrum* (Augsburg: Johann Stridbeck, 1711–1714). Barcelona, Institut Cartogràfic i Geològic de Catalunya. Creative Commons

Music as a symbol of political power and social status 141

Figure 3.6. The gate of Sant Antoni. Detail from: Georg Braun (1541–1622) y Joris Hoefnagel (1542–1601), *Barcino, quae vulgo Barcelona dicitur, urbis est apud Hispanos celebérrima* ([s.l.]: [s.n.], 1572). BNE, R/22249(1) PL. 6

the convent of Santa Maria de Valldonzella serves as one example where the nuns—it is not clear if physically leaving the convent—made a musical contribution which was recognised as a fundamental part of a larger external ceremony. According to custom, the city councillors met the monarchs outside the city walls and accompanied them to the door of the convent, as the councillors were not allowed to enter inside the building (Duran 1930–1947; Raventós 2006: 87–88; Chamorro 2013: 179–180). The royal retinue approached the convent to the sound of trumpets and drums (of both the city council and the king), together with wind-players, usually placed on platforms at strategic points along the route to the convent as an aural symbol of power.[55] For instance, according to the city chroniclers, the Catholic Monarchs arrived in Valldonzella on 23 October 1492, where they stayed before carrying out their triumphal entry into Barcelona through the gate of Sant Antoni accompanied by drums, trumpets, and minstrels the following day.[56] Philip the Handsome also stayed at this convent before his entry in Barcelona in 1503,[57] at which time the singer Caterina Boïl, described in Chapter 1, was abbess (from 1478 to 1503).

The entry of Isabel of Valois and her children on 23 March 1533 must have been spectacular. When they left Valldonzella, the city had prepared a pseudo-theatrical performance at the gate of Sant Antoni, which was located within a distance of less than 700 metres from the convent, which leads to wonder how much could actually be heard in either place of sounds issuing from the other. This spectacle included many performers dressed as angels, who played a variety of musical instruments against a backdrop of decoration which imitated a starry sky. A vocal quartet, situated on a high platform, sang three musical pieces. The lyrics are detailed in the *Dietaris*:

Barcino tribus virtutibus.
Illa potens acies et vincere Barcino classes:

142 *Music as a symbol of political power and social status*

> *Et comitem regum progenuisse patrem.*
> *Vos ergo tergeminas, divina stirpe sorores:*
> *O charitas ardens spesque fidesque precor.*
> *Reddite caelestes morum decorumque parentes:*
> *Sceptra salutifera que ratione regant.*
> *Nam sacer auratos ubi cesar inivit honores:*
> *Castra procul vise cesariana sequi.*
> *Si mea languentis tandem non ora revisant:*
> *Res erit infoelix publica nullus honos.*
> *Tres virtutes Barcinoni.*
> *Barcino clara domi longinquis inclyta bellis:*
> *Quales prestat avos, qui tenet arma nepos.*
> *Spectasti captos quos nemo crederet hostes:*
> *Unus et hic victus littora Turca fugit.*
> *Ecce Augusta potens virtutes conferet omnes:*
> *Sceptraque venturo cesare summa reget.*
> *Tu tantum supplex vultus affare serenos:*
> *Illa parem nusquam sentiat esse fidem.*
> *Quin age clementes veneremur cantibus aures:*
> *Audiat et verum carmen uterque polus.*[58]

A similar musical performance took place in honour of Philip III on 26 March 1626, when a ten-year-old boy dressed as an angel and placed on a crane system sang some *versets* (Parets 1626–1660: fol. 2r–v; Cases *et al.* 1994: vol. 5, 126). Therefore, the music of the nuns of Valldonzella was, on such occasions, an essential part of a wider ceremonial soundscape stretching between the convent and the city. The singing of the nuns, the clamour of the trumpets and drums of the royal train, and the pseudo-theatrical performance of the wind-players and singers hired by the city councillors would have contributed to a vibrant sonic exchange, and crowds and onlookers would undoubtedly have been aware of the role played by the nuns in this grand public occasion.

A printed account of the visit of Philip II in Barcelona in February 1564 (Figure 3.7) offers details on his arrival at the convent of Santa Maria de Valldonzella and the welcome offered there by the nuns, who went out in procession and met the king singing *Tua es potentia*, a responsory from the Book of the Maccabees, together with its verse:

> The abbess and all the nuns left the convent in procession to welcome [the king] [...]. All the nuns came together singing *tua est potentia*, and a choir of nuns replied *por punto tuum regnum domine, tu es super omnes gentes*. Then the nuns said *Da pacem domine in diebus nostris*, and the choir replied *Creator omnium, deus terribilis & fortis, iustus & misericors*.[59]

This text has some connections to expressions of royal power: for example, it was included by Hernando de Talavera (d.1507) in a liturgical Office commissioned

ॐLos triuphos y grandes
recebimientos dela infigne ciudad de
Barcelona ala venida del famofifsimo Phelipe
rey delas Efpañas &c. Con la entrada
de los ferenifsimos principes
de Bohemia.

Compueftos por Balthafar del hierro.

En Barcelona,
En cafa de Iayme Cortey.
Año. 1 5 6 4.

*Venden fe en cafa de Ioan
Trinxer librero.*

Figure 3.7. Baltasar del Hierro, *Los triumphos y grandes recebimientos dela insigne ciudad de Barcelona ala venida del famosissimo Phelipe rey delas Españas &c. Con la entrada de los serenissimos principes de Bohemia* (Barcelona: Iayme Cortey, 1564), title page. Barcelona, Universitat de Barcelona, Biblioteca de Reserva, B-44/3/13-2. Public Domain

by Queen Isabel to commemorate the conquest of Granada (Talavera 1493).[60] In their choice of this text for performance on the occasion of Philip II's visit, the nuns made a musical contribution to this public act of welcome which had significant political overtones; however, it is not specified whether this procession took place inside the convent or beyond the confines of the cloister.

An account of the secret arrival of Philip III at the convent of Valldonzella on 18 May 1599 specifies that the nuns welcomed the king in procession bringing candles 'at the doors of the church':

> At 12 o'clock King Philip III left the palace with four carriages accompanied by his servants and went secretly to the convent of Valldonzella, of nuns of the order of Saint Bernard. Once he arrived in the convent, he was welcomed by the nuns in procession at the doors of the church. Each one brought a candle [...]. Friar Joan Tarrós, the abbot of Poblet, was ready, wearing pontifical clothes, and presented the holy water to the king and also the Cross for adoration. Then the *Te Deum* was sung as the procession was entering the church with the chords of the organ for each verse.[61]

There are some references to nuns' participation in processions outside the convent premises in the sixteenth century.[62] On 10 June 1518 the nuns of Sant Pere celebrated the procession of the 'Octave of the Corpus Christi'. The city chroniclers reported on the itinerary and the musical component of this procession, which is explicitly recorded as having taken place outside the convent (*fora del monastir*):

> On this day [10 June 1518] the nuns of the convent of Sant Pere de les Puel·les of the city of Barcelona celebrated the procession known as that of the Octave of the Corpus Christi. Thus, at six o'clock in the afternoon, the procession left the convent along Sant Pere Street, going up to the street that crosses the lower part of Sant Pere Street, coming out at Fonellar Street and turning left to go back along the said street of Sant Pere the Lower, and returning to the convent. The order of the procession [was] as follows: the flag of the [confraternity of] market gardeners, and the market gardeners themselves in pairs, holding candles; then the banners and the cross of Sant Pere, then the chaplains, who were around thirty, wearing surplices and singing and bearing candles, then the nuns ordered in pairs and carrying lighted white candles in their hands; then seven musicians, dressed in dalmatics, playing string instruments; then the monstrance on a float carried by presbyters wearing white robes and stoles, and the baldachin, which was carried by honourable men of the parish church and others; then the reverend abbess carrying the cross and a white candle in her hand between two presbyters vested as deacon and sub-deacon; then some men of high status and others carrying lighted candles; and many people [followed] out of devotion. All the streets through which this procession passed had been cleaned, swept, and ornamented with canopies and well-ordered devotional altars. May Our Lord accept this service and allow them to maintain it every year so increasing piety in behalf of all. Amen.[63]

On this occasion, therefore, the music of the procession was performed by the chaplains who sang and by musicians who played string instruments, and there is no reference to the nuns making a musical contribution to the event. The same occurs in other references to nuns' processions outside the convent premises. As mentioned in Chapter 1, the celebrations for the foundation of the Elisabets convent were presided by Philip II and his court in March 1564, coinciding with his visit that year.[64] The nuns went in procession from their former house to the new convent:

> The nuns and the mother Fornés left the house and, ordered in procession, continued to their church, where the King [Philip II] with all the greatness of his court and many ecclesiastical prelates were. The Mass was sung and, once it was finished, the nuns made vows before the General Minister.[65]

The participation of Barcelonan nuns in royal burials was also recorded (Costa 1974: 268). For instance, Leonor, Queen of Cyprus, died in Barcelona on 26 December 1417 and, according to two manuscripts cited by Pi i Arimon:

> Her remains were deposited in the church of Sant Francesc d'Assís. In her burial, three queens walked behind her coffin; their heads were covered by mantles. They were Maria, who was the wife of the reigning monarch; Violant, King Jaume's widow; and Margarita, King Martí's widow. Another manuscript from the same archive remarks that the burial was attended by all the secular and regular clergy of the city, and, in addition to this, by the abbess and nuns of the convents of Sant Pere de les Puel·les, Valldonzella, and the prioress and nuns of Jonqueres.[66]

The abbess of Sant Pere and the prioress of Santa Maria de Jonqueres, together with their nuns, were also invited to attend the burial of Mossèn Romeu Llull, head chief councillor (*conseller en cap*) of the city, who died on 19 July 1484.[67]

Likewise, the translation of the convent of Els Àngels to its location inside the city walls on 19 March 1562 was very solemn, with the participation of thirty-six nuns, members of other religious institutions such as the eight oldest chaplains of the parish church of Santa Maria del Pi, sixty knights carrying axes—among them, Gaspar Ferrer, prior of Catalonia, and Onofre de Rocabertí, Viscount of Perelada—the priest of Santa Maria del Pi bringing the Most Holy Sacrament, and the city councillors, carrying the canopy which covered the sacrament. The image of the Our Lady of the Angels was carried by members of the confraternities of ropemakers (*corders*) and of grain-weighers (*mesurers*) (Paulí 1941b: 19–20). The *Dietaris* reported on this event in detail, describing the singing of hymns and responsories by the nuns:

> [On 19 March 1562] [...] they left the convent of Els Àngels, outside this city, and proceeded in this way: first went the banners of Santa Maria del Pi, and then four caskets [*túmols*] or boxes full of bones of dead nuns of the

convent carried by porters [*bastaixos*] on their shoulders, accompanied by many people carrying lanterns; and then came the cross of the parish church of Santa Maria del Pi, and then many chaplains, and then the nuns, in this way: first a nun wearing a veil with a crucifix together with two altar girls with two candelabras and covered faces; then came all the nuns in order, forming eighteen pairs, each wearing a black robe and a thick black veil over her face. Among them went officials with rods to ensure that the nuns' path was not blocked, as those present were so numerous that they proceeded with difficulty. They walked singing many holy hymns and responsories, and behind them came many knights and other important people carrying lighted torches, and then came the Blessed Sacrament with its baldachin carried by the magnificent city councillors [...]. And they proceeded from their [old] convent to the Portal Nou and entered the city, and passed before the convent of Sant Pere, along Sant Pere the Higher Street, past the nunnery of Jonqueres, along Condal Street, along Santa Anna Street, Peu de la Creu Street (or 'd'en Borra'), and entered the [new] convent, which was very small and diminutive, but with plenty of space for building, and [it] already had a chapel and choir with its grille, and the nuns installed themselves as best they could.[68]

Therefore, convents had different strategies to contribute, despite the spatial limitations and enclosure, to the celebrations of their urban surroundings through music. Nunneries used sounds not only as an outward expression of joy, to transmit festive spirit, to attract the ordinary people, and to disseminate religious values. They also sought to stand out in their urban surroundings through sound and worked to acquire prestige for their institutions, which operated within the context of the city's hierarchies of power. Music was used as a means to enhance the status of convents in the context of the urban ceremonies, such as the entries of monarchs into the city. But while the musical performances during these political and religious celebrations might have involved an element of competition between Barcelona's religious houses, the same festivals were perhaps conducive to a sense of cohesion as these institutions worked towards a common cause. The writings explored in this chapter have illustrated the subtle interplay between the music of convents and the political life of the city. But while the writers behind these accounts were aware of the civic ambition motivating these performances, the following chapter gives an account to suggest that the majority of citizens associated the music of convents with a heavenly authority which transcended these temporal concerns.

Notes

1 Cited in Knighton 2014: 208: '¿Quién podrá contar la grandeza, el conçierto de su corte, [...] los cantores, las músicas acordadas de la onrra del culto divino, la solennidad de las misas y oras que continuamente en su palaçio se cantavan; [...] la multitud de poetas e trobadores e musicos de todas artes [...]?'

Music as a symbol of political power and social status   147

2 Translation included in Knighton 2011: 27. For the original text, see Suardo 1935: 157–158: 'Este día, a las dos de la tarde, el señor Virrey y la señora Condessa fueron al Convento de Monjas de Nuestra Señora de la Encarnación, en cuya porteria principal les estava prevenido un recevimiento condigno y, aviendo sus Excelencias tomado sus asientos junto a la puerta que estava avierta de par en par y por de dentro estavan cerca de 30 monjas, empezaron a cantar y tañer diversidad de instrumentos y después les sacaron muchas fuentes allí de muy regalada colación con exquisitos olores, con que los señores Condes estuvieron entretenidos hasta cerca de las ocho de la noche y, aviendose llevado todas las fuentes a Palacio, el señor Virrey las mandó presentar al señor Presidente Vissitador de los Charcas'.
3 Gras 2013b: 121: 'las solemnidades litúrgicas eran también ocasión de encuentro entre familiares, de refuerzo de los lazos de sangre y muestra de apoyo público'.
4 García de Caralps 1617: 145: 'Estas señoras Monjas son todas de muy noble y Illustre sangre. Tienen priuilegio, que siendo professas, pueden casar vna vez, sin dexar la Cruz de la espada: la qual lleuan, no solamente en el manto, mas también en el vestido. En ese Monasterio, se juntan todos los caualleros del habito de Santiago, en ciertas jornadas, para celebrar sus fiestas, confessar y comulgar, vestidos con sus habitos, y capas blancas, con mucha deuuocion'. See also Ibáñez 1966: 98-99.
5 Costa 1974: 266: 'La festa patronal de Sant Jaume tenia també una gran solemnitat. En dóna una idea el compte de las despenses fetes per la del 1436. La vigilia foren cantades les vespres i els preveres reberen una col·lació d'ametlles amb mel i sucre, pinyons, matafaluga i celiandre també ensucrats, melons i vi grec. [...] Dos parells d'ànecs reberen dos tenoristes que havien ensenyat a les monges algunes obres modernes per a l'ofici'.
6 See, among many other examples, AMSP, Llibres d'abadesses, no. 171 (1501–1503), fols. 21v (1503) and 23v (1504); no. 176 (1511–1513), fol. 27r (1511); fol. 28r (1512); and no. 177 (1513–1516), fol. 21r.
7 Paulí 1945: 87: 'Hallándose en Barcelona el rey D. Felipe III y su augusta esposa doña Margarita de Austria, el día de la festividad de San Pedro Apóstol, titular de la iglesia y Convento, según tradicional costumbre, fueron invitadas las reales personas a presidir las solemnidades litúrgicas. Haciendo gala de insignes protectores de la Casa Religiosa, aceptaron deferentes la invitación los Monarcas, presentándose a las once de la mañana a la puerta exterior del Real Monasterio, siendo recibidos por la Comunidad de Presbíteros revestidos de sobrepelliz. En la puerta claustral aguardaban a los Reyes la Iltre. Sra. Abadesa, con el báculo y estolón, y la numerosa Comunidad de Religiosas, acompañando a Sus Majestades por la escalera magna al coro alto, entonándose el Te Deum. Al llegar al Coro la regia comitiva, ofreció la Señora Abadesa el agua bendita a los Soberanos, ocupando luego los magníficos sitiales al efecto preparados. Celebróse misa solemne en el altar de San Pedro, que ofició el Iltre. Abad Presidente de la Orden Benedictina, ceremonia que revistió inusitada pompa, la cual completaron las monjas con sus cantos'.
8 *Manual de novells ardits...*, vol. 5, p. 6.
9 'Llibre dels càrrecs i oficis', p. 62: 'los señors consellers venen en est dia al ofisi en lo cor de les monges'.
10 *Manual de novells ardits...*, vol. 4, pp. 3–5, March 1534; *Ceremonial dels magnífichs consellers...*, vol. 2, p. 35.
11 *Manual de novells ardits...*, vol. 4, pp. 170–172.
12 'Cerimonial Abadesa morta' (1594), AMSBM, box 27, no. 633, fols. 80r–81v.
13 This story is studied in Knighton 2017b: 64–65, taking as a source a *Llibre de difuntes* preserved at the Arxiu de les Carmelites Descalces in Barcelona.
14 Garriga Roca: 1899: 29: 'Sus entradas y profesiones en la misma época, hacíanse con grande ostentación, concurriendo deudos, padrinos, y las familias más distinguidas de la nobleza. Regularmente intervenía la capilla de música, y se adornaban los altares

con multitud de flores y luces. Todos los asistentes llevaban sendas velas, la profesanda de á cuatro libras, la priora de una y las demás religiosas, clérigos y familiares de menos tamaño'.

15 *Ceremonial dels magnífichs consellers...*, vol. 3, p. 71 (14 May 1368): 'foren consecrades en lo Monastyr de S.t Antoni del orde de S.ta Clara 28, monjas, y forenhi lo Rey en Pere, y la Reyna Leonor sa muller, y lo Bisbe de Barcelona, y fouhi feta gentil festa, y bella solemnitat'.

16 AMSBM, box 27, no. 633, fol. 33v ('Forma y modo com se an de vestir las monjas de Nostre Religion del Padre San Benet'); fol. 34r (on the day of the habit, 'el Ofici sol ser a las deu y ab Musica y se diu Missa del Esperit san, y acabat el incarnatus el sacrista presenta al celebrant una fuente ab lo habit per benehirlo').

17 'Llibre dels càrrecs i oficis', pp. 21–22: 'Lo habit sempre se dona en lo offisi maior. Es de costum que lo procurador de la casa diu de ordinari la missa del habit cantada en lo altar major. Los padrins de la que pren lo habit pugen fins a la porta del cap de la schala y alli prenen la monja y la acompanyen al altar major y alli ouhen lo offici en lo qt al offertori la monja dona un ciri de una lliura al vn escut de or lo qual reb la sachristana. Los padrins y los altres offereixen lo que volen y tot es de la monja antigament se deja una missa baxa pero de molts anys en ça se diu offisi cantat [...]. La Rnt. Abadessa la pren de la ma y la posa dintre y totas les monges estan iuntes ab les ciris en les mans y les cantores ab los bordons y comencen a cantar la antiphona veni sponsa christi y entren a lo cor la Abadessa y monja y se agenollen deuant lo altar de nostra señora en lo mig del cor y comencen a cantar la Salue regina y a modo de professo baxen cantant a la stancia al costat del sepulchro que te rexa a la sglesia per la porta y los padrins sen tornen a la sglesia y en dit lloc la Abadessa Priora y thesorera la vesten. Les monges y lo orgue van cantant lo veni creator conforme lo breuiari ab la antiphona confessor domini y una monja diu la oration intercessio nos qus. domine ço es aquella a qui la cantora ha dat lo carrec o la domera la diu'; pp. 24-25 [on professions]: '[...] y la monja se agenolla en lo mig de la capella ab la carta dels vots en les mans y apres del sermo [...] apres del offertori axi agenollada con se esta llig cantant la carta dels vots la qual es del tenor seguent [...] y acabat de cantar la señora que la presentada pren a la monja y la acompanya fins al altar fet en la dita capella y la dita fa de sa ma son signe o senyal e la dita carta que es una creu [...] y les monges canten lo veni creator y dos monges ço es la qui la ha presentada y la alcen de terra y ageollada canta lo vers tres vegades Suspice me domine secundum e lo qui um tuum et vivam / Et non confundas me ab spectatione mea y lo cor prossegueix lo Gloria patri y fet asso se acaba la missa'.

18 'Llibre de les coses dignes de memoria...', pp. 53–54 (1599): 'entraren en lo cor ab lo marques de denia y algunes dames a hont y hauia uns coxins ab son strado a sontse agenollaren y apres se assentaren lo Rey en la cadira de la abadessa y la Reyna al costat y les dames baix lluny // La Reverenda Abadessa se assenta al costat del Rey dexant una cadira en lo mig // Les señores monges se posaren en lo mig del cor cantant // La dita señora abadessa digue al Rey si volia que diguessen vespres o completes y lo Rey respongue que dixessen visperas y axi lo feren'.

19 Among the guidelines of the master of ceremonies was the need for 'two choir directors or singers with cloaks and sticks' (*Item dos cabiscols o cantors ab capes y bordons*). Campruví and Anglès 1743: fol. 154v: 'Item als 19 dia seguent fonch auisat lo pare prior com lo rey vindria a oyr vespras en nostra iglesia juntament ab las personas reals encontinent ampaliarem la iglesia adobantla lo millor que era posible tambe al sacrari y sacristia procurarem adornar lo mes be y al proposit traent [...]. fet asso los dos cantors entonaren lo te deum laudamus y la professo pressegui alternatim ab lo orga, que lo rey expressament no volgue capella de cantoria sino nostro cant; y dura aquest cantar fins lo rey sigue en son strado y assentat juntament ab les personas reals, y aqui matex començarem vespres que era vigilia de la assencio, y lo cantar era tirat un poch, al tercer y quint psalm sonaue lo orga alternatim, quant arribaren al magnificat

lo pare prior ab la capa de broca tana encensar al altar major ab acollits y assistents y turibol [...] Aquí se ha de notar que sta fonch la primera axida de palacio per anar a sentir officis que feu lo dit rey'. During his stay in Barcelona, the king visited the convent again to see the relics of Sant Raimon and the friars sang an antiphon in honour of the saint (*cantarem vna antiphona del Sant*).

20 Campruví and Anglès 1743: fol. 95v: 'fonch sta jornada de molta honrra per al couent'.

21 Díez de Aux 1615: 42: 'aqui se oyeron los Psalmos, compuestos de mas extraordinaria armonia, y cantados con increyble destreza: y grande variedad, assi de vozes como de musica; Suspendian y admirauan las diferencias del Organo, los passos requebrados de garganta, la dulçura de las Cornetillas, la melodia de las Dulçaynas, la profundidad de los Baxones, y la fuga alegre de las Chirimias, que de todo esto huuo mucho, y en estremo bueno. Y tanta gente, assi noble y principal, como mediana y pleueya: que ni en la Iglesia, ni en la plaça della, ni aun en mucha parte del camino, casi no auia lugar desocupado para vna criatura'.

22 Díez de Aux 1615: 44: 'Estos Angeles [monjas de todos los conventos de Zaragoza] dieron increybles muestras de gozosa alegria: Y extraordinariamente aquellas exemplares Religiosas de Ierusalem, y santa Catalina; pues la mayor parte de aquella noche, que a fuerça de luzes era dia claro, la passaron en las mas altas vistas de sus famosos Alcaçares: cantando con celestiales vozes, en concertados Coros, motetes, y Villancicos proporcionados con su alegria y nuestra: De manera cantauan, que con el sosiego que el cielo puso en aquella noche, se oya de muy lexos su melodia. Señaladamente vna voz de las mejores, o quiza la mejor que oy se sabe en España, cantò en santa Catalina a solas, vn *Vn* [sic] *beni sponsa Christi*, tan celestialmente, que parecia imposible no ser de Angel aquella voz'.

23 On Josep Dalmau, see Narváez 1994. See also Dalmau's memoirs preserved in 'Llibre de memorias de cosas particulars del señor Dr. Joseph Dalmau, fundador del convent de Nª Sª de Gràcia de Carmelitas Descalzos fora los murs de Barcelona' (1576), ACA,ORM,Monacales-Hacienda,Volúmenes,1939, fols. 46–49r, 41–44r. These memoirs include some references to expenditure on music, relating to the celebrations of the wedding between Dalmau and Lucretia Balsells in 1584 (fol. 46r).

24 Dalmau 1615: fol. 4v: 'Estauan aguardando en la plaça antes la puerta de la Iglesia, vna gran tropa de menestriles, trompetas, y atabales, todos a cauallo: y en llegando los caualleros, hizieron fiesta, cada qual con la musica de sus instrumentos'.

25 Dalmau 1615: 11r–v: 'Toda esta multitud estuuo muy entretenida con seys coplas de menestriles, que estuuieron repartidos, vnos sobre la Iglesia de san Joseph, otros sobre la de muestra señora del Carmen, otros sobre la Iglesia de las monjas descalças, y otros sobre la torre del Pino: sobre la puerta ferriça otros: y finalmente, sobre la puerta de la boqueria, los quales todos se esmerauan a porfia en tañer motes, madrigals, y batallones, respondiendose vnos a otros, con admirable melodia'.

26 Dalmau 1615: fol. 13r (from ch. 12, devoted to the festivities and ornaments at the convent of Santa Teresa): 'Avnqve las Religosas Carmelitas descalças, como hijas de la madre santa Teresa de Iesus, todos los dias de la octaua en su Iglesia tuuieron fiesta de Officios con grande musica, y sermon; except el primero, que por dar lugar a los Padres, le passaron con sola vna missa, que tres dellos les officiaron por la mañana, cantada por las mesmas Monjas, con su ordinario tono: pero el Lunes se señalaron principalmente, dandoles tambien los padres el lugar, passando esse dia a la sorda, con sola vna missa de la Santa, a canto llano'.

27 Dalmau 1615: fol. 16r–v (from ch. 13, devoted to the 'regozijos y officious de la fiesta principal de las monjas Carmelitas deslcaças'): 'Acabadas las Visperas de la fiesta principal de los padres Carmelitas descalços (que diximos arriba) parò en la Iglesia de san Ioseph la fiesta, hasta el Martes siguiente, y la solenidad de las Completas, fue toda en la Iglesia de las monjas de la mesma orden, con que se dio principio a su fiesta. Acudiò mucha gente, y cantaronse con toda solenidad de musica de cantoria a tres coros: officiòlas el padre Prior de san Ioseph con dos assistentes [...]. Dichas las

Completas, se encendieron en lo de afuera sobre la iglesia y conuento las mesmas luminarias que la noche de la vigilia, a cuya deuocion muchos conuentos de otras monjas hizieron lo mesmo, y tambien muchas casas de personas seculares: particularmente los de la propia calle, en la qual estauan los menestriles, trompetas y atabales de la ciudad, reuezandose en diferentes musicas: muchos caualleros estauan en la calle, esmerandose esta noche en tirar gran copia de coetes tronadores y voladores, con que acudiò gente de suerte, que toda la noche se passo como el dia. Lunes por la mañana hasta la hora del officio, estuuieron los menestriles en la Iglesia, haziendo con sus instrumentos diferentes mudanças: y vinieron a regozijar la fiesta todas las figuras que suelen salir para la procession del Corpus: la briuia, el dragon, el Aguila, y los cauallos que llaman cotoners, haziendo cada qual su bayle, ó dança al son de la mesma musica. Al officio assitiò el señor Virrey, con sus hijas, y muchas damas y caualleros, y nobleza de la ciudad, con mucho concurso de pueblo, mas de lo que podia caber en la Iglesia. Officiò la missa el padre Prior de san Ioseph, con diacono y subdiacono y dos assistentes, con ornamentos de muy rica tela de plata. Cantòla toda la major cantoria de Barcelona a tres coros. Disparòse mucha artilleria. Predicò este dia el R. P. Presentado Fr. Iayme Rebullosa, de la Orden de santo Domingo'.

28 Pujol had been appointed cathedral chapel master in January 1612. A number of his polychoral works for two choirs survive, but, as far as is known, none for three.

29 *Opúsculos espirituales* (MS, 1651–1700), Barcelona, Biblioteca de la Universitat de Barcelona, Ms. 1113, fols. 383r-386r.

30 *Poesías latinas y castellanas de autores diferentes y, especialmente, de fray Lorenzo del Santísimo Sacramento, y Villancicos que se cantaron en la Santa Iglesia Metropolitana de México en la festividad de San Pedro en 1715* (MS, eighteenth century), BNE, MSS/9275.

31 Rebullosa 1601: 472: 'Han sido pocas las calles desta Ciudad, cuyas mugeres no se ayan ayuntado para venir con flores, ramos verdes, velas encendidas, y musica de varios instrumentos al Sepulchro de nuestro Santo, hecho le cantar vna Missa con su Sermon, y ofrecidole vn buen cirio, en prendas de sus desseos'. For a study on the music references included in the *relaciones* of the canonisation of Saint Raimon de Penyafort in Barcelona, see Knighton 2017c.

32 Rebullosa 1601: 473–474: 'Es esto tanta verdad, que sin tener otro impulso que a Dios, la Canonizacion de nuestro Santo a *desterrado de la lengua de los niños las canciones profanas y lasciuas*, que aprendidas del mal exemplo de los mayores, *les oyamos cantar por las calles las noches y dias*; y en su lugar, los à aficionado de suerte á las que tratan de sus alabanças, que *la niña en la labor y el niño por las calles y donde quiera*, ya no sabe sino cantar sus Gozos: y auiendoles sido solo Dios y su afficion maestros (cosa estraña) acuden todas las tardes al anochescer, niños y niñas que apenas saben hablar, delante el sepulcro del Santo, y en capilla formada le cantan variedad de Gozos à concierto y *canto de organo*, que es cosa del *Cielo*' [author's emphasis].

33 In the case of Dominican nuns in late-medieval Castile, Pérez Vidal (2015: 267) points out that they participated in processions outside the cloister, such as that of Corpus Christi.

34 Campruví and Anglès 1743: fol. 267r: 'la missa del dia dia fons solemnissima a tres choros de cantoria; las segonas vespres y completas similiter en fi que tot lo dia era oyr musica que jo crec que esta es un medi per a tenir molta gent'. On the margin: 'a tres choros de cantoria'.

35 Campruví and Anglès 1743: fol. 198r: 'y feren los preparatoris conuenient per a tal remor com es de teya, coets, poluora, atambors, pífanos, trompetas, ministrils, tot aquest aparell era per la vigilia de la present festa [...] y quant agradable y rebuda fonch del poble sta vigilia ab tanta musica al mig dia y a la nit com si no aguessen vista altra nunca en Barcelona'.

36 Cases *et al.* 1994: vol. 3, 395: 'Devant Jonqueres hy havia axí matex un bell altar de diversos retratos y plata, y sobre lo portal del dit monastir de la plassa gran havien fet un corredor de gelosies, a ont estaven les monjas de dit monastir per vèurer la dita professó [...]'.
37 Later, in 1641, the convent of Santa Maria Magdalena received licence to build a viewpoint at the walls of the nunnery. See *Ceremonial dels magnífichs consellers...*, vol. 3, p. 110.
38 *Manual de novells ardits...*, vol. 7, pp. 334–336.
39 Campruví and Anglès 1743: fol. 116r. This celebration was the first of its type in Spain, latterly being replicated in other provinces.
40 Paulí 1941a: 20. It seems that the Jeronymite nunnery had strong connections to the city's rogations; for instance, on 29 April 1628, a procession of rogations proceeded from the cathedral to the convent because of the drought that affected the city. See *Manual de novells ardits...*, vol. 7, p. 260; cited in Vergés 1987: 43.
41 *Manual de novells ardits...*, vol. 3, p. 377. The same ceremony seeking divine intervention in times of drought is recorded in several occasions; see, among other examples, *Manual de novells ardits...*, vol. 3, p. 403 (6 February 1529), and vol. 4, pp. 61 (23 October 1537) and 163–164 (28 April 1545).
42 'Llibre de les coses dignes de memoria...', p. 55 (1613).
43 'Llibre dels càrrecs i oficis', p. 77 (ch. 26, 'del orde se te guardar quant la professo de la seu va al present monestir'). For further examples, see Mazuela-Anguita 2020: 24-28.
44 See, for instance, *Manual de novells ardits...*, vol. 3, p. 319 (7 September 1511, procession to Santa Maria de Jonqueres), p. 378 (17 April 1526, procession to Valldonzella).
45 *Manual de novells ardits...*, vol. 3, pp. 116–117.
46 'Llibre dels càrrecs i oficis', ch. 25 ('de les professons'), p. 76.
47 'Llibre dels càrrecs i oficis', p. 76.
48 'Llibre dels càrrecs i oficis', p. 76. A Benedictine *processionarium* belonging to the Valladolid congregation was printed in Montserrat in 1500 and it includes the musical pieces that might have been performed at the cloister processions in the two Benedictine Barcelonan convents (Sant Pere and Santa Clara) in the sixteenth century. See *Processionarium s[ecundu]m consuetudine[m] monachoru[m] congregationis sancti Benedicti de Valladolid* (Montserrat: Joan Luschner, 1500). A copy is preserved in Barcelona, Universitat de Barcelona, Biblioteca de Reserva, 07 DG-Inc 540.
49 AMSP, Llibres de sagristia, no. 6 (1569–1603).
50 'Llibre de las Ceremonias del Cor fet per Dona Juana de Argensola Religiosa y Cabiscola de esta Casa de nostra señora de Junqueras; fet en lo Any 1640', in *Libro de la fundación, traslado y visitas*, ACA,ORM,Monacales-Universidad,Volúmenes,244, fols. 84r–95v, fols. 92v–93r: 'Benediccio y Professo del Diumenge de Rams: En acabar sexta mi Señora la Priora y totas les Religiosas baixaran a la Reixa de la Yglesia para fer la Ceremonia de la Benedicio del Ram. Comensaran las dos Cabiscolas menors entonar la Antifona que diu *Ossana* y tot lo Cor junt passara avant. Apres de la Epistola las dits dos Cabiscolas entonaran lo respons: *in Monte Oliveti*, y lo Cor passara avant, y las ditas dos Cabiscolas diran lo vers: acabat la Ceremonia, que los Capellans sen Vindran a la Reixa Obriran la Porta y mi Señora la Priora: y totas las demes aniran a pendrer lo Ram; apres totas las Criadas mentras se fara la Ceremonia de anar a pendrer lo Ram las ditas Cabiscolas entonaran lo Verset *Pueri Hebreorum*; ara un vers ara un altre: y tot lo cor junt passara avant. Acabada la Ceremonia lo Capella dara una Oracio y dira *procedamus in pace*, y tot lo Cor junt respondra: y entraran los Capellans, y faran la Professo: y al eixir de la Reixa: entonaran las ditas Cabiscolas *Cum apropim quaret*. La professo ha de anar per lo Claustro de baix, y quant tornara la Professo, que seran a la Porta de la Reixa: La Señora Cabiscola Major; sen entrara a la Reixa en las Religiosas que ella voldra. Tancaran la Porta: y cantaran los versos y tot lo Cor junt respondra. Acabat los versos lo Capella pendra la Creu y donara tres Colps a la Porta:

y entonara *ingrediente Domino* y tota la Professo junta anira cantat lo Respons y sen entraran a la Reixa y las dos Religiosas de Certa llisso las mes antigas una de cada cor cantaran lo vers. Han de advertir que totas las Religiosas que aniran a pendrer lo Ram; y a la professo aniran ab la falda desfeta y no poden aportar Manguito ningunas y las dos Cabiscolas no han de anar al Mitg de la Professo sino cada una a son lloch'. For a transcriptions of the full document, see Mazuela-Anguita 2015b: 61–73.

51 Campruví and Anglès 1743: fol. 175v: 'tot lo dia tinguerem la copla dels ministrils y a completas la capella de cant dels pares del carme los quals voluntariament vingueren y cantaren famosament y per asso auia jo enuiat a suplicarlos que nos fessen exa merce'. There is abundant sixteenth-century documentation from this convent at the ACA which is of musical interest. For example, an account book for the period 1575–1581 includes the purchase of a *monarcort* (36 *sous*) and monthly payments of 2 *sous* to the musicians who played at the procession of the second Sunday of the month. See 'Barcelona, convento del Carme. Libro de gasto' (1575–1581), ACA,ORM,Monacales-Hacienda,Volúmenes,1971.

52 Campruví and Anglès 1743: fol. 116r: 'y axi se es feta la proceso solemne cantant per lo cami vexilla regis fins a la plassa del born [...]. sta nostra professo va causar gran terror al poble'.

53 Zaragoza i Pascual 2005–2006: 309: 'per a assistir a festes, mercats i fer visites, com freqüentment succeïa, i en tot cas havien d'anar acompanyades d'una altra monja designada per l'abadessa'.

54 For a chronology of the entry of royal figures in Barcelona, from the visit of Ferdinand of Aragon in 1479 to that of Margaret Theresa of Spain in 1666, see Chamorro 2013: 427–430.

55 Raventós (2006: 100) presents a diagram with the order of the retinue in royal entries in Barcelona, including the trumpets, clarions, and drums of the city and of the king. For a map of the itinerary of Charles V's entry in Barcelona, see Raventós 2006: 108.

56 Cases *et al.* 1994: vol. 1, 271–272 (see Appendix 4.2) and *Manual de novells ardits...*, vol. 3, p. 96 (23 October 1492). For references to the previous royal stays at the nunnery, see *Manual de novells ardits...*, vol. 3, pp. 8 (21 August 1479), 18 (26 July 1481), and 19-20 (5 November 1481).

57 Paulí 1972: 53; *Ceremonial dels magnífichs consellers...*, vol. 1, p. 245.

58 Cases *et al.* 1994: vol. 1, 421–422. See also *Manual de novells ardits...*, vol. 3, p. 463.

59 Hierro 1564: fol. A3r: 'salio el abadesa con todo el conuento en procesion a recebirle [...]. Venia el conuento junto cantando: tua est potentia, y respondiendo el coro dellas por punto: tuum regnum domine, tu es super omnes gentes: y luego tornaua el convento, y dezia: Da pacem domine in diebus nostris: ha esto respondia el coro. Creator omnium, deus terribilis & fortis, iustus & misericors'. On Philip II's entry in Barcelona, see Raventós 2006: 59 and Appendix 4.2 (5 February 1564).

60 For a study of the links between liturgy, plainchant, and royal power, showing how Hernando de Talavera and Cardinal Cisneros drew on plainchant in order to reinforce the image of the Catholic Monarchs, and how Cisneros attempted to legitimise the process of 'reconquest' through the recovery of the Mozarabic liturgy, see Castillo-Ferreira 2016.

61 Raventós 2006: 60: 'dimarts 18 maig de 1599. Extractada la ressenya de l'arxiu catedralici, diu: que a les dotze del migdia isqué del Palau, S. M. el Rei Felip III, amb quatre carrosses acompanyat dels servidors, i se n'anà secretament al Monestir de Valldonzella, de monges de Sant Bernat. Arribat allí, el reberen en processó a les portes de l'església portant cadascuna a les mans el clpassic ciri de cera blanca. Ja es trobava a punt l'Abat de Poblet, Fran Joan Tarrós, que, revestit de Pontifical, li donava l'aigua beneida amb un "salpasser", ensems que li presentpa per l'adoració, la "Vera Creu", començant tot seguit el cant del "Te Deum", entrant la processó a l'església als acords de l'orgue a cada "verset"'.

62 For an earlier instance of participation of the nuns of Santa Maria de Jonqueres in the procession of the relics of Santa Eulàia in 1334, see *Ceremonial dels magnífichs consellers...*, vol. 3, p. 70.
63 *Manual de novells ardits...*, vol. 3, pp. 276–277: 'En aquest dia las Rev.ts monjas del monastir de Sanct Pere de les puellas de la present Ciutat de Barchinona faheren professo ques diu de les octavas de Corpore Xpi. Axi a las horas sis apres dinar, la qual parti de dit monastir et tira per lo carrer de SAnct Pere subirá fins al carrer qui travessa al carrer de Sanct Pere jussa et ix devant lo carrer den Fonellar et girant a ma Esquerra tira per lo dit carrer de Sanct Peere jussa, e torna en dit monasteir. Lorde de la qual es lo seguent, que primer anave la bandera dels ortolans, e los ortolans de dos en dos ab ciris en las mans, apres anaven los ganfanons y apres la creu de Sanct Pere, apres los capellans qui eren en nombre de XXX poch mes o menyns ab los sobrepellisos cantant, e portant ciris en la ma, apres venien las monjas ordonades de dos en dos ab los ciris blanchs encesos en la ma, apres venien set musichs vestits ab dalmáticas sonant instrument de corda, apres venia la custodia sobre una civera que aportaven preveres ab los camis, e stolas vestits et desus lo talem qui aportaven homens de honor de la parrochia, e altres, apres venie la Rev.t abbadessa ab la crossa y un ciri blanch en la ma en mix de dos preveres vestits com a diacas, e sotsdiacas, apres venien alguns homens de condijo e altres portant ciris encesos, e molta altre gent per devocio. Tots los carrres per hont passa dita professo eren molt regats scombrats, e los enfronts empaliats, e envelats los cels, de loch en loch ab altars molt en orda y cosa de devotio. Placie a N.e S.r deu ho accepte en servey y las deix perseverar quiscun any en auctmentatio de bones obres pera tots amen'.
64 Paulí 1968: 13. He points out that the festivities are described in detail in the convent 'chronicles'.
65 Marca 1764: 352–353: 'salieron las Hermanas con la Madre Fornès de la Casa, y en ordenada Procession se encaminaron à su Iglesia, donde assitia el Rey [Felipe II], con toda la Grandeza de su Corte, y muchos Prelados Eclesiasticos. Se cantò la Missa, y esta concluida; en manos del dicho Ministro General hizieron los Votos essenciales de Religion, con el de Clausura todas las Señoras arriba referidas'.
66 Pi 1854: 240, n. 6: 'fueron depositados sus restos en la iglesia de San Francisco de Asis. En su entierro iban a pie detrás del féretro tres reinas, cubiertas con mantos sus cabezas, Doña María esposa del monarca reinante, Doña Violante viuda del rey D. Jaime, y Doña Margarita, del Rey D. Martin; y en otro manuscrito del mismo archivo se lee, que concurrieron á dicho entierro, á mas de todo el clero secular y regular de la ciudad, la Abadesa y Religiosas del Monasterio de San Pedro de las Puellas y del de Valldoncella, y la Priora y Religiosas del de Junqueras'.
67 *Manual de novells ardits...*, vol. 3, pp. 38–39.
68 See Appendix 4.2. This report is included under the section devoted to 12 March, but on 19 March it is said: '19 de marzo de 1562 Festum beati Josefi. Lo que da dalt stà continuat, a XII del present mes, de les monjes dels Àngells, stà continuat per erra, que ha de star al present dia'. See also *Ceremonial dels magnífichs consellers...*, vol. 3, cap. 42: 'A 19 de Mars 1562: Professó de las Monjas dels Angels quant se mudaren al peu de la Creu'.

4 Music to reach heaven

Music was considered not only a symbol of earthly power, but also as a channel between earth and heaven (Kreitner 2004: 52; Perpiñà 2013). Tess Knighton has demonstrated through an in-depth exploration of notarial documentation that in Barcelona a variety of source material shows a frequent celebration of postmortem Masses and Offices with music endowed by a broad cross-section of citizens in their wills (Knighton 2017a). The various typologies of Masses for the dead were regarded as an efficacious way to relieve the suffering of the souls in Purgatory, and they usually took place on the day of the death, after nine days, thirty days, and on the anniversary of the death. Many of these ceremonies were founded in convent churches and were endowed by individuals, including the nuns themselves and high-status women, and also by confraternities and guilds. Music was commonly stipulated for these celebrations, so that these endowments can be regarded as a kind of 'hidden' music patronage. Only by comparing scattered details in various types of documents—such as wills, account books, bills, and records of anniversaries, among many others—is it possible to assess the extent to which music was present in the post-mortem ceremonies celebrated in urban nunneries and their impact on the aural experience of Barcelona's citizens.

The particular involvement of Barcelona's nuns and noblewomen in devotional activities might have fomented this form of musical patronage. Scholars like Barbara Newman and June Meecham have studied women's concern for the souls of the dead, and their importance in the religious culture of death. While Newman (2013) has theorised about the overlapping between the 'sacred' and the 'secular' in the medieval period, Meecham (2014) has challenged the differences between monastic and lay piety in late medieval Germany, arguing that nuns and laywomen participated in a shared religious culture (Meecham 2014). This is applicable to Barcelona convents, where many nuns belonged to nobility. In the Iberian world, women's participation in the patronage of music in the early modern period was influenced by the particularly strong involvement of women in Christian morality (Marshall 1989: 2; Amelang 1990: 191; Erdman 1999: ix–xii). These moral controversies, together with the problems raised by women's role in a professional sphere, constitute a conceptual framework for an understanding of Iberian women's music-making in the early modern period (Mazuela-Anguita 2016b). However, one way in which women were constantly

DOI: 10.4324/9781003292371-5

pushing the boundaries of what was acceptable was in the patronage of music and the organisation of, as well as participation in, musical events. These organisational activities, which frequently took place in convents' spaces, can, and should, also be seen as a form of music-making, as in the studies undertaken by Therese Martin in the field of art history in which she reconsidered the verb 'to make', arguing that, while the perspective of modern historians has tended to separate patron from artist, the medieval view recognised both as makers (Martin 2012).

Clergymen, nuns, female choristers (*escolanas*), choirboys, deacons, sub-deacons, and organists were usually responsible for the post-mortem musical celebrations in convent churches. They were generally sung in plainchant, so that the cases in which polyphony is referred to must be highlighted because of their significance. The seventeen convents active in sixteenth-century Barcelona were used as performative spaces where it was possible to establish, through the music performed by nuns and clergymen, a connection between the earthly and the celestial worlds. In this way, nuns' music both reflected and influenced a city's spiritual health (Stras 2018: 14, 303). The city councillors usually ordered that the nuns said prayers pleading with God for military victories. For example, the city chroniclers recorded that, on 13 August 1532, the councillors distributed the prayers to ask for the king's victory in Hungary among the different male and female religious institutions of the city so that they were done *sine intermissione* (Table 4.1).

Convents played a mediating role between the citizens and the divine and exerted a social function by celebrating these liturgical ceremonies.[1] One of the reasons for the important role played by convents in urban musical life was related to a popular believe in music as a means to shorten the time the soul would spend in Purgatory and reach heaven safely, both before and after the Council of Trent.[2] This also involves a gendered aspect, namely the 'hidden' nature of nuns, and the identification of their voices with those of asexual angels, which links to a corpus of ideas disseminated in the early modern Iberian world, mentioned above, about women's music-making and morality.

Invisiblis melodia

The experience of sound emanating from high places and the frequent use of adjectives such as celestial or angelic to describe nuns' music in early modern writings suggest that the perception of nuns' voices as belonging to angels was part of popular culture. For example, as shown in Chapter 3, according to a chronicle of the beatification feast of Teresa of Ávila in Saragossa in 1614, nuns spent the night in the upper storeys of their convents singing 'motets and villancicos with celestial voices in concerted choirs' so that their singing could be heard from some distance away, and one nun is recorded as singing the antiphon *Veni sponsa Christi* in such a celestial way that it seemed impossible that her voice did not belong to an angel (Díex de Aux 1615: 44). The use of music at the feasts for the beatification of Saint Teresa in Madrid Carmelite convents was also described as an emulation of the celestial choir: 'who could refer to these days' diversity of

Table 4.1. Prayers *sine intermissione* to be said in Barcelona convents every day to ask God for a victory in Hungary, according to the resolution made by the city councillors on 13 August 1532 (*Manual de novells ardits...*, vol. 3, pp. 453–454)

Time	Performers
10 to 11am	Jerusalem nuns
11am to 12pm	Els Àngels nuns
12 to 1pm	Pedralbes nuns
1 to 2pm	Montsió nuns
2 to 3pm	Montalegre nuns
3 to 4pm	Jonqueres nuns
4 to 5pm	Santa Clara nuns
5 to 6pm	Sant Pere nuns
6 to 7pm	Santa Maria Magdalena nuns
7 to 8pm	Valldonzella nuns
8 to 9pm	Les Jerònimes nuns
9 to 10pm	Sant Agustí friars
10 to 11pm	Santa Caterina friars
11pm to 12am	Carme friars
12 to 1am	Mercè friars
1 to 2am	Sant Francesc friars
2 to 3am	Jesús friars
3 to 4am	Cartoixa de Montalegre friars
4 to 5am	Sant Jeroni de la Murtra friars
5 to 6am	Sant Jeroni de Vall d'Hebrón friars
6 to 7am	Santa Anna canons and benefice-holders
7 to 8am	Sant Pau friars

music, as much of voices as of instruments, which divided into choirs imitated the music of the angels' choirs'.[3] A chronicle about the Dominican convent of Santa Maria Magdalena in Valencia, founded in the thirteenth century and located at what is now Mercado Square until Mendizábal's ecclesiastical dissolution, acts as a further example of the link between nuns' singing and the celestial world, in addition to showing the connection between convents and their social surroundings through music.[4] Caterina de Castro, prioress of this nunnery from 1594, ordered that a 'most solemn' *Salve* was sung at the convent chapel of Our Lady with 'much music' every Saturday. This event was attended by the local residents, who brought candles while, according to the chronicler, the nuns' voices resonated from the choir, emulating those of angels, with the convent even being identified with heaven in the text (Beaumont 1725: 110).

The association of nuns' voices with those of angels was essentially a form of disembodying these female voices as if they did not belong to real women. The dichotomy between celestial and sensual, which was a general issue in religious music from the time of Saint Augustine, acquired more relevance in the case of nuns' voices, to the point that nuns' singing was a constant target for reformers after—but also before—the Council of Trent (Knighton 2017b). In 1494 the Catholic Monarchs appointed Cardinal Cisneros as a reformer and visitor of the Poor Clare nuns in Castile and several case studies show the ways in which his Franciscan spirituality affected musical life and singing in nunneries. In a panegyric written by the humanist Hernando Alonso de Herrera (1460–1527) it is said that women had a debt to Cisneros, since he had taught nuns to live 'more demurely' (*más recatadamente*) and founded convents and schools for young girls (cited in Bataillon 1966 [1937]: 4). These female institutions founded by Cisneros have been considered a reflection of his interest in women's education and seen as radical for its period. For instance, Cisneros founded both the convent of San Juan de la Penitencia in Alcalá de Henares and the school of Santa Isabel—related to the convent of the same name—which was aimed at the education of young girls who would later decide to marry or to become nuns. The same institutional setup was used for the convent of San Juan de la Penitencia in Toledo, which is considered the first educational institution for women in the city. When Cisneros died, the person in charge of giving final form to the project was his secretary, Francisco Ruiz, Bishop of Ávila, a former *seise* (young choirboy) of Toledo Cathedral, very praised for his musical skills, who finalised the rules of the convent and the statutes of the school.[5] The constitutions of the convent, completed in 1520, included a prohibition of singing the Divine Office *por punto*, that is, which melodies, in order to avoid 'human gestures and useless voices', as God delights in 'the purety and devotion of the heart rather than in the sound of the voice'. The Office should be 'prayed or *en tono*', appealing to the abbess's judgement:

> The Divine Office should be celebrated devotionally in the choir at nights and during the day, in such a way that before the beginning of the Hours [...] nuns come to the choir to link their hearts to God and stay there calmly, without noise, far from laughter and vain observance, quietly and peacefully, with the proper seriousness; therefore, beloved sisters, I warned you to praise God in a comprehensive, attentive, and honest way. The Divine Office never will be sung *por punto* [using melodic inflexion], with the purpose of avoiding human gestures and useless voices, which are not pleasant to God, who takes more delight from the pureness and devotion of the heart than from the sound of the voice. You are allowed to say your Office prayed or *en tono*, in the way ordered by the abbess.[6]

In *El Melopeo y maestro* (Naples, 1613), Pietro Cerone explained that, when performing plainchant, 'the rule about accent should be observed when it is sung *sin punto*', while 'this rule did not have to be observed when plainchant is sung *por punto*, since in this case the sounds should be pronounced as indicated by the ligatures or neumes'.[7] Despite this rejection of the voice for its sensuality, a 1666 decree by José de la Cruz, the provincial father, indicates that 'abuses' occurred at the convent of San Juan de la Penitencia in Toledo, such as the learning of polyphonic singing, harp, and other instruments in the parlour and through the grille of the choir.[8]

Likewise, the rules of the convent of the Concepción Francisca in Toledo suggest a similar simplicity regarding the use of music in the divine worship. In 1506 Cisneros established the Franciscan observance in this Poor Clare community. The document that contains the rules and ordinances of this convent was dated in Rome in 1511 and seems to be written by the official visitor to the convent—as it refers to the 'pastoral service to me entrusted'.[9] It is indicated that the nuns had to say the Office according to the Roman breviary as the Franciscan friars did. Following this, the rules of Francisco de Quiñones, great renovator of Poor Clare convents, are included. According to these, the Office had to be celebrated always *en tono* with the prescribed pause in the middle of the verse', except on the main feast days, when it had to be celebrated 'singing devotionally, abandoning all banal chant and augmentation of *puntos*'.[10]

The school of young girls of San Juan de la Penitencia in Toledo was followed by the school of Nuestra Señora de los Remedios (later Real Colegio de Doncellas Nobles), founded by Cardinal Silíceo in 1551—and where he would be buried. At first, it was inhabited by young girls of poor origin who were provided with an education to become Christian wives; subsequently, the school was patronised by Philip II and noblewomen were also received. Its rules establish that the young girls had to read 'books in the vernacular about the lives of saints and about good doctrines' in the refectory; these books would be chosen by the archbishop of Toledo. After lunch and dinner, these girls had to walk together in procession to the choir, singing softly (*en tono bajo*) a hymn composed by the cardinal in praise of the Virgin.[11] However, it seems that this hymn was not never actually composed, due to the illness and death of Silíceo.

One consequence of the reforms fostered by Cisneros, and the musical simplicity they prescribed, might be the absence of references to nuns making music in Franciscan convents in Toledo until the middle of the sixteenth century, as reflected in Colleen Baade's studies. The first Franciscan nun organist identified by Baade is María de Vozmediano, a nun at the convent of San Antonio de Padua between 1553 and 1555 (Baade 2011). These rejections of the voice for its sensuality, which preceded the Council of Trent, evoked Erasmus and Saint Augustine's ideas according to which 'a rumbling of voices and of the organs from which nothing is understood' was not the essence of the divine worship.[12] The twenty-fifth session of the Council, which took place in 1563, addressed convents' musical practices, prohibiting polyphonic singing in convents:

> Let the divine services be accomplished by them with voices raised, and not by professionals hired for that purpose; and in the sacrifice of the Mass let them make the responses that the choir usually makes; but let them not usurp the role of the deacon and sub-deacon of reciting the Lessons, Epistles, and Gospels. Let them abstain from modulating and inflecting the voice or from other artifice of singing, which is called 'figured' or 'instrumental' as much in choir as elsewhere.[13]

However, as Craig Monson indicates, finally 'convent polyphony apparently' was 'saved', since the Council stated that this issue will be left to be decided by the heads of the religious orders and that 'musical singing is not to be prohibited'.[14] The variety of 'attitudes toward the implementation of Tridentine legislation regarding female monasteries' depended on religious attitudes, and the consequence was the 'richly varied practice that would characterize post-Tridentine music in the Catholic world' (Monson 2002: 27–28). Laurie Stras considered that knowledge was key: unison chant did not require knowledge, so no one prevented nuns from singing this.[15] In Spain, restrictions were stricter than elsewhere in the Catholic world, since any type of melodic inflexion was prohibited, probably because the focus of Spanish theologians was not on the nun but on her listener. Thus, the restrictions on nuns' music were an example of masculine control after, but also before, the Council of Trent. At the same time, it is difficult to assess to what extent the prohibitions were observed, since references to the breach of the rules are frequently found in a variety of documentation.

In the case of Barcelona, Diego Pérez de Valdivia, the Franciscan preacher from Baeza (Jaén) who had founded the charity house of the Misericordia in the city (see Chapter 1), wrote a treatise praising chastity which was printed in Barcelona in 1587 (Figure 4.1).[16] This book included a chapter on nuns' singing and playing musical instruments, which referred to the prescriptions of the Council of Trent (Knighton 2017b: 65–66). Pérez de Valdivia stated his preference that nuns did not sing at all—neither polyphony nor plainchant—nor played any musical instruments, including the organ:

> My wish is that everyone does their job. Clergymen's tasks are both to sing for the people and to celebrate the Mass. Singing is not appropriate for virgins, as they use to have such a pleasant voice that it suits the taste of men, and it is not good for them to sing in such a way that men praise their voices and know the identity of each nun through her voice, or that men visit convents to listen to nuns' singing, rather than to attend the Divine Office, as it occurs sometimes, when not very spiritual people prefer women's music (especially when they sing polyphony) to the Word of God which is being sung. My heart would wish that nuns were not identified or seen by men, nor sang polyphony or plainchant nor had organs or another musical instrument. I would like the choir to be a place for pure prayer, where nuns do not pay attention to sing in tune or out of tune, and use a modest, devotional, and low voice, which inspires them to devotion and does not prevent them from contemplation. Nuns must say their canonical Hours for God and for themselves, as it is done in many monasteries in Rome.[17]

This book achieved wide circulation. It was reprinted in Barcelona by Gabriel Graells y Giraldo Dotil in 1608, with a dedication to Juana Pacheco, Countess of Miranda and Vicereine of Catalonia (1583–1586), but also in Baeza by Juan Bautista de Montoya in 1597, at the request of Isabel de Valdivia, the author's sister, in the name of his heirs. However, Pérez de Valdivia's description of

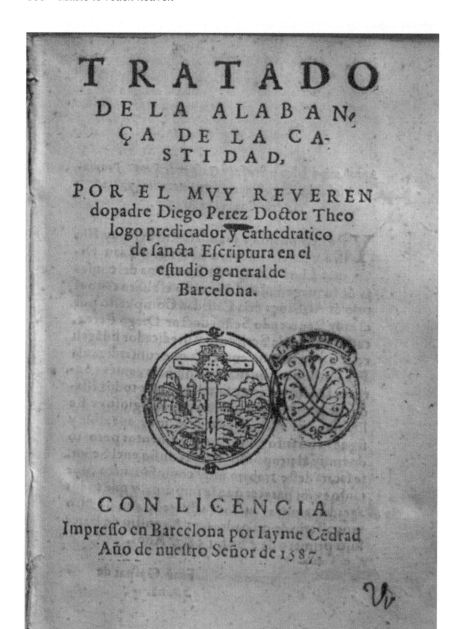

Figure 4.1. Diego Pérez de Valdivia, *Tratado de alabança de la castidad* (Barcelona: Iayme Cendrad, 1587). Rome, Biblioteca Universitaria Alessandrina, Q a 66. Public Domain

nuns' musical practices and his censorship of polyphony—and almost any form of music—may have related to his experience at a particular Barcelona convent, namely the Dominican convent of Els Àngels, where he stayed on his arrival in Barcelona and served as a confessor. Knighton has used a 1635 biography of Pérez de Valdivia written by Luis Muñoz (d.1646) as a source in order to explore how polyphonic singing was a contested issue between the nuns of this convent and external authorities (Knighton 2017b: 67). At this nunnery, which was inhabited by members of Barcelona's social elite (see Chapter 1), the Divine Office was sung in polyphony 'with too much affectation' and using a tune that was 'more pleasant to the ear than decent to the cult'. As a result, the men turned towards the choir to see the nun singers (Figure 4.2). Pérez de Valdivia reprehended this behaviour and some nuns protested to Joan Dimas Loris, the Bishop of Barcelona.[18]

A further source regarding the polyphonic practices at the convent of Els Àngels is the *Tratado de las virtudes* of the mystic writer Isabel de Rocabertí

Figure 4.2. Choir of the convent of the Mare de Déu dels Àngels in Barcelona (photographed in 1918). BC, Fons fotogràfic Salvany. Creative Commons

(alias Hipòlita de Jesús), daughter of Francesc Dalmau, Viscount of Rocabertí.[19] She entered the convent of Els Àngels when she was eleven years old and wrote around twenty works which would be published posthumously by her nephew Joan Tomàs de Rocabertí, Archbishop of Valencia. In her *Tratado de las virtudes* she wrote about her experience singing the verses *O salutaris hostia, / quae caeli pandis ostium, / bella premunt hostilia; da robur, fer auxilium* in the choir with her fellow nuns. She explained that, after this hymn, 'the Benedictus was sung in polyphony, one verse by the choir and the other verse by the organ', and, since she did not have to sing this, she was able to reflect on the hymn's celestial words.[20] These verses are the fifth strophe of Thomas Aquinas's six-stanza hymn *Verbum Supernum Prodiens*, performed at Lauds on the Corpus Christi celebration. This stanza along with the last one (the doxology) was used as an independent hymn sung for the Benediction with the Blessed Sacrament. According to the use of Barcelona Cathedral, this hymn was always sung in *alternatim* with the organ, all the singers on their knees, and the stanza *O salutaris hostia* was always sung— even though it corresponded to the organ (Puentes-Blanco 2018: 379). Polyphonic settings of this hymn are preserved in Catalan sources. For instance, the book of polyphony *E-Bbc 682*, copied between c.1572 and 1597, includes a four-voice setting of this hymn (fols. 39v–40r) ascribed to Jean Maillard (*fl.*1538–1572). However, there is no evidence to relate this book to the convent of Els Àngels. Instead, its origin has been connected to the diocese of Girona.[21] The same hymn appears in the *Musica quinque vocum motteta materna lingua vocata* (Venice, 1543), which is considered the earliest printed polyphonic music for nuns, attributed to Suor Leonora d'Este (1515–1575) and contextualized at the convent of Corpus Domini in Ferrara.[22] Thus, references to Barcelona nuns' polyphonic singing are found in the sixteenth century, although it is difficult to identify the particular repertory associated with these convents.

Pérez de Valdivia's recommendation against any nuns from practising music may well have been the result of the musical practices at a particular convent— Els Àngels—and was motivated by concern for nuns' chastity. This particular fear about music, born out of the alluring aural and visual contact between men and nuns involved in it, was deeper in Iberian lands than elsewhere in Europe. In the case of Italian noblewomen, Laurie Stras has studied how music was affected by the concept of *sprezzatura*, used by Baldasarre Castiglione, that is, 'the art that conceals art' (Stras 2018: 57). The reputation of a courtesan was ambiguous, as she 'relied on cultivating rather than obfuscating her own brilliance' (Stras 2018: 59). Moreover, a noblewoman's virtuosity was an ornament which may become a means by which 'she could be disgraced' (Stras 2018: 74). Likewise, the moral status of music depended on a woman's age: 'the young girl's prodigious accomplishments, acquired as part of her grooming for marriage, might take on an air of desperation or even indecency if practiced by an older woman' (Stras 2018: 144). In the Iberian world, from at least the time of Francesc Eiximenis, whose writings, such as his *Llibre de les dones*—written in c.1396 and printed in Barcelona in 1495—were widely influential, music and dance were traditionally held to exemplify women's loose morality. This attitude continued to prevail in Spanish treatises on female conduct of the sixteenth century, which generally considered that it was unacceptable for women to be associated with public forms of entertainment. According to Pilar Ramos, the moral status of music was lower in the Iberian world 'than in Italian or Franco-Flemish lands mainly because of moralists' criticism of leisure' (Ramos López 2009: 255, 271). Ramos's hypothesis is that the rejection of women practising music in Spain in the context of secular entertainment 'can be partly explained by the context of Muslim and Jewish cultural heritage' (Ramos López 2015: 419).

Elizabeth Eva Leach has analysed the figure of the siren in the medieval period, describing it as 'a hybrid bird-woman with a beautiful but deadly song, which is used to encapsulate the related moral perils of the bestial, the feminine, and the sexual'; Leach has also studied how medieval writers connected 'beautiful but immoral music' to the feminine.[23] Likewise, female musical practices were connected to the idea of the 'savage woman', a character in medieval literature who attracted men through song. The association between women's voices and irrationality is also reflected in seventeenth-century English broadside ballads, as Sarah F. Williams has discussed.[24] Moreover, both demonology treatises and Inquisition records qualified witches' singing as seductive and extremely beautiful, as it was a deception of the Devil (Mazuela-Anguita 2015c). Regarding music in Bologna convents, Craig Monson states that even nuns were said to have charms 'to learn how to sing and play through diabolical arts'.[25]

However, female musical inspiration was understood not only in terms of demonic possession but also as divine intervention, as was reflected in the story of Clara Savall (d.1592), an instructor of novices in the Barcelona convent of Pedralbes. One day, a Mass in the honour of the archangel Saint Michael—to whom Clara Savall had a great devotion—had to be sung, and the singers were not able to do it. However, she made nuns who had never previously sung to perform the Office, and with the archangel's help, the singing was said to be perfect (Anzizu 1897: 149). Another example is that of Saint Christina Mirabilis (c.1150–1224), a German shepherdess who died as a child (Newman 2008; Brown 2009; Figure 4.3). According to legend, after she had visited Purgatory, God gave her an opportunity for resurrection and to do penance for the salvation of souls in Purgatory. As she was able to fly and her body recovered from any pain, her family thought that she was possessed by the Devil and, over her entire life, she suffered from torture, which she accepted offering her pain to souls in Purgatory. What God gave her in return was a soft and melodic inner music, which could be heard between her chest and her throat while she was in silence:

> Surio [Laurentius Surius (1522-1578), a German Carthusian hagiographer] points out that, while she [Saint Christina Mirabilis] was as still as a wood, not moving her mouth or eyelashes, as she was sleeping, those who approached her perceived an angelical music and melody inside her, between her chest and her throat. This music was so soft, sweet, and beautiful that a man with the best musical instruments and voices in the world would not be

Figure 4.3. Portrait of Saint Christina Mirabilis (c.1150–1224). Vienna, Österreichische Nationalbibliothek, PORT_00113353_01. Public Domain

able to imitate the softness that resounded between the chest and the throat of the admirable Christina.[26]

This *exemplum* was included in a book on Purgatory entitled *Tratado del purgatorio contra Luthero y otros herejes con singular y varia dotrina de mucho provecho y muy util para predicadores, curas, religiosos y para todos los estados*, written by Dimas Serpi, the provincial minister of the Franciscan Order in Sardinia (Figure 4.4). It was in Barcelona where this very popular and widely circulated book, which has been considered 'the most popular treatise on Purgatory in the Spanish Golden Age' (Sullivan 1996: 88), was first printed in 1600.[27]

According to Gary Tomlinson, music worked in this period as a form of celestial magic, connected to the concept of the music of the spheres.[28] As discussed in recent studies in the field of Renaissance English literature,[29] sound was regarded as something where the human and nonhuman overlapped, and human singing might be 'an echo of the wordless song of angels'.[30] Consequently, during urban festivities such as those studied in Chapter 3, when nuns' voices reached the people and their surroundings, the chroniclers' identification of nuns' voices with those of angels may be related not only to nuns' musical practices, but also to the reception of women making music in general. If nuns' music was identified with the celestial, it must have fulfilled the demands on women to be humble, modest, and chaste, and satisfied the complaints against women who felt pride in themselves (see Haliczer 2002: 136). Furthermore, this was also connected to the impact of nuns' singing on their audience: nuns' music should have a devotional—not sensual—influence on those who listened to it. Hadewijch, who was a beguine who lived in the mid-thirteenth century in the Low Countries, possibly in Antwerp, drew on the language of courtly love to write this verse: 'Her deepest silence is her sublime song'.[31]

Richard Rolle of Hampole (1290?–1349), recognised as the first mystic in England, received, while singing psalms, 'the gift of mystical *melos* or *canor*, an unearthly spiritual experience of sound with ineffably sweet "harmony"' (Figure 4.5).[32] He describes this first inner musical experience of the *canor* in *Incendium amoris* (Rolle of Hampole 1915: 189). Riehle considers that the *canor* is therefore connected to mysticism as a type of 'auditive vision'. Rolle had received a musical training, which is demonstrated in the detailed references to music included in his writings: 'he sometimes equates *contemplatio* directly with listening to the divine *canor*, and uses terms such as *invisiblis melodia, sonos coelestis, canticum spirituale* as synonyms' (Riehle 2014). Andrew Albin has analysed how the nuns at Hampole Priory 'incarnated' *canor* 'through the performance of liturgy': 'For them, *canor* may very well have been the melodies they themselves sang in the presence of Richard Rolle's tomb, in their capacity as vessels through which inward mystical song graciously flowed into acoustic space' (Albin 2016: 1038). Therefore, the idea that nuns' voices were angelic was deeply embedded in both popular and official religious ideals and practices from the Middle Ages and, not surprisingly, Barcelona convents were frequently employed as 'acoustic spaces' to make a connection to the celestial realm through the foundation of liturgical ceremonies with music at the request of a variety of people.

Figure 4.4. Dimas Serpi, *Tratado del purgatorio contra Luthero y otros herejes con singular y varia dotrina de mucho provecho y muy útil para predicadores, curas, religiosos y para todos los estados* (Barcelona: Iayme Cendrat, 1604 [Barcelona: Gabriel Graells y Giraldo Dótil, 1600]). Monistrol de Montserrat (Barcelona), Biblioteca de la Abadia. Public Domain

Figure 4.5. Richard the Hermit (Richard Rolle), in 'The Desert of Religion', ink and pigments on vellum, 1425. London, British Library, Cotton MS Fastina B VI, vol. II, fol. 8v.

Leaving Purgatory: A form of music patronage for everyone

Barcelona convents were deeply embedded in the citizens' daily life through the 'foundation', that is, the personal funding and institution, of post-mortem ceremonies such as burials and anniversaries, which frequently included music and acted as an interface between nunneries and urban life. The financing of liturgical celebrations for devotional purposes, or to relieve the suffering of the soul in

Purgatory, constituted an indirect but important type of musical patronage which was widely practised in the Iberian world in the early modern period, carried out by citizens from different socioeconomic sectors; this aspect has been generally overlooked in musicological studies. This form of music patronage, linked to popular and official religious practices, was particularly related to women in general and to nuns and powerful women in particular.

Convents were private spaces which served as a public setting in which, for instance, noblewomen were able to display social status through religious patronage. In the Iberian context, from the late fifteenth century the process of constant reform fuelled by the Catholic Monarchs and Cardinal Cisneros promoted an intensification of popular religiosity. This led to the proliferation of liturgical ceremonies with music endowed mostly by women belonging to the circle of Queen Isabel, who both patronised and experimented with music in convents' spaces. Such a socially acceptable activity was, at the same time, a 'hidden' form of music patronage. Noblewomen belonging to the circle of the Catholic Monarchs founded numerous Franciscan convents. For instance, Beatriz Galindo, tutor of the royal house children, founded the convent of the Inmaculada Concepción in Madrid in 1512, among other religious institutions. In 1470, Catalina Núñez, a *converso* and widow of Alfonso Álvarez de Toledo, chief treasurer of Enrique IV and *contador mayor* of Castile at the time of the Catholic Monarchs, founded another emblematic example, the Franciscan convent of Santa Clara in Madrid, originally located between Espejo and Santa Clara Streets and torn down during the French occupation in the nineteenth century. The earliest documents from this nunnery, which form part of a collection preserved at the AHN, provide information on the funding, mostly by women, of post-mortem sung masses.[33] For instance, Catalina Ruiz de Tapia and her husband Juan de Cuervo, both *camareros* of Catalina of Aragon, founded a chapel at the convent of Santa Clara in Madrid, where they wished to be buried. In her 1531 will, Catalina Ruiz stipulated her burial dressed in Franciscan habit and, among the hundreds of masses that she funded, she asked for the celebration of as many masses as possible on the day of her burial for the salvation of her soul, including a Requiem Mass with deacon and sub-deacon.[34] In this way, the documents remaining from the earliest years of this convent reveal a close connection between music patronage, Franciscan devotion, and women in positions of power (Mazuela-Anguita 2016b).

The same connection is found in other regions of Catholic Europe. The Poor Clare convent of Corpus Domini in Ferrara was favoured by the powerful Este family's women from the late fifteenth century (Stras 2018: 22). Eleonora d'Aragona was buried in the choir in 1493, establishing a tradition that lasted until the Estes took leave. Alfonso I left a bequest to these nuns so that they sang perpetually for his soul, and Lucrezia Borgia was buried there dressed in Franciscan habit. It seems that Duchess Margherita Gonzaga and Lucrezia Borgia had distributed the city convents between themselves as regards patronage. Margherita was granted papal permission to enter female and male religious institutes. The analysis of the connections between the Este women and the city convents in the 1580s developed by Stras demonstrates that these noblewomen used convents as extensions of their courts. In particular, Stras draws on Bottigari's treatises to argue that the Este used San Vito convent in that period as an extension of the court for the celebration of courtesan entertainments. Duchess Margherita Gonzaga and her ladies were frequent visitors to the city convents and, although there is no evidence of collaboration between nuns and the duchess's ladies, they accompanied Margherita to the convents, so that they may have sung and played along with the nuns and have had access to nuns as teachers (Stras 2018: 239). Later in Mantua, Margherita 'began the process of establishing a new convent of Sant'Orsola' in 1599 and she put herself at the head of the community. In 1608 she 'petitioned the Pope for permission to participate in the Office with the nuns', which involved 'a significant move away from her lifetime position as a listener to one of physical engagement with music' (Stras 2018: 322–325). Stras has analysed the formation of a reciprocal musical transfer between convents and the noble court, which influenced the music repertory composed in the city and its distinctive musical and performance style:

> Throughout the sixteenth century Italian noblewomen were actively involved [in] the convents of their city, sponsoring musical activity at, and even recruiting musical talent to, their favoured houses. However, Ferrara was unique in that women not only brought musical talent and expertise into the convent, but, as the century wore on, they also brought it out again. In learning to create a new secular form of high-voice ensemble, the Ferrarese women, and the men who composed for them, could draw on their nuns' decades of experience in adapting polyphony for equal-voice performance of moderating and even exploiting the potential for transgressive or dissonant sonorities, of negotiating ensemble ornamentation in a limited tessitura. To this they added the Ferrarese predilection for the dramatic, the musically esoteric, and, perhaps most brilliantly, the new style of solo singing emerging from the south. By the end of the 1570s, these elements had begun to crystalize into a distinctive musical style that merged the art of singing with the practice of polyphony, and a performance style that began to emphasize the distance between musicians and audience. (Stras 2018: 168)

The lack of sources for the repertory performed by Iberian nuns in the sixteenth century, beyond that preserved in chant books (see Chapter 2), makes it difficult to determine if a similar transfer between convents and noble houses developed. However, Iberian cases such as Ana de Mendoza (1540–1592), Princess of Eboli, suggest that these musical transfers might have occurred. She and her husband founded two Carmelite convents in Pastrana (Guadalajara), their ducal village.[35] The princess sought the presence of Teresa of Ávila, who was welcomed with a solemn procession and festivity. After her husband's death, the princess sought consolation by entering this convent, accompanied by her mother and servants. She was accused of 'disrupting' the cloistered life, and Saint Teresa asked the king to intercede to return the princess to secular life. At the end both the Carmelite nuns and the princess left the convent. Then Ana de Mendoza founded a Franciscan convent in the building abandoned by the Carmelite nuns, which was connected to the ducal palace by a passageway,[36] resulting in a blurring between secular and religious spaces. From 1590 she was confined to a few rooms of her palace until the time of her death. During her final captivity, she commandeered a number of chaplains from the collegiate church—which she and her husband had inaugurated in 1573—to celebrate the Mass and Office in her private chapel, which was situated next to her rooms. Thus, Ana de Mendoza pushed at the boundaries of what was acceptable through her patronage of music. Even the private rooms to which she was secluded at the end of her life served as a public arena in which she strove to maintain her social status, and the patronage of religious music was one means of achieving this.

In Barcelona, the Palau de la Comtessa (Palace of the Countess) is another case in which women operated in spaces where a blurring between the private and the public, and the religious and the secular, occurred. It has been studied as an example of where women's contribution to the urban soundscape remaining invisible in the historical records, hidden behind the activities of their husbands and sons (Mazuela-Anguita 2018b). However, most of the time, it was essentially a female space, since the fathers and husbands of the women of the Requesens family who lived there were usually abroad, fulfilling their diplomatic obligations. The palace was centrally located, close to the main centres of musical activity in Barcelona such as the cathedral and main parish churches, and it was an important setting for social networking and meetings between members of the nobility, royalty, and government. The palace chapel was a significant urban focus for liturgical celebrations closely related to women's religious practices, and the Requesens women played an essential role in the foundation and development of this private chapel.

A papal bull dated 24 October 1570 accorded the high altar of the chapel of the Palau de la Comtessa the distinction of being 'privileged'. This means that the altar was granted with a Papal indulgence according to which each time a Mass was celebrated there, a soul would leave Purgatory to reach heaven, among other indulgences for those who received communion at such Masses (March 1921: 32). Given its distinction as a privileged altar, and the importance that popular religious beliefs attributed to Masses and anniversaries as a means of relieving the suffering of the souls in Purgatory, the palace chapel was a major devotional and musical centre in the urban environment. It was also an important focus for polyphonic music outside Barcelona Cathedral.

It was Estefania de Requesens (c.1504–1549), who was the wife of Charles V's *camarero*, Juan de Zúñiga y Avellaneda (1488–1546), who had the earliest known regulations for the chapel choir drawn up in 1548, and who encouraged her son to build an organ and to continue to improve her project. Her granddaughter Mencía de Requesens (1557–1608) was clearly musically educated, even though she was largely absent from Barcelona; she was responsible for the realisation of the project to build a new organ. The insights afforded by archival documents clearly suggest that, as was the case for the princess of Eboli, music played an important role for the Requesens women as a way of expressing religiosity through the patronage of the palace chapel, but also as a means of representing social status and power. Estefania de Requesens had a papal brief which allowed her to obtain licence to enter the convents of Pedralbes and Santa Maria de Jerusalem, which demonstrates not only her religious zeal, but also the porosity of the cloister and the connections between convents—even those outside the city walls—and urban life in early modern Barcelona.[37]

The personal endowment of liturgical celebrations with music in chapels and convents was linked not only with laywomen, but also with the nuns themselves. One of the account books of the nunnery of Sant Pere contains records of the anniversaries to be celebrated there between 1506 and 1540, including the names of the people who endowed them.[38] These records specify the number of nuns, choristers, clergymen, choirboys, and organists who participated, as well as the amount they received. This book also includes documents detailing all the expenses incurred by particular foundations. First of all, we find a list of anniversaries, which were held every year on the feast days of the Saint Cross (14 September) and the Conception (8 December) between 1508 and 1540.[39] On these days, between fifteen and twenty-two nuns and between eleven and nineteen choristers participated, in addition to a priest, deacon, sub-deacon, choirboy, and organist. The highest salary (12 *diners*) was paid to the organist. From 1513 onwards the participation of chaplains is also mentioned. Although the document does not include the name of the person in honour of whom the anniversaries had to be celebrated—she is referred to only as *senyora abadessa*—complementary information from other documents allows us to determine that she was Constança de Peguera, abbess of Sant Pere convent between 1490 and 1504. While this book contains details of the musical components of these foundations, another convent account book of the convent includes receipts of the 'pious cause' of Constança de Peguera alluding to payments for these Masses between 1507 and 1534 without any references to music.[40] Therefore, by consulting only the latter document, it would have been impossible to determine the presence of music in the ceremonies endowed by this abbess,[41] and other records of Mass endowment are likely to be records of musical patronage in many cases.

A further example was Lucrècia Pol, prioress of Sant Pere convent. A workbook (*libro de obra*) of 1588 includes delivery notes (*albaranes*) resulting from payments for anniversaries, *trentenaris* (or *treintanario* in Spanish, that is, a series of Masses celebrated over thirty consecutive days in honour of a deceased person), and other Masses in honour of this prioress's soul, without explicit references to music.[42] However, a book of 'foundations' shows that, for instance, on the Octave of the Corpus Christi, a liturgical ceremony with organ playing was celebrated in honour of Lucrècia Pol.[43]

The account books of Sant Pere convent contain a list of anniversaries founded by Caterina Miquel, sub-prioress of the nunnery until 1535; the expenses are higher on Saint Catalina's feast day, when she asked for the celebration of a Mass and Matins and paid for nuns, choirboys, and organists.[44] There is also an impressive list of anniversaries for the souls of two nuns named Joana and Aldonça de Peguera over a period of thirty years (1506–1536) including payments for singing and organ

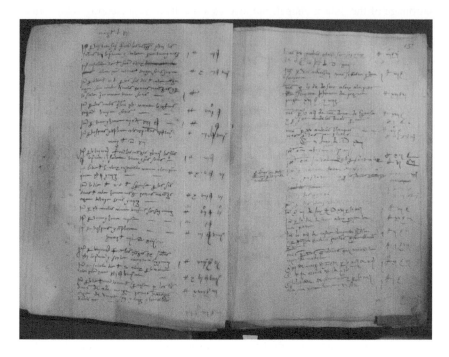

Figure 4.6. Account book containing records of anniversaries celebrated at the Barcelona convent of Sant Pere de les Puel·les between 1506 and 1540. 'Despensa feta per la anima de la señora Johana de Paguera y Aldonsa de Paguera'. AMSP, Llibres d'abadesses, no. 178, fols. 14v–15r. Photograph by the author

playing (*per festegar al orga*) (see Figure 4.6).[45] Marquesa Coloma (d.1580), a nun and member of the confraternity of Sant Magí which had been instituted in the convent, also founded anniversaries with music.[46] Another memory which has been preserved includes the anniversaries celebrated for the soul of Violant Despès, abbess of the convent between 1583 and 1596, with several references to music.[47]

A document which perfectly encapsulates the social dynamics of the celebration of anniversaries is a book in which the liturgical ceremonies to be celebrated each day of the year by the nuns of Sant Pere convent are detailed.[48] Most of the liturgical and musical celebrations recorded in which organists were explicitly referred to as participants were done in honour of the nuns themselves, such as the previously mentioned Marquesa Coloma and Constança de Peguera, as well as other sixteenth-century abbesses (Figure 4.7). These are only a few of the numerous examples of nuns of Sant Pere convent who founded post-mortem liturgical celebrations with music in the sixteenth century, recorded in a variety of documents.

Liturgical ceremonies for deaths and funerals were also extensively celebrated at the convent of Sant Antoni i Santa Clara.[49] A book of rubrics of the convent spanning the years between 1575 and 1586 specifies the arrangements to be made for every festivity as well as the celebration of anniversaries with deacon and

Music to reach heaven 173

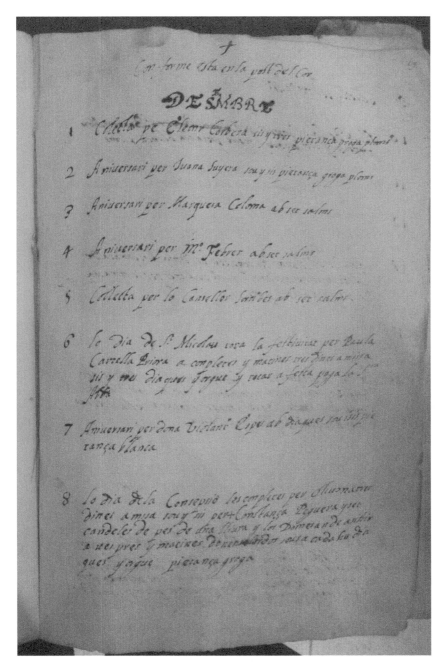

Figure 4.7. 'Llibre en lo qual estan continuats los officis y Aniuersaris que per lo discurs del any celebran la Señora Abadessa y Señoras Monges del Monastir de Sant Pere'. AMSP, Llibres de fundacions, no. 1, fol. 69r. Photograph by the author

sub-deacon. For example, according to this book, it was customary to celebrate eleven masses on the tomb of the abbess—six sung and five said—in addition to this, two Psalms of David and fifteen vigils had to be celebrated—the first vigil would be celebrated while she was dressed, and other vigils would be sung in the same way as on the Day of the Dead.[50] This book also includes a 'memory of the Masses celebrated in honour of Mrs. Vilaplana who is in the glory'. It is interesting that, at the end of this list, it is specified that all are *missas baxas* (low masses, without singing), with the exception of that celebrated on the day of the Saint Cross (3 May), which had been sung by five chaplains.[51]

Some 'ceremonies for the dead abbess' are also recorded for the case of Isabel de Vilallonga (d.1594). Fifteen vigils were prayed when this abbess died, and one was sung on her tomb. Eleven Masses were celebrated by the whole convent and two *salteris* (the complete list of psalms) were said by each black-veiled nun. When black-veiled nuns died, eleven vigils, five Masses, and one psalter had to be celebrated in their honour; in the honour of the *escolanas* (choristers) one Mass and five vigils were customary.[52] This book also includes a series of expenses related to the abbess's burial, including payments to male religious houses of the city—Trinitat, the Mercè, Sant Agustí, Santa Caterina, Sant Francesc, Nostra Senyora del Carme, Betlem, Discalced Carmelite, and Capuchin friars—for a sum of 86 *lliures* and 2 *sous*; for instance, 23 *reales* were paid to the Dominican friars of Santa Caterina for 'the three days when they helped in singing the Offices'.[53] A hundred and sixty chaplains participated in the Office of the abbess Isabel de Vilallonga's burial and another Office was celebrated by the nuns. During these days candles were given to all those who went to the church.

At the convent of Sant Antoni i Santa Clara, it was customary to celebrate a sung *misa conventual* (convent Mass) in the honour of the nuns' parents and siblings. The ceremony would take place on the day the nun who was named as the 'major singer' was available.[54] According to the documents of Sant Pere nunnery, when a lay person wanted to be buried there, if they wanted a Mass of Our Lady, the ceremony would be begun by the nuns, and the two following days Requiem Masses would be celebrated. On these three days there would be *absolta*.[55]

Not only the nuns themselves but a broader cross-section of citizens endowed these musical celebrations at Barcelona nunneries. They stipulated in their wills that they wanted to be buried in a particular convent, in family tombs, and that Masses and Offices were sung for their souls at their burial, on each of the three days after that, a week later, and on the anniversary. Some examples of lay people who founded liturgical celebrations at Sant Pere nunnery, among many others discovered by Tess Knighton in her analysis of notarial documentation, are the wills of Joan Garau de Gualba (1535), a nobleman; Guillermus Salvat (1542), an *oracioner* and member of the confraternity of the Holy Spirit; and Jaume Parera (1544) and Francesc Perit (1552), both priests and benefice-holders at the parish church of Sant Pere.[56] Elisabet Alfonsa (1588), widow of Miquel Alfonso, a pharmacist, and daughter of Miquel Saner, a cloth dyer, required an Office of Our Lady with organ to be celebrated at the church of the monastery of Sant Pere at her burial.[57] Margarida Ametller, wife of Jerònim Ametller, a butcher, stipulated in her 1589 will that, on the day of her burial, an Office had to be sung by twelve chaplains at the chapel of Sant Magí in the church of Sant Pere.[58] The calculation of the devotional and testamentary Masses celebrated at Sant Pere nunnery between June 1671 and May 1672, with a total of 2,206 Masses, gives us an idea, albeit in a later period, of the magnitude of these foundations and their contribution to the sounding life of the city.[59]

Each altar or chapel of the convent of Sant Pere was associated with benefices, which involved a series of obligations, such as the payment for anniversaries with music. Regular oversight of the benefices founded in the chapels and altars of Sant Pere church was carried out by canons chosen by the abbess and their views were recorded in books of visitations. For instance, one book of visitations contains records of the 1585 visitation initiated by Pau Caçador, canon of Barcelona Cathedral, and finished by J. Cordellas, also a canon of the cathedral, both elected by the abbess Violant Despès (1583–1596) to execute the visit.[60] The majority of the benefices recorded in books of visitations included payments for anniversaries, such as the benefice for the invocation of Saint Andrew and Saint Gabriel, instituted at the chapel and altar of Sant Andreu and Sant Sagimon and founded by Mossèn Pere Sendra, a doctor in law (*doctor en drets*), which involved the singing of the Gospel at all convent Masses.[61] At the altar of Our Lady, Juan Llavaneres, a cloth dyer, had founded a benefice in honour of the Visitation of Our Lady; the obligations of this benefice included the celebration of Masses and Offices with music and the payment for the services provided by an organist.[62] These benefices were, therefore, a form of musical patronage.

Other nunnery frequently mentioned in various wills throughout the long sixteenth century is the Poor Clare convent of Santa Maria de Jerusalem. Some of the wills studied by Knighton show that diverse citizens wanted the *assots* (a prayer about the flagellation of Christ) to be prayed for them by these nuns in particular. For example, Eleanor Galiana dels Voltrera, a merchant's widow, stipulated in her 1560 wills (two have been preserved) that, in addition to three *trentenaris* for the souls of her mother and sister in Sant Pere convent, she wanted the nuns of Santa Maria de Jerusalem to sing a Mass of the Conception for her soul, an anniversary the following day, and also 'the *assots*'.[63] Other citizens who wanted the *oracions dels assots* said in the nunnery of Santa Maria de Jerusalem were Bernardus Soler (1530), a tailor; Domingo Moradell (1552), a merchant from Girona; Joana Riera (1566); Francina Font (1566), wife of a fisherman; Àngela Scardona (1568, will read in 1572); and Joan Cerdà Butifulla (1578).[64] Only one of the wills analysed containing benefices for the saying of the *assots* refers to a convent other than Santa Maria de Jerusalem. It is the 1533 will of Alonso de Escobar, the son of a nobleman from Segovia, who gives sums to several monasteries for celebrations with music, including the convent of Santa Maria de Jerusalem to celebrate an anniversary and the *assots*, but also to the Dominican nunnery of Els Àngels where he wanted a sung Mass and also *uns assots*.[65] The custom was that the nuns of Jerusalem prayed the Flagellation of Christ with lighting of candles, as indicated in the 1543 will of Magdalena Úrsula Torredmer, a merchant's daughter and a widow.[66] It is not specified if this prayer devoted to the Flagellation of Christ involved music or not, but it seems clear that it was a competence of the nuns of Santa Maria de Jerusalem, since they also sang Masses for the dead on these occasions. For instance, Anthonius Martorell (1521), a priest and benefice-holder in Barcelona Cathedral, left these nuns 30 *sous* for the singing of a Mass for the dead with deacon and sub-deacon.[67] Likewise, Miquel Ferran (1546) wanted anniversaries and a sung Office of the Conception celebrated at this convent, and Joan Garcia (1546), a royal notary who wished to be buried in Sant Pere convent, gave 40 *sous* to the nunnery of Santa Maria de Jerusalem for lighting of candles and ceremonies, and also 3 *lliures* for the singing of an Office for his soul and that of his wife.[68]

Liturgical celebrations were also a form of economic exchange between convents and Barcelona's citizens. For instance, in 1503, Misser Vallès, a merchant, donated 20 *lliures* to the Jeronymite nuns for the painting of an altarpiece at the high altar, on the condition that the nuns celebrated an anniversary for the dead on 22 October each year.[69] The presence of music in anniversaries to be celebrated in Barcelona convents is frequently mentioned in wills. In her 1546 will, Beatriu Prima, alias Montesa, who was prioress of the convent of Els Àngels when it was located outside the city walls (in the Ciutadella Park), wished to be buried in the nuns' tomb in the convent church and specified several pious acts, including a Mass to be sung by the nuns on the feast of the Assumption of the Virgin.[70] The aforementioned Joana Riera (1566) made several bequests, among them a Requiem Mass sung by the Santa Maria Magdalena nuns with a deacon and sub-deacon.[71] The convent of Montsió also is frequently mentioned. Balthasar Torres (1547) wanted a *Salve Regina* celebrated at this convent on the three days following his death, for the soul of his sister who was a nun of the convent, and Jerònim Moxo (1577), a royal notary, wanted to be buried with his parents in the church of Montsió convent, facing the Roser chapel.[72] He wished the weekly sung Mass, celebrated on Saturdays, founded by his father in that chapel, to be maintained, and urges his heir to ensure its continuity.

A case-study: Music for the dead in Santa Maria de Jonqueres convent

The nunnery of Santa Maria de Jonqueres stood out in the celebration of sung Masses and Offices endowed by citizens, as well as those founded by the nuns themselves. According to the records of the pastoral visitation to the convent in 1605, there was a board hanging in the choir area indicating all the anniversaries and Masses that had to be celebrated, details of the people who had endowed them, and the amount paid:

> there is a board hanging in the choir area to record all the anniversaries and Masses endowed at this convent; details have been provided as to who endowed them, the amount paid for them, and the alms given to both nuns and clergymen for each Mass and anniversary.[73]

This practice of having such a board stemmed from the Council of Trent. As with the cases discussed above, a thick reading of a variety of documents is needed in order to assess the presence of music in these ceremonies celebrated at Santa Maria de Jonqueres nunnery. For instance, according to one of the convent's account books, twenty-seven black-veiled nuns and thirty-three choristers participated in the anniversaries celebrated in 1523 in honour of Antoni Valls, who had served as a priest at this convent.[74] The names of the nuns are recorded, providing an overview of the formation of that year's community of nuns.[75] The nuns were paid 6 *diners* per anniversary and the choristers 3.[76] Although no references to music are included, these quantities coincide with those registered in other documents where it is explicitly indicated that the anniversaries were sung. Similarly, according to the book of 'perpetual' anniversaries founded by the nun Elena Montoliu (d.1593) with 130 *lliures* on 23 July 1589, these anniversaries had to be celebrated in her honour and that of her sister Francisca, also a nun, 'with priest, deacon, sub-deacon, and the solemnity that was customary' twice a year, on 28 February—the day of Francisca's death—and on the day of Elena's own death—which would take place on 14 May.[77] Although there are again no direct references to music in this document, the anniversary in honour of Elena de Montoliu is referred to in this list of explicitly sung anniversaries, Masses, and Offices endowed by earlier nuns of the convent which had to be celebrated in the nunnery in 1661, almost a century after Elena Montoliu's endowment of the anniversary (Table 4.2). Most of the honourees of the liturgical celebrations with music recorded in this list are former nuns of the convent, but there also are many socially distinguished male citizens who used the title *mossèn*, and even a widow named Madalena Llaudis. The case of Elena de Montoliu and these other instances suggest that the indication 'with deacons' (*amb diaques*) implied that the Office or Mass was sung in plainchant.

The existence of a book of *desapropis* (wills) from the community of Santa Maria de Jonqueres nunnery dated from 1411 to 1741 allows a systematic analysis of these nuns' liturgical endowments from the fifteenth to the seventeenth centuries and to establish changes and continuities over the period.[78] Appendix 4.1 presents the details of the foundations of post-mortem ceremonies with music made by some nuns of the convent of Santa Maria de Jonqueres, for themselves and for their relatives, as recorded in their wills. The increase, over the course of the sixteenth century, in the number of liturgical celebrations founded by a single nun is one of the most outstanding features of this data and can be explained by the belief that the 'sacrifice' of the Mass was the best *sufragio*—good work for the relief of souls in Purgatory. This idea is already reflected in *Agonia del transito de la muerte* (Saragossa, 1544), a treatise on death written by Alejo Venegas (c.1498–1562) and which includes a fourteen-chapter section devoted to the various *sufragios*, referring to the efficacy of the Mass as *sufragio*. Likewise, Serpi's treatise of 1600 on Purgatory, described earlier, devoted chapter 53 to an explanation of how the Mass was the best action for the Purgatory souls (*Como el santo sacrifico de la Missa es el primero y mas accepto sufragio, para las almas del Purgatorio*) (Serpi 1604 [1600]: 455). In chapter 57 (*Si por los diffuntos se han de decir solamente Missas de Requiem. O si todas las Missas les aprouechan*) the author argues that every Mass, and not only a Requiem Mass, was beneficial for the souls in Purgatory, referring to the stipulations of the Council of Trent,

178 *Music to reach heaven*

Table 4.2. Examples from: 'Asientos de los aniversarios y misas cantadas de devoción en el año 1661 que se celebran en Santa Maria de Jonqueres, hechos por Sor Agraida Pons y Turell'. ACA,ORM,Monacales-Universidad,Legajos,8,3, fols. 1r–13v

	Honouree	Some of the foundations recorded
January (fol. 2r)	Caterina Marimon	Office of the Most Holy Name of Jesus with deacons
	Marina d'Aragó	Office of Saint Honorat Confessor (16 January). The Mass says *Statuit ei Dominus* including deacons and organ. Also, an anniversary and *absolta*
February (fol. 3r)	Mossèn Pere de Palafox and Mossèn Miquel Coromines [?]	Anniversaries with deacon and *absolta*
	Agraïda Pons and her sister Gerònima de Cardona	Anniversary including deacons and *tomba* ('tomb'). Each nun, while the Office is celebrated, would pray a Miserere and the *Respice*, and the day before each nun in the choir would say a *Nocturno de morts*[a]
March (fol. 4r)	Marquesa de Santa Pau	Anniversary with deacons and *tomba*
	Vitoria Gilabert	Office with deacons and organ
April (fol. 5r)	Rafela Saportella	Office of Saint Catherine of Siena with deacons and organ (29 April)
	Violant de Marimon, a prioress	Office of Saint Catherine of Siena with deacons and organ (30 April)
May (fol. 6r)	Elena Montoliu	Anniversary with deacons and *tomba*; *absolta* in front of Sant Francesc chapel
	Joana de Palafox	Anniversary and *absolta* in front of Sant Miquel chapel
	Santa Fontanet	Office of Saint Monica with organ (4 May)
June (fol. 7r)	Marquesa de Santa Pau	Anniversary with *tomba*, deacons, and *absolta* in front of Santa Magdalena altar
	Mossèn Joan Yars	Anniversary with *tomba* and *absolta* in front of Sant Miquel altar
	Prioress Purgades	Anniversary with deacons and *absolta* in front of Sant Jaume altar
	Magdalena Ballestera	Office of Saint Onofre sung with deacons and organ, which says *Justus ut palma florebit* (Confessors non-Pontiffs) (2 June)
	Madalena Llaudis, a widow	Anniversary with deacons and *tomba*. On that day, all the nuns together will say un *setsams* (seven psalms) and *absolta* in front of Saint Paula chapel (19 June)

(*Continued*)

Table 4.2. (Continued)

	Honouree	Some of the foundations recorded
July (fol. 8r)	Prioress Malla	On the Vigil of Saint Christoph's Day (10 July), all the nuns must sing a *Salva*. On the day of the saint, they must sing an Office with deacons and organ named *In virtute tua*
	Madalena Llaudis, a widow	Office of Saint Magdalena with deacons and organ and an *absolta* at Santa Paula and the *setsams* (22 July)
	Mossèn Pere Garriga	Office of Saint James sung without deacons after Prima
	Madalena Llaudis, a widow	Anniversary with deacons and *tomba*. All the nuns together will say *setsams* and the *absolta* to Saint Paula (30 July)
	Anna Fontanet	Office of Saint Marina with deacon and organ (17 July)
August (fol. 9r)	Mossèn Pere de Palafox	Anniversary with deacons and *tomba*
	Madalena Llaudis, a widow	Sung Mass with deacons and organ (22 August) of the Most Holy Assumption of Maria. All the nuns together will say *setsams* and the *absolta* to Santa Paula. Anniversary with deacons, *tomba*, *setsams*, and *absolta* in front of Saint Paula chapel (23 August)
	Anna Fontanet	Office of Saint Augustin with deacon and organ
September (fol. 10r)	Mossèn Miquel Coromines [?]	Anniversary with deacons
	Marquesa de Santa Pau	Anniversary with deacons, *tomba*, and *absolta* to Saint Magdalene
	Mossèn Joan Yuar	Anniversary with deacons, *tomba*, and *absolta* to Saint Michael
	Joana Palafox	Anniversary *de la tempore* with deacons, and *absolta* to Saint Michael
	Eleonor Sorribas	Anniversary with deacons, *tomba*, and *absolta* to Saint James
October (fol. 11r)	Prioress Desllor	Anniversary with deacons
	Marquesa Meca	Mass of Saint March the Evangelist with deacons, organ (30 October), and *absolta* to Saint Magdalene
November (fol. 12r)	'Nun who made the organ'[b]	Anniversary and *absolta* in front of Sant Francesc
	'Nun who made the silver angel'	Anniversary and *absolta* in front of Santa Paula
	Clara de Argentona	Anniversary with deacons, and *absolta* to Santa Paula (12 November)

(*Continued*)

180 *Music to reach heaven*

Table 4.2. (Continued)

	Honouree	Some of the foundations recorded
	Madalena Llaudis	Anniversary with deacons, *tomba*, and *absolta* to Santa Paula, and all the nuns together will say a *setsams* (9 November)
		Office with deacons and organ on the Octave of All Saints (10 November), and *absolta* to Santa Paula, and all the nuns together will say a *setsams*
	Mossèn Miquel Coromines [?]	Office with deacons and organ of the Octave of All Saints and an *absolta* in front of the high altar
	Francesca de Palafox	Anniversary with deacons and *tomba*
	Anna Fontanet	Office of Saint Gertrudis with deacons and organ
December (fol. 13r)	Pere de Palafox	Anniversary with deacons, *tomba*, and *absolta* in front of Sant Miquel
	Mossèn Miquel Coromines [?]	Anniversary with deacons and an *absolta* at the high altar
	Marquesa de Santa Pau	Anniversary with deacons, *tomba*, and *absolta* to Santa Madalena
	Eugènia Grimau	Anniversary with deacons and *absolta* in front of Santa Paula
		Mass of the Christ's Wounds with deacons
	Joana de Palafox	Anniversary *de la tempore* with deacons
	Caterina Marimon	Mass of the Christ's Wounds with deacons (19 December)
	Lucrècia Brina	Mass of the Most Holy Name of Jesus with deacons

[a] 'Asientos de los aniversarios y misas cantadas de devoción en el año 1661 que se celebran en Santa Maria de Jonqueres, hechos por Sor Agraïda Pons y Turell', ACA,ORM,Monacales-Universidad, Legajos,8,3, fol. 3r: 'Aniversari per la santa senyora doña Graida Pons y su germana doña Geronima de Cardona con diacas y tomba y les religiosses mentres se diu lo Offici diran un miserere cada una y la oracio Respice y lo dia abans dita cada religiosa en lo cor un nocturno de morts'.

[b] It is intriguing that in this case and the following one the names of the nuns are not specified: 'Aniuercari per la Religiosa que a fet lo orga – atsolta deuant Sant Francesh'; 'Aniuersari per la religiosa que a fet lo Angel de Plata – atsolta santa Paula'.

according to which every Mass, although it was celebrated in honour of a particular Saint, was in honour of God. Therefore, the more liturgical ceremonies a person founded, the faster their soul would reach heaven. This led to an increasing number of foundations over the years and to the endowment of hundreds or even thousands of Masses by a single person.

For instance, Eugènia Grimau, the choir director of Santa Maria de Jonqueres nunnery mentioned in Chapter 1, founded in her will (dated 18 August 1636) thousands of ceremonies in a variety of Barcelona churches, it being significant that, excepting her own nunnery, all the monastic churches mentioned belonged to male institutions (Table 4.3).[79] At the nunnery of Santa Maria de

Music to reach heaven 181

Table 4.3. Ceremonies founded by Eugènia Grimau in her will (1636). 'Llibre de desapropis' (1411–1741), ACA, ORM, Monacales-Universidad, Volúmenes, 241, fol. 270r–272r

Ceremonies founded	Convent or church chosen for the ceremonies
Burial assisted by 24 chaplains	Convent of Santa Maria de Jonqueres
Requiem Offices for three days	Convent of Santa Maria de Jonqueres
Trentenari of Saint Amador on the three days following her death	Convent of Santa Maria de Jonqueres
Masses of Saint Gregory on the first day after her death	Male convent of Santa Maria de Jesús
300 Masses (including those of Saint Gregory)	Male convent of Santa Maria de Jesús
50 Masses	Convent of Santa Maria de Montalegre
25 Masses	Male convent of Sant Francesc
25 Masses	Male convent of the Trinitat
25 Masses	Male convent of Sant Agustí
25 Masses	Male convent of the Mare de Déu del Carme
25 Masses	Male convent of Sant Josep
25 Masses	Male convent of the Mercè
25 Masses	Male convent of the Mare de Déu de Bonsuccés
25 Masses	Male convent of Santa Mònica
25 Masses	Male convent of Sant Francesc de Paula
25 Masses	Male convent of Santa Caterina
25 Masses	Monastery of Sant Jeroni de Vall d'Hebrón
25 Masses	Church of Sants Just i Pastor
25 Masses	Church of Sant Miquel
2,000 Masses (including those previously mentioned), 100 of them on the last days of her life	Churches chosen by her executors
Prayed Mass (*Misa baixa*)	Convent of Santa Maria de Jonqueres
3 anniversaries sung perpetually (one of Requiem on the day of her death; other of the Flagellation of Christ on the following Friday; and other of the Assumption of Our Lady eight days later)	Convent of Santa Maria de Jonqueres
Office of the Nativity sung perpetually on the Octave of the festivity	Convent of Santa Maria de Jonqueres
Office of the Most Holy Sacrament sung perpetually on the Octave of the festivity	Convent of Santa Maria de Jonqueres
Other Offices of the Flagellation of Christ sung on the day of her death	Male convent of Santa Maria de Jesús
Requiem anniversary on the day of her death	Male convent of Santa Maria de Jesús

Jonqueres, she endowed, among other ceremonies, three anniversaries to be sung 'perpetually', so that it is not surprising that still in 1661 references to Masses and Offices with deacons, and sometimes also with organ, for the soul of Eugènia Grimau are recorded, specifying that the Requiem anniversaries had to be celebrated in front of Santa Paula chapel, where she was buried (Table 4.2).

The *trentenaris* of Saint Amador and Saint Gregory are among the first ceremonies that Eugènia Grimau stipulated just after her burial. Martí Gelaberto (1994: 340) has indicated that the *trentenari* was the celebration most frequently founded by the nuns of Santa Maria de Jonqueres in the sixteenth century. Groups of Masses such as the so-called Masses of Saint Amador or those of Saint Gregory are frequently mentioned in nuns' wills not only in Barcelona. For instance, references to 'Gregory Masses' have been found by Laurie Stras in account books for Poor Clare institutions in Florence, particularly among nuns endowing their own Masses.[80] These Masses must have been very common, since the nuns asked that they were celebrated with the formalities which were proper for those Masses. In his book on death and society in Hapsburg Spain, historian Fernando Martínez Gil states that both were groups of thirty-three Masses and were deeply associated with the idea of Purgatory from the medieval period. He points out that the Masses of Saint Amador were very popular in the first half of the sixteenth century, and then became less frequent until disappearing completely in the mid seventeenth century.[81] According to Martínez Gil, the distribution of the invocations of these Masses varies in different documents, and the clearest sources concerning their origin—which is virtually unknown—are narratives of Saint Amador's life which stem specifically from Catalonia.[82]

However, the analysis of the wills of Santa Maria de Jonqueres nuns shows that, in Barcelona, both the Masses of Saint Amador and those of Saint Gregory were very popular throughout all of the sixteenth century, and also before and after that century. In the case of Saint Gregory's Masses, their long-lasting reputation among these nuns—and with Barcelona's citizens in general—may be connected to Serpi's book on Purgatory, although the degree of possession of this book by Barcelona's wider citizenry remains to be determined.[83] This treatise provides information on the particular invocations that Barcelona citizens may have been thinking of when founding the Masses of Saint Gregory, and suggests that the total number of Masses reached fifty-two, instead of thirty-three (Figure 4.8). In fact, this particular chapter in Serpi's book is referred to by some nuns in their wills. For example, the will of Margarida de Guimerà (d.1619) indicated that 'details of the Masses of Saint Gregory can be found in chapter 57 of a book entitled Treatise on Purgatory. I want these Masses to be celebrated on the first three days after my death'.[84] Isabel de Marimon (d.1624) also referred to this source (see Appendix 4.1).

Although Saint Gregory the Great's *Dialogues* include the story from which these Masses originated, these nuns may have been thinking of the *exemplum* of Francisca Ferrer. According to Serpi's book, the origin of the tradition of

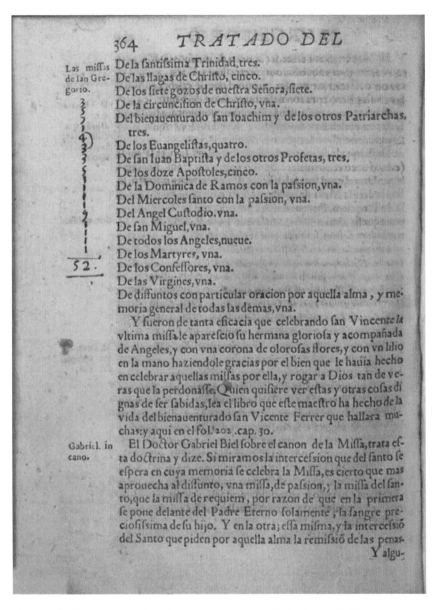

Figure 4.8. Signs of use, calculating the total amount of Saint Gregory's Masses, in a copy of the 1604 edition of Dimas Serpi's *Tratado del purgatorio* (1600), p. 364. Madrid, Universidad Complutense de Madrid. Public Domain

celebrating the Masses of Saint Gregory for souls in Purgatory stems from the case of Francisca, who was the sister of the Valencian saint Vicente Ferrer. She, who was in Purgatory, appeared unto her brother and asked him to celebrate Saint Gregory's Masses, but Saint Vicente did not know what the invocations of these Masses were, so he implored God for help and an angel provided him with the details:

> Francisca Ferrer appeared to her brother Saint Vicente and said to him: if you pray in my honour the Masses of Saint Gregory, they will intercede for me, so that God will relieve me from these pains and torments which I am suffering. The dead woman disappeared, and the saint felt great grief, as he did not know what these Masses asked by his sister were. Saying prayers and multiplying fasts, he begged God to reveal what the Masses said by Saint Gregory for the souls were, in order to help his sister (to whom he had loved so much while she lived). One day, while he was praying, an angel appeared unto him and gave him a parchment, where the invocations of these Masses were written, and the angel disappeared.
> To the Most Holy Trinity, three
> To the Wounds of Christ, five
> To the Seven Joys of Our Lady, seven
> To the Circumcision of Christ, one
> To the Blessed Saint Joaquim and to the other Patriarchs, three
> To the Evangelists, four
> To Saint John the Baptist and to the other Prophets, three
> To the twelve Apostles, five
> To Palm Sunday with the Passion, one
> To Holy Wednesday with the Passion, one
> To the Guardian Angel, one
> To Saint Michael, one
> To all the angels, nine
> To the Martyrs, one
> To the Confessors, one
> To the Virgins, one
> To the Dead, with particular prayer for that soul and general remembrance of all the rest, one
> And the Masses were so efficacious that as fast as Saint Vincent celebrated the last Mass, her sister appeared gloriously accompanied by angels, wearing a crown of fragrant flowers, and handing a lily thanking him for the good he had done for her celebrating those Masses and begging Good her forgiveness.[85]

Moreover, Francisca's story became very popular in the seventeenth century, resulting in the publication of books on the origin of Saint Gregory Masses, which became known as the Masses of San Vicente Ferrer (Martínez Gil 2000: 227), and this story would even form the plot of a subsequent mystical comedy by Fernando de Zárate (Figure 4.9).

None of these books indicates whether these Masses were sung or prayed. Nor do the wills analysed mention any music in connection to Saint Gregory Masses, since nuns only asked that they be celebrated according to custom. However, some evidence hints at the presence of music in these celebrations. Àngela de Guimerá i de Llupià, on her will of 28 July 1628, endowed the Masses of Saint Gregory and Saint Amador, together with other Masses that she specified that had to be prayed and not sung (*misas baixas*).[86] That this detail was missing in the mention of the Masses of Saint Gregory and Saint Amador may indicate that these Masses were customarily sung. Moreover, Serpi's treatise places high importance on the inclusion of music in post-mortem celebrations, using as *exemplum* the Virgin's death ceremonies in which the angels were singing hymns for three days at her grave (Figure 4.10):

> When Our Lady Maria, princess of Heaven, died, the sacred Apostles publicly buried her most holy body singing hymns, along with the angels. [...] They not only accompanied her body to the grave singing hymns, but they also remained there for three days making music and accompanying her most holy body. Three days later, the Apostles realised that the celestial music they have been listening to had stopped, and Saint Thomas arrived to show them that the body was not in the grave. Therefore, now you know that they not only buried the Virgin publicly, but also the angels stay there singing for three days. I believe that this is the origin of such a holy and laudable tradition of celebrating *novenas* or *días séptimos* and anniversaries in honour of the dead, imitating what the Angels did at the Virgin's burial.[87]

The hymn was a musical genre particularly connected to the celestial; according to the early theologian Origen of Alexandria, the 'singing of psalms is fitting for mankind, but the singing of hymns is fitting for the angels and for those who have the essence of angels' (Riehle 2014: 129). The singing of hymns by nuns is also stipulated in some of the wills analysed in preparation for this study. For instance, in the early seventeenth century, the prioress Isabel Dusay (d. 1646) indicated that, on the day of Our Lady of Hope, nine of the youngest choristers would sing the Marian hymn *Alma redemptoris mater* with its antiphon for Vespers in front of her tomb:

> Moreover, on the day of Our Lady of Hope, I want *Alma redemptoris mater* with its antiphon for Vespers (starting *O Virgo Virginum*) to be sung in front of my chapel, which is in the cloister, by nine choristers (those who were the youngest). The choir director [*capiscola*] will say the prayer [...]. Each chorister will be paid 9 *diners*.[88]

The wills of Santa Maria de Jonqueres nuns contain references to those who would perform music and liturgy. Nuns are frequently mentioned as performing psalms—ceremonies reading psalms were frequently endowed in the wills

Figure 4.9. Fernando de Zárate, *Comedia famosa. De las Missas de San Vicente Ferrer* [no editorial details, written in 1661]. Madrid, Real Academia Española, 41-IV-59(7). Creative Commons

Figure 4.10. Fra Angelico, *The Burial of the Virgin and the Reception of Her Soul in Heaven* (1434–1435), tempera and gold on panel, 26 x 53 cm. Philadelphia, Museum of Art, John G. Johnson Collection, 1917, Cat. 15

analysed—while priests from the convent church, and external priests and friars, celebrated the liturgy. Some nuns even pointed out in their wills the names of the priests they wanted or indicated that they would be chosen by a fellow nun. Sometimes it is specified that they wished that the anniversaries were celebrated by both the nuns of the convent and the priests of the convent church. Some nuns also stipulated the number of friars who had to participate in their burial and the religious order to which they would belong. For instance, Marquesa de Santa Pau (d.1500) wanted twenty-five Franciscan friars, twenty-five Dominicans, and all the priests of the convent church to accompany her body to the church.[89] Moreover, she stipulated that the Masses on the day of her burial were celebrated by twenty-five minor friars, twenty-five Dominicans, twenty-two Augustinians, twelve Carmelites, twelve Mercedarians, and all the priests and chaplains of the convent church.

Marianna de Marimon (d.1598) wanted the singing of a Requiem Office on the day of her burial and for the friars of the friary of the Trinitat to go to the convent to sing an *absolta* for her soul.[90] She also wanted the Discalced friars of Barcelona to celebrate a *trentenari* every year for her soul at the chapel of Sant Francesc at the convent. If they were not able to do it, her second option was the friars of the Trinitat. Marianna de Monmany (d.1605) also wanted the friars of the houses of the Trinitat, the Carme, and Sant Francesc de Paula to sing *absoltas* for her.[91] Sometimes it was specified that only the *absolta* should be sung; for example, Anna de Malla (d.1570) ordered that at the Masses and Offices celebrated by the chaplains they only should sing the last *absolta*.[92]

Leonor de Vallseca (d.1538), who served as the convent sacristan, wanted the poor of Santa Creu hospital to accompany her body.[93] Several wills by a variety of Barcelona's citizens stipulated the presence of poor at their burial.[94] For instance, Perot Frualler (1534), nephew of Aldonça Friuellera, abbess of the Trinitarian convent, specified burial in the church of the Franciscan friary, in the family tomb marked by the sign of a lion, and wished for his body to be accompanied to the church by poor people, who were to be given a candle or torch, and who, once they had returned to his house, were to be paid 1 *diner* and given a loaf of bread in return for praying for his soul.[95] He also wanted representatives of all the city's religious orders to attend his burial and to make an *absolta* over his tomb, and for as many Masses as possible to be celebrated at midday by all the orders, and not only on the day of his burial, but on the third day and anniversary. He left 100 *lliures* to cover five *trentenaris*, one of them in Sant Pere nunnery (celebrated by Sebastián Coromines). Likewise, Margarida Lloselles (in a will of 1568) left money to the convents of Els Àngels and Santa Elisabet and wanted her body to be accompanied by the poor.[96] Anthon Joan Moreta (in a will of 1572) stipulated that his body should be buried in the cathedral and to be accompanied by the poor of the city's Hospital and orphans.[97] These are only a few examples of the importance given to the poor accompanying the body at burial. Many wills also were quite specific with regard to the ringing of bells at burials.

Most of the nuns of Santa Maria de Jonqueres—and also the citizens in general—wanted to be buried in churches.[98] Serpi's treatise on Purgatory explained that it was very convenient to be buried in churches, since these were places where people were always praying; for instance, Franciscan friars sang a Mass every Monday and made an *absolta* for those who were buried in their friary church (Serpi 1604 [1600]: 455). Thus, public burials and the inclusion of music—particularly hymns—in the ceremonies on that day and on the following days may have been a result of the wish to follow the model of the Virgin Mary (Figure 4.11). Later, in his *Chronica Seraphica de la Santa Provincia de Cataluña*, Francesco della Marca mentioned listening to angelic singing and to a 'celestial harmony' among the nuns' visions and religious experiences in the convent of Santa Maria de Jerusalem. According to him, Mathea Castellví (d.1600), from Vilafranca del Penedès, died while 'the hymn of the angels was being sung', and Juana Figuerola was also able to listen to the angels' singing.[99]

The only reference to polyphonic singing in the wills of Santa Maria de Jonqueres community is found in the late seventeenth century in the will of Beatris de Lanuça, who founded four Offices on the day of her burial and the following three days, with deacon, sub-deacon, and *a cant d'orga*. Even though most of the post-mortem liturgical celebrations endowed in these wills were performed in plainchant, an account book belonging to the same nunnery and dating from the 1660s suggests that polyphonic singing was particularly present in ceremonies in honour of the souls of the so-called *albats*.[100] *Albats* were children who died before having the use of reason and consequently were free from sin. The Catalan term *albat* comes from the Latin *albatus*, meaning 'dressed in white'.[101] The death of an *albat* was regarded as a source of joy as the *albat* was believed to become an angel who would protect their relatives.

Figure 4.11. Illustration of the burial of Ignatius of Loyola, in Pedro de Ribadeneira (1527–1611), *Vita beati patris Ignatii Loyolae religionis societatis Iesv fvndatoris* (s.n., 1611). BNE, ER/6049 ILUSTRACIONES. Public Domain

The wake of the *albat* was celebrated with a banquet organised by the parents (Pérez Saldanya and Roca Ricart 2018: 145). These wakes included music, dancing, and singing, and the word *albadet* referred to the songs performed on these occasions. These beliefs survived on the Spanish Mediterranean coast and in Latin America until at least the twentieth century (Figures 4.12 and 4.13). This is shown in popular tales which include references to the participation of musicians in ceremonies honouring these children.[102] Moreover, folk song lyrics mention dances performed on the occasion of the death of an *albat*.[103] The burial of an *albat* involved a particular bell ringing style, using smaller bells, so that the sound pitch was higher (Morant and Peñarroya 1995: 275).

Most of these children honoured at the Santa Maria de Jonqueres convent with polyphonic music were the sons and daughters of craftsmen and merchants, who paid for these celebrations (Table 4.4). It is striking that *a cant d'orga* is located above the ruling on the original manuscript, as it was the first phrase to be written. In addition to these *albats*, *a cant d'orga* was also added to Eucharistic sacraments (*combregar*) celebrated in private houses for a variety of citizens, such as Cristofol Riber in the house of Miquel Ribes, a furrier (*assaonador*) in June 1662; Miquel Texidor, a *ciutadà honrat* at Dels Banys Street in July 1662; Pau

Figure 4.12. Engraving by Gustave Doré depicting a festive wake for a child. 'Une danse funébre (*jota*), à Jijona (province d'Alicante)', in Barón Davillier and Gustave Doré, *Le Tour du Monde, Voyage en Espagne 1862 a 1873* (Paris: Typographie Lahure, 1875), p. 317. Creative Commons

Figure 4.13. Francisco Oller, *El velatorio* (The wake) (1893), oil on canvas, 269.5 x 412 cm. Río Piedras (Puerto Rico), Museo de Historia, Antropología y Arte. Creative Commons

Table 4.4. Post-mortem liturgical celebrations in honour of *albats* at the convent of Santa Maria de Jonqueres. 'Barcelona, convento de Santa Maria de Jonqueres. Libro de cuentas'. ACA, ORM, Monacales-Universidad,Volúmenes,381, fols. 1r–6v

Child (dead between 1660 and 1663)	Liturgical celebration
Josep, son of Gabriel Alias, a farmer	*Albat* and *De Angelis* Office *a cant d'orga*
Petronila, daughter of Ventura Alboch	*Albat a cant d'orga*
Anna Maria, the daughter of Pere Pau Balaguer, a ropemaker in Oliver Street	*Albat* and *De Angelis* Office *a cant d'orga*
Caterina, daughter of Gabriel Codina, a shopkeeper	*Albat a cant d'orga*
Baltasar, son of Ventura	*Albat a cant d'orga*
Joabel, daughter of Joseph Gali, a glassmaker	*Albat* and *De Angelis* Office *a cant d'orga*
Maria, daughter of Pau Montegut	*Albat a cant d'orga*
Maria, daughter of Joseph Fábregas, a trader	*Albat a cant d'orga*
Lluís, son of Hièronim Ortou, a farmer	*Albat a cant d'orga*
Francisca, daughter of Mr. Rafel Lemparch, a Barcelona notary	*Albat* and *De Angelis* Office *a cant d'orga*
Eulàlia, daughter of Bartomeu Anglada, a trader	*Albat* and *De Angelis* Office *a cant d'orga*
Olaguer, son of Davit, a merchant from Girona	*Albat a cant d'orga*
Miguel, son of Mr. Boneu	*Albat* and *De Angelis* Office *a cant d'orga*
Mariana, daughter of Franciscà Puig	*Albat a cant d'orga*
Josepa, daughter of Vicente Sebastian, sergeant major	*Albat a cant d'orga*
Joan, son of Joan Pere Albareda, a hosier	*Albat a cant d'orga*
Joseph Antoni, son of Narcís Feliu, a merchant	*Albat* and Office *a cant d'orga*

Rosell Menor, a merchant at Born Street in the same month; Anna Ros, a widow living opposite to Sant Jacint gate in August 1662; and at the funeral of Francisca Rebolledo in January 1663.[104]

The references to polyphonic singing for the souls of children are very common in documents from the early modern period. For instance, Honorat Ciuró, a priest and organist from the nearby region of Roussillon, created a family tree including his brother's children; he indicated that all those who had died at an early age had been commemorated with polyphonic singing at their funerals (Mazuela-Anguita 2016c; Figure 4.14).

Although there is no mention of polyphonic singing in the wills of Santa Maria de Jonqueres nuns until the late seventeenth century, the earliest reference to organ playing in these documents is found in the Magdalena Ballestera's will of 1504. She stipulated the celebration of a Mass on Saint Onofre's day, with a deacon, sub-deacon, and organs; moreover, the nuns would perform the Miserere

192 *Music to reach heaven*

(a)

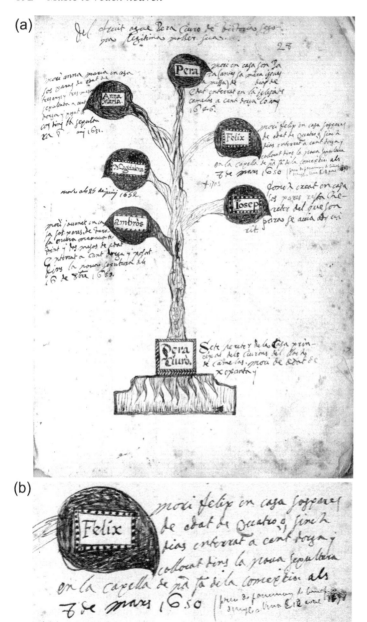

(b)

Figure 4.14. Family tree (and detail) included in Honorat Ciuró (1612–1674), *Camins traçats* (MS, 1642). Perpignan, Archives Communales de Perpignan, Fons Enric Pull, 17 S 1, fol. 26r ['Felix died at his parents' home when he was four or five days old; he was buried with polyphonic singing in the new tomb of the chapel of Our Lady of the Conception on 8 March 1650' (*mori felix en casa sus pares de edat de quatro o sinch dias enterrat a cant dorga y collocat dins la noua sepultura en la capella de n[ostr]a s[enyor]a de la concepcion als 8 de mars 1650*)]

with an *absolta*.[105] The aforementioned book of records of the anniversaries and sung devotional Masses endowed by the nuns themselves and celebrated at Santa Maria de Jonqueres in 1661 (Table 4.2) includes the celebration of these Masses founded by Magdalena Ballestera as late as in June 1661:

> On the 2nd of that month, the feast day of Sant Onofre, it must be sung an Office of that Saint with deacons and organ; the Office says *Justus ut palma florebit* from Confessors non-Pontiffs and it is for the soul of the saint Madelena Bellestera.[106]

This also gives us an idea of the perpetuity of these celebrations with music.

Caterina Duralla—a prioress who died in 1525 and was mentioned in Magdalena Ballestera's will—also stipulated organ playing; she wanted a solemn Mass of the Conception with deacon, sub-deacon, and organs, and the organist would be paid 2 *sous*.[107] Elisabet de Malla (d.1533), also a prioress, founded a solemn Office on Saint Cristopher's feast day with the participation of the nuns, a vicar who would celebrate the Mass, deacon, sub-deacon, organist—to whom 1 *real* would be paid—and choirboy.[108] Prioress Violant de Marimon (d.1593) stipulated the participation of an organist—who would be paid 1 *real* as well—in an Office on Saint Catherine of Siena's feast day (29 April), and she asked her fellow nuns to sing a responsory after the Office in the chapel of Sant Francesc.[109] The records of the devotional Masses celebrated in 1661 (Table 4.3) provide evidence of the importance attributed to Saint Catherine of Siena's feast day and the presence of music on this day: 'on 29 April it must be celebrated an Office of Saint Catherine of Siena with deacons and organ in honour of Mrs. Rafela Zaportella'.[110] The 1661 book also includes a different list made in order to record all the devotional Masses to be celebrated in the Corpus Christi Octave for the nuns themselves and for external citizens, in addition to the convent's Office (Table 4.5).[111] This shows that post-mortem liturgical celebrations had an important presence of music throughout the Octave of the Corpus Christi.

As the case of Eugènia Grimau made clear (Table 4.3), the nuns of Santa Maria de Jonqueres founded ceremonies not only at their convent, but also at other religious institutions in the city. For instance, Anna Marqueta (d.1556) founded fifteen Masses at the high altar of Santa Maria del Mar church, nine Masses at the high altar of Sant Miquel church, *trentenaris* of Saint Amador at the male monastic institutions of Sant Francesc, Jesús, and Trinitat, and a sung Office at the nunnery of Valldonzella.[112] The *desapropis* of the convent of Santa Maria de Jonqueres also refers to the foundation of Masses at altars which had the distinction of being 'privileged'. The first mention of an *altar privilegiado* in Santa Maria de Jonqueres's *desapropis* is found in the 1590 will of the prioress Violant de Marimon (d.1593).[113] Ángela de Vilatorta (d.1595) also founded two *trentenaris* to be 'distributed among all the privileged altars in which a soul is relieved from Purgatory at the discretion of my executors',[114] and Francisca Desbosch i de Sant Vicens (d.1620) founded 200 Masses to be distributed among the privileged altars of the city.[115]

194 Music to reach heaven

Table 4.5. Some of the devotional Masses with music celebrated at Santa Maria de Jonqueres convent at Corpus Christi Octave for the nuns themselves. 'Memoria de totas las misses de deuocio que an de celebrar en la octaua de Corpus de las señoras religiosas de esta casa', in 'Asientos de los aniversarios y misas cantadas de devoción en el año 1661 que se celebran en Santa Maria de Jonqueres, hechos por Sor Agraïda Pons y Turell', ACA,ORM,Monacales-Universidad,Legajos,8,3, fol. 14r

Day	Liturgical celebrations
Corpus Christi Day (Thursday)	Prime: convent Office prayed [this is celebrated every day throughout the Octave] 9 o'clock: Office sung with deacons and organ for the soul of Dalmau de Queralt [1593–1640], Count of Santa Coloma and Viceroy of Barcelona (paid from 1665 onwards)
Friday	Office sung with deacons and organ for Hipòlita Agustín
Saturday	Office sung with deacons and organ for Lluïsa Cepila, sub-prioress
Sunday	Office sung with deacons and organ for Isabel de Marimon, sub-prioress
Monday	Office sung with deacons and organ for Caterina Marimon
Tuesday	Office sung with deacons and organ for Eugènia Grimau
Wednesday	Office sung with deacons and organ for Lluïsa Montornes
Thursday	Office sung with deacons and organ for Eleonor Clariana
Friday	Christ's Would Office with deacons for Elena de Monsuar [d.1636], a prioress
Saturday	Anniversary with deacons and *tomba*, and *absolta* at Santa Teresa altar, for the soul of Jerònima de Cardona i Pons, a widow

Again, the foundation of Masses at privileged altars was a topic included in Serpi's treatise on Purgatory. He devoted chapter 62 to extensively discussing whether the Masses celebrated at privileged altars were more beneficial for the souls than those that took place at ordinary altars (Serpi 1604 [1600]: 394). All the privileged altars mentioned in these *desapropis* belonged to male monasteries: Jesús, Santa Caterina, Sant Agustí, Sant Francesc de Paula, and Trinitat. The cathedral also had a privileged altar, as well as the chapel of the Palau de la Comtessa, as mentioned above. Moreover, the nunnery of Santa Elisabet had a privileged altar and many citizens' wills refers to it. For instance, Caterina Sanctamaria (in a will of 1585) left 500 *lliures* for many pious acts in a variety of religious institutions in the city, including *trentenaris* at the chapel of the Name of Jesus at the convent of Els Àngels, and at the main altar of the Palau de la Comtessa, and fifteen Masses at the privileged altar of the convent of Santa Elisabet.[116] Foundations at specifically privileged altars increased as the century advanced. Enric de Cardona (d.1603), governor of Catalonia, founded 3,000 Masses at privileged altars, among other endowments.[117]

The musical symbiosis between convents and their urban surroundings shows the deep integration of music into the daily life and the aural experience of

Barcelona's citizens and demonstrates that the musical life of Barcelona's nuns and noblewomen was much livelier than previously believed. It is at the points of overlap between religious and civic lives that traces of women's musical practices emerge, challenging the phenomenon of women's voices becoming lost in music history. The financing of liturgical celebrations with music for devotional purposes—and particularly to relieve the suffering of the souls in Purgatory—fuelled convent's economies and constituted an important type of musical patronage, which has been generally overlooked in Spanish musicological studies. This financing was linked to both popular and official religiosity and was carried out by citizens from different socioeconomic sectors. Moreover, it was a morally and socially acceptable form of both music patronage and music-making for women. Widely circulated writings such as Serpi's book on Purgatory—which is even cited in Barcelonan wills—included *exempla* such as Saint Vicente Ferrer's Masses, Christina Mirabilis's inner celestial sound, and the angels' singing at the Virgin's burial, which may have fuelled the identification of nuns' voices with the celestial and the importance of convents for the spiritual health of the city. Beyond networks for the dissemination of music, musicians, and musical discourse within the city, Barcelona convents also formed part of networks involving national and international urban centres, particularly through the different religious orders; comparisons with other countries are, therefore, fundamental in order to evaluate the particularities of Barcelona in the context of European and Latin American cities.

Notes

1 References to this mediating function in the case of the Barcelona convent of Santa Clara are found in Jornet 2007: 126. On the convent of Pedralbes, see Castellano 1996: 328.
2 On the concept of Purgatory, see Chiffoleau 1980; Le Goff 1981; Eire 1995; Tingle 2012; and Booth and Tingle 2020, among others. About the religious beliefs of ordinary people and the devotion to particular saints in sixteenth-century Spain, see Christian 1989. This study takes as main evidence the responses to two questions in Philip II's inquiry known as the *Relaciones topográficas* (1575–1580).
3 San José 1615: fol. 4r: 'Las diferencias de musica destos dias, [¿]quien la referira? Assi de vozes, como de diuersos instrumentos, que repartidos a Coros, imitauan a los de los Angeles, en la musica'. This reference to a division into different choirs might be an oblique reference to the nine choirs of angels.
4 On this convent, see Callado 2013 and 2014.
5 Ruiz signed capitulations with the convent in 1527, according to which he would be buried at the main chapel of the convent; the convent would be the heir of all his belongings; he founded six chaplaincies so that daily Masses were celebrated for his soul and those of his parents, and asked the celebration of the feasts of Corpus Christi, Nativity of the Virgin, and All Saints. Ten years later these stipulations had not been realised yet and Ruiz's servants established, among other terms, the assignation of 2,000 *maravedíes* to the organist. Moreover, the rules of the maid school indicate that 'a sung Requiem Mass' had to be celebrated if some of the girls died.
6 *Constituciones del convento de San Juan de la Penitencia de Toledo* (1520), fols. 10v–11r, transcribed in Abad 1968: 39: 'El Oficio divino siempre se diga devotamente en el choro así de noche como de día en tal manera que antes del principio de las Horas [...] vengan al choro para aparejar sus corazones al Señor y allí estén con

todo sosiego, sin ruydo, apartadas de riso [sic] y de vanos acatamientos, en silencio y paz, con debida gravedad; por lo qual, muy amadas Hermanas, os amonesto en el Señor que los loores divinos entera y atenta y honestamente los digais. Y en ningún tiempo el Oficio divino se diga cantado por punto, por evitar los gestos humanos y vozes inútiles, que no son aplazibles al Señor, el qual se deleita más en la pureza y devoción del corazón, que no en el sonido de la voz. Podréis decir vuestro Oficio rezado o en tono, como la Abadesa lo ordenare'.

7 Cerone 1613: 420: 'En Cantollano *se ha de guardar la regla de los Acentos* en las cosas que se cantan sin punto: como en las Oraciones, Epistolas y Euangelios &c. Si caso (dexando la buena pronuncia de España) no quisiesen tomarse à los barbarismos de Francia; cuyos naturales suelen defenderse muy à propósito, diciendo: *Nos Gallici non cùramus de numèro syllàbarum*. Pero en las cosas que son cantadas por punto, *no se ha de guardar*, sino pronunciarse deuen las notas como estan apuntadas, breues ò luengas que sean, por causa de las ligaduras ò Neumas'. See also Knighton 2017b: 62.

8 *Decreto de José de la Cruz, padre provincial, para el convento de San Juan de la Penitencia de Toledo* (1666), transcribed in Abad 1968: 85.

9 *Regla y ordenanzas del convento concepcionista de la Concepción de la Madre de Dios de Toledo* (MS, siglo XV-1753), AHN, CODICES,L.1029, fol. 2r: 'assi conuiene al officio del seruicio pastoral a nos encomendado'.

10 *Regla y ordenanzas...*, fol. 18v: 'El officio diuino siempre se diga en tono con la pausa devida en medio del verso saluo en las fiestas principales que se dira cantando deuotamente dexando todo canto vano y augmentacion de puntos'.

11 *Constituciones hechas por el cardenal Silíceo, para el Colegio de Nuestra Señora de los Remedios de la ciudad de Toledo, de que fue fundador* [1557] (MS, 18th century), BNE, MSS/11259/52, fols. 6v–7v: 'Iten, que al tiempo del comer, y cenar o hacer colacion se lean en el dicho refitorio libros de romance de vida e de santos, y buenas doctrinas los quales elegira el dicho Reverendisimo Arzobispo de Toledo [...]. Iten despues de hauer comido, cenado o hecho colacion vayan juntas en procesión al choro, cantando en tono bajo el himno por nos [cardenal Silíceo] compuesto en alabanza de la Madre de Dios, y al fin del dira la rectora al mismo tono la oracion, que se sigue despues del dicho himno'.

12 Bataillon 1966 [1937]: 126: 'Es preciso que no se considere como lo esencial del culto divino un estrépito de voces y de órganos del que nada se comprende'.

13 Cited and translated in Monson 2002: 20: 'divina autem officia ab eis alta voce peragantur, non a mercenariis ad id conductis, et in misase sacrificio chorus quidem respondere solet, respondeant; partes vero diaconi vel hypodiaconi in sacri Evangelii vel canonicae Epistolae aut alterius sacrae lectionis recitation non usurpent. Vocis modulation atque inflexione aliove cantus artificio, quod figuratum vel organicum appellatur, tam in choro quam alibi abstineant' [*Concilium Tridentinum...*, 9:1043].

14 Cited and translated in Monson 2002: 22: 'Quo vero ad moniales. Remittatur totum negotium earum generalibus; vel coniungantur canones isti cum superioribus [...] Non prohibeantur cantus musici' [*Concilium Tridentinum...*, 9:1068].

15 Laurie Stras has studied the role of women voices in sixteenth century music, undertaking an exhaustive historical review on the subject, which she presented under the title 'What does it mean when a woman sings?', keynote lecture at the Medieval and Renaissance Music Conference, Edinburgh University, 1 July 2020.

16 On Pérez de Valdivia, see, among others, Pérez Aguilera 2005.

17 Pérez de Valdivia, 1587: 60: 'Mi desseo es, que cada vno haga su officio. El officio de los clerigos es cantar por el pueblo, y officiar el sancto officio de la missa. A las virgines, cuya voz suele ser tan regalada, y tan a gusto de los hombres, parece que no les esta bien cantar de manera que los hombres les alaben las vozes, y conozcan por la voz quien es cada monja: y mas para oyrlas cantar que por oyr los officious

diuinos vayan a los monasterios, como por nuestros pecados alguna vez lo vemos, y tocamos con las manos, y vemos que la gente de menos spiritu gusta mas de musica de mugeres (en especial quando cantan canto de organo) que de lo que se canta, no teniendo cuenta casi ninguna con la palabra de Dios: sino con el canto. Dessea mi coraçon, que las virgines consagradas a Iesu Christo no fuessen conocidas de los hombres ni vistas: que ni cantassen canto de organo, ni llano, ni tuuiessen organos ni otro instrumento musico: sino que el choro les fuesse lugar de pura oracion. En el qual descuydadas de todo cuydado de entonar o desentonarse, con vna voz humilde y deuota y baxita, que les prouocasse a deuocion, y no les impidiesse la contemplacion, dixessen sus horas canonicas para Dios y para ellas: como lo hazen en muchos monasterios de Roma'.

18 Muñoz 1962 [1635]: 360–361: 'Cantaban las religiosas el oficio divino en canto de órgano, con demasiada afectación, y tono más agradable al oído que, por ventura, decente a la majestad del culto: ocasionaba que los hombres volviesen el rostro al coro por mirarlas. Reprendiolo con alguna aspereza el padre Diego Pérez, y pidió se remediase'.
19 For a recent volume on Diego Pérez de Valdivia and Hipòlita de Jesús i Rocabertí, see Giordano 2020.
20 Rocabertí 1684: 199–200: 'y como despues se canto el Benedictus á canto de organo el Coro vn verso, y el organo el otro verso, y yo no huviesse de cantar gustè mas del celestial bocado'.
21 Ros-Fábregas 2015; Puentes-Blanco 2018; Miranda-López 2020. An autograph inscription indicates that, in 1597, the book was in possession of Jeroni Romaguera, a benefice holder and subsequently a succentor at the Cathedral of Castelló d'Empúrias (Girona).
22 Stras 2018: 36–50. For a recording of this repertoire, see *Lucrezia Borgia's Daughter. Princess, Nun and Musician. Motets from a 16th Century Convent*, Musica Secreta and Celestial Sirens, directed by Laurie Stras and Deborah Roberts, CD, Obsidian, 2017.
23 Leach 2007: 239. See also Holford-Strevens 2006; Leach 2006; and Catalunya 2017. The title of Robert Kendrick's paradigmatic book *Celestial Sirens* reflects this controversy (Kendrick 1996).
24 Williams 2015. See also Kay 2016, on troubadours' singing as connected to bestiality.
25 Monson 2010: 41. On diabolic possessions and the interplay between the sacred and diabolical in late medieval European culture, see Katajala-Peltomaa 2020.
26 Serpi 1604 [1600]: 181: 'Hablaua de Dios altissima y diuinamente, y estando callando como arrebatada, se oya entre su pecho y garganta, vna musica y melodia tan suaue, como de Angeles y espiritus seraphicos han oydo los sieruos de Dios muchas vezes. […] Que cumplidissimamente acudia Dios a regalar a su sierua Christina, por lo mucho que ella regalaua y socorria a las benditas animas del purgatorio, con satisfaciones de penas? Dize Surio que estando tan queda como vn leño sin menear boca ni pestaña, como si estuuiera durmiendo, los que se llegauan a ella, oyan que alla dentro entre el pecho y la garganta se entendia vna musica y melodia angelical, muy suaue, muy dulce, muy regalada, tal; que si algun hombre quisiera buscar todos los instrumentos musicos y bozes suauissimas del mundo, y se pusiera a su lado para imitar a aquella melodia, no llegara toda la musica del mundo a la suauidad de la que resonaua entre el pecho y garganta de la admirable Christina'.
27 No copies of the first edition are known. The book was reprinted in 1601, 1603, 1604, 1609, and 1613 in the same Barcelona printing workshop, in 1604 by the widow of Jaume Cendrat, and in 1611 by Jerónimo Margarit. It was also printed in Lisbon by Antonio Álvarez and in Madrid by Luis Sánchez in 1617, and in Girona by Gaspar Garrich in 1620 and 1629. On the Influence of this book on Cervantes, see Sullivan 1996: 88–96. According to Sullivan, the 'huge success' of this treatise 'illustrates the extent of contemporary Spanish interest in the theme of Purgatory' (Sullivan 1996:

90) and 'it remained the most compendious treatise in the vernacular on the subject throughout the seventeenth century' (Sullivan 1996: 91).
28 Tomlinson 1993: 62. See also Gouk 2000; Styers 2004; Gouk and Hills 2005; Brooks 2007; and Gregori 2012.
29 Larson 2019; Wood, 2019; and Richards 2019. Precedents are Gouk 1999 and Smiths 1999. Gouk's review of the three 2019 publications states that 'apart from the creation of uncanny feelings, what is implicit but perhaps underexplored in all three books is the Renaissance assumption that sounds can be magical (of the spiritual or demonic kind), notably in the sense that they can bring about striking effects on people both through the power of the voice alone and also in the form of "harmony", or its opposite, "noise"' (Gouk 2020: 5). On the connection between the Devil to discordant sounds in conventual spaces, see Finley 2019: 76.
30 Boynton 2016: 1000. See also Finley 2019: 78–81.
31 The poem 'Paradoxes of Love' can be read in Hadewijch 1980.
32 Riehle 2014. On Richard Rolle, see Watson 2007, among others.
33 AHN, Legajos:Clero-Secular_Regular,3932-3938 (sixteenth to nineteenth centuries); Legajos:Clero-Secular_Regular,L.6712-6714, 7379-7397, 7974, 19768 (sixteenth to eighteenth centuries); and Legajos:Clero-Secular_Regular,Car.1371 (1503–1684). The collection is formed by seven bundles, twenty-four books, and one folder. See Mazuela-Anguita 2016b.
34 AHN, Legajos:Clero-Secular_Regular,3936.
35 Mazuela-Anguita 2018c. For a recent study on Ana de Mendoza, see Dadson 2021.
36 There are other examples of passageways to link convent to palace, such as that found at the nunnery of La Encarnación in Madrid, founded by Philip III and Margaret of Austria in 1611.
37 ANC1-960-T-43, Lligall 44 ('Documentos referentes á la Excm. Sra. Dña Estefania de Requesens, consorte del Excmo. Sr. Don Juan de Zúñiga y de Avellaneda'), no. 11 ('Licencia concedida por el Rdmo. P. fr. Miguel Capdevila, Superior de los PP. Franciscos de Cataluña, á la Exma. Sra. Dña. Estefania de Requesens de Zuñiga para que, en virtud del Breve Pontificio á ella dado, pueda entrar en los Monasterios de Pedralbes y Jerusalen').
38 AMSP, Llibres d'abadesses, no. 178.
39 AMSP, Llibres d'abadesses, no. 178, fols. 2r–8v.
40 AMSP, Llibres d'abadesses, no. 232.
41 For more details of the ceremonies in honour of this abbess, see AMSP, Llibres de sagristia, no. 6 (1599–1603), s. fol. ('los aparells que a de fer la senora segristana en les vigilies y festes annyalls').
42 AMSP, Llibres d'obras, no. 7 (1588), fols. 1r–8r.
43 AMSP, Llibres de fundacions, no. 1, fol. 23r.
44 'Despenses fetes en la causa pia de la señora catarina miqlla', AMSP, Llibres d'abadesses, no. 178, fol. 10r.
45 'Despensa feta per la anima de la señora Johana de Paguera y Aldonsa de Paguera', AMSP, Llibres d'abadesses, no. 178, fol. 14r. This information can be complemented with the details provided by another account book related to the 'pious causes' instituted by Joana de Peguera between 1507 and 1534; see AMSP, Llibres d'abadesses, no. 232 (1507), fol. 16r.
46 AMSP, Llibres de sagristia, no. 8 (1581–1693), s. fol.
47 AMSP, Llibres de sagristia, no. 7, 1581, fol. [9r].
48 'Llibre en lo qual estan continuats los officis y Aniuersaris que per lo discurs del any celebran la Señora Abadessa y Señoras Monges del Monastir de Sant Pere', AMSP, Llibres de fundacions, no. 1.
49 See, for instance, the 'Llibre en lo qual están continuats los aniversaris y missas y altres divinals oficis instituïdes en la iglesia del monesteir de santa Clara recondit en lo arxiu de aquell' (1598–1599), AMSBM, Manuals, no. 738. A piece of paper inside

the 'Book of memories of the abbess' (1637) indicates that the following expenses were involved in the burial of Adriana Camporélls on 24 February 1642: 16 *sous* for the grave and 12 for the calls, 6 *sous* for the organist, 3 for the dresses, and 6 for the boys. See 'Llibre Memòries Abadessa' (1637), AMSBM, box 8, no. 106. The abbess at that time was Hipòlita de Pujol.
50 'Rubriques visita canónica' (1575–1586), AMSBM, box 27, no. 1262, fol. 8v.
51 AMSBM, box 27, no. 1262, fol. 32r: 'memoria de las missas ques diuen en lany per la señora vilaplana ha en la gloria'.
52 AMSBM, box 27, no. 633. See Chapter 3.
53 AMSBM, box 27, no. 633, fols. 21r–22r ('Item te rebut lo monastir de santa chaterina vint y tres reals y son per los tres dias an ajudat a cantar los oficis). See also fols. 81v–82r ('Lo que diu lo Conuent per la Abbadessa').
54 AMSBM, box 27, no. 1262, fol. 33r. See also 'Llibre de les coses dignes de memoria del monestir de S. Clara de Barcelona' (1599–1895), AMSBM, box 8, no. 742, p. 67.
55 AMSBM, box 8, no. 742, p. 80 (ch. 29, 'Sepultura de secular o altre ques vol sepultar en lo present monestir').
56 See AHPB, 294/70, AHPB, 285/53, AHPB, 292/42, and AHPB, 294/71, respectively.
57 See AHPB, 506/28.
58 AHPB, 506/28.
59 'Calcol de las missas entradas y celebradas de deuotio y testamentarias desde 20 de juny 1671 fins a 6 de maig 1672', AMSP, Llibres de visites, no. 4, fol. 69r.
60 'Libre de les visites dels beneficis y capelles de la esglesia parroquial de Sant Pere Essent abbadesa la Ilustre señora D. Violant Despes any MDLXXXV', AMSP, Llibres de visites, no. 2 (1585–1586), s. fol.
61 AMSP, Llibres de visites, no. 2, fol. 34r–v. Similar information can be found in AMSP, Llibres de visites, no. 3 (1647).
62 AMSP, Llibres de visites, no. 2 (1585–1587), fol. 34r–v.
63 AHPB, 403/01 and 409/77.
64 See AHPB, 285/53, AHPB, 292/42, AHPB, 383/60, fols. 78r–79r, AHPB, 395/65, AHPB, 383/60 fols. 120r–122r, and AHPB, 438/4, respectively.
65 AHPB, 315/8.
66 AHPB, 316/97. She also donated 5 *lliures* for the work on the organ in the church of Sant Miquel to be paid to the organ-builder.
67 AHPB, 292/42.
68 See AHPB, 294/71 and AHPB, 316/97, respectively.
69 Vergés 1987: 28. He refers to a *Calendario de actas* (fol. 80), located at the 'convent archive', as his source.
70 AHPB, 316/97.
71 AHPB, 383/60, fols. 78r–79r.
72 AHPB, 294/71 and AHPB 385/79, respectively.
73 'Libro de visitas hechas por diferentes visitadores' (1536–1726), ACA,ORM,Monacales-Universidad,Volúmenes,169, fol. 102v (pastoral visitation of 1605): '[…] Item ay una Tabla colgada en el coro de todos los aniversarios y missas que estan fundadas en el presente monasterio donde se declara quien los fundo y la renta dexaron para ellos y la limosna que se ha dado por cada missa y aniuersario ansi a las religiosas como a los religiosos'.
74 He might have been a vicar active in 1472 at the convent of Jonqueres who is mentioned in Costa 2005: 53.
75 AMSP, Llibres d'abadesses, no. 185, s. fol. See Mazuela-Anguita 2016a for a list of the nuns who participated.
76 They received *ploms*, a type of coin for internal use that would be changed for ordinary coins at the end of the month; see Estrada-Rius 2014 and Martí 2015.
77 'Barcelona, convento de Santa Maria de Jonqueres. Libro de aniversarios de las señoras Montoliu, religiosas', ACA,ORM,Monacales-Universidad,Volúmenes,218 ('con

presbítero, diácono, subdiácono y la solemnidad que se acostumbra a hacer'). See also 'Orden militar de Santiago. Barcelona, convento de Santa Maria de Jonqueres. Carpetas de cuentas modernas, y escrituras varias fundaciones' (1580–1833), ACA,O RM,Monacales-Universidad,Legajos,36, where wills and foundations are also recorded.

78 'Llibre de desapropis de las señoras religiosas del presnnt [sic] real monastir de nostra señora de jvnqveras de barcelona y de altres personas aderents de dit monastir' (1411–1741), ACA,ORM,Monacales-Universidad,Volúmenes,241. On the concept of *desapropi*, see Costa 2005: 34.
79 'Llibre de desapropis…', fol. 270r–272r. Eugènia Grimau made her will four months before her death (she died on 9 December).
80 I thank Laurie Stras for this information.
81 Martínez Gil 2000: 227–236. He includes tables with the distribution of the Masses according to different sources (Martínez Gil 2000: 235–236).
82 These sources were studied by Llompart 1970.
83 Tess Knighton has found a reference to a 'tratado de purgatorio' among the books included in the inventory—dated on 1 April 1609 and preserved in AHPB 555/74—of Hieronym Sescases, the major sacristan and canon at Vic Cathedral and resident in Barcelona. I am very grateful to her for providing me with this reference.
84 'Llibre de desapropis…', fol. 240r: 'trobaran notades dites missas de st. Gregori en un llibre ques diu lo tratado del purgatorio en lo capitol 57 vull se digan les dites misses los primers tres días de ma mort'.
85 Serpi 1604 [1600]: 363–367: 'Y es que quando Francisca Ferrer aparescio a su hermano san Vincente, y le dixo. Si rezares por mi las missas de san Gregorio, por su intercession me librara Dios destas penas y tormentos en que me vees. Y desapareciendo en aquel punto la difunta, quedo con muy gran congoxa el santo, porque no sabia quales eran las missas que le pedia su hermana. Y haziendo oraciones, y multiplicando ayunos, rogaua a Dios que le reuelasse, que missas eran las que san Gregorio dezia, por las almas; para ayudar a su hermana (a la qual el tanto hauia querido siendo viua) y vn dia estando orando le aparescio vn angel, y le dio vn pergamino, en el qual estauan escritas aquellas missas, y desaparecio; que son estas. De la santissima Trinidad, tres. De las lalgas de Christo, cinco. De los siete gozos de nuestra Señora, siete. De la cicuncision de Christo, vna. Del bienauenturado san Ioachim y de los otros Pattriarchas, tres. De los Euangelistas, quatro. De san Iuan Baptista y de los otros Profetas, tres. De los doze Apostoles, cinco. De la Dominica de Ramos con la passion, vna. Del Miercoles santo con la passion, vna. Del Angel Custodio, vna. De san Miguel, vna. De todos los Angeles, nueue. De los Martyres, vna. De los Confessores, vna. De las Virgines, vna. De diffuntos con particular oración por aquella alma, y memoria general de todas las demás, vna. Y fueron de tanta eficacia que celebrando san Vicente la vltima missa le aparescio su hermana gloriosa y acompañada de Angeles, y con vna corona de olorosas flores, y con vn lilio en la mano haziendole gracias por el bien que le hauia hecho en celebrar aquellas missas por ella, y rogar a Dios tan de versa que la perdonasse'.
86 'Llibre de desapropis…', fol. 255r. See Appendix 4.1.
87 Serpi 1604 [1600]: 457–458: 'quando la Princessa de los cielos Maria Señora nuestra murio, los Apostoles sagrados enterraron publicamente su santissimo cuerpo cantando hymnos, y los Angeles con ellos. […] No solamente acompañeraon cantando hymnos hasta llegar a la sepulture; sino que Tambien quedaron alli los Angeles y los Apostoles tres dias continuos haziendo musica y acompañando aquel santissimo cuerpo. Y como viessen los Apostoles que passados los tres dias cessasse la celestial musica que hasta enetonces hauian oydo; succedio Tambien que vino santo Thomas y para enseñarle el cuerpo que hauian enterrado abriessen la sepulture; no lo hallaron en ella […] Ya haueys oydo que no solo la enterraron publicamente a la santissima virgin; sino que estuuieron alli cantando los Angeles tres dias. De donde creo que ha

venido aquella tan santa y loable costumbre de hazer las nouenas o dias septimos y annuals a los diffunctos, a imitacion de lo que hizieron los Angeles al cuerpo de la Serenissima Princessa'.

88 'Llibre de desapropis…', fol. 277r.
89 'Llibre de desapropis…', fols. 94v–95r.
90 'Llibre de desapropis…', fols. 224r–225r.
91 'Llibre de desapropis…', fol. 230r–v.
92 'Llibre de desapropis…', fol. 195v.
93 'Llibre de desapropis…', fol. 161r.
94 On the composition of the funerary retinues and the inclusion of the poor, see Martínez Gil 2000: 404–405.
95 AHPB, 315/8.
96 AHPB, 395/67.
97 AHPB, 375/36.
98 On the funerary ritual of the nuns of Santa Maria de Jonqueres, see Gelaberto 1994.
99 Marca 1764: 282: 'En una de las dos Festividades, que fuè la de Mayo, hallandose en el Choro la bendita sirva Sor Mathea [Castellví] en oración, à las onze horas oyò Angelicos cantos, y una Celestial armonìa, y juntamente viò un grandissimo resplandòr, y claridad sobrenatural en el Choro'. On Juana Figuerola: 'Era muy devota de los Santos Angeles, a los que con frequencia llamava en su ayuda; de quienes se dize, haver recreado con suave musica alguna vez a esta devota suya'.
100 'Barcelona, convento de Santa Maria de Jonqueres. Libro de cuentas' (seventeenth century), ACA, ORM, Monacales-Universidad,Volúmenes,381. This book is poorly preserved.
101 For a detailed report on the historical development of the meaning of this term, see Pérez Saldanya and Roca Ricart 2018: 143–146.
102 Molí [n.d.]: 49: 'A lo millor, sentía les campanes que tocaven a albat, i com llavors se solia acompañar als albadets, perequè anaven al cel, amb la música tocant valsets, l'home escapava a córrer cap a la cova on vivía pa replegar l'asturment i lo demés'. This refers to Mariano Fontabella, a musician from Paterna (Valencia) in mid-twentieth century. The tale is cited in Pérez Saldanya and Roca Ricart 2018: 145.
103 The Valencian *dansa de la vetla* ('wake dance') refers to 'the dance that is always performed when an *albat* has died': 'La dansa del vetlatori (bis) / dones veniu a ballar (bis) / la dança que sempre es balla / quan es mor un albat'. Cited in Morant and Peñarroya 1995: 274.
104 'Barcelona, convento de Santa Maria de Jonqueres. Libro de cuentas'.
105 'Llibre de desapropis…', fols. 108v–115r.
106 'Asientos de los aniversarios y misas cantadas de devoción…', fol. 14r: 'Als ii de dit mes que es Sant Onofre se ha de cantar un ofici de dit sant ab diacas y orga lofici se diu yusts ut Palma florebit dels confesos, non Pontifice, y es per lanima de la santa Madelena Bellestera'.
107 'Llibre de desapropis…', fol. 136v.
108 'Llibre de desapropis…', fols. 152r–153r.
109 'Llibre de desapropis…', fol. 215r–v.
110 'Asientos de los aniversarios y misas cantadas de devoción…', fol. 14r: 'Als 29 de dit mes se a de celebrar un ofici ab diachas y orga de santa Catherina de Sena per la Señora Rafela Zaportela'.
111 'Asientos de los aniversarios y misas cantadas de devoción…', fol. 14r. Following these records, the book contains notes on the bread (fol. 15r) and candles (fol.16r) to be bought for the Day of the Dead, as well as a memorandum of all of the said Masses to be celebrated on the Day of the Dead in the honour of the nuns themselves, following their wills (fol. 17r). Records of the celebrations during Nativity and its Octave are also detailed, including an Office with deacons and organ for Eugènia Grimau

and other for Mossèn Miquel Coromines (fol. 18r). For the latter, other Offices with deacons and organ are recorded during the Octave of Epiphany (fol. 18v), the Octave of Resurrection Lent (fol. 19r), and the Octave of the Holy Spirit (fol. 20). Josep Zaportella also founded an Office of the Holy Spirit with deacons and organ. During the Octave of Our Lady of August, Offices with deacons and organ were recorded for Miquel Coromines, Madalena Llaudis, and Eugènia Grimau (fol. 21r). The first two also received Offices with deacons and organ on the Octave of All Saints (fol. 21v). On the Octave of the Most Holy Conception, Offices with deacons and organ were sung for Caterina Dusay and Jerònima Barberana (fol. 22r).

112 'Llibre de desapropis...', fols. 184v–186v.
113 'Llibre de desapropis...', fol. 215r.
114 'Llibre de desapropis...', fols. 220r–v: 'repartits per tots los altars priuilegiats en los quals se trau anima de purgatori a conexensa de dits marmesors meu'.
115 'Llibre de desapropis...', fol. 242v.
116 AHPB, 407/56, fols. 68v–72r.
117 AHPB, 506/29.

5 Beyond the city
Religious orders as national and international music networks

Barcelonan religious institutions in general, and nunneries in particular, participated in cultural and liturgical exchanges involving music at national and international levels.[1] Barcelona was a city open to the sea, and historical studies have emphasised the importance of the Mediterranean as a place of positive exchanges between cultures, and not only as a place of conflict (Braudel 1949; Horden and Purcell 2000; Magrini 2003; Salicrú 2008; Broodbank 2014). The importance of interchange in the configuration of early modern European culture has been addressed by cultural historians (Muchembled 2006–2007), and cultural theorists across the humanities have recognised the role of networks of interchange and patterns of borrowing in the formation of cultures. Literary theorists to emphasise cultural interchange include Edward Said, who argued that 'the history of all cultures is the history of cultural borrowing', while Julia Kristeva has stressed the cross-fertilisation of textual tradition as indicative of societal interchange, asserting that 'any text is the absorption and transformation of another'.[2] Likewise, Homi K. Bhabha has observed the relevance of focusing 'on those moments or processes that are produced in the articulation of cultural differences', which he names 'in-between spaces' (Bhabha 1994: 2). Until recently, music was overlooked in these more fundamental studies of cultural networks. However, given the power of music to cross cultural, linguistic, and geographical boundaries, musicology offers a valuable tool for understanding cultural networks, following the pathway traced by studies which show the international matrix in the structure of European musical thought (Agnew 2008). Music, because of its sonic nature, played a unique role in the processes of cultural exchange: music travels readily across the barriers between different languages, and it allows contending religious and cultural identities to be realised in performance.[3]

However, there is a gap in most cultural history, since few accounts of musical networks have addressed Iberian cultures and other countries on the periphery of the continent, and studies of Iberian culture have often suffered from an isolationist mentality. The idea of 'Spanish musical mysticism' (Collet 1913), traditionally encouraged by Spanish musicologists to differentiate Iberian music from that of other European regions, has played a fundamental role in portraying Iberian music as an 'autarchic illusion' (Carreira 1995; Ramos 2008; Llano 2013). Only recently have studies begun to challenge the isolationist view of Iberian musical

DOI: 10.4324/9781003292371-6

life in the modern period by showing the presence and circulation of international music and musicians in Iberian lands.[4]

In the early modern period, Spain formed part of a political network which included Netherlands, Italy, Austria, and the New World (Elliot 1989). In the context of this political union under the control of Habsburg Spain's 'most Catholic kings', music often served as an emblem of Catholic religion, fortifying the shared religious cause of these territories and serving as a diplomatic device to represent their unity abroad. The dynastic alliances that Spanish and Portuguese monarchs made in Europe, such as the marriage between Philip II and Mary Tudor, and that between Catherine of Braganza and Charles II, involved the creation of royal chapels with choral foundations throughout the continent. Portuguese and Spanish musicians were employed at this latter Catholic chapel of Queen Catherine of Braganza in London, where the queen was permitted to exercise her Catholic religion in a period of anti-Catholicism and her chapel 'seems to have been a training ground for young Catholic musicians' (Leech 2001: 584; see also Knighton 2013). Between 1685 and 1689 James II of England had a Catholic chapel at Whitehall and founded Jesuit schools (Leech 2011).

Conversely, William Byrd's son, Thomas, studied at the English College in Valladolid from 1596 (Rees 2010: 271), and Inquisition documents probing religious practices demonstrate the presence of non-Catholic musicians in Iberian lands; an example is the 1583 confession and renouncement from 'the Anglican sect' of Juan Sherwin, an English double-bass player and flautist at the Spanish royal court, who had previously worked in the Spanish region of Galicia as a musician in the service of the Count of Lemos (Mazuela-Anguita 2012b: 195). Spain's link to the Holy Roman Empire involved the circulation of music and musicians between central Europe and the Iberian lands, as exemplified by the *capilla flamenca* (Flemish Chapel), one of the two independent institutions—the other one being the *capilla española* (Spanish Chapel)—into which the Spanish royal chapel was divided until 1634 (Becquart 1967). Likewise, Spanish noblemen occupied positions as viceroys or governors in several territories in Europe and the New World, resulting in musical interchanges (Enciso 2007), such as the circulation of books and musical instruments and the migration of musicians. These interchanges of musical culture played a crucial role in the age of Iberian encounters with the New World (Fenlon and Knighton 2006; Gembero-Ustárroz and Ros-Fábregas 2007; Irving 2010).

The effectiveness of these musical networks in connecting distant religious institutions is reflected in a chronicle of the festivities held in the Jesuit college of Sant Martí in Girona for the beatification of Ignatius of Loyola. This account, which describes how the music honouring Saint Ignatius was rehearsed for months prior to the festivities, notes the presence of Juan Narciso Leysa, the director of the choir at the Colegio de Corpus Christi in Valencia, and describes how the Jesuits had taken advantage of Leysa's visit to Barcelona by bringing him to Girona to lead their musicians. Before taking office at the Colegio de Corpus Christi in 1605, Leysa had participated in the purchase and installation of the organs, the copying of chant books and polyphonic repertoire, and the hiring of the singers for the choir of the Valencian collegiate church. For the acquisition of the organs, he was in contact with the Bordons, the family of organ-builders based in Solsona (see Chapter 2), and the Catalonian town of Lleida was the main centre for the hiring of singers for the Corpus Christi music chapel in Valencia.

Similar inter-city music networks are found in convents. The Barcelonan convent of Santa Maria de Jerusalem, founded in the middle of the fifteenth century under the Franciscan rule, came to belong to the Order of Saint Clare in 1494, and three nuns from the Poor Clare convent of Valencia were brought to lead this transition; among them was Aldonça de Corella, who would serve as the first abbess of the Barcelonan convent between 1494 and 1504. They were welcomed by the Barcelonan nuns in procession singing the hymn *Te Deum laudamus*. It is intriguing that a chant book including a plainchant treatise handwritten in Catalan, dated in the mid-fifteenth century and today preserved in Barcelona, belonged to the Poor Clare convent in Valencia (Figure 5.1).[5] In turn, nuns of the convent of Jerusalem went out with the purpose of founding the convents of Santa Lucia de Caller in Sardinia and San Francisco in Lleida. The transfer of nuns between Barcelona and other regions of the Crown of Aragon was very frequent. The *Dietaris* record the fact that four nuns from Valencia arrived in Barcelona on 23 February 1568, and one of them was to go to the Dominican convent of Montsió (see Appendix 4.2) and, according to Castellano, the singing in Pedralbes must have been very similar to that at the convent of Santa Clara in Oristano in Sardinia (Castellano 1996: 553–554; see also Mele 1985).

Thus, Barcelonan nunneries participated in national and international musical exchanges, particularly through the existing networks of their religious orders. The effectiveness of such networks in diffusing music has been recently illustrated by Tomasz Jeż, who has shown that the forming of an alliance between the Jesuits and Cistercians in the Polish-Lithuanian Commonwealth promptly brought about changes to musical education and increased the speed with which polyphonic repertoire circulated (Jeż 2018). Similar movements are strongly detectable in networks of convents, and the case of Juan Bermudo's *El arte tripharia*, a music treatise printed in Osuna (Seville) in 1550, serves as a prime example of music books moving between religious houses through the established networks of their religious orders. Written in Spanish, this book was dedicated to Isabel Pacheco, abbess of the Poor Clare convent in Montilla (Córdoba), who, according to Bermudo, needed a brief handbook for her nuns' musical training and, in particular, for her niece who was to become a nun and needed to learn to sing and play the organ in a short space of time (Mazuela-Anguita 2012a: 319–333; 2012b). Bermudo accordingly published a brief three-part summary on plainsong, mensural music, and organ playing, which was aimed to be sufficient 'principally for nuns who are studious and only intend to know the Divine Office'.[6] The first eleven chapters of *El arte Tripharia* were translated word-for-word into Catalan and included in the *Ordinarium Barcinonense* (Barcelona, 1569), a liturgical book edited by the bishop of Barcelona, Guillem Caçador, with the aim of improving the training of both nuns and clergymen of his dioceses (Figure 5.2).[7] It was likely

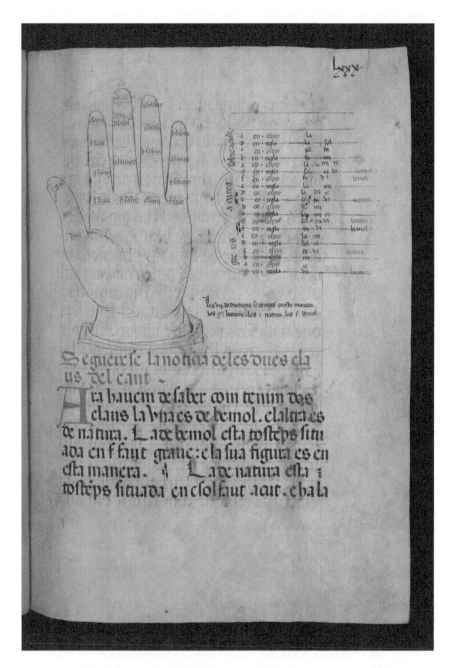

Figure 5.1. Plainchant treatise belonging to the Poor Clare convent in Valencia. *Ars cantus plani*, MS (fifteenth century). BC, M 1327 G. Fol, fols. 72v–89r, fol. 80r. Public Domain

Figure 5.2. Guillem Caçador, *Ordinarium Barcinonense* (Barcelona: Claudium Bornat, 1569), title-page and fol. 246v. BC, 10-III-1. Public Domain

Bermudo himself who sent a copy of the original edition to Pere Alberch Vila, the organist in Barcelona Cathedral (Ester 1985; Otaola 2000: 37–38).

Music as an emblem of cultural identity

Religious institutions drew heavily on local structures of power, and each had its own customs.[8] Convent music and liturgy served as an emblem of local cultural identity, so the musical and liturgical use of nunneries was a constant source of conflict with (male) authorities not only after, but also before, the Council of Trent, as the books of visitations of the convent of Santa Maria de Jonqueres make evident (Mazuela-Anguita 2018a). This nunnery constitutes a paradigmatic example of inter-city networks for the dissemination of musical practices through religious orders.

Music served as an important tool in the continuous process of reformation promoted by the Catholic Monarchs and Cardinal Cisneros from the late fifteenth century, whose objective was the transformation of the Church into a disciplined institution in the service of the Catholic Monarchs. Several case studies have shown how these connections between liturgy, music, and royal power had an impact on convent life. In 1493, Alexander VI granted powers to the Catholic Monarchs to appoint reformers and visitors for the religious orders. In the case of nunneries, this was typically done with the objective of imposing strict enclosure, alongside more rigorous fulfilment of the vows of obedience, poverty, and chastity, and more austere communal living in refectory and dormitory. Cisneros had promoted a reform, particularly of the Franciscan order, concerning the clergy's traditions and training, fuelling the Observant austerity in opposition to the convent brand of the order (see Chapter 4). According to Marcel Bataillon, Cisneros's reform of the Franciscan order aimed more 'to lead the way to an army of reformers which already was strong and popular'; moreover, Bataillon claims that any reforming zeal and successful implementation of significant change in Philip II's Counter-Reformation stemmed directly from pre-existing impulses of the Illuminist movement in the era of Cisneros and Charles V.[9]

As is described in Chapter 1, when the Catholic Monarchs became the administrators of the Order of Santiago at the end of the fifteenth century, visitors were periodically sent to inspect the nuns. Table 5.1 shows that most of these visitors came from Castile. The city councillors usually acted as mediators between the visitors' demanded reforms and the nuns and already in 1467 the councillors were ordered to visit all the nunneries in Barcelona to instruct the nuns to live honestly.[10] They encountered the nuns' resistance when they tried not only to impose enclosure on the convent, but also to 'correct' the particular liturgical practice of these nuns—which followed a 'very different' and 'ancient' style which was so deeply rooted that the nuns knew it by heart—and to replace it by the use of the Castilian monastery of Uclés (Cuenca), the primary seat of the Order of Santiago, and, after the Council of Trent, by the Roman liturgy.[11]

The books of visitations represent a constant polemical attack by the visitors on the nuns' liturgical and musical practices. This disagreement over the program of reforms imposed by visitors of the Order of Santiago and the resistance showed by the nuns to abandon their traditions has been described as a 'progressive dispute' (*contencioso progresivo*) (Altés 1990: 66–67). As early as May 1481, the visitors implemented new measures to make the nuns' liturgy conform to that of the monastery of Uclés: for instance, the nuns had to correct their way of performing the commemoration of the relics at the end of the Office, which supposed a modification of their liturgical and musical use:

> They [the visitors] had noticed that the nuns' performance of the commemoration of the relics was inconsistent, as they say the antiphon and the verse, and sing the prayer. Consequently, [the visitors] ordered the commemorations included in Matins and Vespers to be completely prayed, or else sung in full.[12]

In November of the same year, Alonso de Cárdenas, a general of the Order of Santiago, confirmed the prescriptions of the preceding visitors;[13] in 1495 the necessity for the nuns to conform to the Rule was reiterated, as well as among the orders given in the visit of 1499.[14] According to Diego de Mota, the visitors of 1501 described the nuns as being 'very good in their ecclesiastical practices, as much in singing, as in praying, and they prayed the breviary of the convent of Uclés in an orderly manner and with no discrepancy from the original'.[15]

Table 5.1. Visitors sent to the convent of Santa Maria de Jonqueres[a]

Visitation date	Visitors sent
1401	Juan García de Lisón, commander of Montalbán (Teruel)
	Juan Díez, sub-prior of the monastery of Uclés (Cuenca)
1480	Pedro Ramírez, sent by the monastery of Uclés (Cuenca)
1481, May	Juan Fernando de Pineda, knight and friar
	Juan Martínez, canon of the monastery of Uclés (Cuenca)
	Both appointed by Alonso de Cárdenas, last master of the Order of Santiago
1481, October	Gutierre de Cárdenas, *comendador mayor* of León and *trece* of the Order
	Appointed by the master of the Order
1493	Martí, elected bishop of Messina (Sicily, Italy)
	Galceran Cristófol de Gualbes, a guardian of Sant Francesc friary
	Antoni Joan Major, a priest
1495	Diego de Aguilera
	Diego Chacón, friar and vicar of Caravaca [de la Cruz] (Murcia)
	Sent by the Chapter of Tordesillas, Valladolid (the Catholic Monarchs granted a power of attorney to the visitors which is included in the records of the visitation)
1498–1499	Fernando de Pavía
	Álvaro (or Alonso) López, chaplain of Alcalá de Henares (Madrid)
1501	Francisco (or Fernando) de Villegas, commander of Villoria (Salamanca)
	Juan López de Ponte, rector of Villarejo (La Rioja)
	Sent by the Chapter of Granada (1499)
1504	Juan de Oñón de Ariño, knight of the Order of Santiago
	Pero Gil, rector of Estremera (Madrid)
	Sent by the Chapter of Écija, Seville (1502)
1509	Juan de Oñón de Ariño, knight of the Order of Santiago
	Diego Chacón, in the place of Jerónimo de Cabanillas, commander of Enguera (Valencia), appointed in 1505
1512	No names are recorded
1515	Juan de Oñón de Ariño, knight of the Order of Santiago
	Rodrigo de Monterroso, friar of the monastery of Uclés (Cuenca) and rector of Cehegín (Murcia)
	Sent by Ferdinand the Catholic
1529	Lluís de Gilabert, knight of the Order of Santiago
	Pedro Ramírez Fleyre, rector of Campo de Criptana (Ciudad Real)
	Sent by Charles V
1538	Bartolomé González de Villena, sub-prior of Uclés (Cuenca) and rector of Villamanrique (Ciudad Real)
1549	Bartolomé González de Villena, rector of Socuéllamos (Ciudad Real)
	Juan de Pastrana, rector of Torrenueva (Ciudad Real)
1556	Juan de Quintana, commander of Almendralejo (Badajoz)
	Francisco Sánchez, rector of Campo de Criptana (Ciudad Real)
1560–1561	Pedro Morejón
	Cristóbal Díez, a clergyman

(*Continued*)

210 *Beyond the city*

Table 5.1. (Continued)

Visitation date	Visitors sent
1566	Juan de Grimaldo
	Sebastián de Ruano
1573	Francisco de Mendoza, commander of Fuente del Maestre (Badajoz)
	Francisco de Herrera, rector of Usagre (Badajoz)
1576	Francisco de Zúñiga Valdés
	Alonso Cano, a clergyman
1597	Antonio de Pessoa, commander of Fuente del Maestre (Badajoz)
	Juan Blanco, administrator of the Hospital of Santiago de los Caballeros in Toledo
1605	Juan de Acuña Ulloa
	Jerónimo Romero, rector of Colmenar de Oreja (Madrid)
1628	Francesc de Sagarriga
	Juan Esteban Nieto Ortiz, a clergyman

[a] The names of most of these visitors are mentioned in Costa 1974: 260.

Nevertheless, in 1515 visitors gave instructions to the choir director about liturgical practice. For example, the Offices had to be celebrated solemnly and the psalms well pronounced, and nuns had to observe a pause in the middle of the verse. The last syllables both in the middle and at the end of the verse had to be shortened.[16] Thus, these prescriptions, adjustments, and corrections allow us to obtain a glimpse of the musical practices in Santa Maria de Jonqueres, and the extent to which they were subject to external scrutiny.

While the visitors of 1529 reiterated the orders of the previous visitation,[17] in 1538 Bartolomé González de Villena, sub-prior of the monastery of Uclés, indicated that, although in some things the nuns conformed to the Rule of the Order, 'in other many things they had another way and a very different style', and he concluded it to be 'very difficult to change completely their ancient manner and style'.[18] As a consequence, the records of the 1538 visitation are particularly informative from a musical point of view, as they contain detailed descriptions over the course of ten paragraphs describing aspects of the liturgical practice that needed to be changed, instead of simply imposing the breviary of the Order—it was González de Villena who commanded the two youngest female choristers to learn how to play the organ with the purpose of teaching other girls (see Chapter 2). It was stipulated, for instance, that every Saturday morning the votive Mass of Our Lady had to be sung, as at the time of the visitation it had been necessary for the ceremony to be said 'due to the lack of nuns'.[19] It was further directed that on double feast days the Gloria and the Credo had to be prayed by the choir in alternation with the organ. On days when the organ was not played, the liturgical texts were to be sung throughout:

> When the organs are played, the nun who presides must always perform Kyrie, Gloria, Credo, Sanctus, Agnus, and Magnificat with the choir in *alternatim* with the organ in the way the nuns have been informed. On solemn

double feasts the choir will always perform the Gloria and the Credo in *alternatim* with the organ. On the other days when the organs are played, they should render a spoken recitation of these prayers. When there is no organ, everything will be sung, with the first verse of the Gloria (*Et in terra pax hominibus bonae voluntatis*) and the Credo (*Credo Patrem omnipotemtem*, etc.) by the singers.[20]

It is even specified when the singers were obliged to stand up, kneel, or incline their heads, depending on the text being performed. Bartolomé González himself carried out the visitation of 1549, in which he reiterated the prescriptions of that of 1538, which indicates that the nuns had resisted the prescribed changes to their liturgical and musical use during those eleven years. In addition to repeating the earlier orders, it was added that, 'henceforward, the nuns have to pray according to the festivities of the calendar of the new breviary of the order'.[21] Bartolomé González's very detailed prescriptions with regard to the musical use raise the question of whether he had a particular interest or training in music. There is evidence that he studied in Beas de Segura (Jaén) (Villegas and García 1976: 61), and that, having finished his tasks as a visitor in Castile and Catalonia, he was elected prior of the monastery of Uclés in 1562 (Javierre and Couto 1976: 137).

The following visit to the convent of Santa Maria de Jonqueres took place in 1556, when the visitors approved the convent's practice of the Office, although the nuns still did not follow some aspects of the new breviary of the Order: 'it seemed to them [the visitors] that everything was done well, except for non-conformity in some things to the new breviary of the order, which causes some confusion in the Divine Office'.[22] To solve this problem, the prioress was asked to go to Castile with the purpose of borrowing a missal from the monastery of Uclés (see Chapter 2).[23] The following visit took place between late 1560 and early 1561 and visitors prescribed again that missals and breviaries of the Order be brought from Uclés and used in Santa Maria de Jonqueres.[24] The *Dietaris* record news of a complaint by the nuns addressed to the *Diputació*—they had also appealed to the king and the General Chapter of the Order—on the action of the visitor Pedro Mojerón: on 26 December 1560 it is reported that the visitor 'was the source of some grievance to the nuns', and on 4 March 1561 the same visitor made five nuns to leave the convent (see Appendix 4.2). However, ultimately, the General Chapter of the Order upheld the visitor's injunctions.

In 1566, the visitors indicated that the nuns and vicars still did not sing according to use of the Order, and repeated once again that the prioress, sub-prioress, and *capiscola* had to 'celebrate the sung Masses according to the missal of the Order, which had to be followed also by the vicars when singing the Mass', alleging that not to follow the precepts that had been prescribed was 'a very indecent and disordered thing'. Moreover, the nuns were commanded not to sing or pray from memory: the visitors ordered that, 'before starting to sing Masses or Vespers, [...] the singing nuns must always have written down that which was to be sung and recited in the choir; they were not allowed to say anything by heart even if they knew it'.[25]

It seems probable that the nuns of Santa Maria de Jonqueres never abandoned their liturgical and musical tradition totally in order to conform to the liturgical books of the Order of Santiago, as the Council of Trent would change the paradigm with the prescription of the Roman breviary by Pius V in 1568. The new instructions are reflected in the records of the visitation of 1576, when the visitors required Masses and Offices to be sung according to Roman books as stated at the Council of Trent: they commanded that the prioress, succentor, and nuns of the convent pray in the Roman manner and celebrate 'sung Masses using Roman missals and breviaries as stated now'.[26] The implementation of the decrees of the Council of Trent was slow and partial, not only in nunneries, but also across Spanish religious institutions more generally. Despite the enthusiasm of Philip II for adopting the Tridentine recommendations, numerous clergymen opposed the changes (Kamen 1998: 31).

In the case of Barcelona, it has been argued that nuns were especially resistant to the Tridentine reformations, as they enjoyed the support of influential sectors of society who were similarly unfavourable towards these reforms.[27] For example, the *Dietaris* include an incomplete report from 15 May 1567 on what seems to be the resistance of the nuns of the Dominican convent of Montsió to the decisions of the general of the Order of Preachers (see Appendix 4.2). Likewise, the records of the visitations to the convent of Santa Maria de Jonqueres after 1576 reflect the nuns' resistance to abandoning their own traditions.

The prohibitions on musical activities related to liturgical reforms provide further evidence on the connections of Barcelona nuns and other cities as regards music-making through particular religious orders. The extent to which the prohibitions on types of music-making which were placed on different religious orders across Europe were implemented offers a useful lens for understanding the connections between Barcelonan convents and those further abroad. In the case of Germany, the perception that music-making in convents was constrained while being unhindered in monasteries has been recently challenged,[28] while it has been demonstrated that bishops tolerated or even encouraged music-making by nuns in Ferrara (Stras 2018: 19). Bishop Giambattista Maremonti, as the visitor of the Ferrarese convents after Trent, expressed his worries about the permeability of the cloister, giving instructions to remove all musical instruments besides the organ. However, in Ferrara, the relaxing of the rules was negotiated locally through bishopric. Paolo Leoni, who was appointed as bishop in 1578, fostered musical life in Ferrara convents, but this was not perceived as beneficial by everyone: according to Stras (2018: 225), music after the Council of Trent was seen as a secular threat to the religious discipline, rather than as a means by which the religious ideas might influence the outside world.

At the convent of Sant Antoni i Santa Clara in Barcelona, which used to follow the Benedictine rule, the Roman liturgy was implemented in 1598. A convent book indicates that a Mass was sung daily, with a deacon or sub-deacon on feast days. On Sundays, at six in the morning, a Mass was sung by the chaplains with no participation from the nuns. The Masses and Offices that had to be sung and prayed are specified in detail, as is the celebration of processions. For instance, on the first Sunday after the feast of Saint Francis, an Office of the Guardian Angel was to be performed with organ. The order in which the nuns sat in the choir was also the subject of a separate chapter,[29] while two others are devoted to 'the ceremonies of the choir and the offices sung at this convent' and to the festivities celebrated throughout the year, respectively.[30]

Similarly detailed instructions are given for the convent of Santa Maria de Jonqueres by an equivalent book of choir ceremonies which was compiled in 1640 by Juana de Argençola, director of the choir.[31] This book probably functioned as a guide to the future choir directors and Fontanet's history of this nunnery devoted a chapter to the functions of the *capiscola*, referring to the importance of having a booklet as a guide.[32] This book of ceremonies indicates that the nuns were organised in two choirs placed on the right and on the left of the choir space, respectively. In each choir, distinction was made between the older nuns (*antigas* or *majors*) and choristers (*escolanas*), establishing degrees within a hierarchy (*grados*) based on the seniority and experience of the nuns (*la antiga major, la mès xica de las escolanas*, etc.).[33] When the novices entered the convent, they started as choristers of *tercera lliço*. The soloists were the prioress, the sub-prioress, the president, the hebdomad (*domera* or *semanera*), the major choir director (*capiscola mayor*), the minor choirs directors (*capiscolas menores*), the two 'singers of cross' (*cantoras de Creu*), and the two singer *escolanas*; in the three last cases there was one in each choir. The high level of detail in this document extends even to specifying exact locations of individual singers.[34] Rather than stipulate when the organ should be played, this service book more commonly dictates when the organ should fall silent, which probably indicates that its use in liturgical celebrations was the default custom. For instance, on Christmas Day, 'the first responsory without organ is to be said by the prioress and sub-prioress'; on Holy Thursday, 'the organ must not be played after the Epistle'; and on Eastern Day, 'the organ must not sound in the first responsory'.[35] The occasions when the prioress and sub-prioress, or else two choir directors, had to carry rods (*bordons*) while they sang are also stated.

Although the observation of the Roman liturgy was the theoretical ideal, it is not known if, in practice, the nuns kept their own traditions. In the visitation of 1628 the nuns were still being warned not to pray by heart.[36] The visits of Castilian knights and friars to the convent of Santa Maria de Jonqueres formed part of a programme of constant reform which was functioning from the time of the Catholic Monarchs and the books of visitations reflect the changes and resistances with regard to musical and liturgical practices, in order to unify them according to the practices of the rest of the convents of the Order of Santiago located outside Barcelona. However, the tradition of these nuns was so deeply rooted that it was performed by heart throughout the centuries, which makes it difficult to determine, through written documents alone, the real impact the prescriptions of the visitors from Castile had on the musical life of the Barcelonan convent.

Oral traditions of music

Contemporary reports describing the musical activities of nuns in sixteenth-century Barcelona are relatively common, which is a situation not matched in cities

214 *Beyond the city*

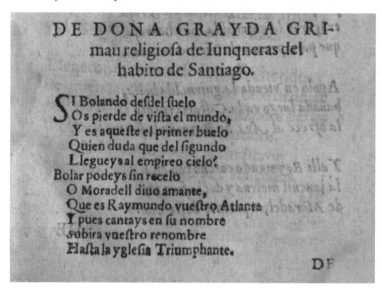

Figure 5.3. Poem by Agraïda Grimau (d.1614), included among the preliminary material of: Vicente Miguel de Moradell, *Historia de S. Ramon de Peñafort frayle de Predicadores en coplas Castellanas* (Barcelona: Sebastián de Cormellas, 1603), s. fol. BC, 8-II-29. Public Domain

like Florence, where the scarcity of such descriptions after the Council of Trent has been ascribed to the influence of the Medici family's own brand of personal piety.[37] However, the wealth of these detailed accounts stands in stark contrast to the dearth of sources of polyphonic music associated with convents, and it seems probable that this imbalance stems from a strongly oral culture of music-making. Likewise, the identity of nuns who acted as composers remains elusive, although poetry written by nun musicians has survived. For instance, the aforementioned Agraïda Grimau owned a harp and a clavichord, but we have no sources for the study of her musical or compositional activities as the choir director of Santa Maria de Jonqueres nunnery. By contrast, her poetic output has been preserved in printed books (Serrano y Sanz 1974: vol. 1, 471–472), and one of her poems is included among the prefatory material of a biography of the friar Raimon de Penyafort printed in Barcelona (Figure 5.3). In this poem she praised the book's author, Vicente Miguel de Moradell, describing the soaring achievement of his first work as a flight through the skies which passes beyond the sight of those on the ground:

> *Si Bolando desde el suelo*
> *os pierde de vista el mundo,*
> *y es aqueste el primer vuelo*
> *quien duda que del sigundo*
> *llegueys al empireo cielo?*

Bolar podeys sin recelo
o Moradell diuo amante,
que es Raymundo vuestro Atlante
y pues cantays en su nombre
subira vuestro renombre
hasta la yglesia Triumphante. (Moradell 1603: s. fol.)

Grimau also entered a sonnet and a gloss in the poetry competition celebrated in Saragossa on the occasion of the beatification feasts of Teresa of Ávila in October 1614 (Figures 5.4a and 5.4b):

Soneto de Doña Grayda Grimau

Dichosa Madre que del alto cielo
conquistays el autor de la grandeza
Virgen que le obligays con la pureza
a que fie su honor de vuestro zelo.

Que mucho que os subays de solo vn vuelo
a pisar de los cielos la belleza
si por mostrar con vos Dios su largueza
os hizo esposa suya, y cielo el suelo.

Mas que a su Madre quiso auentajaros,
pues en Iosef le entrega a ella Esposo
y Dios en Dios, a vos por solo houraros.

El clauo que os ha dado tan costoso
por atrás, y señal que pudo amaros
ponedle a la fortuna victorioso (Díez de Aux 1615: 86).

Glosa de Doña Grayda Grimau

No siendo madre de Dios
no hallo santa a quien le quadre
llamarse Virgen y madre
Teresa major que a uos.

GLOSA
Entoldase el cielo hermoso
de mil diamantes de estrellas
y entre arreboles vistoso
muestra sus luzes mas bellas
y su mouil mas curioso.

a la Beatificacion de la S. M. T. de Iesus.

quien tiene santos como el mar arenas
y ya el mundo con vos le viene estrecho
el remate sereis de su cadena.
  Tiene El principio sin principio hecho
Maria del Pilar de gracia llena
que a tal cadena es justo que le quadre
tener principio y fin de Virgen Madre

GLOSA.
Del Doctor IaymeLuys Ram.

No siendo Madre de Dios,
no hallo santa a quien le quadre
llamarse Virgen y Madre.
Teresa mejor que a vos.
  GLOSA.
AVnque a Dios le consagraron
  su castidad peregrina
muchas que de si triumfaron,
mas madre y Virgen diuina,
sola a la de Dios llamaron.
Y aunque Maria, entre nos
no ay madre Virgen qual vos,
Teresa llega a tener
esso, y quanto puede ser,
no siendo madre de Dios.

  Y si aquello a nadie espanta
por ser sobrenatural
en Maria Virgen santa,
no siendo en vos natural
admira grandeza tanta.
Porque aunque el hereje ladre
obrolo el Eterno Padre
en aquella clara estrella,
mas como a vos Virgen bella
no hallo sancta a quien le quadre.

  Bien serà que esteis gozosa,
pues tal gloria no se dio
si al alua vella y hermosa,
que pariendo al sol, quedó,
madre y Virgen milagrosa
Pero aunque a solas le quadre
para gloria de Dios Padre
auiendo otra que Maria
vos sola sois quien podia

llamarse Virgen y madre.
  Y como aqueste blason
oy el Pontifice os da,
no causarà admiracion,
antes claro se verà
ques en vos celestial don.
Que pues ser Madre de Dios,
no puede estar entre dos
si Maria no lo fuera
no se yo a quien compitiera
Teresa mejor que a vos.

GLOSA.
Del P. F. Bernardo de Iesus Maria Carmelita Descalço.

NO siendo Madre de Dios
  no hallo Santa a quien le quadre
llamarse Virgen y Madre
Teresa mejor que a vos.
  GLOSA.
AQual coraçon no espanta
  Mirar Teresa gloriosa
la alta suerte y venturosa
a que el sumo Dios leuanta
vuestra virtud milagrosa?
quiere que Maria y vos
Madres seais, y las dos
Virgenes tambien seays
ved Teresa a do llegais
no siendo Madre de Dios.

  Soys Virgen intacta y pura
y sois Madre del Carmelo
Luna de su hermoso cielo
que clarificais su hechura
con vuestro encendido zelo
siendo pues Virgen y Madre
de quien Helias fue padre
ser Virgen Madre que cria
despues de vos y Maria
no hallo Santa a quien le quadre

  No solo Madre se llama
la que con leche alimenta

Figures 5.4a and 5.4b. Sonnet and gloss by Agraïda Grimau (d.1614), in Luis Díez de Aux, *Retrato de las fiestas que á la Beatificacion de la Bienaventurada Virgen y Madre Santa Teresa de Iesus, Renouadora de la Religion Primiua del Carmelo, hizo, assi Ecclesiasticas como Militares y Poeticas: la Imperial Ciudad de Zaragoça* (Saragossa: Iuan de la Naja y Quartanet, 1615), pp. 86, 98–99. BNE, R/457. Public Domain

98   *Retrato de las Fiestas hechas*

que détro el coraçon no os tenga impresa.
 De vuestra gloria santa nos holgamos
viendo logrados ya nuestros intentos,
del gozo, y del contéto en que os miramos
tenemos mil alegres sentimientos,
Y estas sagradas Aras frequentamos
alegres, y gozosos, y contentos
porque es contento, gozo, y alegria
a todo el mundo este dichoso dia.

 Y la inuicta ciudad que es gloria imméſa
de todas las que iluſtran nueſtra Eſpaña
a quien sin darle con su furia ofensa
con rapida corriente el Ebro baña
Y la que tiene el cielo por defensa
quando enemigo Rey la inquieta, y daña
iluſtre por la linea de sus Reyes
y por sus francas y seguras leyes.

 Del noble Reyno la cabeça Augusta
en quien no porque Cesar la edifica
mas por la Virgen que amparalla gusta,
Y para templo suyo la dedica,
y porque la bañó la sangre justa,
que su suelo humedece, y santifica,
siempre han tenido con estrecho ñudo
la Religion amparo, y la fe Escudo

 En esta gloria grande que le toca
seguro aliuio del mayor trabajo
con estas sacras fiestas os inuoca
que con razon a todas auentajo
Los Cisnes blancos de su rio conuoca,
que imbidia el Betis y procura el tajo
y al dulce son de su acordado acento,
da muestras de su gloria y su contento.

OCTAVAS.
De Pedro Mongay Despes.

A Y en el apetito sensitiuo
 amor, desseo, y gozo conuenientes
y encierranse tambien en este Archiuo
odio, fuga, y tristeza diferentes.
En lo mejor, amor toma motiuo,
de las cosas que tiene en si presentes
y pues le pone el mundo oy en Teresa,

por lo mejor, sin duda, la confiessa.
 Al punto que el amor la elecion haze
pudiendose alcançar el tal objeto,
el desseo, le sigue, busca, y nace,
y procura gozarle en su conceto.
El mundo que en quanto ay se satisfaze
de Teresa en lo publico y secreto
oy la busca con tales coraçones,
que es milagro, que viua en sus passiones.

 Prosiguiendo el desseo sus intentos,
viene tras sus trabajos à alcançallos,
y metido en sus glorias, por momentos
procura con mil hymnos celebrallos.
Como alcança Salduba oy sus contentos,
dessea hasta los cielos remontallos;
Para que halla los Angeles entienen
lo que aca los ingenios no componen.

 Nace el odio de aquello que no agrada,
y tenemos delante la presencia,
al reues del amor, passion passada
estando ambas a dos en competencia.
La serpiente, Phiton, como turbada
de ver en nuestra santa esta potencia,
como esta halla el odio en lo mas bueno,
dexa de odio el infierno todo lleno.

 Huye luego el encuentro, y se retira
y tras su amarga fuga tan medrosa
de tormento y dolor llena se mira
rabia y gime, vozea y no reposa.
Procura amenazarnos con su ira
detienela Teresa poderosa.
y canta Zaragoça oy su victoria,
con Palma, Lauro, Oliuo, Grama, y Gloria.

 Quien pudiera cantar, o ciudad santa
las muestras que de amor das a Teresa?
mas la Aue, el Bruto, el Pez, todo lo canta
o almenos con señales lo confiessa.
Tu amor, desseo, y gozo, ya me encanta,
y puedes bien creer de que me pesa,
de no auer sido, à aqueste efecto solo,
Mercurio, Pan, Orfeo, Lino, Apolo.

GLOSA.
De doña Grayda Grimau.

NO

Figures 5.4 (Continued)

a la Beatificacion de la S. M. T. de Iesus.

No siendo Madre de Dios
no hallo santa a quien le quadre
llamarse Virgen y madre
Teresa mejor que a vos.

GLOSA.

Entoldasse el cielo hermoso
de mil diamantes de estrellas
y entre arreboles vistoso
muestra sus luzes mas bellas
y su mouil mas curioso,

    Angeles de dos en dos
rompen el ayre velos
lleuando al Eterno Padre
nueuas de vna Virgen Madre
no siendo Madre de Dios.

    Es vn Apostol diuino
la que va a pisar el cielo
vn Profeta pues conuino
serlo para dar al suelo
fruto que es fruto diuino,

    Es Felicissima Madre
con hijos sin tener padre
siendo Virgen en efeto
el ser Madre en vn sujeto
no hallo santa a quien le quadre.

    Que rudo he andado Teresa
en no dezir vuestro nombre
tan digno de aquesta impressa
que no ay hombre a quien no asombre
en vos la naturaleza.

    Pues desde el primero padre
quiso Dios Virgen que os quadre
sin su Madre, que es Esphera
ser sola vos quien pudiera
llamarse Virgen y Madre:

    Soys en estremo dichosa
pues aueys a Dios rendido
y tan santa como hermosa
pues a ser aueys venido
del mismo que os hizo Esposa.

    Y del amor de los dos
me atreuo a dezir de Dios
que si mas gloria tuuiera
a ninguno se la diera
Teresa mejor que a vos.

GLOSA.

Del Padre Fr. Hernando
del Espiritu santo.

No siendo Madre de Dios
no hallo santa a quien le quadre
llamarse Virgen y Madre
Teresa mejor que a vos

GLOSA.

SI vuestro amor puro ardiente
del todo en Dios os transforma
y al inmenso omnipotente
rinde, concibe, e informa
en ser de amado excelente

    Si de esse amor y querer
quiso Dios en vos nacer
(aunque no encarnase en vos)
Madre de Dios podeis ser
no siendo Madre de Dios,

    Mas este pasto diuino
y concepto soberano
abrio en vuestra alma camino
aun concepto y pasto humano
nuebo, raro y peregrino.

    Pues la gracia de Dios Padre
que en vn sexo y otro os hizo
de infinitos hijos Madre
como en vos la solemniço
no hallo santa a quie le quadre

    Estos diuinos fauores
y castissimos amores
Virgen pura en cuerpo, y alma
en la palma, os ponen palma,
en frente y sienes, mil flores

    Y el ser Virgen tan fecunda
primera os haze a quie quadre
despues de la sin segunda
y de humildad mas profunda)
llamarse Virgen y Madre

    Tanto en estas excelencias
Virgen Madre os encumbrais
que la vista deslumbrais
de las mas altas potencias
del cielo adonde morays

    Y assi por cierto tuuiera
si auiendo de nacer Dios
de su madre no naciera
que a ninguna otra escogiera
Teresa mejor que a vos.

Figures 5.4 (Continued)

Angeles de dos en dos
rompen el ayre velos
lleuando al Eterno Padre
nueuas de vna Virgen Madre
no siendo Madre de Dios.

Es vn Apostol diuino
la que va a pisar el cielo
vn Profeta pues conuinò
serlo para dar al suelo
fruto que es fruto diuino.

Es Felicissima Madre
con hijos sin tener padre
siendo Virgen en efeto
al ser Madre env n sujeto
no hallo santa a quien le quadre.

Que rudo he andado Teresa
en no dezir vuestro nombre
tan digno de aquella impressa
que no ay hombre a quien no asombre
en vos la naturaleza.

Pues desde el primero padre
quiso Dios Virgen que os quadre
sin su Madre que es Esphera
ser sola vos quien pudiera llamarse Virgen y Madre.

Soys en estremo dichosa
pues aueys a Dios rendido
y tan santa como hermosa
pues a ser aueys venido
del mismo que os hizo Esposa.

Y del amor de los dos
me atreuo a dezir de Dios
que si mas Gloria tuuiera
a ninguno se la diera
Teresa major que a vos. (Díez de Aux 1615: 98–99)

Although Agraïda Grimau died in August that year, it is possible that she had previously sent her poems to be read in the competition:

> A very high and well-proportioned theatre had been built in the main chapel [of the Carmelite convent] [...]. The best seats were occupied by the bishop,

the bailiff, town councillors, and the judges of the poetry competition. [...] His Lordship and the monks of the friary ordered the verses to be read aloud in public every evening. Thus, after Vespers, two clergymen went up into two pulpits, while the rest of the citizens sat in silence. Poems were read aloud alternatively from the two pulpits. Musical instruments were played when the reading of each poem finished. This [music] and some elegant verses made for a very pleasant and joyful evening.[38]

In the verdict of the competition, Grimau was praised three times for her poetic skills and her noble style, with comments comparing her with the nymphs of the Parnassos.[39] Both her contribution to Moradell's book and her participation in literary events beyond the cloister reflect her integration in wider cultural life with and outside Barcelona. The existence of her poems raises questions of whether some of her poems were intended to be sung, possibly by herself and accompanied on the harp she owned.

The traditional focus of musicological studies on politically significant institutions (such as royal courts, noble houses, and cathedrals), together with the continued application of the contentions categories of 'composer' and 'musical work' in the study of the early modern era, is widely recognised as favouring traditions of written music, inevitably giving rise to the phenomenon of lost women's voices in music history. However, in the period in question, the teaching of music was generally based on oral and memorised practices, and the boundaries between performance and composition were indistinct. Contextual studies considering the coexistence of oral and written traditions, rather than any linear 'progression' to the latter (Berger 2005), tie early modern musicology to much wider debates concerning musical exchange and transmission; for example, the migration of the Sephardi Jewish diaspora in the Mediterranean region following their expulsion from Spain in 1492 offers an important historical example where the experiences of an ethnic community can be interpreted in light of theories around the shaping of new cultural collectives (Shelemay 2011), the relationship between the arts and identity in diaspora communities (Whiteley *et al.* 2004; Ramnarine 2007), and musical-cultural exchange in the refugee experience (Utz 2004). Twentieth-century Spanish collections of traditional music reflect the importance of women in the oral dissemination of folklore music over the centuries (Mazuela-Anguita 2015d), and further research is needed in order to discern how women contributed to the preservation and diffusion of oral national and regional traditions of music in the modern period.

While the pre-Tridentine reforms encouraged by the Spanish crown in the late fifteenth and early sixteenth centuries are predominantly recognised for having promoted simplicity in the Divine Office, they also saw Cardinal Cisneros fuel new forms of spirituality and devotion, as well as the protection of some *beatas* who would later be treated with mistrust in the Counter-Reformation,[40] and also the translation of books into the vernacular to be used in convents. Moreover, the growing prevalence of Franciscan ideals of contemplative devotion outside the formal liturgy resulted in the strong tradition of performing devotional poetry in the vernacular using melodies known by oral transmission. These practices, in which women were heavily involved, were linked to similar customs in Europe such as the Italian *cantasi come* tradition and the *lauda spirituale*,[41] and took place in both convent and court spaces, as a pious entertainment and as part of theatre plays.[42]

Musical repertoires in the oral tradition spanned a wide range of secular genres intended for recreation as well as the sacred genres for divine praise described above; interestingly, the oral repertoires of both convents and domestic spaces typically contained a combination of each. According to Marca, the Valencian noblewoman Eugènia Salzedo i Salazar (1579–1645), who moved to Tortosa (Tarragona) when she was widowed in order to devote herself to works of charity, was known to sing lyrics devoted to Christ and the Virgin in her home, together with little girls to whom she taught as a form of recreation:

> [Eugènia Salzedo i Salazar] used to ask Cándia Borràs—who was one of the girls she taught and had a clear and soft voice—to sing the lyrics. One day, the girl sang a very devout song. With a very sonorous voice, she started the first cuartilla:
>
> *Cordero, y Pan de los Cielos,*
> *Yo te vi recién nacido,*
> *Exemplo de lo que pueden*
> *Las grandezas de ti mismo.*
>
> The venerable Eugènia listened to her with great pleasure and she continued to say:
>
> *Por lo que fuiste primero,*
> *Estàs tan desconocido,*
> *Qué de un Sayal disfrazado*
> *Entre unas pajas te miro.*
>
> Once this was said, and Eugènia enraptured in ecstasy, she continued her singing with more sweetness and softness than before:
>
> *Nació de la Aurora el Sol,*
> *Y de sus rayos vestido*
> *Fuè Ciudadano en la Tierra,*
> *De las Estrellas vezino.*[43]

This might be anecdotal, but it allows us to obtain a glimpse of laywomen's musical practices in the domestic milieu. Fray Antonio de Valenzuela, in his *Doctrina christiana para los niños y para los humildes* (Salamanca, 1556), described how the Catholic Monarchs gave the preachers of their chapel, such as Íñigo de Mendoza (c.1424–c.1508) and Ambrosio Montesino (c.1450–1514), the task of writing devotional romances and villancicos so that only this repertoire was sung 'in the chamber'.[44] Álvaro Bustos, a scholar in the field of literature, emphasises the reference to a 'chamber' where 'these poems were sung before the monarchs themselves' and suggests the possibility that a particular staging took place in which 'musicians and singers must have participated at the request of the friars, who assumed the function of organisers of spectacles'.[45] Bustos also argues that 'the devotional romances and villancicos [...] would not be received as something altogether different from preaching'.[46] In fact, 'many Franciscan theologians were also preachers and song composers' (Loewen 2013: 11).

Cisneros played a central role in restoring the practice of performing these secular songs in the convent setting, but they performed an important role in the theatrical performances with didactic purposes which commonly took place in convents. Before Cisneros's reformation, Gómez Manrique wrote a play entitled *Representación del nacimiento de nuestro Señor* for his sister María, who was the prioress at the convent in Calabazanos (Palencia). The play concluded with a lullaby, probably performed by the full community (Cátedra 1987: 314–315). According to the convent's tradition, the princess Isabel attended the premiere of the play, although there is no documentary evidence testifying to her presence on that occasion (Salvador 2012: 142). Theatrical performances with music in convents served as a type of 'spiritual entertainment and learning for women' (Weaver 2002), and Cisneros's reformation undoubtedly reaffirmed and encouraged the importance of these performances. Later manuscript documents testify to the continued appearance of these songs in the plays which were staged in convents. For instance, in *Fiestecilla del nacimiento* by María de San Alberto (1568–1640), a nun at the Discalced Carmelite convent in Valladolid, it is indicated that two people are to perform a *tonada*, singing and playing the vihuela, respectively, as background music during the play. In this case, a manuscript copy of the music and lyrics of the *tonada* which was performed on this occasion survives in the convent's library (reproduced in Arenal and Schlau 1989: 128).

Thus, in opposition to the simplicity prescribed in liturgical music, the new forms of spirituality promoted by Cisneros fuelled and gave new life to the existent practice of music-making in the oral tradition. The most emblematic example of Cisneros's sponsorship of vernacular styles is his promotion in convents in Toledo of the two *contrafacta* books published by Ambrosio Montesino in 1485 and 1508, respectively.[47] Cisneros and Montesino were both members of the Observant community of San Juan de los Reyes in Toledo, the great religious foundation of the Catholic Monarchs. Montesino has been considered 'a loudspeaker of Cisneros's ideas and proposals' and also a developer of an 'intellectual labour supporting Cisneros's reformist ideology'.[48] Most of the dedicatees of Montesino's poems were women, including the queen and her elder daughter Isabel of Portugal, noblewomen, and nuns in Toledo's convents (Ros-Fábregas 1993 and 2008: 90). Montesino's songbooks served as a type of music book without music notation, and it is probable that women sang Montesino's lyrics at royal rooms and convents as a type of shared entertainment, in a format that might have taken several hours.[49] Therefore, the commissioning of books of devotional lyrics to be sung is a type of unrecorded musical patronage which functioned for women as a way of expressing their piety.

One of the many later examples that reflect the longevity of this tradition promoted by Cisneros in Franciscan convents is *Minerva sacra* (Madrid, 1616), a well-known collection of villancico lyrics published by Miguel Toledano and dedicated to Alfonsa de Salazar (d.1639–1641), a Franciscan nun at the convent of Constantinople in Madrid who was said to sing Toledano's verses.[50] The book includes a sonnet by Miguel de Cervantes praising her musical skills, two poems by her as a token of gratitude to Toledano, and an engraving depicting this nineteen-year-old nun singing the psalm *In conspectus Angelorum* accompanying herself with the harp (Figure 5.5). One wonders whether the powerful imagery of this depiction emulated the same cultural resonances which would have been evoked by Agraïda Grimau when singing with her harp.

Another edition demonstrating the prevalence of vernacular devotional song which replicated traditional oral repertoire is the *Cancionero de Nuestra Señora: en el qual ay muy buenos romances, canciones y villancicos: aora nueuamente añadido*, printed in Barcelona in 1591 (Figure 5.6).[51] Although the book does not contain musical notation, it is indicated in the case of some of the *goigs*, songs, villancicos, and romances which tune is to be sung to the lyrics (Table 5.2). There are also some *coplas* which were 'newly composed' *por sol fa mi re* (fol. 73r), including one forming an acrostic on the names of the degrees of the scale (fol. 75v). Some *coplas* by Ambrosio Montesino are also included at the end. It seems likely that this songbook, which was printed by the aforementioned María Velasco, may well have been used by nuns and noblewomen in Barcelona in the same way as Montesinos's songbooks were in Toledo. Some of the tunes referred to in this publication, such as 'Aquel pastorico', were widely known and circulated throughout the Hispanic world (Knighton and Kreitner 2019). Some of the melodies, such as 'Pedro el Boreguero', 'Cucaracha Martínez', 'Mari García', or 'Mi marido anda cuitato', have been described as highly 'plebeian' and even 'rogue', to the point that it seems unthinkable that they accompanied devotional lyrics.[52]

The connections between Valencia and Barcelona through oral traditions of music are reflected in the case of the poems of Onofre Almudéver, a poet and bookseller in Valencia who was active between 1550 and 1569 (Mahiques 2019). Three of his broadsheets containing song lyrics were printed in Barcelona: two editions of *Silua de varios romances*, printed by Pedro Borin in 1550 (the sole exemplar now being held at the British Library), and by Jaume Cortey in 1552 (in the sole exemplar held at the Herzog August Bibliothek), respectively; and *Coplas en alabança de la Virgen nuestra Señora al tono de ya tiene saya blanca, con otras dos canciones muy deuotas*, printed by Sebastián de Cormellas in 1609 (Figure 5.7), which is believed to be a reprint of an earlier Valencian broadsheet now lost (Mahiques 2019: 149). It contains poems in honour of the Virgin indicating the tunes—of secular origin— which they were to be sung to: 'Ya tiene saya blanca', 'Bella de vos som enamorós', and 'Qué bonita que es la zagala'. The second, 'Bella, de vos som amorós', is an anonymous three-voice Catalan villancico attributed to Mateo Flecha El Viejo and included at the *Cancionero de Uppsala* (RISM 1556/30, fols. 17v–19r; Figure 5.8).

Figure 5.5. Alfonsa de Salazar (d.1639–1641) playing the harp and singing, in Miguel Toledano, *Minerva Sacra* (Madrid: Iuan de la Cuesta, 1616). Santiago de Compostela, Biblioteca de la Universidade, Biblioteca Xeral 8756. Public Domain

Beyond the city 225

Figure 5.6. Title page of *Cancionero de Nuestra Señora: en el qual ay muy buenos romances, canciones y villancicos: aora nueuamente añadido* (Barcelona: en casa de la biuda de Hubert Gotart, 1591). BC, 6-VI-16. Public Domain

In 1578 a group of Carmelite friars from Andalusia complained to the Papal nuncio Filippo Sega over the fact that the Carmelite nuns in the Barcelonan convent of Santa Teresa 'were taught to compose *coplas* and verses'.[53] Verònica Zaragoza's study in the field of Catalan philology also reflects this relationship between poetry written by Barcelonan Carmelite nuns and musical practice in the seventeenth and eighteenth centuries.[54] Her detailed analysis of a songbook belonging to the nunnery of Santa Teresa in Barcelona, preserved at the Arxiu de les Carmelites descalces in Barcelona, shows it to contain poetry dating from between the late sixteenth and the nineteenth centuries which was intended for sung performance as well as other references to singing and dancing in the convent (Figure 5.9).[55] Some of these *coplas* are devoted to the profession of particular nuns, which might indicate that the profession ceremony also included the singing of lyrics written by the nuns themselves, using tunes learned by oral tradition or composed by the nuns for the occasion (Table 5.3).

It appears that religious orders were an important means of dissemination of music and musical discourse and that they might also have been instrumental in the transmission of oral traditions of music across geographical boundaries.[56] The Carmelite Order offers a prime example, in this case stemming from Teresa of Ávila's tradition of composing poems to be sung at daily recreational gatherings. For example, the aforementioned Ana de Mendoza, Princess of Eboli (see Chapter 4), founded a Carmelite nunnery in the Castilian village of Pastrana,

Table 5.2. Lyrics to be sung *al tono de* at the *Cancionero de Nuestra Señora: en el qual ay muy buenos romances, canciones y villancicos: aora nueuamente añadido* (Barcelona: en casa de la biuda de Hubert Gotart, 1591)

Folio	Incipit	To be sung al tono de …
10v	Passe la galena passe	Passe la galana
12v	Bien aya quien a vos pario	Pedro el borreguero
13v	Ya nascio el rey encarnado	Aquel pastorico madre
14v	Bien aya quien hizo	Bien aya quien hizo
15v	Que no es no, que ya no es nada	En bon punt, y en bon ora
16r	En toda natura humana	En toda la trasmontaña
18r	Como estauades sola	Si estauades sola
19v	Sus zagales alaldea	Mariquita y dame ora vn beso
20v	Puse mis amores	Puse mis amores
21v	Virgen madre mia	Cucaracha Martinez
23r	De do vienes Sathanas	Carillo porque te vas
23v	Do venis reyna del cielo	Embiarame mi madre por agua a la fuente frida
27v	A la virgin que es parida	Socorred señora mia
28v	Caminad esposa	Camina señora dize Ioseph a nuestra señora
31r	Parida es la princesa	Los ojos de la niña
32r	Digas pastorico	Ojos morenicos
33r	Vamonos mingo jugando	Con estos ojos que aueys
34v	Iuro a sant botin sagrado	Asserrojar serrojuelas Rite he he, mas el Rite he ha la turula, turule, turula
35v	Dime dime Gil Bragado	Messase mari Garcia
37r	En la ciudad de Bethleem	Rezaremos beaetus vir
38r	Virgen bienauenturada	Si mis amores me han dexado &c
39r	Dime Gil bragado	Messase Mari Garcia
40v	Pascualejo que has hauido	Mi marido anda cuitado, yo jurare que esta castrado
42v	Que le lleuas di polido	Todos duermen coraçon
44v	Debaxo de la peña nace	No quiero que nada sienta
45r	Que hazeys vos Dios mio	Guardame las vacas: dize el hombre y responde el niño
78r	Dentro de Hierusalem	De Antequera sale el moro, de Antequera e Sevilla

and after her husband's death she sought consolation by entering the convent, accompanied by her mother and servants. The princess was accused of disrupting the cloistered life, and Teresa of Ávila asked the king to intercede to return the princess to secular life. A contemporary chronicle describes how the Catalan hermitess Catalina de Cardona, who relied on the princess's favour, visited Pastrana that year. Catalina, who had been educated at a convent in Naples, visited the Carmelite convent, where she sang songs in the Italian manner to the nuns:

> [Catalina de Cardona] had rooms in the Palace that were right by the convent of [Carmelite] nuns, in order to be able to communicate with them more

Coplas en alabança de la Virgen
nuestra Señora al tono de ya tiene saya blanca,
con otras dos canciones muy deuotas,
hechas por Nofre Almodeuar.

Impressas con Licencia en Barcelona en casa Sebastian de Cormellas, al Call Año 1609.

¶ Ya tiene saya blanca
la madre del Redentor
ya tiene saya blanca
y escapulario de amor.

¶ Lalta Reyna soberana
tiene por autoridad
vna saya muy galana
del blanco de castidad.

Broslada de santidad
dentro y fuera al rededor
ya tiene saya blanca
y escapulario de amor.

¶ Tan adornada la hizo
lalta mano poderosa
que viendola tan hermosa
para si solo la quiso.

Retrato

Figure 5.7. Onofre Almudéver, *Coplas en alabança de la Virgen nuestra Señora al tono de ya tiene saya blanca, con otras dos canciones muy deuotas* (Barcelona: Sebastián de Cormellas, 1609). BC, 3-VI-8/12. Public Domain

Figure 5.8. Beginning of the anonymous three-voice Catalan villancico 'Bella, de vos som amorós' at the *Cancionero de Uppsala* (RISM 1556/30), fols. 17v–19r, fols. 17v–18r. Uppsala, Uppsala Universitetbibliotek, Uka Utl.vok.mus.tr. 611. Public Domain

easily [...]. She treated them charitably, cooking for those who were sick, and singing some *coplillas* in the Italian manner for them, with the extraordinary grace that came naturally to her.[57]

This excerpt raises questions over what precisely singing in the Italian manner meant, but it undoubtedly reflects the wider pattern of the transmission through convents of oral repertoires across national and international borders. Moreover, it was Ana de Mendoza who promoted Catalina de Cardona's visit to Pastrana, which suggests that both nuns and laywomen played a role in the oral transmission of music and in the configuration of cultural networks. Studies in the field of Hispanic and Catalan philology have focused on the transnational circulation of poetry which was intended to be sung through the networks traced by religious orders. For example, Daniel John Hanna has analysed the Carmelite tradition of composing poetic verses intended for musical performance, demonstrating that this practice was transferred to Carmelite convents founded in France and the Low Countries in the seventeenth century:

As a general note, in examining these poems it is useful to remember that the *coplas* from the time of Teresa of Avila and the *cantiques* composed by later generations of Carmelites in France and the Spanish Netherlands are texts set to music, and appear to have been intended for singing. It may well be that in some cases, the first version of a 'poem' was actually a song, improvised or

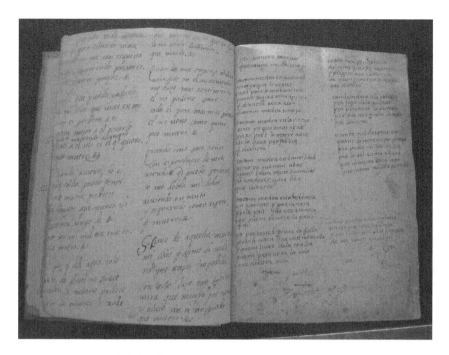

Figure 5.9. Songbook belonging to the Barcelonan Carmelite nunnery (late sixteenth to nineteenth centuries). Barcelona, Arxiu de les Carmelites descalces, Ms. s.n. Photograph by Mercè Gras

composed by singing rather than writing, with a textual record—the written verses—only being created later as a way to remember the text in the future. (Hanna 2012: 23)

A transatlantic rivalry?

While the musical practices of Spanish nuns influenced foreign convents through networks established by religious orders, it is also apparent that the circulation of *relaciones* and chronicles which reported on urban events, and which include references to nuns' music-making, might have had an impact on musical practices as well. According to Tess Knighton, 'many of the *relaciones* printed in Spain in the sixteenth and seventeenth centuries were shipped to the New World, both to convey the news and to reinforce the prevailing ideologies to the lettered Spaniards of the ecclesiastical and governmental hierarchies' (Knighton 2011: 28). Conversely, Spanish nuns' music-making might have been affected in a reciprocal way by the reports on nuns' music in the New World. Colleen Baade suggests that there might have been some form of 'transatlantic rivalry' between convents, speculating whether Spanish nuns 'were inspired by reports of extravagant music on the other side of the Atlantic' (Baade 2013: 242).

Table 5.3. Lyrics devoted to the profession of particular Carmelite nuns in 1603–1608 and 1619 included in the songbook Barcelona, Arxiu de les Carmelites descalces, Ms. s.n.

Pages	Title	Incipit
156	Al ábito de la hermana Arcángela. Coplas	Seay[s], Arcángela, bienvenida
156	Otras al velo	Para siempre le gocéis
157–158	Coplas al ábito de la hermana Madalena de Jesús	Mui bien vengáis, Madalena
158	Coplas al ábito de la hermana clara del Santíssimo Sacramento	Mas que'l sol lindo y hermoso
158–159	Otras	Clara, el niño Jesús
159–160	Otras al ábito de la hermana Gerónima de Jesús María	Bien paresce que Jesús
160	Coplas al ábito de la hermana Teresa de Jesús	Teresa, siempre goséis
160–161	Otras	Pues que el reynar
161	Otras	Qué buscáis, mansa cordera
161–162	Otras al ábito de la hermana Ysabel	Qué buscáis, Ysabel
162–163	Coplas a la profesión de la hermana [en blanc]	Pues con Cristo desposada
163	Otras	Pues que sois de Dios esposa
163–164	Al velo. Coplas	Pues, hermana tan hermosa
164–165	A la profesión de la hermana Ysabel de la Madre de Dios	Oy a muertos an tañido
165	Otras	Dicho me han, Hisabel
165	Al velo de la misma	Velo os ponen, Ysabel
166	A la profesión de la hermana Clara del Santíssimo Sacramento	Pues que quedáis desposada
166	Otras	Pues del grande Hemanuel
167	Otras	Pues que ya sois, Clara
167	Otras para el velo	Pues que, Clara, sois velada
167–168	A la profesión de la hermana Teresa de Jesús. Coplas	Bendesía sienpre al Señor
168–169	Coplas de desafío de la hermana Clara del Santíssimo Sacramento para la hermana Teresa de Jesús	Disen que os alsáys con Dios
169	Respuesta de la hermana Teresa para la hermana Clara	Juráis no us llevaré a Dios
169–170	Al velo de la hermana Teresa de Jesús. Coplas	El Artífice del cielo
170–171	Coplas al ábito de la hermana Catalina de Christo	Oy la Magestad divina
171	Otras	P.: Qué buscáys con tal contento

Geoffrey Baker has compared the wealth of laudatory descriptions of nuns' music in the chronicles of the Perú in comparison with the lack of references to music in male monastic institutions, demonstrating that 'the musical activities of convents were grander and more widely appreciated than those of monasteries'.[58] The extent to which the chronicles studied by Baker generated a transatlantic rivalry between convents is unknown, as they were preserved solely in manuscript form before their first printing in the twentieth century. The Dominican friar Reginal do de Lizárraga (1545–1615) praised the musical skills of the nuns of La Encarnación and those of the nuns of the convent of La Concepción in Lima, while he described how the nuns of La Trinidad 'performed plainchant and organ, preferring a more austere musical approach which excluded polyphony' (Lizárraga 1987 [1908]: 111–114; cited in Baker 2003: 10). However, his chronicle was not published until 1908. The chronicle of the Sevillian Antonio Vásquez de Espinosa (1570–1630) also went unpublished until the twentieth century, and this detailed account evaluated the ceremonial solemnity of Lima as being worthy of competition with the splendour of that in Rome, Toledo, or Seville, offering specific praise for the musical skills of the nuns of Lima.[59] Likewise, Diego de Mendoza (1585–1665), a Franciscan friar from Toledo, described polyphonic and instrumental music at the convent of Santa Clara in equally detailed terms.[60] In contrast with the other two, his chronicle was published in Madrid in 1665 (Figure 5.10).

Baade mentions the observation of the Peruvian Augustin friar Antonio de la Calancha (1584–1654) in his *Coronica moralizada del orden de San Agustín en el Perú* (1638) that the chapel of the convent of La Encarnación in Lima 'was a celebrated event in Europe'.[61] When he commented on music in Lima, Calancha considered Peruvian people to be particularly skilful in music, but he believed that it was the nuns who excelled in this discipline. According to his chronicle, nuns' choirs in Lima were considerably better than both those of Peninsular cathedrals and those of European nuns. Moreover, he added that the choirs of convents in Lima were comparable only with the Chapel Royal in Madrid (Calancha 1638: 69). This transatlantic rivalry is also reflected in his praise of music at the convent of La Encarnación in Lima:

> Its music [that of the convent of La Encarnación in Lima] is the foremost in the Indies, and is celebrated even in Europe. [The chapel] has nine choirs of violones, harps, vihuelas, dulcians, guitars, and other instruments, and more than fifty nuns skilful in music and with celebrated voices. They form the most delightful choir known worldwide.[62]

Francisco Torres's description of the choir of the convent of La Piedad in Guadalajara (see Chapter 3) included a list of eleven nuns who were distinguished for their musical skills and mentioned the existence of twenty-six more (Torres 1647: fols. 208v–209r). Moreover, Torres ranked the choir at La Piedad as being the most skilful in the world. Baade suggests that this statement might reflect a transatlantic rivalry, as Spain did not have convents comparable to, for instance, that of La Encarnación in Lima, where there were more than fifty nuns who sang (Baade 2013: 242). The same rivalry might be observed in the *relaciones* of the beatification of Saint Teresa in Saragossa also mentioned in Chapter 3, when the Carmelite prior noted that at the convents of Jerusalén and Santa Catalina 'more than eighty nuns' sang and played musical instruments.

232 Beyond the city

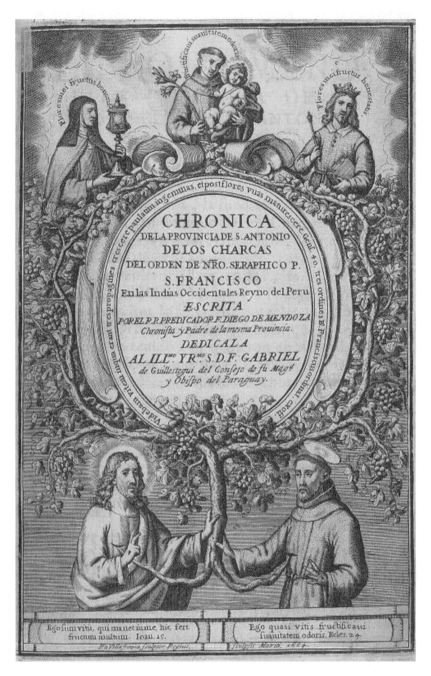

Figure 5.10. Diego de Mendoza, *Chronica de la provincia de San Antonio de los Charcas del orden de nuestro seraphico padre San Francisco en las Indias Occidentales Ryeno del Peru* (Madrid: s.n., 1665), title-page. New York, The New York Public Library, *KB+ 1665. <https://digitalcollections.nypl.org>

Figure 5.11. Antonio de la Calancha, *Coronica [sic] moralizada del orden de San Augustin en el Peru, con sucesos egenplares en esta monarquia* (Barcelona: Pedro Lacavalleria, 1638), frontispiece. Madrid, Biblioteca AECID, 3GR-7118. Creative Commons

234 *Beyond the city*

We do not know if this rivalry was limited to the chroniclers and historians who wrote these accounts, as conventual music offered them an obvious means of exhibiting power, social status, prestige, and influence, or whether there was a wider awareness of such rivalries, and whether the nuns themselves knew of these descriptions. In any case, it was in Barcelona where Calancha's chronicle was printed by Pedro Lacavalleria in 1638 and 1639 (Figure 5.11).[63] The account was subsequently translated into Latin (Antwerp, 1651–1652) and French (Toulouse, 1653), enabling a wide circulation. Various book inventories of European individuals name this edition as being present in a range of collections, such as the list of titles owned by Lorenzo Ramírez de Prado, a knight of the Order of Santiago and Philip IV's advisor.[64]

Further comparison with other countries is fundamental if the musical cultures of Barcelonan convents are to be evaluated more broadly in the context of European and Latin American cities. Writings about women's music might have contributed to the creation of networks of musical discourse within and outside the city of Barcelona. However, the questions raised by this chapter are whether the discourse on women's musical practices in different countries influenced the participation of nuns and women in general in music networks and their experience of music, and how these discourses changed over the centuries because of cultural exchanges. The dispersal of information about convent music in the Hispanic world makes it difficult and laborious to develop a comparative approach. However, the concept of networks and the use of digital tools such as databases and cartographical applications may prove invaluable in the undertaking of future comparative studies with regard to convent sounds between urban centres.

Notes

1 For instance, the project 'Who Were the Nuns? A Prosopographical Study of the English Convents in Exile 1600-1800', ascribed to Queen Mary, University of London, has produced a database <https://wwtn.history.qmul.ac.uk/> as a result of the research into the membership of the English convents in exile, from the foundation of the first new house in Brussels in 1598 until 1800, revealing how nuns' networks spread.
2 Said 1993: 26. Kristeva 1969: 164: 'toute texte est absorption et transformation d'un autre text'.
3 This was illustrated by the research network formed in 2012 to study musical-cultural exchange in the period 1550–1750 by the Royal Holloway, University of London, in conjunction with Uppsala University and the Bach-Archiv Leipzig, funded by the Swedish Foundation for International Co-Operation in Research and Higher Education (STINT network 'Musical-Cultural Exchange in Early Modern Europe, 1550–1750').
4 Volume 12 (1996–1997) of the journal *Artigrama* includes a collection of articles on this topic. See also Leitmeir 2009; Fenlon and Knighton 2006; and, for a later period, Carreras 1995 and Marín 2002, among others.
5 *Ars cantus plani*, MS (fifteenth century), BC, M 1327 G. Fol, fols. 72v–89r.
6 Bermudo 1550: fol. 3v: 'Sufficientes son para dar en alguna manera noticia de la Musica: mayormente a religiosas, que son estudiosas, y no pretenden saber sino el officio diuino'.
7 Caçador 1569: fols. 246r–286r (*Liber sextus, quo agitur de institutione cantus, & intonationibus, quibus Barcinonensis Ecclesia vtitur*).

8 Pérez Vidal has analysed this variety in the case of Castilian Dominican nunneries; see Pérez Vidal 2015: 234.
9 Bataillon 1950 [1937]: 6: 'Pero aquí mismo se trata menos de reformar que de allanar los caminos a un ejército de reformadores que era ya fuerte y popular'.
10 *Ceremonial dels magnífichs consellers...*, vol. 3, p. 77.
11 On the Rule of the Order of Santiago to the fifteenth century, see Gallego 1971.
12 'Protocolo sexto del notario Bartolomé Costa' (1477–1483), ACA,ORM,Monacales-Universidad,Volúmenes,180, fol. 118r (visitation of May 1481): 'Item haviam vist que en la Comemoracio que fan de les relliquies fan difformitat dient la antiphena plana e lo vers e la oracio cantant pro manan sots la dita obediencia que daqui avant quant a matines e a vespres se diran planes les comemoracions sien planes e quant se diran cantades se diguen cantades'.
13 'Protocolo sexto del notario Bartolomé Costa', fols. 127v–130v; 'Libro de visitas antiguas' (1495–1529), ACA,ORM,Monacales-Universidad,Volúmenes,167, s. fol. (visitation of November 1481).
14 Serra Álvarez 1966: 309 (visitation of 1499).
15 Mota 1599: 124–125: 'Tambien notese, que las personas y Monasterios de esta Orden, que tienen obligacion de rezar el offiçio Diuino por el breuiario, aora sea Monasterio de Freyles Clerigos, aora de Freylas, han de reçar de nuestro padre San Agustin a 28 de agosto con su octaua conforme a la costumbre antigua, por ser padre. Y esto entiendo, aunque el Monasterio sea de Freylas de donde salen para casar como son las de Barcelona [...]. La visita del año de 1501 del monasterio de Iunqueras de Barcelona dize, que los visitadores hallaron, que la Priora, supriora è Freyras eran muy buenas Eclesiasticas, assi en el canto, como en el rezar, è rezauan bien ordenadamente el breuiario de el conyuento de Vcles sin discrepar ninguna cosa'.
16 'Libro de visitas antiguas', s. fol. (visitation of 1515).
17 'Libro de visitas antiguas', s. fol. (visitation of 1529).
18 'Libro de visitas hechas por diferentes visitadores', fol. 1v (visitation of 1538): 'en otras muchas tienen otro modo y estilo mui diferente de aquello', por lo que le parecía 'mui dificil mudarles en todo su modo y estilo antiguo'.
19 'Libro de visitas hechas por diferentes visitadores', fol. 2r (visitation of 1538); Fontanet 1686: fol. 12r.
20 'Libro de visitas hechas por diferentes visitadores', fols. 2v–3r (visitation of 1538): 'quando se tañen los organos sienpre diga la que preside con el choro a versos los quirios / gloria yn exçelsisdeo credo santus y agnus y magnificat de la manera que quedan informadas // en fiestas dobles solemnes sienpre dira el choro la gloria yn exçelsis deo y el creo a versos con el organo y en los otros dias que se tañen los organos decirlos an rezados y quando no ay organo todo cantado pero siempre se cante el primero verso de la gloria es a saber et in terra pax ominibus bona voluntatis y el credo patrem omnipotemten etc por las cantoras'.
21 'Libro de visitas hechas por diferentes visitadores', fols. 23v–24r (visitation of 1549): 'de aqui en adelante se conformen en el rezar de las fiestas con el calendario del breviario nuevo de la horden'.
22 'Libro de visitas hechas por diferentes visitadores', fol. 27v (visitation of 1556): 'hauiendo visto los dichos señores visitadores la manera y serimonias y cuidado que las dichas religiosas tienen en el officio diuino parecioles que todo lo hazian bien saluo en no conformarse en algunas cosas con el breuiario nuevo de la dicha orden lo qual causa algunas confusiones en el officio diuino'.
23 'Libro de visitas hechas por diferentes visitadores', fol. 27v (visitation of 1556).
24 'Libro de visitas hechas por diferentes visitadores', fol. 50v (visitation of 1560–1561).
25 'Libro de visitas hechas por diferentes visitadores', fol. 54r (visitation of 1566): 'Ytem mandaron que antes de començar el ofiçio de misa cantada y de bisperas solemnes las cantoras que stubieren diputadas por semanas tengan siempre registrado lo que se a

de cantar y dezir en el dicho coro y en ninguna manera se diga ni reze cosa alguna de cabeça aunque se sepa'.
26 'Libro de visitas hechas por diferentes visitadores', fol. 61v (visitation of 1576): 'las misas cantadas por misales y breviarios romanos como esta dispuesto agora'. For a rule of the Order containing ritual instructions following the Council of Trent, see *Regla de la Orden de la orden y cavalleria de S. Santiago de la Espada...* (Antwerp, 1598).
27 Zaragoza Gómez 2012: 241–242. For instance, the Cistercian nuns of the convent of Vallbona de las Monjas (Lleida) pursued a long court case against the bishop of Lleida between 1606 and 1620 (Cusó 2008: 51–53, 767–777). On the resistance of the nuns of the Dominican convent of Santa María Magdalena in Valencia to reforms, see Callado 2013.
28 Barbara Eichner, 'Same difference? Post-Tridentine Reforms and Music in German Nunneries and Monasteries', paper at the Medieval and Renaissance Music Conference, Basel University, July 2019.
29 'Llibre dels càrrecs i oficis' (ch. 21, 'del orde del assiento del cor'), p. 69.
30 'Llibre dels càrrecs i oficis', pp. 51 (ch. 16, 'De les ceremonies del coro y officis ques canten en la iglesia del present monestir') and 56 (ch. 17, 'De les festes se celebren entre any començat del primer de janer fins al darrer de dezembre'). See also p. 68 (ch. 20, 'Regles generals en esta materia de ceremonies del cor').
31 'Llibre de las Ceremonias del Cor...'. See Chapter 3. There is no reference made to a nun named Juana de Argençola in the convent in the seventeenth century, although several nuns of the Argençola family are mentioned in the convent's documents, such as Anna d'Argençola (d.1662), prioress of the convent from 1648 to her death. See 'Expediente de pruebas de Ana de Argensola de Monsuar de Espes y de Albanell, natural de Las Pallargas, para el ingreso como religiosa en el Convento Santa María de Junqueras de Barcelona de la Orden de Santiago. Año 1606', AHN, OM-RELIGIOSAS_SANTIAGO,Exp.43. Juana de Argençola is not included in the genealogical tree presented in Costa 2005: 118–119. Her will is not found in the aforementioned book of wills of the convent ('Llibre de desapropis...') and the file of the research into her lineage is neither found at the AHN.
32 Fontanet 1686: fol. 20v.
33 See, for example, 'Llibre de las Ceremonias del Cor...', fol. 87v.
34 'Llibre de las Ceremonias del Cor...', fol. 91r.
35 'Llibre de las Ceremonias del Cor...', fols. 84v ('lo primer Responsori que no lo diu lo Orga lo ha de dir la Señora Priora; y Susprior'), 86v ('lo Orga no ha de sonar apres de la Epistola'), and 88r ('lo primer Respons no ha de sonar lo Orga').
36 'Libro de visitas' (1628–1790), fol. 2r-v (visitation of 1628).
37 Lois Breckon, 'The Comparative Silence of Florentine Nuns after the Council of Trent', paper at the Medieval and Renaissance Music Conference, Bassel, 4 July 2019.
38 San José 1615: fol. 125v: 'Estaua en el cuerpo de la Capilla mayor leuantado vno como teatro muy alto y bien proporcionado, cubierto de muchas y buenas alhombras, y repa[r]tidos en el lugares muy graues para el señor Obispo, justicia, jurados, y jueces del Certamen Poetico: y auiendo los Poetas presentado muchos y muy buenos versos, de diferentes poesias, fue gusto de su Señoria, y de los deuotos de casa que se fuessen leyendo cada tarde publicamente, y assi acabadas las visperas, se ponían dos personas Ecclesiasticas, en dos pulpitos, y estando toda la demas gente del pueblo sentados en sus lugares, todos con mucho silencio, se leîa vna poesia en vn pulpito, y otra en el otro, tañendose en acabando cada vno algunos instrumentos, que con estos y algunos versos graciosos tuuieron vn rato de harto gusto y alegria'. See also Díez de Aux 1615: 76.
39 Díez de Aux 1615: 121–122, 127, 134.
40 Bataillon 1950 [1937]. On female mystics in Golden Age Spain, see Haliczer 2002.
41 Pirrotta 1984: 72–79; Wilson 1998, 2009, and 2019.
42 On Caterina Vigri (d.1463), a nun of Corpus Domini convent in Ferrara, and the singing of *laude* at convents, see Stras 2018: 26–28. Likewise, Catherine A. Bradley is

developing a project on 'Music and Poetic Creativity for a Unique Moment in the Western Christian Liturgy c.1000–1500' between 2020 and 2025.
43 Marca 1764: 243: 'Tenia especial consuelo esta Sierva del Señor en oir cantar las Divinas alabanzas; y puesta en el retiro de su Casa, su recreación era cantar algunas letras à Christo su Esposo, y à la Santissima Virgen. Muchas vezes mandava à una Niña de las que enseñava, llamada Candia Borràs, por su voz clara, y suave, que las cantasse; y un dia de orden luyo, cantò una letra muy devota: con voz muy sonora empezò la primera Quartilla [...]. Oyéndola con grande gozo la Venerable Eugenia, continuò diciendo [...]. Dicho esto, se quedó arrobada la Santa Matrona, y estando en el extasi, con mayor dulzura, y suavidad, que antes, continuò su canto'. See also Zaragoza Gómez 2016: 165–166.
44 Valenzuela 1556: fols. k7–k8, cited in Rodríguez Puértolas 1987: 15: 'don Hernando y doña Ysabel [...] mandaron a dos predicadores célebres de su capilla que compusieran romances y villancicos, en romance, de Christo y de su madre y de sus festividades y de los apóstoles. Y otra cosa suya no se cantara en la sala, como parece por el Cancionero de fray Ambrosio y fray Mingo [Íñigo], y otros célebres predicadores de aquel tiempo'.
45 Bustos 2015: 123: 'incluso, se menciona una "sala" donde se cantaban estas composiciones ante los mismos Reyes, lo cual nos lleva a postular, como sucede en los casos de Gómez Manrique o Juan del Encina, una escenificación concreta en la que debieron de participar músicos y cantores a instancias de los propios frailes que asumirían una cierta función de organizadores de espectáculos'.
46 Bustos 2015: 124: 'Los romances y villancicos devotos, en este sentido, no serían recibidos como algo muy diferente de la predicación'.
47 Cátedra 2005: 80. Likewise, Íñigo de Mendoza's *Cancionero* (MS, 1485) was a very popular collection of poetry in the late fifteenth and early sixteenth centuries. Gómez Manrique and Juan Álvarez Gato also composed religious poetry to be sung with secular tunes. On *cancionero* music and verse at the time of the Catholic Monarchs, see Whetnall 2016. See also the classic work on the villancico by Isabel Pope (1954).
48 Bustos 2015: 120–121: 'altavoz de las ideas y propuestas de Cisneros'; 'labor intelectual de apoyo al ideario reformista cisneriano'.
49 Tess Knighton, 'For whom are sweet songs set to music?' Women as performers of and listeners to the *cancionero* repertory', lecture at the conference 'De Canciones y Cancioneros. Music and Literary Sources of the Luso-Hispanic Song Tradition', Taplin Auditorium, Princeton University, 7–8 April 2018.
50 Baade 1997: 226; 2005: 300; and 2008: 94; Aguirre 2004: 287; and Morales 2021: 339. For further examples of songbooks connected to Castilian convents, see Mazuela-Anguita 2012a: 448-456.
51 For an edition of the book, see Pérez Gómez 1952. For a description, see Rodríguez-Moñino 1973: vol. 2, 221–225.
52 Rodríguez-Moñino 1968: 111: 'Inconcebible parece que tonos, a veces enormemente plebeyos y aun bellacos puedan transformarse a lo divino, pero así es'.
53 Gras 2013c: 'a las monjas que han fundado enseñan que hagan coplas y versos y ellos les embían las que hacen'.
54 Zaragoza Gómez 2013. On nun writers at the Dominican convent of Els Àngels, such as Hipòlita de Rocabertí and Contesina Fontanella (Barcelona, 1618–1696), see Zaragoza Gómez 2012.
55 Zaragoza Gómez 2016 and 2017. See also Gras 2013c. Information on this manuscript is provided by the *Manuscrits Catalans de l'Edat Moderna* (MCEM) database, a project of the Institut d'Estudis Catalans <https://mcem.iec.cat/>.
56 On the notion of aurality in historical sound studies for the premodern period—which includes auditory culture and the history of listening—see Boynton *et al.* 2016.
57 Santa María 1644: vol. 1, book 4, 634: 'Tubo aposento en Palacio pegado al Convento de las Monjas, para comunicarlas mas de cerca [...]. Egercitaba con ellas la caridad,

haziendo a las enfermas guisadillos, i cantandoles a lo Italiano algunas coplillas con estraordinaria gracia que para esto tenia'.
58 Baker 2003: 11. On convent music in Peru, see also Knighton 2011 and Stevenson 1960: 56–57. On nunneries and music in the New World, see also Muriel and Lledías 2009; Ortiz 2015; and Finley 2019b.
59 Vásquez 1992: 597–598, 601 (on La Encarnación), and 602 (on La Concepción). Cited in Baker 2003: 10–11, 32, n. 57–58.
60 Mendoza 1976 [1663]: 70. Cited in Baker 2003: 22–23, n. 13.
61 Baade 2013: 242. On the references to the convent of La Encarnación in this chronicle, see Vinatea 2013.
62 Calancha 1638: 432: 'Su musica es la primera de las Indias, i bien celebrada aun en Europa, tiene nueve coros de viguelones, arpas, viguelas, bajones, guitarras i otros instrumentos, que con cinquenta i mas diestras en musica i celebradas en vozes azen el coro mas deleytoso que se conoce en lo mejor del mundo […]'. One wonders if this reference is connected to the idea of the nine choirs of angels.
63 For a description of the processes of printing and publication of this chronicle, see Lohmann 1992. See also MacCormack 1982, among others studies on Calancha's publication.
64 *Inventario de la Librería del Señor D. Lorenzo Ramirrez de Prado Cavallero que fué de la Orden de Santiago de los Consejos de Su Magestad en el Real Svpremo de Castilla y de el de Santa Cruzada* (no editorial details), 'Classe de libros de historia sacra, y profana, annales, y genealogias', fol. 4r.

Epilogue

This study has attempted to use music as a vehicle to construct the histories of the urban nunneries active in sixteenth-century Barcelona and their inhabitants. The disappearance of most of these convents and the scarcity of musical sources from the period which document convents' musical practices in the city in the early modern period have required drawing both on more general archival documents and on more indirect approaches. In other words, very few descriptions of nuns' musical practices survive, and what is known about them comes primarily through documents that prohibit them. For instance, bearing in mind their limitations, the books of visitation records are a particularly special type of music inventory, constituting particularly rich sources that afford a glimpse of the musical life of nunneries. They allow not only knowledge about their collections of music books, but also recreation of performative spaces, identification of female musicians, and, especially, learning about local liturgies and convent's musical traditions. Likewise, the comparative study of several types of documents provides evidence about female musical traditions in Barcelona. For example, the joint analysis both of personal booklets containing notated processional chants and of nuns' legacies in their wills undercovers a tradition of legacies of handwritten music booklets from aunt to niece in nunneries.

Despite the documentary limitations and the fact that no, or few, sources are available, from all the indirect references that have been put together here, it might be possible to hypothesise, even to a limited extent, about the musical repertory that might have been performed and heard in convents. The connections between nun musicians and the production of poetry, the contemporary depictions of nuns singing and accompanying themselves with stringed instruments such as the harp, and the use in convents of songbooks containing lyrics to be sung using well-known tunes reflect the importance of oral traditions of music in cloistered spaces.

The concept of the 'network' has been particularly useful to analyse convent's musical practices within Barcelona and also to preliminarily develop comparative approaches beyond the city. The links between female music patronage in convent and court, and devotional poems set to music, suggest that oral tradition is a key question that must be asked not only to challenge the loss of women's voices in historical accounts and to place women on the map of music history, but also to broaden and deepen historical perspectives on sixteenth-century Hispanic music.

DOI: 10.4324/9781003292371-7

It appears that the convent was a place where, through diverse musics and sounds, the distinction between private and public, and between religious and civic lives, was blurred. The exploration of the participation of convents—where not only nuns but also laywomen operated—in the configuration of Barcelona's music networks allows assessment of the contribution of a broad cross-section of women to the processes of creation and performance of music, to the dissemination of music and musical discourse, and to the promotion of the interaction between musicians, which can also enrich scholarly perspectives on Barcelona's musical life. This might also contribute to broader European studies on cultural networks, in which both women's agency and the Iberian angle have been neglected or insufficiently analysed. The preservation of sources influenced this research, since inevitably the surviving documents form a patchwork with some chronological gaps and variable elements. However, this range can be taken as a useful starting point for understanding the contribution of nunneries to the musical life of sixteenth-century Barcelona, one that may be enriched by further material yet to be unearthed.

Bibliography

Abad Pérez, Antolín. 'San Juan de la Penitencia, obra social del cardenal Cisneros en Toledo'. *Anales toledanos 2* (1968): pp. 1–88.

Abellán, José Luis. *Historia crítica del pensamiento español. II: La Edad de Oro* (Madrid: Espasa-Calpe, 1979–1991), 7 vols.

Additio et indiuidualis satisfactio, pro priore et conuentu Diui Augustini, contra Michaelem Perramon et alios, in hac tertia instantia quae: sub examiné nobilis Narcisi de Anglasell (S.l.: s.n., after 1679). <https://www.worldcat.org/es/title/803918704>.

Additio, pro admodum [...] domina Priorissa et Conventu Beatae Mariae de Junquerijs, Ordinis Sancti Jacobi de Espata contra nobilem matrem et filium Xammars: referente nobili Iacobo de Potau R.A.D., not. Casas (Barcelona?: n.d. [1690 or later]). <https://explora.bnc.cat/permalink/34CSUC_BC/1fpark4/alma991014529719706717>.

Adriazola Acha, Susana. 'Fragmentos de una vida: Ángela Pujades. Escritura y devoción al rosario'. In *Vidas de Mujeres Del Renacimiento*, edited by Ana del Campo Gutiérrez (Barcelona: Publicacions i Edicions, Universitat de Barcelona, 2007): pp. 163–185.

Agnew, Vanessa. *Enlightenment Orpheus: The Power of Music in Other Worlds* (Oxford: Oxford University, 2008).

Aguirre Rincón, Soterraña. 'Sonido en el silencio: monjas y músicas en la España de 1550 a 1650'. In *Políticas y prácticas musicales en el mundo de Felipe II: estudios sobre la música en España, sus instituciones y sus territorios en la segunda mitad del siglo XVI*, edited by John Griffiths and Javier Suárez Pajares (Madrid: ICCMU, 2004): pp. 285–318.

Alabrús Iglesias, Rosa M. *Razones y emociones femeninas. Hipólita de Rocabertí y las monjas catalanas del Barroco* (Madrid: Cátedra, 2019).

Albacete i Gascón, Antoni, and Margarida Güell i Baró. *El Reial Monestir de Santa Maria de Valldonzella de Barcelona (1147–1922). Història i Art en un centre Barceloní d'espiritualitat cistercenca* (Barcelona: Publicacions de l'Abadia de Montserrat, Biblioteca Abat Oliva, 2013).

———. 'Santa Maria de Valldonzella: un monestir sense memòria pròpia. Les destruccions de l'arxiu i les noves troballesdocumentals necessàries per conèixer la història de la comunitat'. *Paratge 27* (2014): pp. 45–58. <https://www.raco.cat/index.php/Paratge/article/view/288469>.

Albin, Andrew. 'Canorous Soundstuff: Hearing the Officium of Richard Rolle at Hampole'. In *'Sound Matters'*, edited by Susan Boynton, Sarah Kay, Alison Cornish and Andrew Albin, *Speculum 91*, no. 4 (2016): pp. 988–1039, pp. 1026–1039. <https://doi.org/10.1086/688003>.

Alcalá, César. *La Música a Catalunya fa 300 anys* (Barcelona: Tibidabo, 1994).

———. 'El Real Monasterio de San Pedro de las Puellas y su Capilla Musical'. *Nassarre* 14, no. 1 (1998), pp. 109–118.

Almudéver, Onofre. *Silua de varios romances, en que están recopilados la mayor parte de los romances castellanos, y agora nueuamente añadidos en esta segunda impresión, que nunca an sido estampados. Hay al fin algunas canciones, villancicos y coplas, y también se an añadido en esta impresion algunas cosas sentidas sacadas de diuersos auctores* (Barcelona: Pedro Borin, 1550) [second edition printed in Barcelona by Jaume Cortey in 1552].

———. *Coplas en alabança de la Virgen nuestra Señora al tono de ya tiene saya blanca, con otras dos canciones muy deuotas* (Barcelona: Sebastián de Cormellas, 1609).

Altés i Aguiló, Francesc Xavier. 'El Breviari per al Monestir de Jonqueres imprès a Lió l'any 1521'. *Miscel·lània litúrgica catalana 4* (1990): pp. 57–79.

Altisent, Agustí. *Monestir de Santa Maria de Valldonzella: 75è aniversari del nou monestir: 1913–1988* (Barcelona: Comunitat de Santa Maria de Valldonzella, 1988).

Alturo i Perucho, Jesús. *L'Arxiu antic de Santa Anna de Barcelona del 942 al 1200: aproximació històrico-lingüística* (Barcelona: Fundació Noguera; Lleida: Virgili & Pagès, 1985), 3 vols.

Amelang, James S. 'Los usos de la autobiografía: monjas y beatas en la Cataluña Moderna'. In *Historia y género: las mujeres en la Europa moderna y contemporánea*, edited by James S. Amelang and Mary Nash (Valencia: Universidad de Valencia, 1990): pp. 191–214.

Analysis por el padre prior y convento de san Agustin de esta ciudad de Barcelona contra Francisco Torrents, maestro de obras de la misma ciudad [...] (Barcelona: Juan Jolis, [1741 or later]).

Angelón, Manuel. *Cronica de la provincia de Barcelona [Cronica general de España, ó sea historia ilustrada y descriptiva de sus provincias, suo poblaciones mas importantes y posesiones de ultramar]* (Madrid: Rubio, Grilo y Vitturi, 1870).

Anglès, Higini. *La música a Catalunya fins al segle XIII* (Barcelona: Biblioteca de Catalunya and Universitat Autònoma de Barcelona, 1988).

Anzizu, Sor Eulàlia. *Fulles històriques del Real Monestir de Santa Maria de Pedralbes* (Barcelona: Estampa de F. Xavier Altés, 1897).

Arana, María J. *La clausura de las mujeres. Una lectura teológica de un proceso histórico* (Bilbao: Mensajero, 1992).

Arenal, Electa, and Stacey Schlau. *Untold Sisters: Hispanic Nuns in Their Own Works* (Albuquerque: University of New Mexico Press, 1989).

Argaiz, Gregorio de. *La perla de Cataluña: historia de nuestra Señora de Monserrate* (Madrid: Andrés García de la Iglesia, 1677).

Arias de Saavedra Alías, Inmaculada, and Miguel L. López-Guadalupe Muñoz. 'Asistencia sanitaria femenina a finales del Antiguo Régimen: el caso del Hospital de la Caridad y Refugio de Granada'. *Cuadernos De Historia Moderna 14 (extra issue)* (2015): pp. 33–61. <https://doi.org/10.5209/rev_CHMO.2015.51178>.

Armanyà i Font, Francesc. *Translacion de los Agustinos Calzados de Barcelona de su antiguo al nuevo real convento de la misma ciudad: relacion de las festivas aclamaciones, con que manifestaron su gratitud à ambas magestades en los dias 30 y 31 de deciembre de 1750, y 1 de enero de 1751, y del regio funeral, con que expressaron su fina memoria a su [...] fundador [...] Don Phelipe V dispuesta por [...] Fr. Francisco Armañá [...]; sacala a luz el mismo Convento de Barcelona [...]* (Barcelona: Pablo Nadal, [1751 or later]).

Armengou, Josep M. *Màgia i misteri dels monestirs catalans* (Barcelona: Institut d'Estudis Històrics Medievals de Catalunya, 1993).

Arnall i Juan, Maria Josepa. *Los Manuscritos, incunables y demás impresos de la Biblioteca del Convento de San José de Barcelona (Carmelitas Descalzos)* (Barcelona: Universidad. Secretariado de Publicaciones, Intercambio científico y Extensión Universitaria, 1976).

_____. 'Aportación de los Carmelitas Descalzos a la cultura catalana, 1586–1835'. In *El Carmelo Teresiano en Cataluña: 1586–1986* (Burgos: Ed. Monte Carmelo, 1986): pp. 55–108. <https://explora.bnc.cat/permalink/34CSUC_BC/1fpark4/alma991011336219706717>.

Atienza López, Ángela. 'De beaterios a conventos. Nuevas perspectivas sobre el mundo de las beatas en la España moderna'. *Historia Social 57* (2007): pp. 145–168.

_____. 'Lo reglado y lo desarreglado en la vida de los conventos femeninos en la España Moderna'. In *La vida cotidiana en el mundo hispánico (siglos XVI-XVIII)*, edited by Manuel Peña (Madrid: Abada Editores, 2012): pp. 445–465.

_____. 'El mundo de las monjas y de los claustros femeninos en la Edad Moderna. Perspectivas recientes y algunos retos'. In *De la tierra al cielo. Líneas recientes de investigación en Historia Moderna*, edited by Eliseo Serrano (Zaragoza: Institución Fernando el Católico, 2013): pp. 89–105.

_____. 'Los límites de la obediencia en el mundo conventual femenino de la Edad Moderna: polémicas de clausura en la Corona de Aragón, siglo XVII'. *Studia historica. Historia moderna 40*, no. 1 (2018a) [Issue entitled *Los límites de la obediencia en el mundo Hispánico de la Edad Moderna: discursos y prácticas*]: pp. 125–157. <https://doi.org/10.14201/shhmo2018401125173>.

_____, ed. *Mujeres entre el claustro y el siglo. Autoridad y poder en el mundo religioso femenino, siglos XVI-XVII* (Madrid: Sílex, 2018b).

Atlas, Allan W. *Music at the Aragonese Court of Naples* (Cambridge: Cambridge University Press, 1985).

Attali, Jacques. *Noise: The Political Economy of Music*, translated by Brian Massumi (Manchester: Manchester University, 1985 [1977]).

Auferil, Jaume. 'La Sort d'Antoni Vallmanya i el cercle literari de Valldonzella'. In *Studia in honorem prof. Martí de Riquer* (Barcelona: Quaderns Crema, 1986): vol. 1, pp. 37–77. <https://explora.bnc.cat/permalink/34CSUC_BC/1fpark4/alma991000804969706717>.

Ausseil, Louis. 'L'orgue en Catalogne et dans les Pyrénées-Orientales'. *L'Orgue, Cahiers et Mémoires 2*, no. 133 (1970). <https://symetrie.com/fr/titres/l-orgue/l-orgue-en-catalogne-et-dans-les-pyrenees-orientales>.

Aviñoa, Xosé, dir. *Història de la música catalana, valenciana i balear* (Barcelona: Edicions, 1999–2004): vol. 62.

Azcona, Tarsicio de. 'Reforma de las clarisas de Cataluña en tiempos de los Reyes Católicos'. *Collectanea Franciscana 27* (1957): pp. 5–51.

_____. 'Reforma de religiosas benedictinas y cistercienses de Cataluña en tiempo de los Reyes Católicos'. *Studia monástica 9*, no. 1 (1967), pp. 75–165.

Baade, Colleen R. 'La "música sutil" del Monasterio de la Madre de Dios de Constantinopla: aportaciones para la historia de la música en los monasterios femeninos de Madrid a mediados del siglo XVI-siglo XVII'. *Revista de Musicología 20*, no. 1 (1997): pp. 221–230. <https://doi.org/10.2307/20797413>.

_____. '"Hired" Nun Musicians in Early Modern Castile'. In *Musical Voices of Early Modern Women. Many-Headed Melodies*, edited by Thomasin K. LaMay (Aldershot: Ashgate, 2005): pp. 287–310.

———. 'Music and Misgiving: Attitudes Towards Nuns' Music in Early Modern Spain'. In *Female Monasticism in Early Modern Europe: An Interdisciplinary View*, edited by C. van Wyhe (Aldershot: Ashgate, 2008): pp. 81–95.

———. 'Monjas músicas y música de monjas en los conventos franciscanos de Toledo, siglos XVI-XVIII'. In *La clausura femenina en el Mundo Hispánico: una fidelidad secular: Simposium (XIX Edición) San Lorenzo del Escorial, 2 al 5 de septiembre*, coordinated by Francisco Javier Campos and Fernández de Sevilla ([San Lorenzo de El Escorial, Madrid]: Real Centro Universitario Escorial-María Cristina, 2011): pp. 545–562.

———. 'Music: Convents'. In *Lexicon of the Hispanic Baroque: Transatlantic Exchange and Transformation*, edited by Evonne Levy and Kenneth Mills (Austin: University of Texas Press, 2013): pp. 240–242.

Bada, Joan. *Situació religiosa de Barcelona en el segle XVI* (Barcelona: Balmes, 1970).

———. *La Inquisició a Catalunya: segles XIII-XIX* (Barcelona: Barcanova, 1992).

———. *Monasterio de Santa María de Jerusalén, 1494–1994* (Barcelona: Monjas Clarisas, 1993).

Badal, Carles. 'Pau Llinàs i la vida a Santa Maria del Pi (1711-1749): biografia i inventari'. *Revista Catalana de Musicologia 9* (2017): pp. 153–173.

Baker, Geoffrey. 'Music in the Convents and Monasteries of Colonial Cuzco'. *Latin American Music Review 24*, no. 1 (2003): pp. 1–41.

Baldelló Benosa, Francesc de Paula. 'La Confraria de Músics de Barcelona'. *La Paraula Cristiana 8* (1928): pp. 134–147.

———. 'Órganos y organeros en Barcelona. Siglos XIII-XIX'. *Anuario Musical 1*, no. 1 (1946): pp. 195–237.

Balltondre, Mònica. 'The Historical Understanding of Female Premodern Possessions. Problematizing Some Gender Assumptions in the Historiography on Teresa de Ávila and Jeanne des Anges'. *Women's History Review 29*, no. 1 (2020): pp. 125–141. <https://doi.org/10.1080/09612025.2019.1595209>.

Baranda Leturio, Nieves. *Cortejo a lo prohibido: lectoras y escritoras en la España moderna* (Madrid: Arco, 2005).

Barraquer y Roviralta, Cayetano. *Las casas de religiosos en Cataluña durante el primer tercio del siglo XIX* (Barcelona: F. J. Altés y Alabart, 1906): vol. 1.

Bassa i Armengol, Manuel. *L'heràldica del monestir de Valldonzella* [Estudis Cistercencs 5] (Barcelona: Germandat de Valldonzella, 1969).

Bassegoda i Nonell, Joan. 'Nous documents sobre Santa Maria de Jonqueres de Barcelona'. *Butlletí del Museu Nacional d'Art de Catalunya 1* (1993): pp. 275–280.

Bassegoda i Nonell, Joan, et al. *La parròquia de la Puríssima Concepció en el seu 125è aniversari. Barcelona 1871–1996. Parròquia de la Puríssima Concepció* (Barcelona: Parroquia de la Puríssima Concepció, 1997).

Bataillon, Marcel, *Erasmo y España, estudios sobre la historia espiritual del siglo XVI*, translated by Antonio Alatorre (Mexico and Buenos Aires: Fondo de Cultura Económica, 1966 [1937]).

Batlle, Josep, *Chrónica seraphica de la provincia de Cataluña de la regular observancia* (MS, 1710). Barcelona, Biblioteca de la Universitat de Barcelona, Ms. 994.

Bazinet, Geneviève. 'The Musical Encart of the Royal Printers Le Roy & Ballard in the 1583 Hours of Jamet Mettayer Held in the Musée de l'Amérique française in Quebec City'. *Renaissance & Reformation 39*, no. 4 (2016): pp. 253–283.

Beaumont de Navarra, Vicente. *Compendio historico del Real Convento de Santa Maria Madalena, de Religiosas del Gran Patriarca Santo Domingo de la Ciudad de Valencia* (Valencia: Juan Gonçalez, 1725).
Becquart, Paul. *Musiciens néerlandais à la cour de Madrid: Philippe Rogier et son école (1560–1647)* (Brussels: Palais des Académies, 1967).
Bejarano Pellicer, Clara. 'El paisaje sonoro de la ciudad de Sevilla en las fiestas públicas de los siglos XVI y XVII'. In *Paisajes sonoros medievales*, directed by Gerardo Rodríguez, Éric Palazzo, and Gisela Coronado Schwindt (Mar del Plata: Universidad Nacional de Mar del Plata, 2019): pp. 113–138.
Bel Bravo, María Antonia. *Mujeres españolas en la historia moderna* (Madrid: Sílex, 2002).
Bennassar, Bartolomé. *Reinas y princesas del Renacimiento a la Ilustración: el lecho, el poder y la muerte* (Barcelona: Paidós, 2007).
Berger, Anna Maria Busse. *Medieval Music and the Art of Memory* (Berkeley: University of California Press, 2005).
Bermudo, Juan. *Comiença el arte Tripharia* (Osuna: Juan de León, 1550).
Bernadó, Màrius. 'Impresos litúrgicos: algunas consideraciones sobre su producción y difusión'. In *Fuentes Musicales en la Península Ibérica (ca. 1250-1550)*, edited by Maricarmen Gómez and Màrius Bernadó (Lleida: Universitat de Lleida-Institut d'Estudis Ilerdencs, 2001): pp. 253–270.
Bertran, Lluís. 'Musique en lieu: une topographie de l'expérience musicale à Barcelone et sur son territoire (1760–1808)' (PhD dissertation, Université de Poitiers and Universidad de La Rioja, 2017).
Bhabha, Homi K. *The Location of Culture* (London and New York: Routledge, 1994).
Bingen, Hildegard of. *Selected Writings* (London: Peguin, 2009).
Blázquez Miguel, Juan. 'Catálogo de los procesos inquisitoriales del Tribunal del Santo Oficio de Barcelona'. *Espacio, Tiempo y Forma 3* (1990a): pp. 11–158.
Boada, Coloma, and Irene Brugués. *Monasterios urbanos en tiempos de guerra: Sant Pere de les Puel·les y Santa Clara de Barcelona, 1691–1718* (Barcelona: Ajuntament de Barcelona, Institut de Cultura, MUHBA, 2014).
_____. *La Inquisición en Cataluña. El Tribunal del Santo Oficio de Barcelona (1487–1820)*, with a prologue by Henry Kamen (Toledo: Arcano, 1990b).
Boadas Llavat, Agustín. 'Notas para una Historia de la música franciscana'. In *Los Franciscanos Conventuales en España. Actas del II Congreso Internacional sobre el Franciscanismo en la Península Ibérica: Barcelona, 30 de marzo-1 de abril de 2005*, edited by Gonzalo Fernández-Gallardo Jiménez (Madrid: G. Fernández-Gallardo, 2006): pp. 219–244.
Boer, Antonio. *Jardin mystico plantado en el nuevo Real Monasterio de Santa Isabel de la ciudad de Barcelona de religiosas de la Tercera Orden de penitencia de el grande S. P. S. Francisco [...]* (Barcelona: Jayme Surià, 1735).
Boer, Wietse, and Christine Göttler. *Religion and the Senses in Early Modern Europe* (Boston: Brill, 2013).
Bohigas, Pere. 'Les Miniatures dels cantorals de Pedralbes'. In *Miscelánea en Homenaje a Monseñor Higinio Anglès* (Barcelona: CSIC, 1958–1961): vol. 1, pp. 135–150. <https://explora.bnc.cat/permalink/34CSUC_BC/1fpark4/alma991004731679706717>.
Bohigas, Pere. 'Inventario de códices miniaturados o iluminados de procedencia catalana o existentes en bibliotecas catalanas'. In *La ilustración y la decoración del libro manuscrito en Catalunya* (Barcelona: Asociación de Bibliófilos, 1960–1967): vol. 3, pp. 145–223.

Bombi, Andrea. '"The Third Villancico Was a Motet": The Villancico and Related Genres'. In *Devotional Music in the Iberian World, 1450–1800: The Villancico and Related Genres*, edited by Tess Knighton and Álvaro Torrente (Aldershot: Ashgate, 2007): pp. 149–187.

Bonaissie, Pierre. *La organización del trabajo en Barcelona a finales del siglo XV* (Barcelona: CSIC, 1975).

Bonsante, Annamaria, and Roberto Matteo Pasquandrea, eds. *Celesti sirene II: musica e monachesimo dal Medioevo all'Ottocento: atti del secondo seminario internazionale: San Severo, 11–13 ottobre 2013* (Barletta: Cafagna, 2015).

Booth, Philip, and Elizabeth Tingle, eds. *A Companion to Death, Burial, and Remembrance in Late Medieval and Early Modern Europe, c.1300–1700* (Leiden: Brill, 2020).

Bordoy Bordoy, Maria José. *Algunes notes sobre les possessions del monestir de Santa Maria de Jonqueres de Barcelona a Mallorca* (Palma, Mallorca: Societat Arqueològica Lul·liana, 2001).

Botinas i Montero, Elena, Julia Cabaleiro i Manzanedo, and Maria dels Àngels Duran i Vinyeta. *Les beguines. La Raó il·luminada per Amor* (Barcelona: Publicacions de l'Abadia de Montserrat, 2002).

Boynton, Susan, Sarah Kay, Alison Cornish, and Andrew Albin, eds. 'Sound Matters'. *Speculum 91*, no. 4 (2016): pp. 988–1039. <https://doi.org/10.1086/688003>.

Braudel, Fernand. *La Méditerranée et le monde méditerranéen à l'époque de Philippe II* (Paris: Armand Colin, 1949).

Bravo de Saravia Sotomayor, Alonso. *Relacion de las fiestas qve en la civdad de Lima se hizieron por la Beatificacion del Bienaventvrado Padre Ignacio de Loyola, fundador de la Religion de la Compañia de Iesus, hechas imprimir por D. Alonso Brauo de Sarauia Soto Mayor. Alcalde de Corte, de la Ciudad de los Reyes* (Lima: Francisco del Canto, 1610).

Bridenthal, Renate, and Claudia Koonz, eds. *Becoming Visible: Women in European History* (Boston: Houghton Mifflin, 1977).

Briz i Franández, F. P. *Lo Llibre dels poetas: cansoner de obras rimadas dels segles XII, XIII, XIV, XV, XVI, XVII y XVIII* (Barcelona: Salvador Manero, 1867).

Broodbank, Cyprian. *Making of the Middle Sea: A History of Mediterranean from the Beginning to the Emergence of the Classical World* (London: Thames & Hudson, 2014).

Brooks, Jeanice. 'Music as Erotic Magic in a Renaissance Romance'. *Renaissance Quarterly 60*, no. 4 (2007): pp. 1207–1256. <https://doi.org/10.1353/ren.2007.0367>.

Brown, Jennifer N. *Three Women of Liège: A Critical Edition of and Commentary on the Middle English Lives of Elizabeth of Spalbeek, Christina Mirabilis, and Marie d'Oignies* (Turnhout: Brepols, 2009).

Burke, Peter. *Popular Culture in Early Modern Europe* (London: Temple Smith, 1978).

Burn, David J., Grantley McDonald, Joseph Verheyden, and Peter De Mey, eds. *Music and Theology in the European Reformations* (Tournhout: Brepols, 2019).

Burns, Kathryn. *Colonial Habits: Convents and the Spiritual Economy of Cuzco, Peru* (Durham: Duke University Press, 1999).

Bustos, Álvaro. 'El Romance de la sacratísima Magdalena de Ambrosio Montesino: escritura (1508), reescritura y censura'. *Medievalia 18*, no. 2 (2015): pp. 119–151.

Cabot Roselló, Salvador. 'Reforma de las monjas terciarias por Felipe II (1567–1570)'. In *El Franciscanismo en Andalucía: Clarisas, Concepcionistas y Terciarias regulares (Priego de Córdoba, 26 a 30 de julio de 2004)*, edited by Manuel Peláez del Rosal (Córdoba: Asociación Hispánica de Estudios Franciscanos, 2004): pp. 269–298.

Cabré i Pairet, Montserrat. 'El monacat femení a la Barcelona de l'alta Edad Mitjana: Sant Pere de las Puel·les, segles X-XI' (Bachelor dissertation, Universitat de Barcelona, 1985).

_____. 'De la leyenda a la autoría colectiva. A propósito de la versión aragonesa de la "Crónica de Sant Pere de les Puel·les"'. In *Mujeres de la Edad Media: actividades políticas, socioeconómicas y culturales*, coordinated by María del Carmen García Herrero and Cristina Pérez Galán (Saragossa: Institución Fernando el Católico, 2014), pp. 51–68.

Caçador, Guillem. *Ordinarium Barcinonense* (Barcelona: Claudium Bornat, 1569).

Calancha, Antonio de la. *Coronica [sic] moralizada del orden de San Augustin en el Peru, con sucesos egenplares en esta monarquia* (Barcelona: Pedro Lacavalleria, 1638).

Callado Estela, Emilio. 'Mujeres, reforma y resistencia. Las dominicas valencianas de Santa María Magdalena en los siglos XVI y XVII'. In *La vida cotidiana y la sociabilidad de los dominicos: entre el convento y las misiones (siglos XVI, XVII y XVIII)*, coordinated by Rosa María Alabrús Iglesias (Barcelona: Arpegio, 2013): pp. 73–103.

_____. *Mujeres en clausura. El convento de Santa María Magdalena de Valencia* (Valencia: Universidad de Valencia, 2014).

Camós i Cabruja, Lluís, and Josep M. Marquès. 'Pergamins de Santa Maria de Palamós'. *Estudis del Baix Empordà 7* (1988): pp. 101–146.

Campruví, Francesc, and Pere Màrtyr Anglès. *Lumen domus o Annals del c[onve]nt de S[an]ta Catha[rin]a. Tom I: des de 1219 fins 1634 inclusive* (MS, 1743). Barcelona, Universitat de Barcelona, Biblioteca de Reserva, 07 Ms 1005.

Canabal Rodríguez, Laura. 'Beaterio y convento. Origen, evolución y desarrollo de las comunidades regulares de la Orden Franciscana en Toledo'. In *El franciscanismo: identidad y poder. Libro homenaje al P. Enrique Chacón Cabello*, coordinated by Manuel Peláez del Rosa (Córdoba: Asociación Hispánica de Estudios Franciscanos, Universidad Internacional de Andalucía, 2016): pp. 317–330.

Cano Roldán, Imelda. *La mujer en el reino de Chile* (Santiago: Gabriela Mistral, 1981).

Cárcel Ortí, María Milagros. 'Hacia un inventario de visitas pastorales en España de los siglos XVI-XX'. *Memoria ecclesiae 15* (1999): pp. 9–135.

Cárcel Ortí, María Milagros, and José Trenchs Odena. 'Una visita pastoral del pontificado de San Juan de Ribera en Valencia (1570)'. *Estudis: Revista de historia moderna 8* (1979–1980): pp. 71–86.

Carreira, Xoán M. 'La musicologia Spagnola: Un'Illusione Autarchica?' *Il Saggiatore Musicale 2* (1995): pp. 105–142.

Carreras, Juan José. '"Conducir a Madrid estos moldes": Producción, dramaturgia y recepción de la fiesta teatral 'Destinos vencen finezas' (1698/9)'. *Revista de musicología 18*, nos. 1–2 (1995): pp. 113–143. <https://doi.org/10.2307/20797044>.

Carreras, Juan José, and Bernardo García García, eds. *The Royal Chapel in the Time of the Habsburgs: Music and Ceremony in the Early Modern European Court*, translated by Yolanda Acker (Woodbridge: The Boydell Press, 2005).

Carreras i Candi, Francesc, dir. *Geografia general de Catalunya: Ciutat de Barcelona* (Barcelona: Albert Martín, [1908–1918?]).

Carreras i Candi, Francesc, and Pablo Vinyoles i Torres. 'Agregación del monasterio de San Antón y Santa Clara a la Orden de San Benito'. *Revista Montserratina 7*, no. 12 (1913): pp. 581–583.

Carreres i Péra, J. 'Santa Maria de Jonqueres'. *Assemblees d'estudis 6* (1988): pp. 1–6.

Casas i Homs, Josep Maria. 'Elecció d'una abadessa de Valldonzella l'any 1476'. In *I Col·loqui d'història del monaquisme català Santes Creus, 1966* (Santes Creus,

Tarragona: Publicacions de l'arxiu bibliogràfic de Santes Creus, 1967): vol. 1, pp. 63–84. <https://usuaris.tinet.cat/absc/catala/arxiu/publi/2publi/1%20col_loqui%20%201.pdf>.

Casas Nadal, Montserrat. 'Los Fondos italianos de la biblioteca del Convento de San Agustín de Barcelona'. In *X Congreso Internacional de Historia de la Orden de San Agustín 'Conventos agustinos' (Madrid, 20–24 de octubre de 1997). Actas del Congreso* (Rome: Institutum Historicum Augustinianum, 1998): pp. 213–259.

Casas-Gras, María del Carmen. 'La música en el Monasterio de Uclés conservada en sus fuentes originales' (PhD dissertation, Universidad Pública de Navarra, 2003).

Cases i Loscos, Luïsa, *et al.*, eds. *Dietaris de la Generalitat de Catalunya* (Barcelona: Generalitat de Catalunya, 1994), 10 vols.

Castellano i Tresserra, Anna. 'Origen i formació d'un monestir femení, Pedralbes al segle XIV (1327–1411)' (PhD dissertation, Universitat Autònoma de Barcelona, 1996).

_____. *Pedralbes a l'edad mitjana. Història d'un monestir femení* (Barcelona: Publicacions de l'Abadia de Montserrat, 1998).

_____. *El Monestir de Pedralbes* (Barcelona: Ajuntament de Barcelona, Districte de les Corts, 2003).

Castellano i Tresserra, Anna, *et al. Petras Albas. El monestir de Pedralbes i els Montcada (1326–1673). Guia-Catàleg* (Barcelona: Ajuntament de Barcelona, 2001).

_____. *El Monestir de Pedralbes: la recuperació d'una joia de l'art català* [exhibition catalogue] (Barcelona: Museu d'Història de la Ciutat, 2003).

Castillo Bejarano, Rafael. 'Erotismo, éxtasis, tormento: la música vocal femenina en la poesía del conde de Villamediana (entre Marino y Góngora)'. *Bulletin of Spanish Studies* 97, no. 7 (2020): pp. 1079–1101. <https://doi.org/10.1080/14753820.2020.1791529>.

Castillo-Ferreira, Mercedes. 'Chant, Liturgy and Reform'. In *Companion to Music in the Age of the Catholic Monarchs*, edited by Tess Knighton [Brill's Companions to Musical Culture 1] (Leiden: Brill, 2016): pp. 282–322.

Catalunya, David. 'Nuns, Polyphony, and a Liégeois Cantor: New Light on the Las Huelgas "Solmization Song"'. *Journal of the Alamire Foundation* 9 (2017): pp. 89–133. <https://doi.org/10.1484/J.JAF.5.114051>.

Cátedra García, Pedro Manuel. 'Fundación y dote del convento de la Visitación de Madrid de monjas clarisas'. *Archivo Ibero-Americano* 47, nos. 185–188 (1987): pp. 307–329.

_____. *Liturgia, poesía y teatro en la Edad Media: estudios sobre prácticas culturales y religiosas* (Madrid: Gredos, 2005).

Cátedra García, Pedro Manuel, and Anastasio Rojo Vega. *Bibliotecas y lecturas de mujeres: s. XVI* (Salamanca: Instituto de Historia del Libro y de la Lectura, 2004).

Cebrián Ferreros, Carlos Francisco. 'Misericordia recuperada. Historia y arte de la antigua casa de la Misericordia'. *Ars Longa* 16 (2007): pp. 93–103.

Cecilia del Nacimiento. *Journeys of a Mystic Soul in Poetry and Prose*, translated by Kevin Connelly and Sandra Sider (Tempe: Arizona Center for Medieval and Renaissance Studies, 2012).

Ceremonial dels magnífichs consellers y regiment de la ciutat de Barcelona: Rúbriques de Bruniquer (Barcelona: Imprempta de'n Henrich y Companyia, 1912–1916), 5 vols.

Cerone, Pietro. *El Melopeo y Maestro* (Naples: Iuan Bautista Gargano y Lucrecio Nucci, 1613).

Chamorro Esteban, Alfredo. 'Ceremonial monárquico y rituales cívicos: Las visitas reales a Barcelona desde el siglo XV hasta el XVII' (PhD dissertation, Universitat de Barcelona, 2013).

_____. *Barcelona y el Rey. Las visitas reales de Fernando el Católico a Felipe V* (Barcelona: Ediciones La Tempestad, 2017).
Chartier, Roger. *Les usages de l'imprimé (XVe-XIXe siècle)* (Paris: Fayard, 1987).
Chiffoleau, J. *La comptabilité de l'au-delà: Les hommes, la mort et la religion dans la region d'Avignon à la fin du Moyen Âge (vers 1320-vers 1480)* [Collection de l'École française de Rome 47] (Rome: École française de Rome, 1980).
Christian, William A. *Local Religion in Sixteenth-century Spain* (Princeton: Princeton University Press, 1989).
Citron, Marcia. *Gender and the Musical Canon* (Cambridge: Cambridge University Press, 1993).
Civil Castellví, Francisco. 'Compositores y organistas gerundenses en el siglo XVII'. *Anales del Instituto de Estudios Gerundenses 21* (1972–1973): pp. 117–169.
Clark, Alice. *Working Life of Women in the Seventeenth Century* (London: Routledge, 1919).
Clay, Catherine, Christine Senecal, and Chandrika Paul, eds. *Envisioning Women in World History: Prehistory to 1500* (New York: McGraw-Hill, 2008).
Codina, Jaume. *Bàndols i bandolers al Baix Llobregat (1580–1630)* (Barcelona: Publicacions de l'Abadia de Montserrat, 1993).
Codina y Formosa, Juan Bautista, and Gumersindo Alabart y Sans. *Efemérides para la historia del Seminario conciliar de Barcelona* (Barcelona: Imprenta de la Casa Provincial de Caridad, 1908).
Coll i Alentorn, Miquel. 'La crònica de Sant Pere de les Puelles'. In *I Col·loqui d'història del monaquisme català Santes Creus, 1966* (Santes Creus, Tarragona: Arxiu bibliogràfic de Santes Creus, 1969): vol. 2, pp. 35–50. <https://usuaris.tinet.cat/absc/catala/arxiu/publi/2publi/1%20col_loqui%202.pdf>.
Collet, Henri. *Le Mysticisme musical espagnol au XVIe siècle* (Paris: Félix Alcan, 1913).
Concilium Tridentinum: Diariorum, actorum, epistularum, tractatuum, nova collection, edidit Societas Goerresiana (Freiburg: Herder, 1901–2001), 13 vols.
Conde, Antónia Fialho. 'O modelo da *perfeita religiosa* e o monaquismo cisterciense feminino no contexto pós-tridentino em Portugal'. In *Mosteiros Cistercienses. Histórica, Arte, Espiritualidade e Património*, directed by José Albuquerque Carreiras (Alcobaça: Jorus, 2013): vol. 2, pp. 397–412.
_____. 'Ambiência monástica e prática litúrgico-musical pós-tridentinas no mosteiro de S. Bento de Cástris'. In *Do Espírito do Lugar – Música, Estética, Silêncio, Espaço, Luz I e II Residências Cistercienses de São Bento de Cástris (2013, 2014)*, directed by Antónia Fialho Conde and António Cãmoes Gouveia (Évora: Publicações do Cidehus, 2016).
_____. 'Do tanger e do cantar no mosteiro cisterciense de S. Bento de Cástris no período moderno'. *Paisagens sonoras urbanas: História, Memória e Património* (Évora: Publicações do Cidehus, 2019): pp. 207–222. <http:// books.openedition.org/cidehus/8886>.
Conde, Antónia Fialho, and Isabel Maria Botelho de Gusmão Dias Sarreira Cid da Silva. 'Os Livros de Coro do mosteiro cisterciense de S. Bento de Cástris: análise codicológica de um Antifonário'. *Mirabilia Ars 2*, no. 1 (2015) [*El Poder de la Imagen. Ideas y funciones de las representaciones artísticas*, directed by José María Salvador González]: pp. 59–83.
Conde, Antónia Fialho, and Margarida Sá Nogueira Lalanda, 'The Monastery of St. Benedict of Cástris as a Space of Assertion and Power: From the Mystic Marriage to

Musical Praxis'. *European Scientific Journal 11*, no. 10 (2015): pp. 401–408. <https://eujournal.org/index.php/esj/article/view/6164>.

Constituciones en forma de capítulos y artículos extractados del Derecho Canónico vigente, de los decretos pontificios, de la Regla de san Benito y de las Definiciones, Costumbres y Ritual de la Orden Cisterciense, para el uso de las religiosas del real monasterio de Santa María de Valldoncella de Barcelona (Poblet: Impr. Monástica, 1947).

Constituciones para los monasterios de religiosas de la Congregacion Benedictina Claustral Tarraconense y Cesar-Augustana: hechas y mandadas observar por el Sagrado Capitulo General celebrado en la ciudad de Barcelona (Barcelona: Lorenzo Deu, 1615).

Convent de Sant Agustí (Barcelona). *Manifiesto por el padre prior y Convento de San Agustin de esta ciudad contra Francisco Torrents [...]* (Barcelona: Juan Jolis, [1740 or later]).

Conte Aguilar, Lucía. 'Formes de transgressió a les parròquies de Barcelona segons les visites pastorals de principis del segle XIV'. In *El món urbà a la Corona d'Aragó del 1137 als decrets de Nova Planta: XVII Congrés d'Història de la Corona d'Aragó = Congreso de Historia de la Corona de Aragón: Barcelona. Poblet. Lleida, 7 al 12 de desembre de 2000*, coordinated by Salvador Claramunt Rodríguez (Barcelona: Universitat de Barcelona, 2003): vol. 2, pp. 87–106.

Coolidge, Grace E. *Guardianship, Gender and the Nobility in Early Modern Spain* (Aldershot: Ashgate, 2010).

Corona, Ignacio, and Alejandro L. Madrid. *Postnational Musical Identities: Cultural P'roduction, Distribution, and Consumption in a Globalized Scenario* (Lanham: Lexington Books, 2007).

Costa i Paretas, Maria Mercè. 'El Monestir de Jonqueres: història d'un edifici desaparegut'. *Cuadernos de arqueología e historia de la ciudad 15* (1973a), pp. 95–119.

_____. 'Un Conflicte monàstic: Valldonzella i Jonqueres'. *Estudis Cistercencs Germandat de Valldonzella 9* (1973b), pp. 5–24.

_____. 'Les dames nobles de Jonqueres'. In *II Col·loqui d'història del monaquisme català: Sant Joan de les Abadesses 1970* (Poblet: Abadía de Poblet, 1974): vol. 2, pp. 253–309. <https://explora.bnc.cat/permalink/34CSUC_BC/1fpark4/alma991007472569706717>.

_____. 'Els llibres notarials del Monestir de Jonqueres'. *Estudios históricos y documentos de los archivos de protocolos 7* (1979), pp. 59–74.

_____. 'Les eleccions priorals al monestir de Santa Maria de Jonqueres'. *Quaderns d'arqueologia i història de la ciutat 18* (1980): pp. 153–169.

_____. 'Les monges de la família Llull en el monestir de Jonqueres'. In *Miscel·lània Fort i Cogul. Història Monàstica Catalana. Història del Camp de Tarragona*, edited by Miquel Coll i Alentorn (Barcelona: Publicacions de l'Abadia de Montserrat, 1984): pp. 103–127.

_____. 'Els esclaus del monestir de Jonqueres'. In *De l'esclavitud a la llibertat: esclaus i lliberts a l'edat mitjana. Actas del col·loqui internacional celebrat a Barcelona, del 27 al 29 de maig de 1999*, coordinated by María Teresa Ferrer i Mallol and Josefina Mutgé i Vives (Barcelona: CSIC, Institución Milá y Fontanals, 2000): pp. 297–308.

_____. *El món de les dames de Jonqueres* (Lleida: Pagès, 2005).

_____. 'Les Dames gironines del Monestir de les Jonqueres'. *Annals de l'Institut d'Estudis Gironins 49* (2008): pp. 123–133.

Courcelles, Dominique de, and Carmen Val Julián. *Des femmes et des livres: France et Espagnes, XIVe-XVIIe siècle: Actes de la Journée d'Étude organisée par l'École Nationale des Chartes et l'École Normale Supérieure de Fontenay Saint-Cloud (Paris, 30 avril 1998)* (Paris: École des Chartes, 1999).

Cowan, Alexander, and Jill Steward, eds. *The City and the Senses: Urban Culture Since 1500* (Aldershot: Ashgate, 2007).

Crispí i Canton, Marta. 'La iglesia del monasterio de Sant Pere de les Puel·les a través de la visita pastoral de la abadesa Violant d'Espés (1585–1587)'. *Anuario de Estudios Medievales 50*, no. 1 (2020): pp. 93–125.

Cruz, Anne J. 'Las formas de vida religiosa femenina en la época de Teresa de Jesús y Catalina de Cardona'. *eHumanista 33* (2016): pp. 246–265.

Cummings, Anthony. *The Lion's Ear: Pope Leo X, the Renaissance Papacy, and Music* (Ann Arbor: University of Michigan Press, 2012).

Cusó Serra, Marta. 'Un monestir cistercenc femení català durant el primer segle borbònic espanyol: Santa Maria de Vallbona (1701–1802)' (PhD dissertation, Universitat Autònoma de Barcelona, 2008).

Dadson, Trevor J. *Libros, lectores y lecturas. Estudios sobre bibliotecas particulares españolas del Siglo de Oro* (Madrid: Arco libros, 1998).

_____. 'Ana de Mendoza y de la Cerda, Princess of Éboli: Image, Myth, and Person'. In *Representing Women's Political Identity in the Early Modern Iberian World*, edited by Jeremy Roe and Jean Andrews (London: Routledge, 2021).

Dalmau, José. *Relacion de la solemnidad con que se han celebrado en la ciudad de Barcelona, las fiestas a la beatificacion de la Madre S. Teresa de Iesus...* (Barcelona: Sebastián Matevad, 1615).

Darna Galobart, Leticia. 'Emblemas de gremios y cofradías en la ciudad de Barcelona'. *Anales de la Real Academia Matritense de Heráldica y Genealogía 6* (2000–2001): pp. 7–28.

Darna Galobart, Leticia. 'Heráldica en las cartas de profesión del monasterio de Santa Clara de Barcelona'. *Paratge: quaderns d'estudis de genealogia, heràldica, sigil·lografia i nobiliària 27* (2014): pp. 157–202.

Darnton, Robert. 'What Is the History of Books?' *Daedalus 111*, no. 3 (1982): pp. 65–83.

Davies, Natalie Zemon. *Women on the Margins: Three Seventeenth-Century Lives* (Cambridge, MA: Harvard University Press, 1995).

Davy-Rigaux, B. Dompnier, and D.-O. Hurel, eds. *Les cérémoniaux catholiques en France à l'époque moderne: Une littérature de codification des rites liturgiques* (Turnhout: Brepols, 2009).

Delgado Casado, Juan. *Diccionario de impresores españoles* (Madrid: Arco Libros, 1996), 3 vols.

Dell'Antonio, Andrew. *Listening as Spiritual Practice in Early Modern Italy* (Berkeley: University of California Press, 2011).

DePrano, Maria. *Art Patronage, Family, and Gender in Renaissance Florence: The Tornabuoni* (Cambridge: Cambridge University Press, 2018).

Diago, Francisco. *Historia de los victoriosissimos antiguos Condes de Barcelona* (Barcelona: Sebastián de Cormellas, 1603).

Diccionari d'Història Eclesiàstica de Catalunya (Barcelona: Generalitat de Catalunya, Claret, 1998–2001), 3 vols.

Die 21 Ianuarii 1693, Nos Petrus Roig & Morell Sacrista major & Canonicus Sedis Barcin[onensis] Decretorum Doctor, pro [...] Capitulo Canonicorum ejusdem Sedis, Sede vacante, V.G. & Off. electus & deput (Barcelona?: s.n., 1693).

Díez Borque, José María. *El libro. De la tradición oral a la cultura impresa* (Barcelona: Montesinos, 1985).

Díez de Aux, Luis. *Retrato de las fiestas que á la Beatificacion de la Bienaventurada Virgen y Madre Santa Teresa de Iesus, Renouadora de la Religion Primiua del Carmelo, hizo, assi Ecclesiasticas como Militares y Poeticas: la Imperial Ciudad de Zaragoça* (Saragossa: Iuan de la Naja y Quartanet, 1615).

──────. *Compendio de las fiestas que ha celebrado la Imperial ciudad de Çaragoça. Por auer promouido la Magestad Catholica del Rey nuestro Señor, Filipo Tercero de Castilla, y Segundo de Aragon: al illustissimo Señor don Fray Luys Aliaga su Confessor, y de su Real Consejo de Estado, en el Oficio y Cargo Supremo de Inquisidor General de España. Ordenado, por orden y comission de la mesma Ciudad, por Luys Diez de Aux Hijo suyo. Con la version de tres hymnos que Aurelio Prudencio hizo en su alabança y de sus Martyres* (Saragossa: Iuan de la Naja y Quartanet, 1619).

Discurso en derecho en favor de las muy ilustres y muy reverendas señoras abadesas y conventos de N. Señora de S. Pedro de las Puellas de Valdoncella y de S. Clara de la ciudad de Barcelona (Barcelona?: [s.n.], 1665). <https://explora.bnc.cat/permalink/34CSUC_BC/1fpark4/alma991000891169706717>.

Ditchfield, Simon, and Helen Smith, eds. *Conversions: Gender and Religious Change in Early Modern Europe* (Manchester: Manchester University Press, 2017).

Donovan, R. *The Liturgical Drama in Medieval Spain* (Toronto: Pontifical Institute of Medieval Studies, 1958).

Dunn, Leslie C., and Nancy A. Jones, eds. *Embodied Voices: Representing Female Vocality in Western Culture* (Cambridge: Cambridge University Press, 1996).

Duran i Sanpere, Agustí. *Barcelona i la seva historia* (Barcelona: Curial, 1972–1975), 3 vols.

Duran i Sanpere, Agustí, and J. Sanabre, eds. *Llibre de les Solemnitats de la ciutat de Barcelona: edició completa del manuscrit de l'Arxiu Històric de la Ciutat* (Barcelona: Institut d'Estudis Catalans, 1930–1947), 2 vols.

Echániz Sans, María. *Las mujeres de la Orden Militar de Santiago en la Edad Media* (León: Junta de Castilla y León, 1992).

Edelstein, Bruce L. 'Nobildonne napoletane e committenza: Eleonora d'Aragona ed Eleonora di Toledo a confronto'. *Quaderni Storici 104*, no. 2 (2000): pp. 295–330.

Edwards, Robert R., and Vickie Ziegler. *Matrons and Marginal Women in Medieval Society* (Woodbridge: The Boydell Press, 1995).

Eichner, Barbara. 'Sweet Singing in Three Voices: A Musical Source from a South German Convent?' *Early Music 39*, no. 3 (2011): pp. 335–348. <https://doi.org/10.1093/em/car051>.

──────. 'The Woman at the Well: Divine and Earthly Love in Orlando di Lasso's Parody Masses'. *Revue belge de Musicologie 72* (2018): pp. 31–52.

Eidsheim, Nina Sun. *Sensing Sounds: Singing and Listening as Vibrational Practice* (Durham: Duke University Press, 2015).

Eire, Carlos M. N. *From Madrid to Purgatory: The Art and Craft of Dying in Sixteenth-Century Spain* (Cambridge: Cambridge University Press, 1995).

Eisenbichler, Konrad, ed. *The Cultural World of Eleonora di Toledo: Duchess of Florence and Siena* (Aldershot: Ashgate, 2004).

Eisenstein, Elizabeth Lewisohn. *The Printing Press as an Agent of Change: Communications and Cultural Transformations in Early-Modern Europe* (Cambridge: Cambridge University Press, 1979).

Eiximenis, Francesc. *Llibre de les dones* (Barcelona: Johann Rosembach, 1495).

Elliott, John Huxtable. *Spain and Its World, 1500–1700* (New Haven: Yale University Press, 1989).
Enciso Alonso-Muñumer, Isabel. *Nobleza, poder y mecenazgo en tiempos de Felipe III: Nápoles y el Conde de Lemos* (San Sebastián de los Reyes: Actas, 2007).
Epítome de memorias del Convento de Santa Maria de Jesus de la orden de menores observantes extramuros de Barcelona y noticia de la bendicion y colocacion de la primera piedra para su segundo restablecimiento: hecha pontificalmente por el [...] señor don Pablo de Sichar obispo de Barcelona, del Consejo de S. M. &c. en el dia 1 de enero de ese año 1817 lo escribio un Sacerdote Catalán i Natural de la Villa de Olot (Barcelona: Impr. de Agustin Roca, 1817).
Erdmann, Axel. *My Gracious Silence: Women in the Mirror of 16th Century Printing in Western Europe* (Lucerne: Gilhofer & Ranschburg, 1999).
Establés Susán, Sandra. *Diccionario de mujeres impresoras y libreras de Españae Iberoamérica entre los siglos XV y XVIII* (Saragossa: Universidad de Zaragoza, 2018).
Ester Sala, María Asunción, and Josep Maria Vilar y Torrens. 'Arxius Musicals a Catalunya (XX). Barcelona. Arxiu de l'Escola Pia de Catalunya, Arxiu Històric dels Franciscans de Catalunya, Arxiu dels Carmelites Descalços de Catalunya i Balears, i Arxiu dels Caputxins de Sarrià'. *Revista Musical Catalana* 64 (1990). 'Difusió en català de l'obra de J. Bermudo a l'*Ordinarium Barcinonense* de 1569'. *Recerca Musicològica* 5 (1985): pp. 13–43.
Estévez Monagas, Jesús Enrique. 'Documentación musical en el Convento de San Francisco de quito: libros litúrgico-musicales, órganos y coristas'. *Acta Musicologica* 93, no. 1 (2021): pp. 43–66.
Esthér elegida por esposa de Asuero. Drama, que en la solemne profesion, y velo de la señora sor Maria Benita Lacóma, y Martí, se cantó en el sacro, y real convento de religiosas franciscas de Jerusalen de la ciudad de Barcelona, por la capilla de la santa iglesia cathedral, siendo su maestro el licenciado Joseph Pujol (Barcelona: en la imprenta de Maria Angela Martí viuda, [1769]). <https://cercabib.ub.edu/permalink/34CSUC_UB/13d0big/alma991006655009706708>.
Estill, Laura, *et al. Early Modern Studies After the Digital Turn* (Toronto and Tempe: Iter Press, in collaboration with Arizona Center for Medieval and Renaissance Studies, 2016).
Estrada-Rius, Albert. *Pellofes & ploms eclesiàstics. Un patrimoni numismàtic per descobrir* (Barcelona: Museu Nacional d'Art de Catalunya, 2014).
Ettinghausen, Henry, *et al.*, coords. *Las relaciones de sucesos en España 1500–1750: actas del primer Coloquio Internacional* (Alcalá de Henares: Universidad de Alcalá, 1996).
Evangelisti, Silvia. *Nuns: A History of Convent Life, 1450–1700* (New York: Oxford University Press, 2007).
Fàbrega i Grau, Àngel. *La vida quotidiana a la catedral de Barcelona en declinar el Renaixement Any 1580* (Barcelona: Arxiu Capitular de la S. E. Catedral Basílica de Barcelona, 1978).
Fabris, Dinko. *Music in Seventeenth-Century Naples: Francesco Provenzale (1624–1704)* (Aldershot: Ashgate, 2007).
Federación de monjas cistercienses de España. *Breve noticia histórica de los monasterios pertenecientes a la Federación de Monjas Cistercienses de España* (Tarragona: Federación de Monjas Cistercienses de España, 1974).
Fenlon, Iain. 'Urban Soundscapes'. In *The Cambridge History of Sixteenth-Century Music*, edited by Iain Fenlon and Richard Wistreich (Cambridge: Cambridge Univesrity Press, 2018): pp. 209–259.

Fenlon, Iain, and Tess Knighton, eds. *Early Music Printing and Publishing in the Iberian World* (Kassel: Reichenberger, 2006).

Fernández Terricabras, Ignasi. 'Un ejemplo de la política religiosa de Felipe II: el intento de reforma de las monjas de la Tercera Orden de San Francisco, 1567–1571'. In I Congreso Internacional del Monacato femenino en España, Portugal y América, 1492–1992 (León: Universidad, 1993): vol. 3, pp. 159–172.

Finley, Sarah. 'Más allá de la sonoridad: huellas del pensamiento musical en el convento de Jesús María de México'. *Boletín de monumentos históricos* 45 (2019a): pp. 68–81.

_____. *Hearing Voices: Aurality and New Spanish Sound Culture in Sor Juana Inés de la Cruz* (Lincoln and London: University of Nebraska Press, 2019b).

Fita, Fidel. 'Fundación y primer período del monasterio de Santa Clara de Barcelona'. *Boletín de la Real Academia de la Historia* 27 (1895): pp. 272–314, 436, 489; 28 (1896): pp. 54–62.

Flores, Cándido. 'Dos discursos en griego de la Barcelona del siglo XVI'. *Suplemento de Estudios Clásicos*, third series, *no. 2* (1980): pp. 31–57.

Fons, Iván Pablo, and Miguel Torbavi. *Historia y vida de la venerable madre Angela Margarita Serafina, Fundadora de religiosas capuchinas en España y de otras sus primeras hijas, hasta el año de mil 1622. En que la dexò escrita el P. Ivan Pablo Fons, de la Compañía de Iesus. Revista por el P. Miguel Torbavi de la misma Compañía. Dedicanla a la christianissima magestad de Doña Ana de Austria, Reyna Madre de Francia. La Abadessa, y Relgiosas de su Primario Convento de santa Margarita la Real de Barcelona* (Barcelona: En casa de Maria Dexen viuda, 1649).

Fontanet, Joan Baptista. 'De la Fundacion de la Real Casa de Nuestra Señora de Junqueres de la Inclita Orden y Cavalleria del Glorioso Apostol Santiago de la Espada de Ucles en la Ciudad de Barcelona instituida y Fundada'. In *Barcelona, convento de Santa Maria de Jonqueres. Libro de la fundación, traslado y visitas* (MS, 1686). Barcelona, Arxiu de la Corona d'Aragó, ORM,Monacales-Universidad,Volúmenes244, fols. 1r–69v.

Fox, Gwyn. *Subtle Subversions: Reading Golden Age Sonnets by Iberian Women* (Washington, DC: Catholic University of America Press, 2008).

Freed, John B. *The Friars and German Society in the Thirteenth Century* (Cambridge: The Medieval Academy of America, 1977).

Fuhse, Jan. 'The Meaning Structure of Social Networks'. *Sociological Theory* 27 (2009): pp. 51–73. <https://doi.org/10.1111/j.1467-9558.2009.00338.x>.

Gaffarot, Jacinto. *Evidencia Historica-Canonica, de la Ordinaria, y Omnimoda Jurisdicion que a la Muy Ilustre Señora Abadesa del Real Monasterio de San Pedro De las Puellas de esta Ciudad, compete y ha Competido en su Iglesia, y Beneficiados de las mas remotas edades...* (Barcelona: Imprenta de María Ángela Martí, viuda, 1756).

Gallego Blanco, Enrique, ed. *The Rule of the Spanish Military Order of St. James: 1170-1493* (Leiden: Brill, 1971).

García de Caralps, Antonio Juan. *Historia de S. Oleguer arçobispo de Tarragona y obispo de Barcelona* (Barcelona: Sebastian Matevad Impressor de la Vniuersidad, 1617).

García Mercadal, José. *Viajes de extranjeros por España y Portugal: desde los tiempos más remotos hasta comienzos del siglo XX* (Madrid: Aguilar, 1952–1962).

García Oro, P. José O.F.M. *La reforma de los religiosos españoles en tiempo de los Reyes Católicos* (Valladolid: Instituto Isabel la Católica, 1969).

_____. *Cisneros y la reforma del clero español en tiempo de los Reyes Católicos* (Madrid: CSIC, 1971).

———. 'Conventualismo y observancia. La reforma de las órdenes religiosas en los siglos XV y XVI'. *Historia de la Iglesia en España 3*, no. 1 (1980) [issue directed by R. Garcia Villoslada]: pp. 211–350.

———. 'La Corte de España y las cofradías inmaculistas de los siglos XVI y XVII'. In *De cultu mariano saeculis XVII-XVIII. Acta congressus mariologici-mariani internationalis in republica melitensi anno 1983 celebrati. Vol. 6: The cultur mariano saeculis XVII et XVIII apud varias nationes*. Pars prior (Rome: Pontificia Academia Mariana Internationalis, 1988): pp. 449–471. <https://worldcat.org/es/title/43992162>.

———. 'Reforma y reformas en la familia franciscana del Renacimiento. Cuadro histórico del tema'. In *El franciscanismo en la Península Ibérica. Balance y perspectivas*, edited by María del Mar Graña Cid (Barcelona: GBG Editora, 2005): pp. 235–254.

García-Arenal, Mercedes, ed. *After Conversion Iberia and the Emergence of Modernity* (Leiden: Brill, 2016).

Garí, Blanca, *et al.* 'CLAUSTRA. Propuesta metodológica para el estudio territorial del De monacato femenino'. *Anuario de estudios medievales 44*, no. 1 (2014): pp. 21–50.

Garriga Roca, Miquel. *Monografía del Monasterio de Santa María de Junqueras de Barcelona ó sea memoria descriptiva, histórica y arqueológica del mismo de su iglesia y de su claustro acompañada de los respectivos dibujos de plantas alzados, secciones y detalles todo con arreglo al programa de la digna Sociedad Económica Barcelonesa de Amigos del País y en opción al premio 5º de los que ofrece adjudicar el día 19 de Noviembre del presente año de 1864* (Barcelona: Tipografía La Academia, de Serra hermanos y Russeli, 1899).

Gelaberto Vilagran, Martí. 'Ritual funerario y contrarreforma: El Monasterio de Nuestra Señora de Junqueras (siglos XVI-XVII)'. *Analecta Sacra Tarraconensia 67*, no. 2 (1994): pp. 333–343.

Gembero-Ustárroz, María, and Emilio Ros-Fábregas, eds. *La Música y el Atlántico* (Granada: Universidad de Granada, 2007).

Gilchrist, Roberta. *Gender and Material Culture: The Archaeology of Religious Women* (London and New York: Routledge, 1994).

Giordano, Maria Laura. 'Cuando los católicos eran paulinos: Diego Pérez y Sor Hipólita de Jesús en Barcelona (1578–1624)'. In *Reforma católica y disidencia conversa: Diego Pérez de Valdivia y sor Hipólita de Jesús y Rocabertí en Barcelona (1578–1624)*, edited by Maria Laura Giordano (Vigo: Editorial Academia del Hispanismo, 2020): pp. 33–106.

Glixon, Jonathan E. *Mirrors of Heaven or Worldly Theaters? Venetian Nunneries and Their Music* (Oxford: Oxford University Press, 2017).

Goigs de la gloriosa verge, y Martyr Santa Polonia, ques cantan en la sua Capella, fundada en la Iglesia de las Religiosas de Monte-Syon, de la Ciudad de Barcelona (Barcelona: Joan Piferrer, [c.1740]).

Goigs del Glorios Sant Nicasi Bisbe y Martyr advocat contra la peste: Los quals se cantan en lo Monestir de Religiosas Dominicas de Mo[n]tesion de Barcelona, que està la sua Santa Reliquia (Barcelona: En casa Antoni Lacavalleria, 1651). <https://bd.centrelectura.cat/items/show/19157>.

Gómez Fernández, Lucía. *Música, nobleza y mecenazgo. Los duques de Medina Sidonia en Sevilla y Sanlúcar de Barrameda (1445–1615)* (Cádiz: Universidad de Cádiz, 2017).

Gómez Muntané, Maricarmen. *La música medieval en España* (Kassel: Reichenberger, 2001).

González Peña, María del Val, ed. *Mujeres y cultura escrita. Del mito al siglo XXI* (Gijón: Trea, 2005).
González Sugrañes, Miquel. *Contribució a la història dels antichs gremis dels arts y oficis de la ciutat de Barcelona* (Barcelona: Henrich y Com., 1915–1918), 2 vols.
Gordon, Bonnie. *Monteverdi's Unruly Women: The Power of Song in Early Modern Italy* (Cambridge: Cambridge University Press, 2009).
Gouk, Penelope. *Music, Science and Natural Magic in Seventeenth-Century England* (New Haven: Yale University Press, 1999).
_____, ed. *Musical Healing in Cultural Contexts* (Aldershot: Ashgate, 2000).
_____. 'Book Review Essay: Embodying the Voice'. *Renaissance Studies 35*, no. 4 (2020): pp. 722–728. <https://doi.org/10.1111/rest.12676>.
Gouk, Penelope, and Helen Hills, eds., *Representing Emotions: New Connections in the Histories of Art, Music and Medicine* (Aldershot: Ashgate, 2005).
Graduale Romanum De Tempore, et Sanctis, Ad ritum Missalis, ex decreto sacrosancti Concilij Tridentini restituti, Pii Quinti Pontificis Maximi iussu editi, Et Clementis viij. auctoritate recogniti (Venice: Iuntas, 1618).
Graña Cid, María del Mar, ed. *Las sabias mujeres: educación, saber y autoría (siglos III-XVII)* (Madrid: Asociación Cultural Al-Mudayna, 1994).
_____. 'Espacios de vida espiritual de mujeres (Obispado de Córdoba, 1260–1550)' (PhD dissertation, Universidad Complutense de Madrid, 2008).
Gras Casanovas, Maria Mercè. 'Patronatge femení i fundació de convents: el convent de la Immaculada Concepció de carmelites descalces de Barcelona (1589)'. In *Redes femeninas: de promoción espiritual en los reinos peninsulares, s. XIII-XVI*, edited by Blanca Garí (Rome: Viella, 2013a): pp. 251–266.
_____. 'Familia y clausura. El monasterio de Nuestra Señora de los Ángeles y Pie de la Cruz de Barcelona (1485–1750)'. In *La vida cotidiana y la sociabilidad de los dominicos*, edited by Rosa Maria Alabrús (Sant Cugat del Vallès, Barcelona: Arpegio, 2013b): pp. 117–132.
_____. 'L'escriptura en el carmen descalç femení: la província de Sant Josep de Catalunya (1588–1835)'. *Scripta, Revista internacional de literatura i cultura medieval i moderna 1* (2013c): pp. 302–332. <https://doi.org/10.7203/SCRIPTA.1.2587>.
_____. 'Música per carmelites descalces'. *Castell Interior* [Blog] (2015). <https://castellinterior.com/2015/03/10/musica-per-a-carmelites-descalces/>.
_____. 'Música de Francesc Valls per a una Carmelita descalça: sor Teresa de Crist (1697)'. *Castell Interior* [Blog] (2021). <https://castellinterior.com/2021/03/01/musica-de-francesc-valls-per-a-una-carmelita-descalca-sor-teresa-de-crist-1697/#_ftn2>.
Gregori i Cifré, Josep Maria. 'Pere Alberch artífex de la relació musical entre les seus de girona i barcelona en el renaixement tardà'. *Annals de l'Institut d'Estudis Gironins 28* (1985–1986): pp. 281–298.
_____. *La música del Renaixement a la catedral de Barcelona, 1450–1580* (Barcelona: Universitat Autònoma de Barcelona, 1987).
_____. 'La controvertida preeminència musical de la Seu dins la Barcelona de la segona meitat del segle XVI'. *Anuario Musical 46* (1991): pp. 103–126.
_____. 'Joan Ferrer, mestre de cant i organista de la Catedral de Barcelona (1513–1536), autor del motet 'Domine non secundum' del Cancionero Musical de Segovia (CMS) (E: SegC, s. s.)'. *Revista Catalana de Musicologia 10* (2017): pp. 45–65. <https://doi.org/10.2436/20.1003.01.52>.

Griffin, Clive. *The Crombergers of Seville: The History of a Printing and Merchant Dynasty* (Oxford: Clarendon Press, 1988).

_____. *Journeymen-Printers, Heresy, and the Inquisition in Sixteenth-Century Spain* (Oxford: Oxford University Press, 2005).

Griuppaudo, Ilaria. 'Music, Religious Communities, and the Urban Dimension: Sound Experiences in Palermo in the Sixteenth and Seventeenth Centuries'. In *Hearing the City in Early Modern Europe*, edited by Tess Knighton and Ascensión Mazuela-Anguita (Turhout: Brepols, 2018): pp. 309–326.

Gschwend, Annemarie Jordan. 'The Monastery I Have Built in this City of Madrid: Mapping Juana of Austria's Royal Spaces in the Descalzas Reales Convent'. In *Representing Women's Political Identity in the Early Modern Iberian World*, edited by Jeremy Roe and Jean Andrews (London: Routledge, 2021).

Gudayol, Anna, and M. Rosa Montalt, with the collaboration of Sergi Zauner. 'Música litúrgica a la Biblioteca de Catalunya I: Llibres de cant litúrgic manuscrits'. *Miscel·lània Litúrgica Catalana XXV* (2017): pp. 137–289. <https://doi.org/10.2436/20.1002.01.29>.

Hadewijch. *The Complete Works*, translated by Mother Columba Hart (New York: Paulist Press, 1980).

Haliczer, Stephen. *Between Exaltation and Infamy. Female Mystics in the Golden Age of Spain* (Oxford: Oxford University Press, 2002).

Hall, Dianne. *Women and the Church in Medieval Ireland, c.1140-1540* (Dublin: Four Courts Press, 2003).

Hamilakis, Yannis. *Archaeology and the Senses: Human Experience, Memory, and Affect* (Cambridge: Cambridge University Press, 2013).

Hampton, Timothy. *Fictions of Embassy: Literature and Diplomacy in Early Modern Europe* (Ithaca: Cornell University Press, 2009).

Hanna, Daniel John. 'Carmelite Poetry in France and the Low Countries: The Tradition of Teresa of Avila' (PhD dissertation, Princeton University, 2012).

Hathaway, Janet. *Cloister, Court and City: Musical Activity of the Monasterio de las Descalzas Reales (Madrid), c.1620–1700*. Ann Arbor: UMI, 2005.

_____. '"Music Charms the Senses…": Devotional Music in the Triunfos festivos of San Ginés, Madrid, 1656'. In *Devotional Music in the Iberian World, 1450-1800: The Villancico and Related Genres*, edited by Tess Knighton and Álvaro Torrente (Aldershot: Ashgate, 2007): pp. 219–230.

Head, Matthew. *Sovereign Feminine: Music and Gender in Eighteenth-Century Germany* (Berkeley: University of California Press, 2013).

Hernández Cabrera, María Soledad. 'Montesión, una comunidad de dominicas en Barcelona, siglos XIV-XVI' (Bachelor dissertation, Universitat de Barcelona, 1997), 2 vols.

_____. 'La celda del convento una habitación propia. La vivencia de la clausura en la comunidad de dominicas de Montesión'. *Duoda. Revista de Estudios feministas 22* (2002): pp. 19–40.

Hierro, Baltasar del. *Los triumphos y grandes recebimientos de la insigne ciudad de Barcelona a la venida del famosissimo Phelipe rey de las Españas &c. Con la entrada de los serenissimos principes de Bohemia* (Barcelona: Iayme Cortey, 1564).

Hills, Helen. *Invisible City: The Architecture of Devotion in 17th-Century Neapolitan Convents* (Oxford: Oxford University Press, 2004).

Holford-Strevens, Leofranc. 'Sirens in Antiquity and the Middle Ages'. In *Music of the Sirens*, edited by Linda Austern and Inna Naroditskaya (Bloomington: Indiana University Press, 2006): pp. 25–50.

Horden, Peregrine, and Nicholas Purcell. *The Corrupting See: A Study of Mediterranean History* (Oxford: Blackwell, 2000).
Howard, Deborah, and Laura Moretti. *The Music Room in Early Modern France and Italy* (Oxford and New York: Oxford University Press, 2012).
Howe, Elizabeth Teresa. *Education and Women in the Early Modern Hispanic World* (Aldershot: Ashgate, 2008).
Huglo, Michel. *Les manuscrits du processional* (Munich: Henle, 1999).
Ibáñez Lería, María Pilar. 'El monasterio de Santa María de Junqueres. Estudio histórico y colección diplomática (1212–1389)' (Bachelor dissertation, Universitat de Barcelona, 1966).
_____. 'La fundación y primera época del monasterio de Jonqueres (1212–1389)'. *Anuario de Estudios Medievales 11* (1981): pp. 362–382.
Indulgencias concedidas a los Congregantes de la Inmaculada Concepcion de Maria SS. baxo el titulo de la Corona de las siete Alegrias principales que tuvo la Divina Reyna (Barcelona: s.n., 1793). <https://explora.bnc.cat/permalink/34CSUC_BC/1fpark4/alma991004311429706717>.
Inventario de la Librería del Señor D. Lorenzo Ramirrez de Prado Cavallero que fué de la Orden de Santiago de los Consejos de Su Magestad en el Real Svpremo de Castilla y de el de Santa Cruzada (no editorial details, n.d.). <http://bdh.bne.es/bnesearch/detalle/bdh0000173525>.
Iranzo y Eiras, Ubaldo de. 'El claustro del monasterio de San Pedro de las Puellas. Memoria descriptiva'. In *Anuario para 1903. Asociación de Arquitectos de Cataluña*, edited by the Asociación de Arquitectos de Cataluña (Barcelona: Imprenta y Litografía de Henrich y Cia., 1903): pp. 69–122 [republished by the Asociación de Arquitectos de Cataluña in 1950].
Irving, David R. M. *Colonial Counterpoint: Music in Early Modern Manila* (Oxford: Oxford University, 2010).
Iuris responsum in causa educationes nobilium pupillarum Mendoças (Barcelona: ex typographia Stephani Liberôs, 1617).
Iuris responsum pro monesterio et conventu beatae Mariae de Montesion contra [...] Franciscum Gamis (S.l.: s.n., after 1655). <https://explora.bnc.cat/permalink/34CSUC_BC/1fpark4/alma991014833259706717>.
Janini, José. *Manuscritos litúrgicos de las bibliotecas de España* (Burgos: Aldecoa, 1980), 2 vols.
Jaspert, Nikolas. *Stift und Stadt: das Heiliggrabpriorat von Santa Anna und das Regularkanonikerstift Santa Eulàlia del Camp im mittelalterlichen Barcelona: 1145–1423* (Berlin: Duncker & Humblot, cop. 1996).
Javierre Mur, Aurea L., and María Dolores Couto de León. *Los religiosos de la Orden de Santiago* (Madrid: Servicio de Publicaciones del Ministerio de Educación, 1976).
Jerusalén librada de los asirios por el angel del Señor: drama sacro-alegorico, que en las fiestas celebradas en el convento de Santa Madrona de [...] Barcelona, con motivo de la beatificacion del [...] Fr. Lorenzo de Brindis [...] en los dias 9 y 10 de maio de 1784 cantó la capilla de la santa iglesia de Barcelona / siendo su maestro [...] Francisco Queralt [...] (Barcelona: Bernardo Pla, [1784]).
Jeż, Tomasz. 'The Jesuit Musical Tradition in the Polish-Lithuanian Commonwealth'. *Journal of Jesuit Studies 5*, no. 3 (2018), pp. 385–403. <https://doi.org/10.1163/22141332-00503003>.
Jones, Pamela. 'Envisioning a Global Environment for Blessed Teresa of Avila in 1614: The Beatification Decorations for S. Maria della Scala in Rome'. In *Mapping Gendered*

Routes and Spaces in the Early Modern World, edited by Merry E. Wiesner-Hanks (Farnham, Surrey: Ashgate, 2015): pp. 131–156.
Jornet i Benito, Núria. 'Guia de l'Arxiu del Monestir de Sant Benet de Montserrat'. <http://www.benedictinescat.com/montserrat/htmlfotos/Arxiu.html>.
_____. 'Agnès de Peranda i Clara de Janua: dues figures carismàtiques o la fundació del monestir de Sant Antoni de Barcelona'. *Duoda. Revista d'estudis feministes 22* (2002): pp. 41–57.
_____. 'Sant Antoni i Santa Clara de Barcelona: origen d'un monestir i configuració d'un arxiu monàstic (1236–1327)' (PhD dissertation, Universitat de Barcelona, 2005).
_____. 'Memoria y genealogía femeninas: la leyenda fundacional del primer monasterio de clarisas de Catalunya'. In *La historia de las mujeres: perspectivas actuales. XIII Coloquio Internacional de la Asociación Española de Estudios de Historia de las Mujeres* (Barcelona, 19-21 octubre, 2006). CD-Rom edition.
_____. *El monestir de Sant Antoni de Barcelona. L'origen i l'assentament del primer monestir de clarisses a Catalunya* (Barcelona: Publicacions de l'Abadia de Montserrat, 2007).
_____. 'Memoria, historia y archivo en el monasterio de Sant Antoni i Santa Clara de Barcelona'. *Boletín de la ANABAD 4* (2008): pp. 297–305.
_____. 'Sant Antoni i Santa Clara de Barcelona, 1513: De clarisas a benedictinas, un paso a esclarecer'. *Itinerantes. Revista de Historia y Religión 2* (2012): pp. 173–188.
Kamen, Henry. *The Phoenix and the Flame: Catalonia and the Counter Reformation* (New Haven and London: Yale University Press, 1993).
_____. 'La política religiosa de Felipe II'. *Anuario de historia de la Iglesia 7* (1998): pp. 21–33.
Katajala-Peltomaa, Sari. *Demonic Possession and Lived Religion in Later Medieval Europe* (New York: Oxford University Press, 2020).
Kay, Sarah. 'The Soundscape of Troubadour Lyric, or, How Human Is Song?' In *'Sound Matters'*, edited by Susan Boynton, Sarah Kay, Alison Cornish and Andrew Albin, *Speculum 91*, no. 4 (2016): pp. 988–1039, pp. 1002–1015. <https://doi.org/10.1086/688003>.
Keathley, Elizabeth Lorraine. *Revisioning Musical Modernism: Arnold Schoenberg, Marie Pappenheim, and Erwartung's New Woman* (New York: State University of New York, 1999).
Kehr, Paul Fridolin. *Papsturkunden in Spanien, I. Katalonien* (Berlin: Weidmannsche Buchhandlung, 1926).
Kendrick, Robert. *Celestial Sirens: Nuns and Their Music in Early Modern Milan* (Oxford: Clarendon Press, 1996).
Keym, Stefan, and Peter Schmitz. *Das Leipziger Musikverlagswesen: Innerstädtische Netzwerke und international Ausstrahlung* (Hildesheim, Zurich; New York: Georg Olms Verlag, 2016).
Kirk, Douglas. 'Instrumental Music in Lerma, c.1608'. *Early Music 33*, no. 3 (1995): pp. 393–408. <https://doi.org/10.1093/earlyj/XXIII.3.393>.
Kisby, Fiona, ed. *Music and Musicians in Renaissance Cities and Towns* (Cambridge: Cambridge University Press, 2001).
Kleinberg, Jay S., ed. *Retrieving Women's History: Changing Perceptions of the Role of Women in Politics and Society* (Oxford: Berg, 1988).
Knighton, Tess. 'La circulación de la polifonía europea en el medio urbano: libros impresos de música en la Zaragoza del siglo XVI'. In *Música y cultura urbana en la*

Edad Moderna, edited by Andrea Bombi, Juan José Carreras, and Miguel Ángel Marín (Valencia: Universitat de València, 2005): pp. 337–350.

———. 'Isabel of Castile and Her Music Books: Franco-Flemish Song in Fifteenth-Century Spain'. *Queen Isabel I of Castile: Power, Patronage, Persona*, edited by Barbara F. Weissberger (Woodbridge: Tamesis, 2008): pp. 29–52.

———. *Catálogo de los impresos musicales de la colección Uclés* (Cuenca: Diputación Provincial de Cuenca, 2009).

———. 'Music and Ritual in Urban Spaces: The Case of Lima, c.1600'. In *Music and Urban Society in Colonial Latin America*, edited by Geoffrey Baker and Tess Knighton (Cambridge: Cambridge University Press, 2011): pp. 21–42.

———. 'Victoria and the English Choral Tradition'. *Tomás Luis de Victoria Studies*, edited by Manuel del Sol and Javier Suárez-Pajares (Madrid: ICCMU, 2013): pp. 455–476.

———. '"Rey Fernando, mayorazgo/ de toda nuestra esperanza/ ¿tus favores a do están?': Carlos V y la llegada a España de la capilla musical flamenca'. In *La Casa de Borgoña. La Casa del rey de España*, directed by José Eloy Hortal Muñoz and Félix Labrador Arroyo (Leuven: Leuven University Press, 2014): pp. 205–228.

———. 'Music for the Soul: Death and Piety in Sixteenth-Century Barcelona'. In *Listening to Early Modern Catholicism: New Perspectives from Musicology*, edited by Daniele V. Filippi (Leiden: Brill, 2017a), pp. 233–258.

———. 'Voces angélicas, voces femeninas: música y espiritualidad en la época de Santa Teresa'. In *Santa Teresa o la llama permanente. Estudios históricos, artísticos y literarios*, directed by Esther Borrego and Jaime Olmedo (Madrid: Centro de Estudios Europa Hispánica, 2017b): pp. 57–70.

———. 'Relating History: Music and Meaning in the *relaciones* of the Canonization of St Raymond Penyafort'. In *Música e História: Estudos em homenagem a Manuel Carlos de Brito*, coordinated by Manuel Pedro Ferreira and Teresa Cascudo (Lisbon: Colibri/CESEM, 2017c): pp. 27–51.

Knighton, Tess, ed. *Iberian Confraternities and Urban Soundscapes*, special issue of *Confraternitas 31*, no. 2 (2020).

Knighton, Tess, and Ascensión Mazuela-Anguita. 'The Soundscape of the Ceremonies Held for the Beatification of St Teresa of Ávila in the Crown of Aragon, 1614'. *Scripta: Revista internacional de literatura i cultura medieval i moderna 6* (2015): pp. 225–250. <https://doi.org/10.7203/SCRIPTA.6.7831>.

———, eds. *Música i política a l'època de l'arxiduc Carles* (Barcelona: Museu d'Història de Barcelona, 2017).

———, eds. *Hearing the City: Musical Experience as Portal to Urban Soundscapes* (Turnhout: Brepols, 2018).

Knighton, Tess, and Kenneth Kreitner. *The Music of Juan de Anchieta* (New York: Routledge, 2019).

Kottmann, Aline. *St. Walburga in Meschede: der karolingische Bau und das Schalltopfensemble* (Büchenbach: Faustus, 2015).

Kreitner, Kenneth. 'The City Trumpeter of Late-Fifteenth-Century Barcelona'. *Musica Disciplina 46* (1992): pp. 133–167.

———. 'Music in the Corpus Christi Procession of Fifteenth-Century Barcelona'. *Early Music History 14* (1995), pp. 153–204. <https://doi.org/10.1017/S0261127900001467>.

———. *The Church Music of Fifteenth-Century Spain* (Woodbridge: Boydell Press, 2004).

_____. 'The Ceremonial Soft Band of Fifteenth-Century Barcelona'. In *'Uno gentile et subtile ingenio' Studies in Renaissance Music in Honour of Bonnie Blackburn*, edited by Gioia Filocamo and M. Jennifer Bloxam (Turnhout: Brepols, 2008): pp. 147–154.
Kristeva, Julia. *Séméiotiké* (Paris: Ed. Du Seuil, 1969).
La devoció a Sant Magí a Catalunya i a la ciutat de Mallorca: IV centenari de la Confraria de Sant Magí: 1580–1980 (Barcelona: Altés, 1980). <https://explora.bnc.cat/permalink /34CSUC_BC/1fpark4/alma991016042319706717>.
La Nave del alma sacada de la tempestad del siglo por el mejor piloto San Francisco, a influxos de la hermosa estrella Maria Señora Nuestra. Drama, que en la solemne profesion, y velo de la señora sor Maria Josepha Esquis, y Prats, se cantò en el sacro, y real convento de religiosas clarisas de Jerusalen de la ciudad de Barcelona, siendo su abadesa la R. M. sor Francisca Llauder, por la capilla de la Sta. iglesia cahtedral, siendo su maestro el licenciado Joseph Pujol. Dia 29 de junio de 1772 (Barcelona: por los herederos de Bartholomé, y Maria Angela Girált, [1772]). <https://cercabib.ub.edu/ permalink/34CSUC_UB/13d0big/alma991007074859706708>.
Labelle, Brandon. *Accoustic Territories: Sound Culture and Everyday Life* (New York and London: Bloomsbury, 2010).
LaMay, Thomasin K., ed. *Musical Voices of Early Modern Women. Many-Headed Melodies* (Aldershot: Ashgate, 2005).
Lambea, Mariano. 'Los villancicos de Joan Pau Pujol (1570–1626). Contribución al estudio del villancico en Catalunya, en el primer tercio del siglo XVII' (PhD dissertation, Universitat Autònoma de Barcelona, 1999), 2 vols. <http://hdl.handle.net/10261 /26866>.
Laningham, Susan Diane, ed. *María Vela y Cueto: Autobiography and Letters of a Spanish Nun*, translated by Jane Tar (Tempe: Arizona Center for Medieval and Renaissance Studies, 2016).
Larson, Katherine R. *The Matter of Song in Early Modern England: Texts in and of the Air* (Oxford: Oxford University Press, 2019).
Las Gracias y indultos concedidos por el pontifice Pio VII a la Real Congregacion de la Purissima Concepcion bajo el titulo de las siete alegrias de Maria Santissima (Rome: Luis Lazzarini, 1802). <https://explora.bnc.cat/permalink/34CSUC_BC/1fpark4/alm a991009343489706717>.
Le Goff, Jacques. *La naissance du Purgatoire* (Paris: Editions Gallimard, 1981).
Leach, Elizabeth Eva. '"The Little Pipe Sings Sweetly While the Fowler Deceives the Bird": Sirens in the Later Middle Ages'. *Music and Letters 87* (2006): pp. 187–211. <https://doi.org/10.1093/ml/gci250>.
_____. *Sung Birds: Music, Nature, and Poetry in the Later Middle Ages* (Ithaca: Cornell University Press, 2007).
Leech, Peter. 'Musicians in the Catholic Chapel of Catherine of Braganza, 1662–92'. *Early Music 29*, no. 4 (2001): pp. 570–87. <https://doi.org/10.1093/earlyj/XXIX.4 .570>.
_____. 'Music and Musicians in the Catholic Chapel of James II at Whitehall, 1686–1688'. *Early Music 39*, no. 3 (2011): pp. 379–400. <https://doi.org/10.1093/em/car072>.
Lehfeldt, Elizabeth A. 'Baby Jesus in a Box: Commerce and Enclosure in an Early Modern Convent'. In *Mapping Gendered Routes and Spaces in the Early Modern World*, edited by Merry Wiesner-Hanks (Farnham, Surrey: Ashgate, 2015): pp. 203–211.
Leppert, Richard. *Music and Image: Domesticity, Ideology and Socio-Cultural Formation in Eighteenth-Century England* (Cambridge: Cambridge University Press, 1993).

Lehfdelt, Elizabeth. 'Uneven Conversions: How Did Laywomen Become Nuns in the Early Modern World?'. In *Conversions: Gender and Religious Change in Early Modern Europe*, edited by Simon Ditchfield and Helen Smith (Manchester: Manchester University Press, 2017): pp. 127–143.

Leitmeir, Christian Thomas. *Jacobus de Kerle (1531/2-1591): Komponieren im Brennpunkt von Kirche und Kunst* (Turnhout: Brepols, 2009).

Lester, Anne E. *Creating Cistercian Nuns: The Women's Religious Movement and Its Reform in Thirteenth-Century Champagne* (Ithaca: Cornell University Press, 2011).

Leyshon, Andrew. *Reformatted: Code, Networks, and the Transformation of the Music Industry* (Oxford: Oxford University, 2014).

Lizárraga, Reginaldo de. *Descripcion del Perú, Tucuman, Río de la Plata y Chile* (Madrid: Historia 16, 1987 [1908]).

Llano, Samuel. *Whose Spain? Negotiating Spanish Music in Paris, 1908–1929* (Oxford: Oxford University, 2013).

Llompart, Gabriel. *Aspectos populares del purgatorio medieval* (Madrid: Vda. De C. Bermejo, 1970).

Loewen, Peter V. *Music in Early Franciscan Thought* (Leiden and Boston: Brill, 2013).

Lohmann Villena, Guillermo. 'Nuevos datos sobre fray Antonio de la Calancha y la impresión de la *Coronica moralizada*'. *Revista Peruana de Historia Eclesiástica 2* (1992): pp. 233–245.

Lomax, Derek W. *La Orden de Santiago (1170–1275)* (Madrid: CSIC, Escuela de Estudios Medievales, 1965).

López, Atanasio. 'Crónica franciscana inédita'. *Archivo ibero-americano 11* (1919): pp. 439–447.

López de la Plaza, Gloria. *Las mujeres en una orden canonical. Las religiosas del Santo Sepulcro de Zaragoza (1300–1615)* (Saragossa: Institución Fernando el Católico, 2020).

Lorea, Antonio de. *La venerable madre Hipolita de Iesus, y Rocaberti religiosa de la orden de N.P. S. Domingo [...] Epitome de su prodigiosa vida, virtudes, y admirables escritos sacado de los procesos de su beatificación [...]* (Valencia: Vicente Cabrera, 1679).

Lorenzo Pinar, Francisco Javier. 'Monjas disidentes. Las resistencias a la clausura en Zamora tras el Concilio de Trento'. In *Disidencias y Exilios en la España Moderna*, edited by Antonio Mestre Sanchís and Enrique Giménez López (Alicante: Universidad de Alicante, 1997), pp. 71–80.

_____. *La monja organista y cantora: una voz y una identidad silenciada* (Salamanca: Universidad de Salamanca, 2019).

Luis Iglesias, Alejandro. 'El maestro de capilla Diego de Bruceña (1567/71-1623) y el impreso perdido de su libro de *Misas, Magnificats y Motetes* (Salamanca: Susana Muñoz, 1620)'. In *Encomium Musicae: Essays in Memory of Robert J. Snow*, edited by David Crawford (Hillsdale: Pendragon, 2002): pp. 435–469.

MacCormack, Sabine. 'Antonio de la Caclancha. Un agustino del siglo XVIII en el Nuevo Mundo'. *Bulletin hispanique 84*, nos. 1–2 (1982): pp. 60–94.

Maclean, Ian. *The Renaissance Notion of Woman. A Study in the Fortunes of Scholasticism and Medical Science in European Intellectual Life* (Cambridge: Cambridge University Press, 1980).

Madre di Dio, Fra Marcello della. *De' Nove Chori De Gli Angioli. Cioè De' Componimenti Poetici Del P.F. Marcello della Madre di Dio Carmelitano Scalzo Choro Primo. Che Contiene La Corona della B.V. Teresia Fondatrice de' Padri, e delle Monache*

Carmelitane Scalze. *Overo Raccolta delle Compositioni, che per la Festa della sua Beatificatione si posero, nella Chiesa della Madonna della Scala di Roma, a dì 5. d'Ottobre 1614* (Rome: Guglielmo Faciotti, 1615).
Madurell i Marimón, José María. 'Documentos para la historia de maestros de capilla, infantes de coro, maestros de música y danza y ministriles en Barcelona (siglos XIV-XVIII)'. *Anuario musical 3* (1948): pp. 218–234.
_____. 'Documentos para la Historia de Maestros de capilla, organistas, órganos, organeros, músicos e instrumentos (siglos XIV-XVIII)'. *Anuario musical 4* (1949): pp. 198–220.
_____. 'Documentos para la Historia de músicos, maestros de danza, instrumentos y libros de música (siglos XIV-XVIII)'. *Anuario musical 5* (1950): pp. 199–212.
_____. 'Documentos para la historia de los maestros de capilla, cantores, organistas, órganos y organeros (siglos XIV-XVIII)'. *Anuario musical 6* (1951), pp. 205–215.
_____. comp. *Documentos para la historia de la imprenta y librería en Barcelona (1474-1553), anotados por Jordi Rubió i Balaguer* (Barcelona: Gremios de Editores y Libreros y de Maestros Impresores, 1955).
_____. 'Documentos de archivo. Libros de canto (siglos XIV-XVI)'. *Anuario musical 11* (1956): pp. 219–232.
_____. 'Documentos de archivo: manuscritos e impresos musicales (siglos XIV-XVIII)'. *Anuario musical 23* (1968): pp. 199–221.
_____. 'Hubert Gotard'. *Gutenberg Jahrbuch* (1972): pp. 188–196.
_____. *Micel·lània de notes històriques del monestir de Valldonzella* (Barcelona: Estudis Cistercenes Germandat de Valldonzella, 1976).
Magrini, Tullia, ed. *Antropologia della musica e culture mediterranee* (Bologna: Il Mulino, 1993).
_____, ed. *Music and Gender: Perspectives from the Mediterranean* (Chicago: The University of Chicago Press, 2003).
Mahiques Climent, Joan. 'Sobre la Epístola proemial y las obras poéticas de Onofre Almudéver'. *Revista de Cancioneros Impresos y Manuscritos 8* (2019): pp. 128–209. <https://doi.org/10.14198/rcim.2019.8.05>.
Manual de novells ardits vulgarment apellat Dietari del Antich Consell Barceloní (Barcelona: Imprempta de'n Henrich y Companyia, 1892–1975), 28 vols.
Marca, Francesco della. *Chronica Seraphica de la Santa Provincia de Cataluña de la Regular Observancia de Nuestro Padre S. Francisco: parte Segunda contiene desde los años 1400 hasta los de 1759* (Barcelona: Imprenta de los Padres Carmelitas Descalzos, 1764).
Marcer, Antoni. *Allegatio facti, et iuris, pro Anthonio, Iacobo, Francisco, et Iosepho Marcers fratribus, contra, Priorem, et Conventum de Sanctae Monicae praesentis civitatis / relatore Nob. Domino Hieronymo de Magarola [...]; Rufasta Nott* (S.l.: s.n., after 1682). <https://explora.bnc.cat/permalink/34CSUC_BC/1fpark4/alma991014248809706717>.
March, José María. *La Real Capilla del Palau en la ciudad de Barcelona: breve reseña* (Barcelona: Residencia del Palau, de la Compañía de Jesús, 1921).
Marín López, Miguel Ángel. *Music on the Margin: Urban Musical Life in Eighteenth-Century Jaca* (Kassel: Reichenberger, 2002).
Marquès, Josep M. 'Organistes y mestres de Capella de la Diòcesi de Girona'. *Anuario Musical 54* (1999): pp. 89–130.
Marshall, Kimberly, ed. *Rediscovering the Muses: Women's Musical Traditions* (Boston: Northeastern University Press, 1993).

Marshall, Sherrin, ed. *Women in Reformation and Counter-Reformation Europe: Public and Private Worlds* (Bloomington: Indiana University Press, 1989).

Martí i Bonet, Josep Maria. *El Convent i Parròquia de Sant Agustí de Barcelona: notes històriques* (Barcelona: Arxiu Diocesà i Biblioteca Pública Episcopal de Barcelona, 1980).

_____. *Les pellofes. Antecedents, context i evolució histórica i económica* (Barcelona: Arxiu Diocesà de Barcelona, 2015).

Martin, Therese, ed. *Reassessing the Roles of Women as 'Makers' of Medieval Art and Architecture* (Leiden and Boston: Brill, 2012).

Martínez Gil, Fernando. *Muerte y sociedad en la España de los Austrias* (Cuenca: Universidad de Castilla-La Mancha, 2000).

Martínez López, Cándida, and Purificación Ubric Rabaneda, coords. *Cartografías de género en las ciudades antiguas* (Granada: Universidad de Granada, 2017).

Mas Domènech, Joseph. 'Notes històriques del monesteir de Sta. Maria de Valldonzella de Barcelona'. *Butlletí de l'Acadèmia de Bones Lletres de Barcelona 1* (1901–1902): pp. 303–308.

_____. *Notes històriques del Bisbat de Barcelona* (Barcelona: Jaume Vives, 1906–1907).

_____. 'Notes sobre antichs illuminadors a Catalunya'. *Butlletí de la Reial Acadèmia de Bones Lletres de Barcelona 7*, no. 53 (1914): pp. 280–284.

_____. 'Notes documentals de llibres antichs a Barcelona (Conclusió)'. *Butlletí de la Reial Acadèmia de Bones Lletres de Barcelona 8*, no. 63 (1916): pp. 444–463.

Masabeu Tierno, Josep. *Santa María de Montalegre: església de l'antiga Casa de Caritat: centenari 1902-2002* (Terrasa: Albada, 2004).

Massot, José (O.S.A.). *Compendio historial de los hermitaños de Nuestro Padre San Agustin, del Principado de Cataluña; desde los años de 394 que empeçó San Paulino à plantar Monasterios en dicho Principado, y de los que después se han plantado: Como también de los Varones Ilustres, que han florecido, assi en letras, puetos, y virtudes, hasta los años de 1699* (Barcelona: Juan Jolis, 1699).

Mazuela-Anguita, Ascensión. 'Artes de canto (1492–1626) y mujeres en la cultura musical del mundo ibérico renacentista' (PhD. dissertation, Universitat de Barcelona, 2012a). <http://hdl.handle.net/2445/35622>.

_____. 'Women as Dedicatees of *Artes de canto* in the Early-Modern Iberian World: Imposed Knowledge or Women's Choice?'. *Early Music 40*, no. 2 (2012b): pp. 191–207. <https://doi.org/10.1093/em/cas038>.

_____. 'Mujeres músicas y documentos de la Inquisición: Isabel de Plazaola y la IV Duquesa del Infantado'. *Revista de Musicología 36*, nos. 1–2 (2013): pp. 17–55. <https://doi.org/10.2307/24245716>.

_____. ''Una Celestial armonía': los conventos femeninos en la vida musical de Barcelona en el siglo XVI'. *Quadrivium. Revista Digital de Musicologia 6* (2015a). <http://bit.ly/2gpc1v7>.

_____. 'La vida musical en el monasterio de Santa Maria de Jonqueres en los siglos XVI y XVII: Agraïda y Eugènia Grimau'. *Revista Catalana de Musicologia 8* (2015b): pp. 37–79. <https://doi.org/10.2436/20.1003.01.35>.

_____. '¿Bailes o aquelarres? Música, mujeres y brujería en documentos inquisitoriales del Renacimiento'. *Bulletin of Spanish Studies: Hispanic Studies and Researches on Spain, Portugal and Latin America 92*, no. 5 (2015c): pp. 725–746. <https://doi.org/10.1080/14753820.2015.1039391>.

_____. *Las mujeres y la transmisión del repertorio andaluz en el Fondo de Música Tradicional del CSIC-IMF (1945–1960)* (Badajoz: CIOFF, 2015d).

_____. 'El monasterio de Sant Pere de les Puel·les en el paisaje sonoro de la Barcelona del siglo XVI'. In *El sons de Barcelona a l'edad moderna*, edited by Tess Knighton [MUHBA Textures 6] (Barcelona: Museu d'Història de Barcelona, 2016a): pp. 91–112.

_____. 'Lost Voices: Women and Music at the Time of the Catholic Monarchs'. In *Companion to Music in the Age of the Catholic Monarchs*, edited by Tess Knighton [Brill's Companions to Musical Culture 1] (Leiden: Brill, 2016b): pp. 549–578.

_____. 'Polifonía, redes musicales y ceremonias rurales en las crónicas de Honorat Ciuró (1612–1674)'. *Revista de Musicología 39*, no. 2 (2016c): pp. 411–454. <https://doi.org/10.2307/24878568>.

_____. 'Música y paisaje sonoro en las fiestas de beatificación de Santa Teresa en 1614'. In *Santa Teresa o la llama permanente. Estudios históricos, artísticos y literarios*, directed by Esther Borrego and Jaime Olmedo (Madrid: Centro de Estudios Europa Hispánica, 2017a): pp. 109–126.

_____. 'Música para los reconciliados: Music, Emotion, and Inquisitorial Autos de fe in Early-Modern Hispanic Cities'. *Music and Letters 98*, no. 2 (2017b): pp. 175–203. <https://doi.org/10.1093/ml/gcx056>.

_____. 'Controverses liturgiques et musicales au convent Santa Maria de Jonqueres de Barcelone: réformes et résistances de la première modernité'. In *Réalités et fictions de la musique religieuse à l'époque moderne. Essais d'analyse des discours*, directed by Thierry Favier and Sophie Hache (Rennes: Presses Universitaires de Rennes, 2018a): pp. 273–287.

_____. 'The Contribution of the Requesens Noblewomen to the Soundscape of Sixteenth-Century Barcelona Through the Palau de la Comtessa'. In *Hearing the City in Early Modern Europe*, edited by Tess Knighton and Ascensión Mazuela-Anguita (Turnhout: Brepols, 2018b): pp. 197–217.

_____. 'Pushing Boundaries: Women, Sounding Spaces, and Moral Discourse in Early Modern Spain Through the Experience of Ana de Mendoza, Princess of Eboli (1540–92)'. *Early Modern Women 13*, no. 1 (2018c): pp. 5–29. <https://doi.org/10.1353/emw.2018.0049>.

_____. 'La música en el ceremonial jesuita: Granada y las fiestas de beatificación de Ignacio de Loyola, 1610'. In *Poder, identidades e imágenes de la ciudad: Música y libros de ceremonial religioso en España (siglos XVI-XIX)*, coordinated by María José de la Torre Molina and Alicia Carmen Marchant Rivera (Madrid: Síntesis, 2019): pp. 149–184.

_____. 'Confraternities as an Interface Between Citizens and Convent Musical Ceremonial in Sixteenth-Century Barcelona'. *Confraternitas 31*, no. 2 (2020) [Special issue on *Iberian Confraternities and Urban Soundscapes*]: pp. 14–35.

McClary, Susan. *Feminine Endings. Music, Gender, and Sexuality* (Minnesota: University of Minnesota Press, 1991).

_____. 'Feminine Endings at Twenty'. *Trans-Revista Transcultural de Música 15* (2011). <http://www.sibetrans.com/trans/a348/feminine-endings-at-twenty>.

McGowan, Keith. 'The Prince and the Piper: *Haut, bas* and the Whole Body in Early Modern Europe'. *Early Music 27* (1999): pp. 211–232. <https://doi.org/10.1093/earlyj/XXVII.2.211>.

McMillin, Linda A. 'Cloister and Society in Thirteenth-Century Barcelona: The Women of Sant Pere de les Puelles' (PhD dissertation, University of California Los Angeles, 1990).

_____. 'Sacred and Secular Politics: The Convent of Sant Pere de les Puelles in Thirteenth-Century Barcelona'. In *Iberia and the Mediterranean World of the Middle Ages*, edited by Paul E. Chevedden, Donald J. Kagay and Paul G. Padilla (Leiden: Brill, 1995): vol. 2, pp. 225–239.

———. 'Sant Pere de les Puelles: A Medieval Women's Community'. *American Benedictine Review* 47, no. 2 (1996): pp. 200–222.

McNamara, Jo Ann Kay. *Sisters in Arms. Catholic Nuns Through Two Millenia* (Cambridge, MA, and London: Harvard University Press, 1996).

McVay, Pamela. *Envisioning Women in World History: 1500-Present* (New York: McGraw-Hill, 2008).

Meecham, June L. *Sacred Communities, Shared Devotions: Gender, Material Culture, and Monasticism in Late Medieval Germany* (Turnhout: Brepols, 2014).

Mele, Giampaolo. *Un manoscritto arborense inedito del Trecento: il códice 1bR del monastero di Santa Chiara di Oristano* (Oristano: Editrice S'Alvure, 1985).

Mendoza, Diego de. *Chronica de la Provincia de S. Antonio de los Charcas* (La Paz: Casa Municipal de la Cultura 'Franz Tamayo', 1976 [1663]).

Mendoza, Íñigo. *Cancionero* (MS, 1485). San Lorenzo de El Escorial, Monasterio de El Escorial, Sig. EM6.

Mestre i Godes, Jesús. *Monestirs de Catalunya* (Barcelona: Edicions 62, 2003 [2001]).

Millares Carlo, Agustín. 'La imprenta en Barcelona en el siglo XVI'. In *Historia de la Imprenta Hispana* (Madrid: Editora Nacional, 1982): pp. 491–643. <https://explora.bnc.cat/permalink/34CSUC_BC/1fpark4/alma991005429919706717>.

Minnis, Alastair, and Rosalynn Voaden, eds. *Medieval Holy Women in the Christian Tradition c.1100-c.1500* (Turnhout: Brepols, 2010).

Miquel Rosell, Francisco. 'Inventario de manuscritos de la Biblioteca Universitaria de Barcelona referentes a Ordenes religiosas'. *Hispania Sacra 2* (1949), pp. 209–220.

Miranda López, Mar. 'Música i cerimònia a Girona, 1500–1650' (PhD dissertation, Universitat de Giroina, 2020), 2 vols.

Molí, Ernest del. *Una llocà. 21 contets amb hitòria paternera, publicats en 'llibres de festes' de dos parròquies* (S.l.: s.n., s.d. [it contains accounts dated between 1956 and 1971]). <https://books.google.es/books?id=E4JvDwAAQBAJ&pg=PA153&lpg=PA153&dq=Una+lloc%C3%A0.+21+contes+amb+%22hist%C3%B2ria+paternera%22,+publicats+en+%E2%80%98llibres+de+festes%E2%80%99+de+dos+parr%C3%B2quies&source=bl&ots=_je_QUywwg&sig=ACfU3U3LZFbw17WR-7Qgl3ij0QAe98PEAA&hl=es&sa=X&ved=2ahUKEwi5wN_G4uH6AhVLhc4BHZKxDL8Q6AF6BAgJEAM#v=onepage&q=Una%20lloc%C3%A0.%2021%20contes%20amb%20%22hist%C3%B2ria%20paternera%22%2C%20publicats%20en%20%E2%80%98llibres%20de%20festes%E2%80%99%20de%20dos%20parr%C3%B2quies&f=false>.

Monestir de Sant Pere de les Puel·les: en el marc del monacat femení, hereves de tota una tradició (Barcelona: Museu d'Història de Catalunya, Generalitat de Catalunya, Departament de Cultura i Mitjans de Comunicació, 2008).

Monson, Craig A., ed. *The Crannied Wall: Women, Religion and the Arts in Early Modern Europe* (Ann Arbor: University of Michigan Press, 1992).

———. *Disembodied Voices: Music and Culture in an Early Modern Italian Convent* (Berkeley and London: University of California Press, 1995).

———. 'The Council of Trent Revisited'. *Journal of the American Musicological Society* 55, no. 1 (2002): pp. 1–37. <https://doi.org/10.1525/jams.2002.55.1.1>.

———. *Nuns Behaving Badly. Tales of Music, Magic, Art, and Arson in the Convents of Italy* (Chicago: The University of Chicago Press, 2010).

_____. *Divas in the Convent: Nuns, Music, and Defiance in Seventeenth-Century Italy* (Chicago: The University of Chicago Press, 2012).

Montllor i Pujal, Joan. 'El Monestir de Santa Maria de Jonqueres'. *Alba: Revista de la Parroquia de la Purísima Concepción de Sabadell 10*, no. 109 (1959): pp. 311–312.

Moradell, Vicente Miguel de. *Historia de S. Ramon de Peñafort frayle de Predicadores en coplas Castellanas* (Barcelona: Sebastián de Cormellas, 1603).

Morales, Luisa. 'Ángeles y anónimas: la profesión de monja música y sus límites espacio-sonoros en conventos y monasterios femeninos castellanos (siglos XVI a XVIII)'. *Hipógrifo 9*, no. 2 (2021), pp. 327–343. <https://doi.org/10.13035/H.2021.09.02.25>.

Morales Abril, Omar. 'El esclavo negro Juan de Vera. Cantor, arpista y compositor de la Catedral de Puebla (fl.1575–1617)'. In *Música y catedral. Nuevos enfoques, viejas temáticas*, coordinated by Jesús Alfaro Cruz and Raúl H. Torres Medina (Mexico D.F.: Universidad Autónoma de la Ciudad de México, 2010): pp. 43–59.

Morant, Ricard, and Miquel Peñarroya. *Llenguatge i culture: per a una ecologia lingüística* (Valencia: Universitat de València, 1995).

Moreno, Doris, ed. *The Complexity of Hispanic Religious Life in the 16th–18th Centuries* (Leiden: Brill, 2019).

Morris, María, Rebeca Sanmartín Bastida, and Yonsoo Kim, eds. *Gender and Exemplarity in Medieval and Early Modern Spain* (Leiden: Brill, 2020).

Mota, Diego de la. *Libro del principio de la Orden de la Cauallería de S. Tiago, del Espada, y vna declaracion de la Regla y tres votos substanciales de religión [...] y la fundacion del Conuento de Vcles, cabeça de la Orden: con un catalogo de los Maestres, y Priores, y de algunos Caualleros* (Valencia: Álvaro Franco, 1599).

Muchembled, Robert, ed. *Cultural Exchange in Early Modern Europe* (Cambridge: Cambridge University Press, 2006–2007), 4 vols.

Muñoz, Luis. *Vida y virtudes del venerable varón el Maestro Juan de Ávila, predicador apostólico, con algunos elogios de las virtudes y vidas de algunos de sus más principales discípulos*, ed. Luis Sala Balust (Barcelona: Juan Flors, 1964 [Madrid: Imprenta Real, 1635]).

Muñoz Fernández, Ángela. 'El monacato como espacio de cultura femenino. A propósito de la Inmaculada Concepción de María y la representación femenina'. In *Pautas históricas de sociabilidad femenina: rituales y modelos de representación: actas del V Coloquio Internacional de la Asociación Española de Investigación Histórica de las Mujeres, Cádiz, 5, 6 y 7 de junio de 1997*, edited by Mary Nash, María José de la Pascua, and Gloria Espigado (Cádiz: Universidad de Cádiz, 1999): pp. 71–89.

Muriel, Josefina, and Luis Lledías. *La música en las instituciones femeninas novohispanas* (Mexico D.F.: Universidad Nacional Autónoma de México, 2009).

Mutgé Vives, Josefina. 'El convento de agustinos de Barcelona en el siglo XIV'. In *Conventos agustinos (Madrid, 20-24 de octubre de 1997): actas del congreso*, coordinated by Rafael Lazcano González (Rome: Institutum Historicum Agustinianum, 1998): vol. 1, pp. 497–528.

_____. 'Noticias y documentos sobre las Órdenes Militares en Barcelona durante el reinado de Alfonso el Benigno (1327–1336)'. *Revista de las Órdenes Militares 1* (2001): pp. 33–61.

Nader, Helen. *Power and Gender in Renaissance Spain: Eight Women of the Mendoza Family, 1450–1650* (Urbana: University of Illinois Press; Bristol: University Presses Marketing, 2003).

Narváez Cases, Carme. 'Josep Dalmau, promotor dels convents de carmelites descalços de Barcelona'. *Analecta sacra tarraconensia: Revista de ciències historicoeclesiàstiques* 67, no. 1 (1994): pp. 589–597.

Newman, Barbara, ed. *Thomas of Cantimpré: The Collected Saints' Lives: Abbot John of Cantimpré, Christina the Astonishing, Margaret of Ypres, and Lutgard of Aywières*, translated by Margot H. King and Barbara Newman (Turnhout: Brepols, 2008).

_____. *Medieval Crossover: Reading the Secular Against the Sacred* (Notre Dame: University of Notre Dame Press, 2013).

Nienhuis, Nancy E., and Beverly Mayne Kienzle. *Saintly Women: Medieval Saints, Modern Women, and Intimate Partner Violence* (London: Taylor and Francis, 2017).

Nieva, Pilar, et al., eds. *Género y exilio teatral republicano: entre la tradición y la vanguardia* (Amsterdam and New York: Rodopi, 2014).

Noguera, Marta. *La enamorada del home més hermós del món. Autobiografia de Na Maria [Sor Marta] Noguera y Valèri, Religiosa Caputxina de Manresa (1774–1830)* (Barcelona and Manresa: Foment de Pietat Catalana i Imp. Catòlica de Domingo Vives, 1911).

Noone, Michael. *Music and Musicians in the Escorial Liturgy Under the Habsburgs, 1563–1700* (Rochester: University of Rochester Press, 1998).

_____. 'Susana Muñoz, *ympressora de los libros de musica*, y el *Libro de canto de misas y magnificas y motetes y una salue* (Salamanca, 1620) de Diego de Bruceña'. *Anuario Musical* 75 (2020): pp. 23–60.

Order of Santiago. *Regla de la Orden y cavalleria de S. Santiago de la Espada. Con la glosa y declaracion del Maestro Ysla, Freyle de la misma orden, professo en el conuento de Vcles, y capellan de su Magestad. Va añadida una Tabla de las materias, con un Tratado de la Nobleza, compuesto por el Doctor Francisco de la Portilla, Freyle de la mesma orden* (Antwerp: Emprenta Plantiniana, 1598).

O'Regan, Noel. 'Music at Roman Confraternities to 1650: The Current State of Research'. *Analecta Musicologica* 45 (2011): pp. 132–158.

_____. 'Confraternity Statutes in Early Modern Rome: What Can They Tell Us About Musical Practice?'. In *Atti del Congresso Internazionale di Musica Sacra in occasione del centenario di fondazione del PIMS Roma, 26 maggio–1 giugno 2011*, edited by Antonio Addamiano and Francesco Luisi (Vatican City: Libreria Editrice Vaticana, 2013): vol. 1, pp. 487–501.

Obiols Bou, Montserrat. 'El monacat femení en la Catalunya medieval: Santa Maria de Valldaura (1241–1399)' (PhD dissertation, Universitat de Barcelona, 2005).

Olivar, Alexandre. 'Noves notícies de manuscrits litúrgics i a propòsit d'ells'. *Miscel·lània litúrgica catalana* 2 (1983): pp. 131–143.

Ong, Walter. *Orality and Literacy: The Technologizing of the World* (London: Routledge, 1995).

Orden, Kate van, ed. *Music and the Cultures of Print* (New York and London: Garland, 2000).

Ortiz, Mario. *La musa y la melopea: la música en el mundo conventual, la vida y el pensamiento de Sor Juana Inés de la Cruz* (Mexico D.F.: Universidad del Claustro de sor Juana, 2015).

Ortoll i Martín, Ernest. 'Algunas consideraciones sobre la iglesia de Santa Caterina de Barcelona'. *Locvs amcenvs* 2 (1996): pp. 47–63.

Otaola González, Paloma. *Tradición y modernidad en los escritos de Juan Bermudo: del 'Libro primero' (1549) a la 'Declaración de instrumentos musicales' (1555)* (Kassel: Reichenberger, 2000).

Owens, Sarah E. *Madre María Rosa: Journey of Five Capuchin Nuns* (Tempe: Arizona Center for Medieval and Renaissance Studies, 2009).

_____. *Nuns Navigating the Spanish Empire* (Albuquerque: University of New Mexico Press, 2017).

Páez de Valenzuela y Castillejo, Juan. *Relacion Brebe de las fiestas, que en la ciudad de Cordoua se celebraron à la Beatificacion de la gloriosa Patriarcha santa Theresa de Iesus [...]. Con la justa Literaria, que en ella vuo y sermon que predico el Doctor Aluaro Piçaño de Palacios [...]* (Córdoba: Viuda de A. Barrera, 1615).

Page, Janet K. *Convent Music and Politics in Eighteenth-Century Vienna* (Cambridge: Cambridge University Press, 2014).

Palau y Dulcet, Antonio. *Manual del librero hispanoamericano: bibliografía general española e hispanoamericana desde la invención de la imprenta hasta nuestros tiempos* (Barcelona: Librería anticuaria de A. Palau, 1948–1977), 28 vols. [Barcelona: Librería Anticuaria, 1923–1927, 7 vols.].

Parets, Miquel. *De molts sucsesos que han sucseyt dins Barselona y en molts altros llochs de Catalunya, dignes de memòria, en los dies y anys han sucseyt* (MS, 1626–1660) (Barcelona: Biblioteca de la Universitat de Barcelona, n.d., Ms. 224–225), 2 vols.

Paulí Meléndez, Antonio. *Efemérides históricas del monasterio de San Matías de Barcelona* (Barcelona: el Monestir, 1941a).

_____. *Resumen histórico del Monasterio de Nuestra Señora de los Ángeles y pie de la Cruz de Barcelona* (Barcelona: s.n., 1941b).

_____. *El monasterio de religiosas Agustinas de Santa María Magdalena, vulgo 'Arrepentidas', fundado y protegido por el municipio barcelonés* (Barcelona: Altés, 1942).

_____. *El Real Monasterio de San Pedro de las Puellas* (Barcelona: Bartrés, 1945).

_____. *El Real Monasterio de Nuestra Señora de Monte-Sión* (Barcelona: Bartrés, 1952).

_____. *El Real Monasterio de Santa Isabel de Barcelona, 1564–1964* (Barcelona: Tipografía del Monasterio de Santa María de Poblet, 1968).

_____. *El Reial Monestir de Santa Maria de Jerusalem de Barcelona (1454–1970)* (Barcelona: Emporium, 1970).

_____. *Santa Maria de Valldonzella* (Barcelona: Emporium, 1972).

Pedrell, Felip. *Diccionario técnico de la música* (Barcelona: Isidro Torres Oriol, 1897 [2nd ed.]).

Pedrell, Felip, and Higini Anglès, eds. *Els Madrigals i la Missa de difunts d'en Brudieu* (Barcelona: Institut d'Estudis Catalans, 1921).

Pena Sueiro, Nieves. 'Estado de la cuestión sobre el estudio de las Relaciones de sucesos'. *Pliegos de Bibliofilia 13* (2001): pp. 43–66.

Peña Díaz, Manuel. 'Un librero-editor en la Barcelona del XVI: Joan Guardiola'. In *1490, En el umbral de la modernidad*, edited by José Hinojosa Montalvo and Jesús Pradells Nadal (Valencia: Consell Valencià de Cultura, 1994), 2 vols.: vol. 2, pp. 311–332.

_____. *El laberinto de los libros. Historia cultural de la Barcelona del Quinientos* (Madrid: Fundación Germán Sánchez Ruipérez, 1997).

Peñarroja, Jordi. *Edificis viatgers de Barcelona* (Barcelona: Llibres de l'Índex, 2007).

Pérez Aguilera, P. M. 'De Sacra ratione concionandi de Diego Pérez de Valdivia (Baeza, 1524 – Barcelona 1589)'. *Boletín del Instituto de Estudios Giennenses 191* (2005): pp. 119–135.

Pérez Castañeda, de María Ángeles, and María Dolores Couto de León. *Pruebas para ingreso de religiosas en las órdenes de Santiago, Calatrava y Alcántara* (Madrid: Ministerio de Cultura, 1980).

Pérez de Valdivia, Diego. *Tratado de alabança de la castidad* (Barcelona: Iayme Cendrad, 1587 [colophon indicates 1582]).

Pérez Gómez, Antonio, ed. *Cancionero de Nuestra Señora: en el cual ay muy buenos romances, canciones y villancicos (1591)* (Valencia: Castalia, 1952).

Pérez Saldanya, Manuel, and Rafael Roca Ricart, eds. *Del manuscrit a la paraula digital / From Manuscript to Digital Word: Estudis de llengua i literatura catalanes / Studies of Catalan language and literature* (Amsterdam and Philadelphia: John Benjamins Publishing Company, 2018).

Pérez Sedeño, Eulalia, *et al*. *Ciencia, tecnología y género en Iberoamérica* (Madrid: CSIC, 2006).

Pérez Vidal, Mercedes. 'Between the City and the Cloister. Saints, Liturgy and Devotions in the Dominican Nunneries in Late Medieval Castile'. In *Saints and the City: Beiträge zum Verständnis urbaner Sakralität in christlichen Gemeinschaften (5.-17. Jh.)*, edited by Michele C. Ferrari (Erlangen: FAU University Press, 2015): pp. 233–267.

Perpiñà García, Candela. 'Música angélica en la imagen mariana. Un discurso visual sobre la esperanza de salvación'. *ACTA ARTIS: Estudis d'Art Modern 1* (2013): pp. 29–49. <https://doi.org/10.1344/actaartis.1.2013.9917>.

Peters, Gretchen. *The Musical Sounds of Medieval French Cities: Players, Patrons, and Politics* (Cambridge: Cambridge University Press, 2012).

Pi i Arimon, Andrés Avelino. *Barcelona antigua y moderna, descripción e historia de esta ciudad desde su fundación hasta nuestros días* (Barcelona: Tomás Gorchs, 1854).

Piquer i Jover, Josep Joan. *Santa Maria de Vallbona. Guía histórico descriptiva del monasterio cisterciense y del pueblo* (Barcelona, 1957 [unpublished]).

_____. *Etapas progresivas de la vida cisterciense: ensayo sobre liturgia y usos de los monasterios de monjas* (Barcelona: Balmesiana, 1968a).

_____. *Restauració de la vida comunitària íntegra al cenobi de Valldonzella* (Barcelona: Germandat de Valldonzella, 1968b).

_____. *Vallbona de les Monges: Monestir de Santa Maria de Vallbona, Lleida-Espanya* (Vallbona de les Monges, Lleida: Comunitat Cistercenca de Santa Maria de Vallbona, 1981).

Pirrotta, Nino. *Music and Culture in Italy from the Middle Ages to the Baroque: A Collection of Essays* (Cambridge, MA: Harvard University Press, 1984).

Pizarro Carrasco, Carlos. 'Imprenta y gobierno municipal en Barcelona. Sebastián y Jaime Matevat al servicio del Consell de Cent (1631–1644)'. *Hispania 63*, no. 213 (2003): pp. 137–159. <https://doi.org/10.3989/hispania.2003.v63.i213.236>.

Pladevall i F. Catalá Roca, Antoni. *Els monestirs catalans* (Barcelona: Destino, 1974 [1968]).

Planas Badenas, Josefina. 'Llibres de cor'. In *Pedralbes, els tresors del Monestir*, edited by Marià Carbonell i Buades *et al*. (Barcelona: Museu d'Història de la Ciutat, 2004): pp. 136–147.

_____. 'Incanto catalano. I Corali del monastero di Santa María de Pedralbes'. *Alumina 43* (2013), pp. 22–29.

Pons i Turell, Miquel de. *Iuris responsum pro Michaele de Pons et Turell, auunculo, tutore & curatore pupillarum Mendoças contra alios tutores et curatores dictarum pupillarum: Super earum educatione* (Barcelona: ex typographica officina Sebastiani à Cormellas, [c.1617]).

Pontón, Gonzalo. 'Sebastián de Cormellas, mercader de libros'. In *La comedia española en la imprenta catalana. Coloquio internacional. Barcelona, 11 y 12 de abril de 2013*, edited by Felipe B. Pedraza Jiménez and Almudena García González ([Cuenca]: Universidad de Castilla-La Mancha, 2015): pp. 15–33.

Pope, Isabel. 'Musical and Metrical Form of the Villancico'. *Annales Musicologiques* 2 (1954): pp. 189–214.

Por la muy illustre doña Maria Josepha de Magarola y de Zaportella, en nombre de priora del Real Convento de Nuestra Señora de Junqueras de la ciudad de Barcelona [...], con el muy illustre don Miquel [...] (Barcelona: Martin Gelabert, 1696). <https://explora.bnc.cat/permalink/34CSUC_BC/1fpark4/alma991014774699706717>.

Pro ciuitate Barcinonae contra patrem Honofrium de Sancto Thomas Religiosum Descalciarum Ordinis Sanctiss. Trinitatis [Iofreu aduo. subroga civi, Guell aduocatus ciuitatis, Fontanella V.I.D.] (S.l.: s.n., after 1634). <https://explora.bnc.cat/permalink/34CSUC_BC/1fpark4/alma991014915439706717>.

Pro insigni communitate, et operariis Ecclesiae Sanctae Mariae de Mari, [et] Priore Monasterij Sancti Augustini Ciuitatis Barcinonae, aduersus Venerabiles Clericos Minores Nuncupatos, pro demolitione (Barcelona?: s.n., 1638 or later).

Pro Mariangela Lafont vidua [...] contra [...] Monasterij Sancti Augustini [...] (S.l.: s.n., after 1654).

Pro priorissa et conventu monialium de Monte-Sion praesentis ciuitatis Barcinonae & Iacobo Llobet & Bollò agricola, contra Sebastianum de Portoles et Bresco domicellum Gerundae domiciliatum, in causa suplicationis ad relationem [...]D. Iosephi de Pastor et Mora (Barcelona: ex. typ. Iosephi Llopis, 1688).

Pro revdis. rectore et communitate presbyterorum beneficiatorum ecclesiae parochialis B. Mariae de Pinu civitatis Barchinonae, cum revdo. P. ministro et conventu ordinis Ss. Trinitatis excalceatorum ejusdem civitatis: in actis officialatus curiae ecclesiasticae Barchinonensis: coram admodum [...] Iosepho de Amigant et de Olzina [...] ac pro [...] Philippo de Aguado & Requexo [...], apud doctorem Franciscum Vila [...] (Barcelona: ex typogr. Jacobo Surià, [1736 o post.]).

Processionarium s[ecundu]m consuetudine[m] monachoru[m] congregationis sancti Benedicti de Valladolid (Montserrat: Joan Luschner, 1500). <https://www.cervantesvirtual.com/obra/processionarium-secundum-consuetudinem-monachorum-congregationis-sancti-benedicti-de-valladolid--0/>.

Puentes-Blanco, Andrea. 'Música y devoción en Barcelona (ca.1550–1626): Estudio de libros de polifonía, contextos y prácticas musicales' (PhD dissertation, Universitat de Barcelona, 2018).

Pujades, Jeroni. *Dietari de Jeroni Pujades*, edited by Josep M. Casas i Homs (Barcelona: Fundació Salvador Vives Casajuana, 1975–1976), 4 vols.

Ramnarine, Tina K., ed. *Musical Performance in the Diaspora* (London and New York: Routledge, 2007).

Ramos López, Pilar. 'Music and Women in Early Modern Spain: Some Discrepancies Between Educational Theory and Musical Practice'. In *Musical Voices of Early Modern Women. Many-Headed Melodies*, edited by Thomasin K. LaMay (Aldershot: Ashgate, 2005): pp. 97–118.

_____. 'Mysticism as a Key Concept of Spanish Early Music Historiography'. In *Early Music. Context and Ideas. II International Conference in Musicology* (Cracovia: Universidad de Cracovia, 2008): pp. 1–14. <https://plus.cobiss.net/cobiss/ul/sl/bib/COBIB/28591661>.

_____. 'The Spanish Prohibition on Women Listening to Music: Some Reflections on Juan Luis Vives and the Jewish and Muslim Legacy'. In *New Perspectives on Early Music in Spain*, edited by Tess Knighton and Emilio Ros-Fábregas (Kassel: Reichenberger, 2015), pp. 418–432.

_____. 'Musical Practice and Idleness: A oral Controversy in Renaissance Spain'. *Acta Musicologica 81* (2009): pp. 255–274.

Raventós i Freixa, Jordi. 'Manifestacions musicals a Barcelona a través de la festa: les entrades reials (segles XV-XVIII)' (PhD dissertation, Universitat de Girona, 2006).

Reardon, Colleen. *Holly Concord within Sacred Walls: Nuns and Music in Siena, 1575–1700* (New York: Oxford University Press, 2001).

Rebullosa, Fray Jaime. *Relacion de las grandes fiestas que en esta ciudad de Barcelona se han echo à la canonizacion de su hijo San Ramon de Peñafort, de la Orden de los Predicadores: Con vn sumario de su Vida, Muerte y Canonizacion, y siete Sermones que los Obispos han predicado en ellas* (Barcelona: En la Emprenta de Iayme Cendrat, 1601).

Rees, Owen. 'Luisa de Carvajal y Mendoza and Music in an English Catholic House in 1605'. In *Essays on the History of English Music in Honour of John Caldwell: Sources, Style, Performance, Historiography*, edited by Emma Hornby and David Maw (Woodbridge: Boydell, 2010): pp. 270–280.

Regia sententia lata die 6 Aprilis 1699, in Regia Audientia Cathaloniae [...] in secunda instantia, referente [...] D. Petro de Amigant [...] in [...] causa praetensae nullitatis, [et] falsitatis instrumenti donationis, inter sororem Mariam Agnetem Riambau et Sulla, religiosam conventus monialium de las Madalenas Barchinonae et nobiles conjuges Jacobum Puig de Perafita, et D. Eulaliam Puig et de Sorribas, ac Alios / actuario Forès & Cortell (S.l.: s.n., 1699 or later). <https://explora.bnc.cat/permalink/34CSUC_BC /1fpark4/alma991014350479706717>.

Regla de la orden de la caualleria de señor Santiago del espada (Toledo: Micer Lazaro Saluago Ginoues, 1529).

Regla primera de la gloriosa madre Santa Clara, y estatutos, y constituciones de las Monjas Capuchinas (Seville: Juan Francisco Blas de Quesada, 1693).

Riambau, Maria Ines. *Per la priora sor Maria Ines Riambau y Convent de Religiosas Madalenas de Barcelona ab los coniuges Iaume Puig de Perafita y D. Eularia Puig y de Sorribes, y altres: a relacio del... senador D. Pedro de Amigant: nott. Forès y Cortell* (Barcelona?: s.n., 1587 [i.e. 1687?]).

Ricconboni, Bartolomea. *Life and Death in a Venetian Convent: The Chronicle and Necrology of Corpus Domini, 1395–1436*, edited and translated by Daniel Bornstein (Chicago: University of Chicago Press, 2000).

Richards, Jennifer. *Voices and Books in the English Renaissance: A New History of Reading* (Oxford: Oxford University Press, 2019).

Riehle, Wolfgrang. *The Secret Within: Hermits, Recluses, and Spiritual Outsiders in Medieval England*, translated by Charity Scott-Stokes (Ithaca and London: Cornell University Press, 2014).

Ríos Hevia Cerón, Manuel de los, *Fiestas que hizo la [...] ciudad de Valladolid, con poesias y sermones en la Beatificacion de la Santa Madre Teresa de Iesus* (Valladolid: Francisco Abarca de Angulo, 1615).

Robledo Estaire, Luis. 'Música y cofradías madrileñas en el siglo XVII: Los Esclavos del Santísimo Sacramento de la Magdalena y los Esclavos del Santo Cristo de San Ginés'. *Revista de Musicología 29*, no. 2 (2006): pp. 481–520. <https://doi.org/10.2307 /20798196>.

———. 'Hacer choro con los ángeles. El concepto de polifocralidad en la teoría musical Española de Cerone a Nassarre'. In *Polychoralities. Music, Identity and Power in Italy, Spain and the New World*, edited by Juan José Carreras and Iain Fenlon (Venice: Fondazione Ugo e Olga Levi; Kassel: Reichenberger, 2013): pp. 181–208.

Rocabertí, Hipòlita de Jesús. *De los sagrados huessos de Christo señor nuestro* (Valencia: Viuda de Benito Macè, 1679).

———. *Tratado de las virtudes dividido en quatro libros, el primero del santo silencio. El segundo de la virtud de la esperança. El tercero de la caridad y el quarto de las divinas alabanças* (Valencia: Imprempta vda. Benito Macè, 1684).

Rodríguez-Moñino, Antonio. *Poesía y cancioneros (Siglo XVI). Discurso leído ante la Real Academia Española el día 20 de octubre de 1968 en su recepción pública por el Excmo. Sr. D. Antonio Rodríguez-Moñino y contestación del Excmo. Sr. D. Camilo José Cela* (Madrid: s.n., 1968).

Rodríguez Puértolas, Julio, ed. *Cancionero de Fray Ambrosio Montesino* (Cuenca: Diputación Provincial, 1987).

Roig i Torrento, M. Assumpta. *Iconografia del retaule a Catalunya (1675–1725)* (PhD dissertation, Universitat Autònoma de Barcelona, 1990).

Roldán Herencia, Gonzalo. 'Music and Ceremony in Granada Cathedral Following the Council of Trent'. In *New Perspectives on Early Music in Spain*, edited by Tess Knighton and Emilio Ros-Fábregas (Kassel: Reichenberger, 2015), pp. 256–275.

Roldán Panadero, Concha. 'Transmisión y exclusión del conocimiento en la Ilustración: Filosofía para damas y *Querelle des femmes*'. *Arbor: Ciencia, pensamiento y cultura* 184, no. 731 (2008), pp. 457–470. <https://doi.org/10.3989/arbor.2008.i731.196>.

Rolle of Hampole, Richard. *Incemdium amoris of Richard Rolle of Hampole*, edited by Margaret Deanesly (Manchester: Manchester University Press, 1915).

Ros-Fábregas, Emilio. 'The Manuscript Barcelona, Biblioteca de Catalunya, M.454: Study and Edition in the Context of the Iberian and Continental Manuscript Traditions' (PhD dissertation, The City University of New York, 1992).

———. 'Canciones sin música en la corte de Isabel la Católica: "Se canta al tono de"'. *Revista de Musicología 16*, no. 3 (1993): pp. 1505–1514.

———. 'Libros de música en bibliotecas españolas del siglo XVI'. *Pliegos de Bibliofilia 15, 16, 17* (2001–2002): pp. 37–62, 33–46, 17–54.

———. 'Melodies for Private Devotion at the Court of Queen Isabel'. In *Queen Isabel I of Castile: Power, Patronage, Persona*, edited by Barbara F. Weissberger (Woodbridge: Tamesis, 2008): pp. 83–107.

———. 'Dos manuscrits de polifonia del Renaixement amb connexions gironines: E-Boc 5 i E-Bbc 682'. In *La música culta a les comarques gironines. Dels trobadors a l'electroacústica*, edited by Mari Carmen Pardo Salgado and Miquel Cuenca i Vallmajó (Banyoles: Centre d'Estudis Comarcals de Banyoles, 2015): pp. 21–36.

Rose, Stephen. 'Trumpeters and Diplomacy on the Eve of the Thirty Years' War: The *album amicorum* of Jonas Kröschel'. *Early Music 40*, no. 3 (2012): pp. 379–392. Print. <https://doi.org/10.1093/em/cas075>.

Ruiz Jiménez, Juan. 'Fémina inquieta y andariega: Paisajes sonoros del itinerario fundacional de Teresa de Jesús'. In *El Libro de la 54 Semana de Música Religiosa de Cuenca* (Cuenca: Semana de Música Religiosa de Cuenca, 2015): pp. 62–89.

———. 'La transformación del paisaje sonoro urbano en la Granada conquistada (1492–1570)'. In *Paisajes sonoros medievales*, directed by Gerardo Rodríguez, Éric Palazzo, and Gisela Coronado Schwindt (Mar del Plata: Universidad Nacional de Mar del Plata, 2019): pp. 139–185.

———. 'Chanzonetas y romances compuestos para la profesión de Francisca de Córdoba y Ribera (1634)', *Paisajes Sonoros Históricos*, 2020. <http://www.historicalsoundscapes.com/evento/1086/montilla/es>.
Said, Edward W. *Culture and Imperialism* (London: Chatto and Windus, 1993).
Sáinz de la Maza Lasoli, Regina. *La Orden de Santiago en la Corona de Aragón* (Saragossa: Institución Fernando el Católico, 1980–1988), 2 vols.
Salazar, Alonso de. *Fiestas que hizo el insigne Collegio de la Compañia de Iesus de Salamanca a la Beatificación del glorioso Patriarca S. Ignacio de Loyola* (Salamanca: viuda de Artus Taberniel, 1610).
Salicrú, Roser. 'Crossing Boundaries in Late Medieval Mediterranean Iberia: Historical Glimpses of Christian-Islamic Intercultural Dialogue'. *International Journal of Euro-Mediterranean Studies 1*, no. 1 (2008): pp. 33–51.
Salvador Miguel, Nicasio. 'Gómez Manrique y la Representación del nacimiento de nuestro Señor'. *Revista de Filología Española 92*, no. 1 (2012): pp. 135–180. <https://doi.org/10.3989/rfe.2012.v92.i1.240>.
San José, Diego de, *Compendio de las solenes fiestas que en toda España se hicieron en la Beatificacion de N. M. S. Teresa de Iesus [...]* (Madrid: viuda de Alonso Martín, 1615).
Sanahuja, Pedro. *Historia de la Seráfica Provincia de Cataluña* (Barcelona: Edit. Seráfica, 1959).
Sanjust i Latorre, Cristina. 'L'obra del Reial Monestir de Santa Maria de Pedralbes des de la seva fundació fins al segle XVI. Un monestir reial per a l'orde de les clarisses a Catalunya' (PhD dissertation, Universitat Autònoma de Barcelona, 2008).
Santa María, Fray Francisco de. *Reforma de los Descalzos de Nuestra Señora del Carmen* (Madrid: Diego Díaz de la Carrera, 1644).
Saurí, Manuel, and José Matas. *Guía general de Barcelona* (Barcelona: Imp. de Manuel Saurí, 1849).
Scarci, Manuela, ed. *Creating Women: Representation, Self-Representation, and Agency in the Renaissance* (Toronto: Centre for Reformation and Renaissance Studies, 2013).
Scedula resolutiva donada per lo ministre y convent de la Santissima Trinitat, Redempciò de Cautius, de Religiosos Calçats de la ciutat de Barcelona, en la causa aporta en la R. Audiencia, contra la Universitat de la vila de la Roca, Bisbat de Barcelona y altres, a relació del noble don Pere de Amigant, meritissim Doctor de la Real Audiencia: not. Pere Pau Ribes (Barcelona?: s.n., after 1689). <https://explora.bnc.cat/permalink/34CSUC_BC/1fpark4/alma991014436219706717>.
Schwartz, Roberta Freund. 'En busca de liberalidad: Music and Musicians in the Courts of the Spanish Nobility, 1470–1640' (PhD dissertation, University of Illinois at Urbana-Champaign, 2001).
Serpi, Dimas. *Tratado del purgatorio contra Luthero y otros herejes con singular y varia dotrina de mucho provecho y muy útil para predicadores, curas, religiosos y para todos los estados* (Barcelona: Gabriel Graells y Giraldo Dótil, 1600).
Serra Álvarez, Isabel. 'Dos visitas de la orden de Santiago al Monasterio de Junqueras (1495–1499)' (Bachelor dissertation, Universitat de Barcelona, 1966).
Serra de Manresa, Valentí. *Les clarisses-caputxines a Catalunya i Mallorca: de la fundació a la guerra civil (1599–1939)* (Barcelona: Facultat de Teologia de Catalunya, 2002).
———. 'Alguns aspectes de la primitiva legislació de les clarisses caputxines: espiritualitat i vida quotidiana'. *Analecta sacra tarraconensia: Revista de ciències historicoeclesiàstiques 76* (2003): pp. 183–212.

Serrano Martín, Eliseo. *El Pilar, la historia y la tradición. La obra erudita de Luis Díez de Aux (1562-ca.1639)* (Saragossa: Mira Editores, 2014).
Serrano y Sanz, Manuel. *Apuntes para una biblioteca de escritoras españolas desde el año 1401 al 1833* (Madrid: Establecimiento tipolitográfico 'Sucesores de Rivadeneyra', 1974), 2 vols.
Shelemay, Kay Kaufman. 'Musical Communities: Rethinking the Collective in Music'. *Journal of the American Musicological Society 64*, no. 2 (2011): pp. 349–390. <https://doi.org/10.1525/jams.2011.64.2.349>.
Shemek, Deanna, ed. *Isabella d'Este: Selected Letters* (Tempe: Arizona Center for Medieval and Renaissance Studies, 2017).
Sigüenza, José de. *Historia de la Orden de San Jerónimo* (Madrid: Bailly Baillière e Hijos, 1907–1909), 2 vols.
Smith, Bruce R. *The Acoustic World of Early Modern England: Attending to the O-Factor* (Chicago: University of Chicago Press, 1999).
Smith, David J., and Rachelle Taylor, eds. *Networks of Music and Culture in the Late Sixteenth and Early Seventeenth Centuries: A Collection of Essays in Celebration of Peter Philips's 450th Anniversary* (Farnham, Surrey: Ashgate, 2013).
Sohrabi, Naghmeh. *Taken for Wonder: Nineteenth-Century Travel Accounts from Iran to Europe* (Oxford: Oxford University Press, 2012).
Solà, Àngels. 'Las mujeres como productoras autónomas en el medio urbano (siglos XIV-XIX)'. In *La historia de las mujeres: perspectivas actuales*, edited by Cristina Borderías (Barcelona: Icaria, 2009): pp. 225–267.
Soler i López, Núria. *Maria de Jonqueres: un personatge a l'ombra de la historia* (Planes d'Hostoles: Ajuntament de les Planes d'Hostoles, 2007).
Solsona i Coiment, Francina. 'El monestir de Sta. Maria de Jonqueres (Barcelona) durant la lloctinència de Joan d'Aragó, Duc de Lorena (1467–70)'. *Medievalia 2* (1984): pp. 313–329.
Soto, Francisco. *Destierro de los malos cantares, con que nuestro Señor se ofende: y para que canten los niños en las calles y escuelas dejando los del mundo por los de Dios* (Seville: Bartolomé Gómez de Patrana, 1621).
Stevenson, Robert. *The Music of Peru: Aboriginal and Viceroyal Epochs* (Washington, DC: Pan American Union, 1960).
Stras, Laurie. 'Le nonne della ninfa: Feminine Voices and Modal Rhetoric in the Generations Before Monteverdi'. In *Gender, Sexuality and Early Music*, edited by Todd Borgerding (New York: Routledge, 2002): pp. 123–165.
_____. 'Musical Portraits of Female Musicians at the Northern Italian Courts in the 1570s'. In *Art and Music in the Early Modern Period: Essays in Memory of Franca Trinchieri Camiz*, edited by Katherine A. McIver (Aldershot: Ashgate, 2003): pp. 145–172.
_____. 'The Performance of Polyphony in Early 16th-Century Italian Convents'. *Early Music 45*, no. 2 (2017a): pp. 195–215. <https://doi.org/10.1093/em/cax023>.
_____. '*Voci pari* Motets and Convent Polyphony in the 1540s: The *materna lingua* complex'. *Journal of the American Musicological Society 70*, no. 3 (2017b): pp. 617–696. <https://doi.org/10.1525/jams.2017.70.3.617>.
_____. *Women and Music in Sixteenth-Century Ferrara* (Cambridge: Cambridge University Press, 2018).
Strocchia, Sharon. *Nuns and Nunneries in Renaissance Florence* (Baltimore: The Johns Hopkins University Press, 2009).
Stroccia, Sharon, and Julia Rombough. 'Women Behind Walls. Tracking Nuns and Socio-Spatial Networks in Sixteenth-Century Florence'. In *Mapping Space, Sense, and*

Movement in Florence: Historical GIS and the Early Modern City, edited by Nicholas Terpstra and Colin Rose (London: Routledge, 2016): pp. 87–106.

Strohm, Reinhard. *Music in Late Medieval Bruges* (Oxford: Clarendon Press, 1985).

Styers, Randall. *Making Magic: Religion, Magic, and Science in the Modern World* (Oxford: Oxford University Press, 2004).

Suardo, Juan Antonio. *Diario de Lima de Juan Antonio Suardo (1629-1634)*, introduced and annotated by Rubén Vargas Ugarte S. J. (Lima: Imp. C. Vásquez L., 1935).

Sullivan, Henry W. *Grotesque Purgatory. A Study of Cervantes's Don Quixote, Part II* (Pennsylvania: The Pennsylvania State University Press, 1996).

Surtz, Ronald. 'Iberian Holy Women: A Survey'. In *Medieval Holy Women in the Christian Tradition c.1100-c.1500*, edited by Alastair Minnis and Rosalynn Voaden (Turnhout: Brépols, 2010): pp. 499–528.

Talavera, Hernando de. *Oficio de la toma de Granada* (MS, 1493). Sources: Santa Fe (Granada), Archivo Parroquial, chant book no. 20; Simancas (Valladolid), Archivo de Simancas, sección Patronato Real, sign. 25–41.

Santa Teresa, Anastasio de. *Reforma de los Descalzos de Nuestra Señora del Carmen de la Primitiva Observancia, VII* (Madrid: Imprenta Real; Miguel Francisco Rodríguez, 1739).

Terni, Clemente. 'L'espressione musicale francescana, povera e per tutti: Giuliano da Spira'. *Storia della Città 26–27* (1983): pp. 91–94.

Terpstra, Nicholas, ed. *The Politics of Ritual Kinship: Confraternities and Sacred Order in Early Modern Italy* (Cambridge and New York: Cambridge University Press, 2000).

Tingle, Elizabeth C. *Purgatory and Piety in Brittany, 1480–1720* (Farnham and Burlington: Ashgate, 2012).

Tintó i Sala, Margarita. 'Les cases gremials de Barcelona i el seu entorn urbà'. In *El món urbà a la Corona d'Aragó del 1137 als decrets de Nova Planta: XVII Congrés d'Història de la Corona d'Aragó = Congreso de Historia de la Corona de Aragón: Barcelona. Poblet. Lleida, 7 al 12 de desembre de 2000*, coordinated by Salvador Claramunt Rodríguez (Barcelona: Universitat de Barcelona, 2003): vol. 2, pp. 895–901.

Tobella, Antoni M. 'Cronologia dels capítols de la Congregació Claustral Tarraconense i Cesaraugustuna (1219–1661)'. *Anuario Montserratensia 10* (1964): p. 304.

Toledano, Miguel. *Minerva Sacra* (Madrid: Iuan de la Cuesta, 1616).

Tomlinson, Gary. *Music in Renaissance Magic: Toward a Historiography of Others* (Chicago: University of Chicago Press, 1993).

Torra, Alberto. 'Fondos documentales monásticos en el Archivo de la Corona de Aragón'. *Memoria ecclesiae 6* (1995): pp. 121–146.

_____. 'Fondos documentales de los conventos de Barcelona en el Archivo de la Corona de Aragón'. *Quaderns d'història 7* (2002): pp. 307–323.

Torremocha Hernández, Margarita. *De la mancebía a la clausura. La Casa de Recogidas de Magdalena de San Jerónimo y el convento de San Felipe de la Penitencia (Valladolid, siglos XVI-XIX)* (Valladolid: Universidad de Valladolid, 2014).

Torrente, Álvaro. 'Sacred Villancico in Early Eighteenth-Century Spain: The Repertory of Salamanca Cathedral' (PhD dissertation, University of Cambridge, 1997).

Torrente, Álvaro, and Miguel Ángel Marín. *Pliegos de villancicos en la British Library (Londres) y la University Library (Cambridge)* (Kassel: Reichenberger, 2000).

Torres Fernández, Milagros de. *El ceremonial de Granada y Guadix y los espectáculos religiosos en Castilla a fines del medievo* (Madrid: Fundación Universitaria Española, 2006).

Torres, Francisco. *Historia de la mui nobilissima ciudad de Guadalajara* (MS, 1647). Madrid, Biblioteca Nacional de España, MSS/1690, fols. 208v–209r.

Tristany Boffill i Benach, Bonaventura de. *Corona benedictina* (Barcelona: Rafael Figueró, 1677).
Triunfos en Jerusalen. Epinicio sacro, que en la solemne profession, y velo de la señora Sor Maria Teresa Sociats, y Guitart, en el religiosissimo real convento de N. Señora, de Jerusalèn de la ciudad de Barcelona, orden del serafico P.S. Francisco de Assis, y de la V. Madre S. Clara, cantò la capilla de la santa iglesia cathedral, siendo su maestro el licenciado Joseph Pujol, en 29. de deciembre de 1765 (Barcelona: herederos de Bartholome Giralt, [1766?]).
Truax, Barry. *Acoustic Communication* (Westport: Ablex, 2001 [1984]).
———. 'Acoustic Space, Community, and Virtual Soundscapes'. In *The Routledge Companion to Sounding Art*, edited by Marcel Cobussen, Vincent Meelberg, and Barry Truax (New York and London: Routledge, 2017): pp. 253–263.
Turbaví, Miguel. *Relacion de las fiestas que hizo el colegio dela conpañia de Iesus de Girona, en la canonizacion de su patriarca San Ignacio, i del apostol de la India San Francisco Xavier, i beatificacion del angelico Luis Gonzaga. Con el torneo poetico mantenido i premiado por don Martin de Agullana, cavallero del abito de Santiago, señor de las baronias de Liguerre, i Mipanas, en el reino de Aragon, etc. Por Francisco Ruiz natural de la noble ciudad de Loja, en el reino de Granada. Dirigida al reverendisimo P Mucio Viteleschi preposito general de la conpania de Iesus* (Barcelona: Sebastian i Iaime Matevad, 1623).
Turino, Thomas, and James Lea, eds. *Identity and the Arts in Diaspora Communities* (Warren: Harmonie Park Press, 2004).
Tylus, Jane. *Reclaiming Catherine of Siena: Literacy, Literature, and the Signs of Others* (Chicago and London: The University of Chicago Press, 2017).
Uberti da Cesena, Gratioso. *Contrasto musico: Opera dilettevole* (Rome: Lodovico Grignani, 1630).
Udina Martorell, F. 'El milenario del Real Monasterio de San Pedro de las Puellas y el acta de consagración de su primitivo templo'. *Boletín de la Real Academia de buenas Letras de Barcelona 18* (1945): pp. 217–244.
Utz, Christian. 'Cultural Accommodation and Exchange in the Refugee Experience: A German-Jewish Musician in Shanghai'. *Ethnomusicology Forum 13*, no. 1 (2004): pp. 119–51. <https://doi.org/10.1080/1741191042000215309>.
Valenzuela, Antonio de. *Doctrina christiana para los niños y para los humildes* (Salamanca: Andreas de Portonariis, 1556).
Vallmanya, Antonio. *Poesies*, critical edition by Jaume Auferil (Barcelona: Fundació Noguera, 2007).
Vásquez de Espinosa, Antonio. *Compendio y descripción de las Indias Occidentales* (Madrid: Historia 16, 1992).
Vendrix, Philippe, Marlène Britta, and François Turellier. 'La vie musicale à Orléans de la fin de la Guerre de Cent Ans à la Saint-Barthélemy'. In *Orléans, une ville de la Renaissance*, directed by Clément Alix, Marie-Luce Demonet, David Rivaud, and Philippe Vendrix (Orléans: Ville d'Orléans, 2009): pp.120–131.
Venegas, Alejo. *Agonia del transito de la muerte: con los auisos y consuelos que cerca della son prouechosos* (Saragossa: George Coci, 1544).
Vera, Alejandro. *The Sweet Penance of Music: Musical Life in Colonial Santiago de Chile* (Oxford: Oxford University Press, 2020).
Vergés i Forns, Tomàs. *Les jerònimes de Barcelona i la seva historia (1475–1980)* (Barcelona: Santjer, 1987).

Vicente Delgado, Alfonso de. 'Diez años de investigación musical en torno al Monasterio de Santa Ana de Ávila'. *Revista de Musicología 23*, no. 2 (2000): pp. 509–562. <https://doi.org/10.2307/20797667>.

_____. 'Música, propaganda y reforma religiosa en los siglos XVI y XVII: cánticos para la 'gente del vulgo' (1520–1620)'. *Studia Aurea 1* (2007). <http://www.studiaaurea.com/articulo.php?id=47>.

_____. 'Los cargos musicales y las capillas de música en los monasterios de la orden de San Jerónimo (siglos XVI-XIX)' (PhD dissertation, Universidad Complutense de Madrid, 2010).

Vigil, Mariló. *La vida de las mujeres en los siglos XVI y XVII* (Madrid: Siglo XXI de España Editores, 1994).

Vilarrúbia i Estrany, Josep Maria, and Jordi Jové i Permanyer. *Els Carrers de Ciutat Vella* (Barcelona: Fundació La Caixa, 1990).

Villegas Díaz, Luis Rafael and Rafael García Serrano. 'Relación de los pueblos de Jaén, de Felipe II'. *Boletín del Instituto de Estudios Giennenses 88–89* (1976): pp. 9–304.

Vinatea Recoba, Martina. 'Ficción y realidad en la crónica de la fundación del convento de la Encarnación de Lima'. *Hipogrifo: Revista de literatura y cultura del Siglo de Oro 1*, no. 2 (2013): pp. 125–133. <https://doi.org/10.13035/H.2013.01.02.11>.

Vinyolas y Torres, Pablo. 'Santa Inés Peranda de Asís y Santa Clara de Janua en Barcelona. Su culto inmemorial'. *Revista Montserratoma 7*, no. 3 (1913): pp. 147–153.

Wagner, Lavern John. 'Franciscan Chant as a Late Medieval Expression in the Liturgy'. *Essays in Medieval Studies 5* (1988): pp. 45–56.

Warren, Nancy Bradley. *Spiritual Economies: Female Monasticism in Later Medieval England* (Philadelphia: University of Pennsylvania Press, 2001).

Watkins, John. 'Toward a New Diplomatic History of Medieval and Early Modern Europe'. *Journal of Medieval and Early Modern Studies 38*, no. 1 (2008): pp. 1–14. <https://doi.org/10.1215/10829636-2007-016>.

Watson, Nicholas. *Richard Rolle and the Invention of Authority* (Cambridge: Cambridge University Press, 2007).

Weaver, Elissa B. *Convent Theatre in Early Modern Italy: Spiritual Fun and Learning for Women* (Cambridge: Cambridge University Press, 2002).

Weissberger, Barbara F. *Isabel Rules: Constructing Queenship, Wielding Power* (Minneapolis: University of Minnesota Press, 2003).

Wendling, Miriam. 'Music, Death and Women's Communities in Late Medieval Europe', paper at the Annual Meeting of the American Musicological Society, Minneapolis (online), 15 November 2020.

Whetnall, Jane. 'Secular Song in Fifteenth-Century Spain'. In *Companion to Music in the Age of the Catholic Monarchs*, edited by Tess Knighton [Brill's Companions to Musical Culture 1] (Leiden: Brill, 2016): pp. 60–96.

Whiteley, Sheila, Andy Bennett, and Stan Hawkins, eds. *Music, Space and Place: Popular Music and Cultural Identity* (Burlington, VT: Ashgate, 2004).

Wiesner-Hanks, Merry E. *Women and Gender in Early Modern Europe* (Cambridge: Cambridge University Press, 1993).

_____, ed. *Mapping Gendered Routes and Spaces in the Early Modern World* (Farnham, Surrey: Ashgate, 2015).

Wilson, Blake. 'Song Collections in Renaissance Florence: The *cantasi come* Tradition and Its Manuscript Sources'. *Recercare 10* (1998): pp. 69–104.

_____. *Singing Poetry in Renaissance Florence: The 'Cantasi Come' Tradition and its Sources* (Florence: Olschki, 2009).

_____. *Singing to the Lyre in Renaissance Italy: Memory, Performance, and Oral Poetry* (Cambridge: Cambridge University Press, 2019).
Williams, Sarah F. *Damnable Practises: Witches, Dangerous Women, and Music in Seventeenth-Century English Broadside Ballads* (Farnham and Burlington: Ashgate, 2015).
Wood, Jennifer Linhart. *Sounding Otherness in Early Modern Drama and Travel: Uncanny Vibrations in the English Archive* (New York: Palgrave Macmillan, 2019).
Woshinksky, Barbara R. *Conventual Spaces in France, 1600–1800: The Cloister Disclosed* (New York: Routledge, 2016).
Wyhe, Cordula van. *Female Monasticism in Early Modern Europe: An Interdisciplinary View* (Aldershot: Ashgate, 2008).
Zamora Bretones, Montserrat. 'La clausura femenina: religión cívica en la Barcelona moderna (siglos XV-XVII)'. In *Providencialisme i secularització a l'Europa moderna (segles XVI-XIX): moment maquiavel·lià o macabeu?*, directed by Xavier Torres i Sans (Girona: Universitat de Girona, Institut de la Recerca Històrica, 2018): pp. 121–136.
_____. 'La ciudad y el templo: religión cívica en la Barcelona moderna (XVI-XVIII)' (PhD dissertation, Universitat de Girona, 2020).
Zaragoza Gómez, Verònica. 'La obra literaria de los Fontanella al entorno del monasterio dominico de Nuestra Señora de los Ángeles y pie de la Cruz (Barcelona, siglo XVII)'. *Archivum Fratrum Praedicatorum 82* (2012): pp. 217–266.
_____. 'Historiar les protragonistes absents. La poesia femenina de l'edat moderna a l'àmbit català'. In *'Allegro con brio'. I Encuentro 'Aula Música Poética' de Jóvenes Humanistas (Barcelona, 9 y 10 de octubre de 2012)*, edited by Lola Josa and Mariano Lambea (Barcelona: CSIC, 2013): pp. 146–159.
_____. '"En vers vull desafiar...". La poesia femenina a l'àmbit català (segles XVI-XVIII). Edició crítica' (PhD dissertation, Universitat de Girona, 2016).
_____. 'El Cancionero poético del Carmelo descalzo femenino de Barcelona (ca.1588-ca.1805)'. *eHumanista: Journal of Iberian Studies 35* (2017), pp. 615–644.
Zaragoza i Pascual, Ernest. 'Reforma de las benedictinas de Cataluña en el siglo XVI (1589–1603)'. *Analecta Sacra Tarraconensia 49–50* (1976–1977): pp. 177–204.
_____. 'Documentos inéditos referentes a la reforma monástica en Cataluña durante la segunda mitad del siglo XVI (1555–1600)'. *Studia Monastica 19*, no. 1 (1977): pp. 93–203.
_____. 'Reforma de las benedictinas en Cataluña en el siglo XVII'. *Anuario S. Tarraconensia 51–52* (1978–1979): pp. 170, 190.
_____. *Catàleg dels monestirs catalans* (Barcelona: Publicacions de l'Abadia de Montserrat, 1997).
_____. 'Músicos benedictinos españoles (siglos XV-XX)'. *Analecta sacra tarraconensia: Revista de ciències historicoeclesiàstiques 76* (2003): pp. 45–182.
_____. 'Documentació inèdita sobre la reforma de Sant Pere de les Puel·les (1563–1602)'. *Analecta Sacra Tarraconensia 78–79* (2005–2006): pp. 309–321.
_____. 'Fernando el Católico y la reforma de los benedictinos y benedictinas españoles (1474–1516)'. *Anuario de Historia de la Iglesia 26* (2017): pp. 157–184. <https://doi.org/10.15581/007.26.157-184>.

Index

Abarca y Velasco, Teresa **90**
absolta 121, 174, **178–180**, 187–188, 193, **194**
acoustic community 2
acoustic jars 85, 113n84
Acuña Ulloa, Juan de **210**
Advent 69, 137
Agnus Dei **70**, 71, 210, 235n20
Aguilar, Bernardino de 11, 45n6
Aguilera, Diego de **209**
Aguiló i Aloi, Maria Rosa **78**, **80**
Agustín, Hipòlita **194**
Alana, lord of 52n130
Albareda, Joan Pere **191**
albat 58, 188–189, **191**, 201nn102–103
Albert VII of Austria, Archduke 145, 148n19
Albiá i Fayet, Maria Clara **91**
Alboch, Ventura **191**
Alcalá de Henares (Madrid) 73, **209**; Santa Isabel school 157; San Juan de la Penitencia convent 157
Alcántara, Order of 29, 48n67
Alexander III (the Great) of Macedonia 71
Alexander IV, Pope 21
Alexander VI, Pope 207
Alexandria, Origen of 185
Alfons III of Aragon 124
Alfons IV of Aragon 124
Alfonsa, Elisabet 174
Alfonso, Miquel 174
Algasia, Catalina 35
Alias, Gabriel **191**
Alicante *190*
All Saints' feast day 137, **180**, 195n5, 202n111
Alm, Mossèn Nicolau **62**
Alma redemptoris mater 185
Almansor 13
Almendralejo (Badajoz) **209**

Almudéver, Onofre 223, *227*
Alpicart, Elisabet 21
Altabàs, Manuel 63
alternatim performance 37, **123**, 124–125, 139, 148n19, 162, 210–211
Álvarez, Antonio 197n27
Álvarez de Toledo, Alfonso 168
Álvarez Mendizábal, Juan 156
Amat, Caterina 104
Amat, Joan Carles **100**
Amat i de Iunyent, Francesca Gaetana **91**
Ametller, Jerònim 174
Ametller, Margarida 174
Amorós, Juan Carlos: widow of **100**
Andrew, Saint: feast day 55, 107
Angelico, Fra *187*
Angelina (widow of Guillem de Santcliment) 113n94
Anglada, Bartomeu **191**
Anglí Street (Barcelona) 24
Anna Maria (daughter of Pere Pau Balaguer) **191**
Anna of Austria 43
Anne, Saint: feast day 105
antiphon 66, 68–69, 71–74, 76, *77*, 107, 112n71, 112n75, 123, 135, 137, 148n17, 149n19, 155, 185, 208
antiphonal performance 131
antiphonary 65–66, 69–73, 112n66, 112n69, 112n71
Antonian Order **12**
Antonina 21
Antwerp 165, 234, 236n26
Anzizu, Sor Eulàlia 65, 110n46
Apolonia, Saint 105; confraternity (Barcelona) **102**, 105
Aquinas, Thomas 162
Aragó, Marina d' **178**
Aragó Street (Barcelona) 16
Aragon, Kingdom of 44, 126

Index 281

Aragona, Eleonora d' 168
archaeology of the senses 126
Argençola, Anna d' 236n31
Argençola, Francesca 121
Argençola, Juana de *138*, 151n50, 213, 236n31
Argentona, Clara de **179**
Armendia, Pere 60–61
Armengol, Bartomeu 111n60
Armengol, Galceran de 52n121
Armengol y Prado, Magdalena 38, 51n121
Arrabasa, Pedro 59–61
Artís/Abril, Mossèn Miquel 61, **62**, 109n32
Artufel, Dámaso 112n79
Ascension's feast day 137
Asperges me 71
Aspiciens (responsories) 73, **74**
Assots 175
Assumption of the Virgin: feast day 176, **179**, **181**
Astor, Joan **62**
Auditexaudi (female choir) 112n63
Augustine, Saint 20, 156, 158
Augustinian Order **7–8**, 9, **12**, 19–21, 59, **86**, 187, 231, *233*
Auro Bello, Marcial de 42, 53n140
auto de fe 139
Ávila, Teresa of 126–129, 133, 155, 169, 215, *216*, 225–226, 228, 231

Badia, Francesc 63
Baeza (Jaén) 22, 159; University of 22
Balaguer, Pere Pau **191**
Balducci, Giovanni, 'il Cosci' *136*
Ballester family 52n124
Ballestera, Magdalena **178**, 191, 193
Baltasar, son of Ventura **191**
Bárbara (daughter of Sor Àngela Serafina Prat) 43–44
Barbarà, Baltasar 112n64
Barcelona entre muralles Project 45n1
Barter, Joan **90**
Bassecourt i Briás, Sor Maria Benita 112n79
Bassel 236n37
Bassols i Rafart, Augustina **91**
battle musical pieces 129
Beas de Segura (Jaén) 211
beatas 6, **8**, 19, 21–22, 24, 35, 220
beaterio 22, 46n24
Beates de Santo Domingo (Barcelona) 6, **8**, 21, 24
beatification 118, 125–129, 133–135, 139, 155, 204, 215, 231

beguines **7**, 35, 165
'Bella, de vos son amorós' 223, *228*
Bellafilla, Joseph de 29, 48n68
Bello, Guillem **63**
belloc 36, 50n104
bells 56, 108n10, 127, 188–189
Benedict, Saint: feast day 66
Benedictine Order 6, **8**, 11–12, 14, 16, 24, 34, 71, **78–79**, 120, 212
Benedictus 162, 197n20
benefice-holder 56, **57–58**, 60, 104, **156**, 174, 176
Berardo i Morera, Antonia **90**
Berardo i Morera, Josefa **90**
Berart i de Ramon, Maria Magdalena **91**
Berenguer de Castell-Germà i Areny, Zeferina **90**
Berga (Barcelona): Santa Maria de Montbenet convent 51n109
Bergadá i de Taraval, Maria Ignacia **92**
Bermudo, Juan 205, 207, 234n6
Bernáldez, Andrés 117
bernardas (Cistercians) **7**, 11
Besora, José Jerónimo 46n22
Bible **74**
Bisbe Laguarda Street (Barcelona) **7**
Blanch, Domingo 61, **62**, 109n32
Blanco, Juan **210**
Blessing of the Palms ceremony 137
Bodet Garcia, Diego **39**
Boïl de Boixadors, Caterina 38, 51n115, 141
Boïl de Boixadors, Joan 38, 51n115
Boïl de Boixadors, Pere 38, 51n115
Boisseau, Jean *15*
Boixò i de Francolí, Francesca **91**
Bologna 163
Bonamich, Tomàs 112n64
Boneu **191**
book of hours 65, 84
booksellers 56, 85, 97, 99–103, 115n112, 223
Boqueria gate (Barcelona) 129, 149n25
Bordons, Josep 48n68, 59–61, 205
Bordons, Pierre 60, 205
boreriorum (wine-skin makers) guild confraternity (Barcelona) 99
Borgia, Lucrezia 168, 197n22
Borgó i Roger, Beatriu de l'Encarnació 43
Borgunyó, Joan 9
Borin, Pedro 223
Borja, Francisco de **123**, 124
Borrell II, Count 13
Borrell Street (Barcelona) 45n13

Boscà, Antoni 59
Boscà, Josep 59
Bottigari, Hercole 169
Braganza, Catherine of 204
Braun, Georg *17*, *141*
Bravo, Juana 35, 44
breviary 65, **74**, 84–85, 88, *89*, 123, 158, 208, 210–212, 232
Brina, Lucrècia **180**
broadside ballads 163
brothels 18
Bru, Joan 112n64
Brudieu, Joan 99
Bruguera y Pallós, Teresa (professed as Teresa del Cor de Jesús) **93**
Brugués, Irene 24, 47n50
Bruniquer i Riera, Gilabert 29
Brussels 234n1
Burgos: Most Pure Conception confraternity 105
Burguera, Jacobus **58**
burial ceremonies 40, 58, 76, 104, 121–122, 125, 145, 158, 167–168, 174, 176, **181**, 182, 185, 187–189, *192*, 195
Byrd, Thomas 204
Byrd, William 204

Cabanillas, Jerónimo **209**
Cabanyes i Boet, Maria Gertrudis **93**
Cabessa, Salvador 56
cabiscol/capiscol/sochantre (succentor) 37, **57–58**, 139, 148n19, 197n21, 212
cabiscola/capiscola 40, 111n56, 113n92, *138*, 151–152n50, 185, 211, 213
Caçador, Guillem 19, 120, 205, *207*
Caçador, Jaume 9, 35
Caçador, Pau 175
Calabazanos (Palencia) 222
Calàbria Street (Barcelona) 45n13
Calancha, Antonio de la 231, *233*, 234, 238nn62–63
Calatrava, Order of 29, 48n67
Calcer, Jaume 41
calends 128
Callar, Felícia **90**, 94
Cammsa.[Camarasa?], Mossèn **62**
Camp de Galvany (Sant Gervasi, Barcelona) 23
Campo de Criptana (Ciudad Real) **209**
Camporélls, Adriana 199n49
cancionero (songbook) 95, 99, 222–223, **225**, **226**, *228*, 229, **230**, 237n44, 237n47, 237nn49–50, 239
Cano, Alonso **210**

Canonesses **7**, 19, 20, 46n30
Canónigos del Santo Sepulcro (religious Order) **12**
canonisation 118, 125–126, 133–134, 139, 150n31
Canons regular **12**
cantasi come tradition 221
cantatrice 37
Canuda Street (Barcelona) 22
Capbreu 31, 47n55, 48n57, 48–71, 109n36, 114n104
Capella Reial **12**
capilla española (Spanish chapel) 204
capilla flamenca (Flemish chapel) 204
capilla real see Chapel Royal
capitoler (book) 73, **74**
Capuchin Order **7**, **12**, 23, 43, 53n148, 65, 76, *102*, 135, 174
Çaragoça, Diego **39**
Caravaca de la Cruz (Murcia) **209**
Carcer i de Martí, Maria Flora **90**
Cardedeu (Barcelona) 59
Cárdenas, Alonso de 208, **209**
Cárdenas, Gutierre **209**
carders (makers of brushes to card the wool) guild confraternity (Barcelona) 99, 114n105
Cardona, Anna de, Countess of Aytona 44
Cardona, Catalina de 226
Cardona, Enric de 194
Cardona, Gerònima/Jerònima de **178**, **180**, **194**
Cardona, Teresa de 65
Cardona i Pinós, Anna de 42
Cardona i Pons, Jerònima de
Cardona-Rocabertí, Joan de
Caridad house (Barcelona) **27**
Carme church (Barcelona) **7**, 22, *23*
Carme Street (Barcelona) **7**, 20
Carreira, Isabel 38
Cartellà, Cecília de 51n109
Cartellà Fons i Sebastida, Teresa de **91**
Casa de la Bolla (Barcelona) 121
casa d'En Porta (Barcelona) 18, 21
Caselles, Jaume **91–92**, 94
Castellarnau, Blanca 35
Castellbisbal (Barcelona): Santa Magdalena i Santa Margarida convent 20
Castelldosrius, Marquises of **80**, **93**
Castelló d'Empúries (Girona): cathedral 197n21
Castellví, Mathea 201n99
Castiglione, Baldasarre 162

Castro, Caterina de 156
Catalina of Aragon 168
Catalina of Austria 114n101
Caterina, daughter of Gabriel Codina **191**
Cathedral (Barcelona): Santa Eulàlia chapel 59; Canónica of **12**
Cavaller i Ratès, Maria Agustina **91**
Cehegín (Murcia) **209**
celestial choir 126–127, 155
Cellers, Joan **63**
Cendrat, Jaume 166; widows of 197n27
censal 25, 111n60
Centre de Cultura Contemmporània (Barcelona) **7**, 21
Cepila, Lluïsa **194**
Cerda, Francisca de la 42
Cerdà Butifulla, Joan 175
Cerone, Pietro 157, 196n7
Cervantes, Miguel de 197n27, 223
Cervera 111n60
Cervera, Berenguera de 37
Cervera, Juan Francisco 73
Chacón, Diego **209**
chanzoneta 94
Chapel Royal 125, 127, 136, 139, 204, 231
Charles II 204
Charles V 21, **123**, 152n55, 170, 208, **209**
Chicago: Art Institute *136*
Christina Mirabilis, Saint 163–165, 195, 197n26
Christmas Day 137, 213
Christmas Eve 128
Christopher, Saint **102**, 104; feast day 179
cinc nafres (five wounds of Christ) procession 134
Circumcision of Christ 184
Cisneros, Cardinal 152n60, 157–158, 168, 207–208, 220, 222–223, 237n48
Cistercian Order 6, **7**, 11, **12**, 37, 51n110, *81*, 205
Ciuró, Honorat 191, *192*
Ciutadella chapel (Barcelona) **8**, 14
Ciutadella Park (Barcelona) **8**, 14, 176
Claramunt parish church (Barcelona) 108n16
Clare, Saint: feast day 36, 120, 137
Clarí, Jeroni 71–72, 111n58, 111nn60–62
Clariana, Eleonor **194**
clarion 152n55, 127
CLAUSTRA Project 2, 5n4
clavichord 40–41, 43, 52n134, 53n144, 108n23, 214
Clement VIII, Pope 70, 104, 111n57, 112n69

cobla (group of instrumentalists) 129, 149n25
Codina, Gabriel **191**
Col, Mossèn Pere **62**
Colmenar de Oreja (Madrid) **210**
Coloma, Alfons, Bishop 23
Coloma, Marquesa 172
Comes, Mossèn Vicens **62**
Common of the Saints *89*
Commune Confessoris 66
Compline Office 55, **57–58**, 65, **123**, 124, 132–133, 139
Compte i Reyón, Eulàlia (professed as Eulàlia del Cor de Jesús) **92**
Conceptio Tua Dei genitrix 107
Condal Street (Barcelona) 146
Conditor alme 72
Confessor Domini 123
Consell de Cent 19, 36, **100**
consellers (city councillors) 21–22, 29, 33, 38, 55, 102, 107, 118–121, 129, 135, 141–142, 145–147n9, 155, **156**, 208, 220
continuo instruments 95
contrafacta 222
converso 29, 168
coplas/coplillas 214, 223, 225, *227*, 228, 230
Copons i Cordelles, Maria Antonia **91**
Cordellas, J. 175
Córdoba: Carmelite convent 128
Córdoba y Ribera, Francisca de 94
Corella, Aldonça de 21, 205
Corens, Antonio **58**
Cormellas, Sebastián de 99, *214*, 223, *227*
Cormellas family 97
cornet 127, 149n21
Coromines, Mossèn Miquel **178–180**, 202n111
Coromines, Ramon 59
Coromines, Sebastián 188
Corpus Christi 66, 125, 162, 195n5; Octave of 99, 144, 171, 193, **194**; procession of 132, 137, 150n27, 150n33
Cors i Pinyana, Gerònima de **91**
Cortada i Bru, Maria Teresa **79–80**
Cortés y Dalmau, Josefa (professed as Josefa del Santíssim Sacrament) **92**
Cortey, Jaume *143*, 223
Cots, Esperança (professed as Esperança de Jesús Maria) **93**
Council of Trent 3–5n8, 19–21, 26, 38, 46n33, 49n78, 69, 118, 121, 140, 155,

284 Index

157–159, 176–177, 207, 208, 212, 214, 236n26, 236n37
counterpoint 124
Counter-Reformation 5n8, 126, 208, 220
countertenor 95
Credo 66, **70**, 122, 210–211, 235n20
Creu Corbeta (Barcelona) **7**, 15
Cross of the Sword 119
Cruïllas i Zarriera, Emanuela **91**
Cruz, José de la 157, 196n8
Cuervo, Juan de 168
Cum ad propinquaret 137
Cuzco 1, 118

Dalmau, Francesc, Viscount of Rocabertí 162
Dalmau, Josep 129–131, 133, 149nn23–27
Damians, Jaume 114n109
Davillier, Barón *190*
Davit (father of Olaguer) **191**
De Angelis Office **191**
De profundis clamavi ad te 66
Deacon 55, **57–58**, 76, 101, 132, 144, 155, 158, 168, 171–172, 176, **178–180**, 182, 188, 191, 193, **194**, 201n111, 212
Delamare, Adolphe Hedwige Alphonse *11, 18*
Dels Àngels Square (Barcelona) **7**, 19
Dels Banys Street (Barcelona) 191
demonology treatises 163
Denia, Marquis of 124, 148n18
desapropis (wills) 26, **74**, **83**, 177, **181**, 193–194
Desbosch, Anna 56
Desbosch i de Sant Vicens, Francisca 193
Descros, Costanç **83**
Desllor, Prioress **179**
Desllor, Violant **83**
Despalau, Violant 35
Despès, Violant 172, 175, 199n60
Deu, Llorenç **100**
Devil 163, 198n29
Dexen, Maria **100**
Dexen, Pedro Juan **100**
Diago, Francisco 19–21
diaspora 220
Díez, Cristóbal **209**
Díez, Juan **209**
Díez de Aux, Luis 126–128, 215, *216*, 219, 155
digital humanities 3
Diputació (Deputation house) 121, 211
diputats (representatives of the church) 120

Discalced Carmelite Order **8**, 9, **12**, 18, 22, 31, 36, 46n22, 53n144, 101, 121, 127–129, 131–133, 135n13, 155, 169–170, 174, 187, 219, 222, 225–226, 228–231
disentailment 26, 156
Dolcet i Baliart, Cayetana **93**
Dolor Monserdá Street (Barcelona) **8**
dominical (book) 65, 71, 73, **74**, 85–**87**
Dominican Order **7–8**, 9, **12**, 18–19, 21, 35, 42, 56, 64, 95, 104, 114n102, 121, 125, 133–134, 139, 150n33, 156, 161, 174–175, 187, 205, 212, 231, 235n8, 236n27, 237n54
Dominus secus mare Galilaeae 72
Doré, Gustave *190*
Dotil, Giraldo 159, *166*
doxology 162
drought 135, 151nn40–41
drums 104, 127, 129, 132, 134, 141–142, 152n55
Dulach, Elisabet **100**
dulcian 127, 231
Dulcissim Nom de Iesus (Most Sweet Name of Jesus): confraternity (Barcelona) **102**; feast 120, **178**, **180**
dulzaina 127
Durall/Duralla, Caterina 85, 193
Duran, Josep 94–95
Dusay, Caterina 202n111
Dusay, Isabel 185

Eastern Sunday 60, 213
E-Bbc 587 32
E-Bbc 682 162
Écija (Seville) **209**
Eiximenis, Francesc 162
election of abbess/prioress 31, 49n87, 120–121
Elena (widow of Llorenç Deu) **100**
Elisabets Street (previously named *d'en Borra* Street) (Barcelona) **7**, 22, 35, 146
Elm, Saint **102**, 107
Els Segadors, war of 16
Encomienda de Sant Joan de Jerusalem **12**
Enguera (Valencia) **209**
Enrique IV 168
Epiphany 69, 137, 202n111
Epistle 56, 137, 158, 213
epistoler (book) 65
Erasmus 158
Erill i Cardona, Maria d' 40, 52n124
Escobar, Alonso de 175

Index   285

escolà/monaguillo (acolyte) 56, 58–59, 66, 108nn10–11, 110n51
escolana (chorister) 41, 109n37, 110n40, 155, 174, 213
escolano (choir boy) 56
Església Street (Barcelona) **8**
Espanya Square (Barcelona) 45n13
Espanyol y Ardenuy, Teresa (professed as Teresa de Crist) 114n98
Esperança (widow of Bartomeu Armengol) 111n60
Esplugues de Llobregat (Barcelona) **8**, 19, 25
Esquis i Prats, Maria Josefa **93**
estament mercantívol (merchant class) 120
Este, Alfonso I d' 168
Este, Suor Leonora d' 162
Estremera (Madrid) **209**
Et incarnatus 122, 148n16
Eulàlia (daughter of Bartomeu Anglada) **191**
Eulàlia (widow of Pere Montpezat) **100**
Eulàlia (wife of Juan Carlos Amoros) **100**
expedientes de pruebas de sangre 29, 51nn120–121, 52n126, 52nn128–129, 236n31
Extreme Unction 58–59

Fábregas, Joseph **191**
fadrines 73, **74**
Falgueras, Francisco 109n26
Fallcó, Simón 112n64
Farrera/Balle, Elisabet 41
Feliu, Narcís **191**
Ferdinand the Catholic 21, 65, 85, 152n54, **201**
Fernández de Córdoba, Alonso, fifth Marquis of Priego 94
Ferran, Miquel 176
Ferran I 124
Ferran i Fivaller, Magdalena de
Ferran Street (Barcelona) **8**
Ferrando, Joan 59
Ferrara 117, 212; Corpus Domini convent 88, 162, 168, 236n42; San Vito convent 169
Ferrer, Francisca 182, 184, 200n85
Ferrer, Gaspar 145
Ferrer, Vicente 184, *186*, 195
fife 127, 134
Figueres, Salvador **92**, 94
Figueró, Rafael 95
Figuerola, Juana 35, 188, 201n99
Fivaller i de Rub, Ignacia de **92**

Flecha El Viejo, Mateo 223
Flos Santorum **74**
Fluvia i de Aguilar, Inés **90**
Foix i de Pi, Clemencia **90**
Folch de Cardona, Joana, Duchess of Cardona and of Segorbe 113n94
folia 43
Fondo de Música Tradicional IMF-CSIC project 46n35
Fonellar Street (Barcelona) 144, 153n63
Fons, Iván Pablo 43
Font, Francina 175
Fontabella, Mariano 201n102
Fontana i Coixet, Maria **92**
Fontanella, Contesina 237n54
Fontanet, Anna **179–180**
Fontanet, Joan Baptista 26, 48n61, 48n64, 123–124, 213, 235n19, 236n32
Fontanet, Santa **178**
Fornés, Juana 22, 35, 145, 153n65
Forroll, Pere **58**
Foxà i de Mora, Maria Victòria **92**
Francis, Saint 14, **102**, 105; feast day 212
Francisca (daughter of Rafel Lemparch) **191**
Franciscan Third Order 7, 22
'Francisce cantricis' 37
Friuellera, Aldonça 188
Frualler, Perot 188
Fuente del Maestre (Badajoz) **210**
fusters (carpenters) guild confraternity (Barcelona) **102**, 116n127

Gabriel, Saint 175
Gali, Joseph **191**
Galiana dels Voltrera, Eleonor 175
Galindo, Beatriz 168
Garau de Gualba, Joan 174
Garcia, Joan 60, 176
García de Caralps, Antonio Juan 119, 147n4
García de Lisón, Juan **209**
Gardunya Square (Barcelona) 7, 18
Gargallo, Lluís Vicenç 94–95
Garrich, Gaspar 197n27
Garriga, Mossèn Pere **179**
Gaspar (organist) 63
General house (Barcelona) 121
Genloch, Ana 35
Genoves, Berengarius **58**
Gertrudis, Saint **180**; feast day 72
Giberga, Joannes **58**
Gil, Pero **209**
Gilabert, Joana de **83**

Gilabert, Lluís de **209**
Gilabert, Vitoria **178**
Ginebret, Dalmau **63**
Giralt, Bartomeu 95
Girau, Juan **39**
Girona 13, 23, 29, 48n68, 59, 162, 175, 191, 197n27, 204; Cathedral 60, 108n22, 112n66; Sant Daniel convent 24, 34; Sant Martí Jesuit college 204
Gispert i Illa, Teresa Maria **93**
Gloria **70**, 123, 148n17, 210–211, 235n20
Gloria, laus et honor 75, **78**, **80**
gloss 42, 215, *216*
goigs 105, 115n124, 133, 223
Gonçal, Mestre Joan 65
Gonçalo, Diego **39**
Gonser, Pere **58**
Gonzaga, Duchess Margherita 168–169
González, Elena 35
González de Villena, Bartolomé **209**, 210
Gospel/*Evangelio* 56, **74**, 85, 158, 175
Gotart, Hubert 99, **100**, *225*, **226**
governor's palace (Barcelona) 14
Gràcia, Eduard *20*, *24*
gradual (book) 65, **66**, 69–70
Graell i de Anglassell, Maria Anna de **92**
Graells, Gabriel 159, *166*
gramallas (mourning robes) 121
Granada 5n1, 50n96, **209**; conquest of 144
Grases i Cortès, Teresa **93**
Green Cross procession 139
Gregory, Saint: Masses of **181**, 182–185
Gregory XIV, Pope 104
Grimaldo, Juan de **210**
Grimau, Agraïda *30*, 40–41, 52nn127–128, 52n130, *214*, 214–215, *216*, 219–220, 223
Grimau, Àngela 40–41
Grimau, Eugènia 40–41, 180–182, 193, **194**, 200n79, 201n111
Grimau, Francesc de 40
Grimau, Isabel 52nn129–130
Grimau, Joan 40
Guadalajara: La Piedad convent 135–136, 231
Gualbes, Galceran Cristófol
Gualbes, Isabel de **83–84**, 84
Gualbes, Leonor **83–84**, 84
Gualbes, Luisa de 64, **84**
Guancer, Pere 104
Guardi, Francesco 118
Guardian Angel, Saint 184, 212; confraternity (Barcelona) **102**
Guardiola, Joan 103

Guardiola, Violant de 103
Guimerà, Àngela 35
Guimerà, Margarida de 40, 182
Guimerá i de Llupià, Àngela 185
Guitar 43, 53n144, 53n146, 72, **100**, 118, 231, 238n62
Guzmán, Juan Alonso de, sixth Duke of Medina Sidonia 49n82

Habsburg Spain 204
Hadewijch 165
Hampole Priory 165
harp 40–42, 118, 127, 158, 214, 220, 223, *224*, 231, 239
hebdomadaria/hebdomadario (hebdomad) 26, 42, 56, **57–58**, 65, 71, 104, 123, 213
Helena (slave) 64
Herrera, Francisco **210**
Herrera, Hernando Alonso de 157
Hierro, Baltasar del *143*
Hoc est praeceptum meum 68
Hoefnagel, Joris *17*, *141*
Holy Spirit confraternity (Barcelona) 174
Holy Week 118
Homobonus, Saint **102**
Honorat Confessor, Saint **178**
horn 95
hortelans (market-gardeners) guild confraternity (Barcelona) **102**, 104, 144
Hosanna 137
Hospitalarian Order **12**
Huesca: Santa Clara Square **7**
Hyacinth, Saint 134
hymn 71–75, 111n62, 119, 127, 134, 139, 145–146, 158, 162, 185, 188, 200n87, 205

Iacob autem genuit 68
IES Verdaguer (Barcelona) **8**, 14
Illuminist movement 208
Immaculate Conception: confraternity (Barcelona) 101, 105; feast day 22, 171, 202n111
In conspectus Angelorum 223
In exitu Israel 121
In Monte Oliveti 137, 151n50
In virtute tua **179**
Ingrediente Domino **78**, 137, 152n50
Inquisition 29, 126, 163, 204
Institut Cartogràfic i Geològic de Catalunya (Barcelona) *15–16*, *140*
Instituto Español de Musicología (Barcelona) 46n35

Intercessio nos quaesumus, Domine 123, 148n17
Iofre, Gaspar 129
Iradier Street (Barcelona) 22
Isabel I of Castile 117, 168, 222
Isabella Clara Eugenia 125
Isabel of Portugal 222
Isabel of Valois 141
Isnardi, Paolo 88

Jaca 5n1
Jacob, Saint: feast day 68
James, Saint 85, **179**; feast day 119, 124, 137
James II of England 204
Jaume I of Aragon 124
Jaume II of Aragon 15, 17
Jerome, Saint **102**; feast day 101–103, 120
Jeronymite Order **7**, 11, 22, *23*, 31, 35, 44, 47n43, 48n73, 60, *61*, 95, 101, 115n112, 120, 135, 151n40, 176
Jerusalem 21, 120
Jesuit Order 204–205
Jesús friary (Barcelona) **12**, 49n76, 59, **156**, **181**, 193–194
Jews 20, 29, 162, 220
Joabel (daughter of Joseph Gali) **191**
Joan (slave) 38
Joan (son of Joan Pere Albareda) **191**
Joan I of Aragon 16
Joan II of Aragon 20
Joana of Aragon 21
Joaquim, Saint 184
John, Saint: Order of 129
John the Baptist, Saint 56, **57–58**, **102**, 107, 184; feast day 56, **57–58**
Jonqueres, Bastion of 6, *11*
Jonqueres Street (Barcelona) **8**, 16
Jorba el Mayor, Luis 48n59
Jorba el Menor, Luis 48n59
Jordana, Violant 35
Jordi, Sant: feast day 125
José Cupertino, Saint: feast day 66
Josep (son of Gabriel Alias) **191**
Josepa (daughter of Vicente Sebastian) **191**
Joseph, Saint: feast day 120
Joseph Antoni (son of Narcís Feliu) **191**
Josquin des Prez 113n94
Juan of Austria 124
Julián, Francisco **39**
Justus ut palma florebit **178**, 193

knightly tournament 127
Kyrie **70**, 71, *72*, 210

La Bisbal (Girona) 63
Lacavalleria, Pere/Pedro **100**, *233*, 234
La Central del Raval bookshop (Barcelona) **7**
Lacóma i Martí, Maria Benita **93**
lamentations 63, *69*
La Nouë, Guillaume de la 73
Lanuça, Beatris de 188
lauda spiritual 105, 221
Laudate Dominum omnes gentes 124
Lauds Office 162
Lemos, Count of 204
Lemparch, Rafel **191**
Lentorn i de Civilla, Francesca de **90**
León, Kingdom of 16
Leoni, Paolo 212
Leonor of Cyprus 145
Les Jerònimes (or Santa Margarida or Sant Maties) convent (Barcelona) 6, **7**, 11, 22, *23*, 31–32, 35, 44, 48n73, 60, *61*, **90**, 95, 101, **102**, 115n112, 120, 135, 137, 151n40, **156**, 176
Les Rambles (Barcelona) 6, 18, 21, 135
Lescuyer, Bernard *89*
Leysa, Juan Narciso 204
Libera me 121
Liberal Triennium 26
liceu 18
Lima 128, 135, 231; *Diario de Lima* 118; La Concepción convent 135, 231; La Encarnación convent 118, 231
litany 73, 137, 139
Lizárraga, Reginaldo de 231
Llauder i Duran, Maria Francesca **92**
Llauder i Duran, Maria Teresa **92**
Llaudis, Madalena 177, **178–180**, 202n111
Llaurador i de Vilana-Perlas, Gerònima **91**
Llavaneres, Joseph **58**
Llavaneres, Juan 175
Lleida 34, 44, 205, 236n27; Franciscan convent 205
llibreters (booksellers) guild confraternity (Barcelona) 97, 99, 101–103, 115n112
Llinàs, Pau **91–92**, 94, 113n95
Llinàs i de Lapeyra, Maria de **92**
Lloselles, Margarida 188
Lluís (son of Hierònim Ortou) **191**
Lluís el Piadós Steet (Barcelona) **8**
Llull, Constança 84
Llull, Mossèn Romeu 56, 145
Llull, Yolant **83**
Llull/Lulla, Isabel 85, **87**
Lo Frasso, Antonio 42
Locutus 73, **74**

288 Index

Loeches (Madrid): Carmelite convent 127
London *81*, *167*, 204, 234n1, 234n3; Whitehall 204
López, Álvaro (or Alonso) **209**
López de Ponte, Juan **209**
Lorenç, Ramira **62**
Lorente, Andrés 73
Loris, Joan Dimas 19, 42, 161
Low Sunday procession 136
Loyola, Ignatius of 49n77, 135, *189*, 204
lullaby 222
Lumen ad revelationem Gentium 76
Lunes, Juan/Joan 108n17, 113n89
Lupià, Angelina de 38–40
Lupià, Francesc de **39**, 40
Lupià, Isabel de 40
Lupià, Lluís de **39**
Lupià/Sancha, Àngela de 40
Lyon *89*

Maccabees, Book of the 142
Madre de Dios, Isabel de la **91**
Madrid 2, 29, 35, 197n27, *224*, 231, *232–233*; Carmelite convents 94, 155; confraternities 101, 114n102; Constantinople convent 223; Espejo Street 168; Inmaculada Concepción convent; La Encarnación convent 198n36, 223; Santa Clara convent 168; Santa Clara Street 168
madrigal 99, 129, 149n25
Madrona Surià, Maria **91**
Magarola i Clariana, Maria Antonia **92**
Magarola i Clariana, Maria Josefa **92**
Magarola i de Reart, Francesca de **91**
Magarola i de Reart, Maria Gertrudis de **92**
Magí Martyr, Saint: confraternity (Barcelona) **102**, 104, 115n116, 172
Magnificat 66, 68, 149n19, 210, 235n20
Maillard, Jean 162
Major, Antoni Joan **209**
Maldá, Baron of 38
Malla, Anna de 187
Malla, Elisabet de 121, 193
Malo family 97
manacort see clavichord
mancebías 19–20
Manresa (Barcelona) 19, 23
Manrique, Gómez 222, 237n45, 237n47
Mantua: Sant'Orsola convent 169
manxaires 59
Marca, Francesco della 21–22, 34–35, 44, **102**, 188, 221
March the Evangelist, Saint **179**

Mare de Déu de Bonsuccés friary (Barcelona) **181**
Mare de Déu del Carme friary (Barcelona) 12, 129, 139, **181**
Mare de Déu del Roser Avenue (Barcelona) 7
Mare de Déu dels Àngels convent (Barcelona) 6, **7**, 19, 32, 35, 42, 49n77, 99, **102**, 112n79, 119–120, 124, 136, 145, 153n68, **156**, 161–162, 175–176, 188, 194, 237n54; Name of Jesus chapel 194
Mare de Déu Street (Barcelona) 22
Maremonti, Bishop Giambattista 212
Marganell (Barcelona): Sant Benet de Montserrat convent **8**, 14, 25
Margaret of Austria 119, **123**, 124, 198n36
Margaret Theresa of Spain 152n54
Margarit, Jerónimo 197n27
Margarita (Juan Carlos Amoros's wife) **100**
Margarita (widow of King Martí) 145
Margherita of Austria 23, 147n7
Marí i de Vilana, Teresa de (professed as Teresa de Jesús) **91**
Maria (daughter of Joseph Fábregas) **191**
Maria (daughter of Pau Montegut) **191**
Maria of Aragon 17–18, 65
Maria of Austria **123**, 124
Maria of Hungary 124
Mariana (daughter of Franciscà Puig) **191**
Mariana Luisa 124
Marimon, Caterina **178**, **180**, **194**
Marimon, Isabel de 40, 182, **194**
Marimon, Marianna de 187
Marimon, Violant de **178**, 193
Marina, Saint **179**
mariners (sailors) guild confraternity (Barcelona) **102**
Mark, Saint: feast day 137
Marqueta, Anna **84**, 193
Martí, Bishop of Messina **209**
Martí i Baseya, Antonia **92**
Martí i Baseya, Josefa **91**
Martí i Baseya, Maria Àngela **91**
Martí I of Aragon 16
Martínez, Juan **209**
Martínez de Bizcargui, Gonzalo 99, **100**
Martorell, Anthonius 176
Martorell i Reyt, Eulàlia Francesca **92**
martyrology 65, 110n44
Mary Magdalene, Saint 43, 85
masquerade 127
Massot, José 35, 42–43

Index 289

Mataró (Barcelona): Capuchin convent 23; Sant Benet convent 14
Matevad, Catalina **100**
Matevad, Jaime: widow of **100**
Matevad, Paula **100**
Matevad, Sebastiá **100**, *130*
Mathoses, Jaime 108n16
Matins Office 59, 65–66, 110n51, 120, 127, 171, 208
Maubuisson (France): Notre-Dame-la-Royale Cistercian nunnery *81*
Maurice, Saint **102**, 104, *105*
Meca, Marianna 73
Meca, Marquesa **179**
Meca de Vilana, Dionísia (professed as Teresa de Jesús) 121
Mediterranean sea 189, 203, 220
melismata 69
Mella, Isabel de 35
melos or *canor* 165
Mendoza, Ana de, Princess of Eboli 49n82, 169–170, 198n35, 225, 228
Mendoza, Brianda de 135
Mendoza, Diego de 221, 231
Mendoza, Francisco de **210**
Mendoza, Íñigo de 237n47
Mercè friary (Barcelona) **12**, 59, **156**, 174, **181**
Mercè Rodoreda Street (Barcelona) 7, 22
Mercedarian Order **12**, 187
Mersenne, Marin 73
Messina (Sicily, Italy) **209**
mestres d'obra i molers (master builders and millstone makers) guild confraternity (Barcelona) 99
mesurers (grain-weighers) guild confraternity (Barcelona) **102**, 145
Mexico: Metropolitan Cathedral 133
Mey, Pedro Patricio 73
Michael, Saint 163, **179**, **184**; feast day 137
Miguel (son of Boneu) **191**
Miguel, Andreas **58**
Milá y Fontanals school (Barcelona) 7
Milan 23
Milans, Tomàs **90–91**, 94
Millàs, Brígida 104
Mimo, Antich 59
Mingalla, Flavià **63**
Minims (religious Order) **12**
Minstrel 107, 131–132, 134, 139, 141
Miquel, Caterina 171
Miquela, Isabel **84**

Miser, Pau **63**
Miserere 43, 139, **178**, **180**, 191
Missa pro infirmis 76
Missa pro Mulieribus Pregnantibus 76, *82*
missal 65–66, 73, **74**, 88, **100**, 211; Roman missal 65, 212
Mitjans, Ana 44
Moixò i de Francolí, Maria Teresa de **92**
Molí d'en Carbonell (Clot, Barcelona) 16
Moliner, Juana 34
Mollar i Mitjans, Teresa **90**
Mollar i Roig, Esperança **92**
Mollar i Roig, Maria Gertrudis **91**
Moncada/Montcada, Elisenda de, Queen of Aragon 15, 110n46
Moncada/Montcada, Juan de 44
Moncayo, Mathias 44
Monells, Clara 35
Monica, Saint **178**
Monistrol de Montserrat (Barcelona): abbey 11–12, 60, *166*; Santa Cecília convent 14
Monlleó, Pere Antoni **93**
Monmany, Francisca 25
Monmany, Isabel de 84
Monmany, Margarita de **83**
Monmany, Marianna 187
Monsuar/Montsuar, Elena/Helena de 40, **194**
Montalbán (Teruel) **209**
Montalegre Street (Barcelona) **7**
Montblanc (Tarragona): Franciscan convent 44
Montcalvari friary (Barcelona) **12**
Montegut, Pau **191**
Montepoliciano/Montepulciano, Saint Agnes of 134
Monterroso, Rodrigo de **209**
Montesclaros, Marquise of 43
Montesino, Ambrosio 221–223
Montilla (Córdoba): Poor Clare convent 94, 205
Montoliu, Elena 177, **178**
Montoliu de Segarra (Lleida): castle 38
Montornes, Lluïsa **194**
Montoya, Juan Bautista de 159
Montpezat, Pere **100**
Montserrat, Pau **93**
Montserrat Xemallau, Gaspar 113n94
Montsió convent 6, **8**, 17–19, 21, 25, 41–42, 47n55, 56, 64, **90–91**, 95, **102**, 104, *106*, 110n42, 120, 134, 137, 156, 176, 205, 212; Roser chapel 176

290 *Index*

Montsió Street (Bacelona) **8**
Mora, Ginés de 41
Moradell, Domingo 175
Moradell, Vicente Miguel de 214–215, 220
Morales, Cristóbal de 113n94
Mordenayrs, Anthony 61
Morejón, Pedro 33, **209**
Morell, Sor Joana 22
Moreta, Anthon Joan 188
Moreta, Pere **63**
Morisco 29
Most Holy Trinity **102**, 184
Mota, Diego de 208
motet 88, 124, 127–129, 136, 149n22, 155, 197n22
Moxo, Jerònim 176
Moxò i de Ninot, Maria Eulàlia **93**
Moxò i de Ninot, Maria Ignacia **93**
Mozarabic liturgy 152n60
Muñoz, Luis 161
Muntaner Street (Barcelona) 19
Museu d'Art Contemporani (Barcelona) **7**
Museu Nacional d'Art de Catalunya (Barcelona) *11*, 13, *14*
Musica Secreta (music group) 197n22
musicians confraternity (Barcelona) 99

Nájera, Bartolomé de 73
Nájera, Duke of 124
Naples 23, 49n78, 157, 226
Nativity's feast day **57**, 181, 195n5, 201n111
Naves, Stephani 113n94
New World 4, 32, 49n82, 71, 94, 133, 195, 204, 229, 234, 238n58
New York *232*
Nicholas, Saint: confraternity (Barcelona) 101
Nieto Ortiz, Juan Esteban **210**
Nin, Francesc **62**
Nin i Steva, Anna Maria **92**
Nocturno de morts **178**, **180**
Noguera (Lleida): Les Avellanes convent 45n1
Noguera, Marta 43, 53n146
Nogués, Joan **79**
Nostra Senyora de la Misericordia house (Barcelona) 6, **7**, 22, 24, 159
Nostra Senyora de la Victòria convent (Barcelona) 6, **7**, 20, 24, 35
novices 11, 21, 23, 34–35, 42, 45n5, 49n87, 50n98, 73, 85, *136*, 163, 213
Nuça, Anna de la 40–41

Nuévalos (Saragossa): Pedra monastery 37
Núñez, Catalina 168
Nunyes, Gracia **100**
Nunyes, Pere Joan 71, 111n61

O sacrum convivum 66, 74
O salutaris hostia 162
O Virgo Virginum 185
oboe 95
obsequies 9, 120
Observant Carmelite Order 129
Offertory 122, 148n17
oïdors (royal judges) 120
oïdors de comptes (account judges) 121
Olaguer (son of Davit) **191**
Olivelles, Felipe **90**, 94–95
Oliver, Isabel de 71
Oliver i de Miralles, Cecília **90**
Oliver Street (Barcelona) **191**
Oller, Francisco *190*
Olvia, Aldonça de 71
Onofre, Saint: feast day **178**, 191, 193, 201n106
Oñón de Ariño, Juan de **209**
oracioner 174
ordinary (book) 65
organ-builder 55, 59–60, 199n66, 205
organist 29, 32, 37, 39, 55, 59–64, 105, 107, 109n33, 155, 158, 171–172, 175, 191, 193, 195n5, 199n49, 207
Ortou, Hierònim **191**
Osuna (Seville) 205
Our Lady: confraternity (Barcelona) **102**, 105, 107; feast day 55, 105, 107, 137, **181**, 202n111
Our Lady of the Carmen confraternity (Barcelona) 101

Pacheco, Isabel 205
Pacheco, Juana, Countess of Mirando and Vicereine of Catalonia 159
Padró Square (Barcelona) 22
Pagès, Rafaela 21
Paguera/Peguera, Aldonsa/Aldonça de 171, *172*, 198n45
Paguera/Peguera, Constança de 171–172
Paguera/Peguera, Johana de 171, *172*, 198n45
Palafox, Francesca de **180**
Palafox, Joana de **178–180**
Palafox, Mossèn Pere de **178–180**
Palau, Berenger de, Bishop 15–16
Palau, Joana de 121
Palau, Petronilla 44

Index 291

Palau de la Comtessa (Barcelona) 32, 170, 194; Our Lady of the Palau chapel 88, **90–93**, 94
Palau de la Generalitat (Barcelona) 27
Palau Reial (Barcelona) 14
Palma (Mallorca) 23
Palm Sunday 74, 76, **78–80**, 137, 139, 184
papal nunciature 133
parade 127
paraires (wool makers) guild confraternity (Barcelona) 99, 104, 114n103
Parera, Jaume 174
Paris *11*, *15*, *18*, 73, *190*
parlour 34, 44, 118, 121, 158
Pascali i Sanpere, Maria Bàrbara (Maria Magdalena de Pascali i Sanpere) **93**
Passatge Mare de Déu de l'Estrella (Barcelona) **7**
Passions 73, 184
Pastrana (Guadalajara): Carmelite convents 169, 225–228; collegiate church 170; Franciscan convent 169–170
Pastrana, Juan de **209**
Paterna (Valencia) 201n102
Paul V, Pope 38
Paulet, Luis **39**
Pavía, Fernando de **209**
pellers (second-hand clothe sellers) guild confraternity (Barcelona) 99, 114n104
Peñarroja, Gerónima de 21
Pentecost 137
Penyafort, Raimon de 133–134, 150n31, 214
Perallada, Silvestre 59
Pere II 124
Pere III 124
Pérez de Valdivia, Diego 22, 159–162, 196nn16–17, 197n19
Perit, Francesc 174
Perpignan 35, 38, 40–41, 107, *192*; Poor Clare convent 35; Saint-Jean church **39**; Sant Joan Cathedral 60
pescadors (fishermen) guild confraternity (Barcelona) **102**, 107
Pessoa, Antonio de **210**
Peter, Saint **79**, **102**, 107; feast day 56, **57**, 119–120, 133
Petronila (daughter of Ventura Alboch) **191**
Peu de la Creu Street (Barcelona) **7**, 19, 146, 153n68
Philadelphia: Museum of Art *187*
Philip I 50n99

Philip II 22, 35, **39**, **123**, 124–125, 142, 144–145, 152n59, 158, 195n2, 204, 208, 212
Philip III 119, **123**, 124–125, 142, 144, 198n36
Philip IV 124, 234
Philip V 124
Philip the Handsome 141
Pi, Paulo **58**
Picanyes, Gabriel 59
Picanyol, Josep **91–92**, 94
Piferrer i Pou, Eulàlia (professed as Eulàlia de Crist) 92
Piñatelli/Pignatelli i Aymerich, Catalina **90**
Piñatelli/Pignatelli i Aymerich, Gertrudis **90**
Piñatelli/Pignatelli i Aymerich, Isabel **90**, 94
Piñatelli/Pignatelli i de Rubí, Maria Ignacia **93**
Pineda, Juan Fernando **209**
Pinós, Sor Maria Dominga 76, *82*, 112n76
Pisa 21
Pius V 212
Pla, Antoni 204
plague 20, 135
Planella, Maria Francisca **78**, **80**
pliegos **100**
Poblet (Tarragona): abbey of 144
poetic competition 127
Pol, Dionisa 35
Pol, Lucrècia 171
Polish-Lithuanian Commonwealth 205
polychoral performance 131–133, 150n28
Pomaret Street (Barcelona) 23
Pons y Turell, Agraïda **178**, **180**, **194**
Poor Clare Order **7–8**, 13–14, 19, 21, 34–35, 65, 76, *77*, 128, 157–158, 168, 175, 182, 205–*206*
Populum tuum obliviscere 77
Porn, Joannes **58**
Portaferrissa (Barcelona) 129
Portal de l'Àngel Avenue (Barcelona) **8**
Pou i Çanou, Maria Orosia Pou i Çanou **91**
Prat, Sor Àngela Serafina 23, 43
Prats, Franciscus 59
Preachers (religious Order) 212, 221
precentor (or chantre) 37
precentrix 37
presbyter 76, 144
Prima, Beautriu (alias Montesa) 176
Prima Office **179**
privileged altar 170, 193–194
Procedamus in pace 137

Index

processional (book) 74, *75*, *76*, *77*, 122, 239
Propheta magnus surrexit 72
prostitutes 19–21
Psalms of David 174
psalter 65, 71, 73, 109n36, 110n44, 174
psaltery (musical instrument) 43
Public Credit, offices of the 26
Puebla: Cathedral 49n82
Pueri Hebraeorum 137
Puig, Franciscà **191**
Puig, Montserrat 40, 52n135
Puig, Pere **100**
Puig Cabrer, Montserrat, a priest 52n135
Pujades, Àngela 104
Pujades, Jeroni 112n70
Pujol, Hipòlita de 199n49
Pujol, Joan Pau 133, 150n28
Pujol, Josep **93**, 94–95, *97*
Purgades, Prioress **178**
Purgatory 4, 104, 154–155, 163, 165, 167–168, 170, 177, 182, 184, 188, 193–195
Purification of Our Lady's feast day 74, **78**, 137
Puríssima Concepció basilic (Barcelona) 16

Queralt, Dalmau de **194**
Queralt, Francesc **93**
Queralt Reart i de Xatmar, Anna **91**
Quiñones, Francisco de 158
Quintana, Juan de **209**
Quinze Graons festivity 120
Quirra, Count of 42

Rabasa, Joan **62**
Rambla de Catalunya (Barcelona) 18
Ramírez, Pedro **209**
Ramírez de Prado, Lorenzo 234
Ramírez Fleyre, Pedro **209**
Ramis, Josep 59
Raval (Barcelona) **7**, 18, 20
Rebolledo, Francisca 191
Rec Comtal (Barcelona) 14
refugee 220
Regner, Llorens 112n64
Reial Acadèmia de Belles Arts de Sant Jordi (Barcelona) 45n1
relación (chronicle) 126, 128–129, *130*, 133, 150n31, 229, 231
repentant women, houses for 18–20, 35, 43
Requesens, Estefania de 170–171
Requesens, Mencía de 170

Requiem Mass **70**, 105, 107, 168, 174, 176–177, 195n5
rescluses see beguines
Respice **178**, **180**
Riba, Bartolomeu **58**
Riba, Joannes **58**
Ribadeneira, Pero de *189*
Ribafort, Nicolau 59
Riber, Cristofol 189
Ribes, Miquel 189
Riera, Bartomeva 97, **100**
Riera, Joana 175–176
Riera, Miquel 97, **100**
Riera Alta Street (Barcelona) **7**
Riera de Sant Joan Street (Barcelona) **8**, 19
Riera i Vidal, Maria Inés **90**
Rifé, Jordi 51n106
Río Piedras (Puerto Rico): Museo de Historia, Antropología y Arte *190*
Ripoll (Girona) 25
Riquida, Countess 13
Rius i de Falguera, Inés de **90**
Roca, Catalina 35
Roca, Jacobus **58**
Rocabertí, Estefania 22, 36
Rocabertí, Isabel de (alias Hipòlita de Jesús) 42, 161, 237n54
Rocabertí, Joan Tomàs de, Archbishop of Valencia 162
Rocabertí, Onofre de, Viscount of Perelada 145
Rocabertí y de Soler, Jerónima 35
Roch, Saint: feast day 135
Rodés, Caterina 101, 103
rogativas (rogations) procession 134
Roger, Sebastià 25, 34, 36, 137
Rolle of Hampole, Richard (Richard the Hermit) 165, *167*, 192n32
Romaguera, Jeroni 197n21
Roman curia 34
romance 43, 94, 99, 135, 222–223, *225*, **226**
Rome 43, 73, 158–159, *160*, 231
Romero, Jerónimo **210**
Ros, Anna 191
Rosa, Count and Countess de la **90**
Rosary, Our Lady of the 22; *Roser* confraternity (Barcelona) 101, **102**, 104, 125
Rosell Menor, Pau 191
Rosselló Street (Barcelona) 18
Rossinès i Fontllonga, Arcàngela **91**
Rossinès i Fontllonga, Francesca **91**
Roussillon 107, 191

Rovira, Magdalena 34
royal crier 129
royal entry 118, 125, 139, 152n55
Ruano, Sebastián de **210**
Ruiz, Francisco, Bishop of Ávila 157, 195n5
Ruiz de Tapia, Catalina 168

Sabadell (Barcelona) 16
Sabater i de Oriol, Maria Teresa de **92**
Saboya/Savoy, Duke of 114n101, 120, 125
Saboya/Savoy, Princes of 124
Sacerdos in aeternum 72
Sacris Solemnis **123**, 124
Sagarriga, Francesc **210**
Saint Cross's feast day 171, 174
Saiol, Guiomar de 39, 63–64
Sala, Joannes **58**
Sala i de Pujades, Marianna **93**
Salazar, Alfonsa de 223, *224*
Salcedo, Jerónimo de 40
salteris 174
Salvat, Antoni 9
Salvat, Guillermus 174
Salve crux pretiosa 66
Salve Regina 123, 176
Salzedo i Salazar, Eugènia 221
San Alberto, María de 222
San Baudilio de Llobregat parish church (in the province of Barcelona) 59
San Lorenzo de El Escorial (Madrid): monastery 31
San Vicente, Marquises of **90**, 94
Sancha, Àngela **39**
Sánchez, Francisco **209**
Sánchez, Luis 197n27
Sanctamaria, Caterina 194
sanctorale (book) 72–73, 85
Sanctus **70**, 71, 210
Saner, Miquel 174
Sans, Luis, Bishop of Barcelona 129
Sans, Maria Francisca **78**
Sans i Montrodon, Teresa de **92**
Sant Agustí Vell friary (Barcelona) **12**, 21
Sant Àngel college and convent (Barcelona) **12**
Sant Antoni, gate of (Barcelona) 15, 141
Sant Antoni Abat friary (Barcelona) **12**
Sant Antoni i Santa Clara convent (Barcelona) 4, 6, **8**, 13, *15*, 24–25, 71, *72*, 74, *75*, *76*, **74**, **78**, **90**, **93**, **102**, 105, 120, 124, 172, 174, 212
Sant Boi de Llobregat (Barcelona) 52n135

Sant Cugat del Rec church (Barcelona) 59, 99
Sant Cugat del Vallès (Barcelona): Sant Domènec convent 59
Sant Daniel, gate of (or Portal del Mar) 14, *15*
Sant Francesc de Paula friary (Barcelona) 187, 194
Sant Francesc/Sant Nicolau de Bari friary (Barcelona) **12**, 49n76, 101, **156**, 174, **181**, 193, **209**
Sant Gervasi (Barcelona) 22–23
Sant Guillem d'Aquitània college and convent (Barcelona) **12**, 22
Sant Jacint, gate of 191
Sant Jeroni de la Murtra friary (Barcelona) 11, **156**
Sant Jeroni de Vall d'Hebrón friary (Barcelona) 47n43, **156**
Sant Joan y de Planella, Maria **78**
Sant Josep, Maria Àngela de **90**
Sant Josep, Maria Ignacia de **93**
Sant Josep friary (Barcelona) **12**, 18, 60, 101, 129, 131–133, **181**
Sant Just Desvern (Barcelona): Sant Joan de l'Erm convent 20
Sant Maties hospital (Barcelona) 22
Sant Miquel church (Barcelona) 60, **181**, 193, 199n66
Sant Pau del Camp friary (Barcelona) **12**
Sant Pere de les Puel·les convent (Barcelona) 6, **8**, 9, 12, *14*, 18, 24, 31–32, 34, 48n73, 55–62, 65–66, 69–72, 88, **90**–**93**, 95, *98*, **102**, 117–121, 124, 135–137, 140, 144–146, **156**, 171–176, 188; high altar of Our Lady 104, 123, 175; Sant Andreu chapel 175; Sant Sagimon chapel 175
Sant Pere the Higher Street (Barcelona) 146
Sant Pere the Lower Street (Barcelona) 144
Sant Vicenç de Jonqueres (near Sabadell, Barcelona) 16
Santa Anna friary (Barcelona) **12**, **146**
Santa Anna Square (Barcelona) 18, 21
Santa Anna Street (Barcelona) 146
Santa Caterina friary (Barcelona) **12**, 18, 56, 73, 97, 101, 112n70, 125, 133–135, 139–140, 156, 174, **181**, 194
Santa Creu hospital (Barcelona) 187
Santa Eulàlia del Camp friary (Barcelona) **12**
Santa Madrona friary (Barcelona) **12**
Santa Margarida hospital (Barcelona) 35
Santa Margarida la Reial convent (Barcelona) 6, **7**, 24, 43, 65

Index 293

Santa Maria de Jonqueres convent
  (Barcelona) 4, 6, **8**, *11*, 16, *18*, 26–34, 40–41, 59–64, 69, 76, **83**, 84–89, 117–124, 134–137, 140, 145–146, **156**, 176–195, 207–214; Sant Francesc chapel 59, **178**; Sant Jaume chapel **178**; Sant Miquel chapel **178**; Santa Magdalena chapel **178**; Santa Paula chapel 40, **179**, 182
Santa Maria de Natzaret priory
  (Barcelona) **12**
Santa Maria de Pedralbes convent
  (Barcelona) **7**, 14, 32, 34, 36, 52n134, 55, 65, **156**, 163, 171, 195n1, 205
Santa Maria de Valldaura convent
  (Barcelona) 51n109
Santa Maria de Valldonzella convent
  (Barcelona) 5n1, 6, **7**, 15–16, 31–32, 37–38, 88, **90–93**, 94, 135–136, 140–145, **156**, 193
Santa Maria del Mar parish church
  (Barcelona) 9, 19, 59–60, 71, 88, **90–93**, 94, 140, 193
Santa Maria del Pi parish church
  (Barcelona) 9, 32, 60, 88, **91–92**, 94, 129, 145–146
Santa Maria Magdalena convent (Barcelona) 6, 8, **18**, 19–20, 24, 31, 35, 42, 48n73, **92**, 94, 134–136, 151n37, 156, 176
Santa Mònica friary (Barcelona) **79**, **181**
Santa Pau, Marquesa de **178–180**
Santa Regla 65
Santa Teresa, Anastasio de 43
Santa Teresa, Maria Ignacia de **91**
Santcliment, Guillem de 113n94
Santiago de Chile 1, 22, 71, 49n81
Santiago de Compostela (A Coruña) *224*
Santíssima Trinitat, Maria Gracia de la **92**
Sants Just i Pastor parish church
  (Barcelona) 60, **181**
Saportella, Rafela **178**
Saragossa 23, 73, 97, 99, **100**, 114n101, 126, 133, 155, 177, 215, *216*; Basilica of the Pilar 126; Carmelite friary 127–128; Carmelite nunnery 127–128; Jerusalén convent 128, 231; La Seo 126; Santa Catalina convent 128, 231
Saragossa, Pedro 108n19
Saragossa Cabeça, Violant **39**
Sardinia 165; Santa Clara in Oristano convent 205 Santa Lucia de Caller convent 205;
Sarrià (Barcelona) 13, 22–24
sastres (tailors) guild confraternity
  (Barcelona) **102**, 104

savage woman 163
Savall, Clara 163
Savoy **100**
Scardona, Àngela 175
Scotto 88
Scribes 25, **63**, 71, 112n66
Sebastian, Saint: feast day 135
Sebastian, Vicente **191**
Secular canons **12**
Sega, Filippo 225
Segols, Francisco **58**
Segovia 175
Seguí i Rovira, Jacinta **91**
seise (young choirboy) 157
Sendra, Mossèn Pere 175
Sentmanat i de Oms, Francisca de **79–80**
Sentmenat, Anna Maria 40
Sentmenat, Casilda 40–41
Sentmenat, Elizabet de **83**
Sentmenat, Galceran de 41
Sentmenat i de Bach, Maria Francesca de **93**
Seo de Urgel 99
Serafina, Juana 35, 44
Serdanya, Miquel 59
Serpi, Dimas 165, *166*, 177, 182, *183*, 185, 188, 194–195
Serra, Lluís 94
Serra i Postius, Maria Rosa **90**
Sescases, Hieronym 200n83
Setantí family 36
Setmana Tràgica 19, 22–24, 50n98
Setsams **178–180**
Seven Joys of the Virgin 76, 184
Seven Sorrows of the Virgin 135
Severus, Saint 135
Seville 5n1, 231
shawm 127–128
Sherwin, Juan 204
Sicily 22, **209**
Siena: Santa Maria degli Angeli convent 136; Santa Monaca convent 136
Siena, Saint Catherina of **178**, 193
Sigüenza, José de 11
Silíceo 158
Simancas (Valladolid) 25, 47n54
siren 163
Sisterbooks 121
Sisters of the Third Order of Penance 35
Sixtus IV, Pope 22
Slaves 3, 32–33, 38, 44, 49nn81–82, 64, 127
Sociats i Guitart, Maria Teresa **93**
Socuéllamos (Ciudad Real) **209**
Solanell, Teresa de **90**, 94
Soldevila, Bartolomé 104

Soler, Bernardus 175
Soler, Mossèn 59
Soler Rovirosa, Francesc 17, *61*
Solsona (Lleida) 60, 205
song 105, 118, 133, 163, 165, 189, 221–223, 225–226, 228
songbook *see cancionero*
sonnet 42, 215, *216*, 223
Sorribas, Eleonor **179**
Sorribes, Serapi de 104
Spanish Civil War 22
spinet 43
Spinosa, Andreu 112n64
sprezzatura 162
Statuit ei Dominus **178**
Stridbeck, Johann *15*, *16*, *140*
Suardo, Juan Antonio 118
sub-deacon 56, **57–58**, 101, 132, 144, 155, 158, 168, 171, 174, 176, 177, 188, 191, 193, 212
subprecentrix 37
sufragio 104, 177
Sunday of Lent 137
Sunyer, count 13
Surius, Laurentius 163
Suspice me, Domine 123

Talavera, Hernando de 142, 152n60
Tarragó i Puigibet, Apolonia **78**, 80
Tarragona 38, 85
Tarrós, Joan 144
Te Deum laudamus 21, 74, 119–120, **123**, 124–125, 134, 144, 205
Tenebrae responsories 118
tenoristes 119
Terra Santa (Holy Land) confraternity (Barcelona) **102**
Terrasa, Maria de 16
Terrassa 19
Terré, Brígida 22, 35
terreres 35
Terreros, Luisa de 35
Texidor, Miquel 189
Thomas, Antonio **100**
Tiana (Maresme) 20; cartoixa de Montalegre **156**
tintorers i bugaders (cloth dyers) guild confraternity (Barcelona) **102**, 104, *105*
tiple 95, *96*
Toledano, Miguel 223, *224*
Toledo 94, 223, 231; Cathedral 11, 157; Concepcón Francisca convent 158; Nuestra Señora de los Remedios school (later Real Colegio de Doncellas Nobles) 158; San Antonio de Padua convent 158; San Juan de la Penitencia convent 157–158; San Juan de los Reyes Observant community 222; Santiago de los Caballeros hospital **210**
Tomasa, Elisabet **100**
tonada/tono 4, 95, *96*, 222
Torbavi, Miguel 43
Torcuato, Saint **79**
Tord, Raimunda **90**, 94
Tordesillas (Valladolid) **209**
tornera 35
torno (convent revolving window) 45
Torre Sarjalet (Gràcia, Barcelona) 19
Torredmer, Magdalena Úrsula 175
Torrenueva (Ciudad Real) **209**
Torres, Balthasar 176
Torres, Francisco 135, 231
Tort i de Llar, Maria Josefa de **92**
Torta, Eleonor/Leonor 35, 59
Tortosa (Tarragona) 19, 221
Toulouse (France) 234
Tovella i Fauli, Joan 72
trece of the Order of Santiago 124, **209**
trentanari 101, 171, 175, 187–188, 194; of Saint Amador **181–182**, 193
Tria, Bernat **92–93**, 95
Trinitarian Order **8**, 9
Trinitat friary (Barcelona) 174, **181**, 187, 193–194
Trinxer, Joan 85
troubadours 117, 197n24
trumpet 104, 127–129, 132, 134, 141, 142, 152n55
Tua es potentia 142
Tudor, Mary 204
Tunisia 44

Uclés (Cuenca): monastery of 88, 208–211
Umbert, Paula **100**
Uppsala 234n3; *Cancionero de* (RISM 1556/30) 223, *228*
Urban Convents and Music Networks in Early Modern Barcelona online application 5n10
URBANMUSICS project 2, 4
Urquinaona Square (Barcelona) 16
Usagre (Badajoz) **210**

Valderrábano, Enríquez de 73
Valdivia, Isabel de 159
Valencia 23, 73, 94–95, 124, 162, 184, 221, 223; Colegio de Corpus Christi 204–205; Collegiate chuch 205; Mercado Square 156; Misericordia house 47n40; Poor Clare convent 205,

206; Santa Catalina de Siena convent 94; Santa Maria Magdalena convent 94, 156, 236n27; Trinitat convent 21
València Street (Barcelona) 19
Valenzuela, Fray Antonio de 221
Valeriola, Vicente 127
Valla, Giorgio 73
Valladolid 73; Aprobación house 43; Discalced Carmelite convent 128, 222; English College 204; Magdalena de San Jerónimo (house for repentant women) 19, 43; Poor Clare convent; San Felipe de la Penitencia convent 19
Vallaro, Fernando **39**
Vallbona de las Monges (Lleida): Cistercian convent 37, 236n27
Valldonzella Street (Barcelona) **7**
Vallès, Miquel 85
Vallès, Misser 176
Vallmajor Street (Barcelona) **8**, 19
Vallmanya, Antoni 38
Valls, Antoni 177
Valls, Francesc 94–95, *96*
Valls, Miquel **63**
Vallseca, Leonor de 187
Vallseca, Serena de 38
Vallvidrera (Barcelona) **7**, 21
Vásquez de Espinosa, Antonio 231
Vega, Lope de 133
Vega i Copons, Maria Agustina de **90**
Vega i Copons, Teresa de **90**
Velada, Marquis of 124
Velasco, María 99, **100**, *225*, **226**
Venegas, Alejo 177
Veni Creator 123
Veni sponsa Christi 123, 128, 155
Venice 70, 73, 162; Fondazione Musei Civici 118
Ventura (father of Baltasar) **191**
Vera, Antonio de 49n82
Vera, Juan de 49n82
Verbum Supernum Prodiens 162
Verger (organist) **63**
verguers i porters (municipal rod-bearer and gatekeepers) guild confraternity (Barcelona) **102**, 104, *106*
versets 73, 142, 151n50, 152n61
Vexilla Regis 139
Via Laietana (Barcelona) **8**, 16
Vic (Barcelona) 19; catedral 200n83
Vicar 9, 21, 35, 44, 140, 193, 199n74, **209**, 211
Vidal Grimau, Jaume/Diego 40

Vienna 117; Österreichische Nationalbibliothek *164*
Vigri, Caterina 236n42
vihuela 71–72, 222, 231
Vila, Pere Alberch 59, 108n22, 207
Vila de Madrid Square (Barcelona) **8**
Vilafranca del Penedés (Barcelona) 34, 188
Vilalba, Abbess Elisabet de 56
Vilallonga, Isabel de 121, 174
Vilallonga i Ialpi, Maria Josefa **90**, *98*
Vilanova, Aldonça de **83**
Vilanova, Bartolomé 104
Vilanova, Elionor de **83**
Vilanova, Joana de **83**
Vilanovo, Bartolomeu 58
Vildig, Eleonor 21
Villa de Caldes (Barcelona) **7**, 19
Villamanrique (Ciudad Real) 209
villancico 4, 32, 88, **90**, 94–99, 113n96, 114n98, 122–124, 127–128, 133, 155, 222–223, 225–226, *228*
Villanova, Fernando de 39
Villarejo (La Rioja) 209
Villegas, Francisco (or Fernando) 209
Villoria (Salamanca) 209
Vinyals, Ramon **63**
viola 41
Violant of Aragon 47n43
Violant of Hungary 124
violer/lutier 61
violin 95
violon 127, 231
Virgin of Hope's feast day 107, 185
Visitation of Our Lady 175
Viver, Constança **39**
Viver y Sors, Maria Antonia (professed as Maria Bàrbara Sant Joan de la Creu) **93**
Vives, Ángela de 40
Vozmediano, María de 158

watermarks 76
wind-player 129, 132, 141–142
witch 163
Wolfenbüttel: Herzog August Bibliothek 223

Yars/Yuar, Mossèn Joan **178–179**

Zaportella, Josep 202n111
Zaportella, Rafaela 193
Zárate, Fernando de 185, *186*
Zúñiga Valdés, Francisco de **210**
Zúñiga y Avellaneda, Juan de 170
Zurita, Nicasio 99